ABBA

All The Top 40 Hits

Craig Halstead

First Edition

By the same author:

Michael, Janet & The Jackson Family – All The Top 40 Albums
Michael, Janet & The Jackson Family – All The Top 40 Singles
Donna Summer: For The Record
Whitney Houston: For The Record

With Chris Cadman:

Janet Jackson: For The Record
Michael Jackson: For The Record (2ⁿᵈ Edition)
ABBA Gold Hits
Jacksons Number Ones
Michael Jackson – The Early Years
Michael Jackson – The Solo Years

www.cadman-halstead-musicbooks.com

Fiction:

Tyranny
The Secret Library (James Harris 1)
Shadow Of Death (James Harris 2)

for Aaron

ACKNOWLEDGEMENTS

Once again, I would like to acknowledge the support and encouragement of my co-writer, Chris Cadman ~ although we're working on individual projects at the moment, I'm looking forward to the time we are both free to start work on the 3rd edition of *Michael Jackson: For The Record*. Good luck with Vol.2 of 'Maestro', Chris ~ I'm sure you will have another winner on your hands!

A big thank you to Christopher Kimberley, for digging out chart runs for your homeland, Zimbabwe, and South Africa for me. Not forgetting pre-1975 chart action from Sweden ~ much appreciated.

I would like to thank the online music community, who so readily share and exchange information at: Chartbusters (chartbusters.forumfree.it), ukmix (ukmix.org/forums), Haven (fatherandy2.proboards.com) & Buzzjack (buzzjack.com/forums). In particular, I would like to thank:

- 'zeus555' & 'Benny' for sharing ABBA information on ukmix;
- 'BrainDamageII' & 'Wayne' for posting current Canadian charts on ukmix;
- 'flatdeejay' & 'ChartFreaky' for posting German chart action, and 'Indi' for answering my queries regarding Germany, on ukmix;
- 'mario' for posting Japanese chart action, and 'danavon' for answering my queries regarding Japan, on ukmix;
- 'Davidalic' for posting Spanish chart action on ukmix;
- 'Shakyfan', 'CZB' & 'beatlened' for posting Irish charts on ukmix;
- 'Hanboo' for posting and up-dating on request full UK & USA chart runs on ukmix.

Not forgetting Trent Nickson's excellent, and regularly up-dated, ABBA Charts site which you will find at **home.zipworld.com.au/~callisto/abba.html** ~ fantastic job, Trent!

If you can fill any of the gaps in the chart information in this book, or have chart runs from a country not already featured in the book, I would love to hear from you. You can contact me via **www.cadman-halstead-musicbooks.com** ~ thank you!

CONTENTS

INTRODUCTION   7

ALL THE TOP 40 SINGLES   13

THE ALMOST TOP 40 SINGLES   195

THE TOP 40 ABBA & ABBA-RELATED SINGLES   197

SINGLES TRIVIA   203

ALL THE TOP 40 ALBUMS   229

THE ALMOST TOP 40 ALBUMS   395

THE TOP 40 ABBA & ABBA-RELATED ALBUMS   397

ALBUMS TRIVIA   401

INTRODUCTIO

Before they won the Eurovision Song Contest in A........... .... people outside Scandinavia had heard of ABBA – indeed, before *Waterloo*, the quartet were credited as 'Björn Benny & Agnetha Frida' on the few singles they released and on their debut album, as the name ABBA hadn't yet been coined.

Björn, Benny, Agnetha and Frida were all successful musicians in their own right, before they formed a group together, and they continued to enjoy success after ABBA ceased to exist, and the quartet went their separate ways. Incredibly, the four members of ABBA have scored more than a hundred Top 40 singles and eighty Top 40 albums between them over the years, if their pre-ABBA and post-ABBA recordings are taken into account.

Introducing ABBA

Björn Kristian Ulvaeus was born on 25th April 1945 on the Island of Hisingden, near Gothenburg, Sweden. He started his musical career as a member of a Swedish folk group the West Bay Singers, who found success as the Hootenanny Singers – the group released their debut single and album in 1964. Surprisingly, Björn is the only member of ABBA who has never released a solo album.

Anni-Frid Synni Lyngstad was born on 15th November 1945 in Ballangen, near Narvik in Norway. However, Frida's father was a German soldier and fearing reprisals following German occupation, Frida's maternal grandmother took her to Sweden in early 1947, where Frida's mother soon joined them. Tragically, her mother was just 21 when she succumbed to kidney failure, so Frida was raised by her grandmother. Frida released her debut solo single in 1969, followed by her self-titled debut album in 1971.

Göran Bror Benny Andersson was born on 16th December 1946 in Stockholm, Sweden. Like Björn, he first tasted success as part of a group, as the keyboard player with the Hep Stars – Sweden's most successful rock band of the mid-to-late 1960s. The Hep Stars released their debut album in 1964, and their debut single early the following year.

Agneta (later Agnetha) Åse Fältskog was born on 5th April 1950 in Jönköping, Sweden. She composed her debut single, *Jag Var Så Kär* ('I Was So in Love'), herself, after she broke up with her boyfriend at the time, Björn Lilja – released in 1968, it gave Agnetha her first no.1 in Sweden.

Stig Anderson, ABBA's manager and co-founder of Polar Records, has often been described as the fifth member of ABBA. Born on 25th January 1931, Stig wrote or co-wrote the lyrics to many of ABBA's early recordings – sadly, he died of a heart attack on 12th September 1997.

Björn and Benny first met while the Hootenanny Singers and Hep Stars were touring southern Sweden in 1966 – that summer, they composed their first song together, *It Isn't Easy To Say*, which the Hep Stars recorded. Björn and Benny continued to write songs together, and they eventually recorded an album, *LYCKA* ('Happiness'), as a duo in 1970.

Benny met Frida, and Björn met Agnetha, in early 1969.

Björn and Agnetha were married on 6th July 1971, and had two children together, Linda Elin in February 1973 and Peter Christian in December 1977. Just a year after Christian's birth, the couple separated, and their divorce was finalised in June 1980.

When she first met Benny, Frida was still married to – but separated from – her first husband, Ragnar Fredriksson, with whom she had two children, Hans Ragnar in January 1963 and Ann Lise-Lotte in February 1967.

Before meeting Frida, Benny had two children with his girlfriend Christina Grönvall, a son Peter and a daughter Hélene. Benny and Christina separated in 1966, with Christina keeping custody of the children.

Frida and Benny became engaged in August 1969 but, although Frida's divorce from Ragnar Fredriksson was made final in May 1970, the couple didn't marry until October 1978. Just over two years later, in February 1981, Frida and Benny separated and in November the same year they divorced.

All The Top 40 Hits

For the purposes of this book, to qualify as a Top 40 hit, a single or album must have entered the Top 40 singles/albums chart in at least one of nineteen featured countries: Australia, Austria, Belgium (Wallonia), Canada, Finland, France, Germany, Ireland (singles only), Japan, the Netherlands, New Zealand, Norway, South Africa, Spain, Sweden, Switzerland, the United Kingdom, the United States and Zimbabwe.

The Top 40 singles and albums are detailed chronologically, according to the date they first entered the chart in one or more of the featured countries. Each Top 40 single and album is illustrated and the catalogue numbers and release dates are detailed, for both Sweden and the UK, followed by the chart runs in each featured country, including any chart re-entries. Where full chart runs are unavailable, peak position and weeks on the chart are given.

For both singles and albums, the main listing is followed by 'The Almost Top 40 Singles/Albums', which gives an honorable mention to ABBA and ABBA-related singles/albums that peaked between no.41 and no.50 in one or more countries. There is also a points-based list of the Top 40 ABBA and ABBA-related Singles and Albums,

plus a fascinating 'Trivia' section at the end of each section which looks at the most successful ABBA and ABBA-related singles and albums in each of the featured countries.

The Charts

The charts from an increasing number of countries are now freely available online, and for many countries it is possible to research weekly chart runs. Although this book focuses on Top 40 hits, longer charts runs are included where available, up to the Top 100 for countries where a Top 100 or longer is published.

Nowadays, charts are compiled and published on a weekly basis – in the past, however, some countries published charts on a bi-weekly or monthly basis, and most charts listed far fewer titles than they do today. There follows a summary of the current charts from each country featured in this book, together with relevant online resources and chart books.

Australia
Current charts: Top 100 Singles & Top 100 Albums.
Online resources: current weekly Top 50 Singles & Albums, but no archive, at **ariacharts.com.au**; archive of complete weekly charts dating back to 2001 at **pandora.nla.gov.au/tep/23790**; searchable archive of Top 50 Singles & Albums dating back to 1988 at **australian-charts.com**.
Books: 'Australian Chart Book 1970-1992' & 'Australian Chart Book 1993-2009' by David Kent.

Austria
Current charts: Top 75 Singles & Top 75 Albums.
Online resources: current weekly charts and a searchable archive dating back to 1965 for singles and 1973 for albums at **austriancharts.at**.

Belgium
Current charts: Top 50 Singles & Top 200 Albums for two different regions, Flanders (the Dutch speaking north of the country) and Wallonia (the French speaking south).
Online resources: current weekly charts and a searchable archive dating back to 1995 at **ultratop.be**.
Book: '*Het Belgisch Hitboek – 40 Jaar Hits In Vlaanderen*' by Robert Collin.
Note: the information in this book for Belgium relates to the Wallonia region.

Canada
Current charts: Hot 100 Singles & Top 25 Albums.

Online resources: weekly charts and a searchable archive of weekly charts from the Nielsen SoundScan era at **billboard.com/biz** (subscription only); incomplete archive of weekly RPM charts dating back to 1964 for singles and 1967 for albums at **collectionscanada.gc.ca/rpm** (RPM folded in 2000).

Book: 'The Canadian Singles Chart Book 1975-1996' by Nanda Lwin.

Finland

Current charts: Top 20 Singles & Top 50 Albums.

Online resources: current weekly charts and a searchable archive dating back to 1995 at **finnishcharts.com**.

France

Current charts: Top 200 Singles & Top 200 Albums.

Online resources: current weekly charts and a searchable archive dating back to 1984 for singles and 1997 for albums at **lescharts.com**; searchable archive for earlier/other charts at **infodisc.fr**.

Book: '*Hit Parades 1950-1998*' by Daniel Lesueur.

Note: Compilation albums were excluded from the main chart until 2008, when a Top 200 Comprehensive chart was launched.

Germany

Current charts: Top 100 Singles & Top 100 Albums.

Online resources: current weekly charts (Top 10s only) and a searchable archive dating back to 2007 (again, Top 10s only) at **germancharts.com**; complete Top 100 charts are usually posted weekly in the German Charts Thread on **ukmix.org**.

Books: '*Deutsche Chart Singles 1956-1980*', '*Deutsche Chart Singles 1981-90*', '*Deutsche Chart Singles 1991-1995*' & '*Deutsche Chart LP's 1962-1986*' published by Taurus Press.

Note: music videos are allowed to chart on the German album chart, but have been excluded from this book.

Ireland

Current charts: Top 100 Singles & Top 100 Albums.

Online resources: current weekly charts are available at **irma.ie**; there is a searchable archive for Top 30 singles (entry date, peak position and week on chart only) at **irishcharts.ie**; weekly singles chart from 1967 to 1999 have been posted in the Irish Chart Thread on **ukmix.org**.

Note: the Irish album chart launched much later than the singles chart, and there is no online archive, so only chart information for singles is included in this book.

Japan
Current charts: Top 200 Singles & Top 300 Albums.
Online resources: current weekly charts (in Japanese) at **oricon.co.jp/rank**; selected information is available on the Japanese Chart/The Newest Charts and Japanese Chart/The Archives threads at **ukmix.org**.

Netherlands
Current charts: Top 100 Singles & Top 100 Albums.
Online resources: current weekly charts and a searchable archive dating back to 1956 for singles and 1969 for albums at **dutchcharts.nl**.

New Zealand
Current charts: Top 40 Singles & Top 40 Albums.
Online resources: current weekly charts and a searchable archive dating back to 1975 at **charts.org.nz**.
Book: 'The Complete New Zealand Music Charts 1966-2006' by Dean Scapolo.

Norway
Current charts: Top 20 Singles & Top 40 Albums.
Online resources: current weekly charts and a searchable archive dating back to 1958 for singles and 1967 for albums at **norwegiancharts.com**.

South Africa
Current charts: no official charts.
Online resources: none known.
Book: 'South Africa Chart Book' by Christopher Kimberley.
Notes: the singles chart was discontinued in early 1989, as singles were no longer being manufactured in significant numbers. The albums chart only commenced in December 1981, and was discontinued in 1995, following re-structuring of the South African Broadcasting Corporation. The information presented in this book was obtained through personal correspondence with Christopher Kimberley.

Spain
Current charts: Top 50 Singles & Top 100 Albums.
Online resources: current weekly charts and a searchable archive dating back to 2005 at **spanishcharts.com**.
Book: *'Sólo éxitos 1959-2002 Año a Año'* by Fernando Salaverri.

Sweden
Current charts: Top 60 Singles & Top 100 Albums.

Online resources: current weekly charts and a searchable archive dating back to 1975 at **swedishcharts.com**.

Note: before 1975, a weekly Top 20 *Kvällstoppen* charts was published, which was a sales-based, mixed singles/albums chart.

Switzerland

Current charts: Top 75 Singles & Top 100 Albums.

Online resources: current weekly charts and a searchable archive dating back to 1968 for singles and 1983 for albums at **hitparade.ch**.

UK

Current Charts: Top 200 Singles & Top 200 Albums.

Online resources: current weekly Top 100 charts and a searchable archive (Top 40s only) dating back to 1960 at **officialcharts.com**; weekly charts are posted on a number of music forums, including ukmix (**ukmix.org**), Haven (**fatherandy2.proboards.com**) and Buzzjack (**buzzjack.com**).

Note: weekly Top 200 single and album charts are only available via subscription from UK ChartsPlus (**ukchartsplus.co.uk**).

USA

Current charts: Hot 100 Singles & Billboard 200 Albums.

Online resources: current weekly charts are available at **billboard.com**, however, to access Billboard's searchable archive at **billboard.com/biz** you must be a subscriber; weekly charts are posted on a number of music forums, including ukmix (**ukmix.org**), Haven (**fatherandy2.proboards.com**) and Buzzjack (**buzzjack.com**).

Note: older 'catalog' albums (i.e. albums older than two years) were excluded from the Billboard 200 before December 2009, so the chart didn't accurately reflect the country's best-selling albums. Therefore, in this book Billboard's Top Comprehensive Albums chart has been used from December 2003 to December 2009, as this did include all albums. In December 2009 the Top Comprehensive Albums chart became the Billboard 200, and Billboard launched a new Top Current Albums chart – effectively, the old Billboard 200.

Zimbabwe

Current charts: no official charts.

Online resources: none known.

Books: 'Zimbabwe Singles Chart Book' & 'Zimbabwe Albums Chart Book' by Christopher Kimberley.

Note: Zimbabwe was, of course, known as Rhodesia before 1980, but the country is referred to by its present name throughout this book. The information presented in this book was obtained through personal correspondence with Christopher Kimberley.

All The Top 40 Singles

1 ~ *Jag Väntar Vid Min Mila* by the Hootenanny Singers

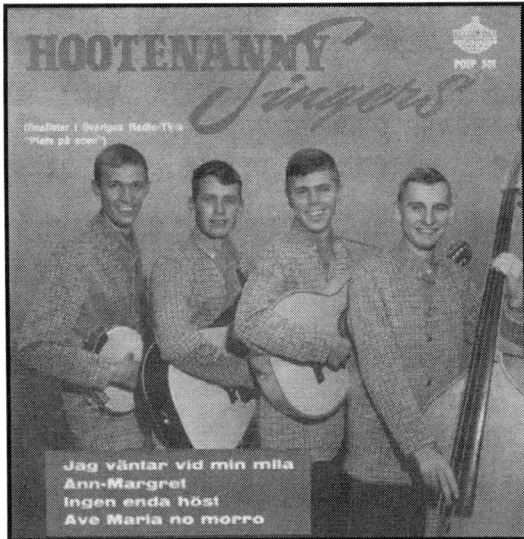

Sweden: Polar POEP 501 (1964).

13.04.64: peaked at no.**7**, charted for 16 weeks

Founded in 1961 as the Westbay Singers, Björn Ulvaeus, Johan Karlberg, Tony Rooth and Hansi Schwarz found success as the Hootenanny Singers, a name chosen for them when they signed with Polar shortly after the quartet formed. It was, Björn has confirmed, a name every single member of the folk group hated.

Jag Väntar Vid Min Mila, which translates as 'I'm Waiting At the Charcoal Kiln', was written by Swedish poet Dan Andersson. The Hootenanny Singers performed the song when they made their TV debut on the Swedish show *Hylands Hörna* in 1964, and it was the lead track on an EP that was the very first release on the Polar label, which went on to release all ABBA's singles and albums in Sweden.

Jag Väntar Vid Min Mila gave the Hootenanny Singers their first chart hit, when it rose to no.7 on the Sweden's *Kvällstoppen* chart, which featured both singles and albums.

2 ~ Gabrielle by the Hootenanny Singers

Sweden: Polar POEP 505 (1965).

10.11.64: peaked at no.**5**, charted for 12 weeks

Finland
01.65: peaked at no.**3**, charted for 20 weeks (monthly chart)

Norway
19.12.64: 8-**6**-7-8-7-7-**6-6**

The Hootenanny Singers released two self-titled albums in Sweden in 1964, and *Gabrielle* was taken from the second of them.

As well as Swedish, the group translated and performed *Gabrielle* in English, Dutch, Finnish, German and Italian, using the tune of the Russian song *May There Always Be Sunshine*, which was composed by Arkady Ostrovsky. However, for political reasons, Ostrovsky was never credited on *Gabrielle*.

Gabrielle charted at no.3 in Finland, no.5 in Sweden and no.6 in Norway.

3 ~ Cadillac by the Hep Stars

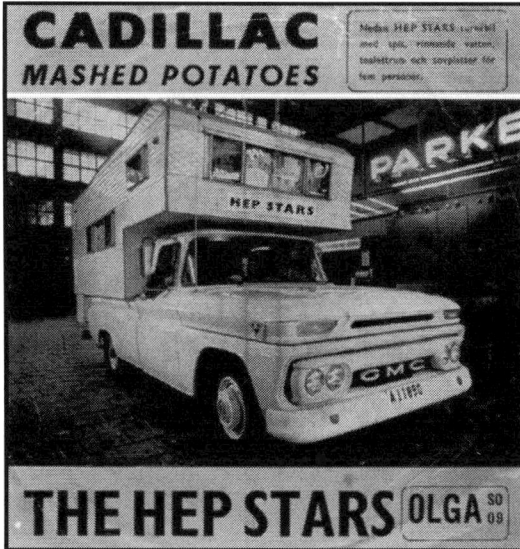

Sweden: Olga SO 09 (1965).

13.04.65: peaked at no.**1** (1 week), charted for 14 weeks

Norway
5.06.65: 8-4-3-**1**-2-2-2-2-2-3-5-6-7-6-8-7

Originally called Quartet Ye, the Hep Stars were a Swedish rock group formed in 1963 in the Swedish capital, Stockholm. The quartet was founded by Jan 'Janne' Frisk, Christer 'Chrille' Pettersson, Lennart 'Lelle' Hegland and Hans Östlund. Lead vocalist Sven 'Svenne' Hedlund joined soon afterwards, and when disagreements within the band led to keyboard player Östlund leaving, Benny Andersson – who was playing with a group called Elverkets Spelmanslag at the time – was invited to take his place.

Brand New Cadillac was originally recorded by Vince Taylor & His Playboys in 1959. The Renegades, a British band, covered the song in 1964, and shortened the title to *Cadillac*. The Hep Stars recorded a version of *Cadillac*, based on the Renegades cover, for their 1965 album, *WE AND OUR CADILLAC*, and it gave them their debut hit, hitting no.1 in both Norway and Sweden.

On 18th May 1965, the Hep Stars had three singles in the Swedish Top 5, with *Cadillac* at no.1, *Farmer John* at no.2 and *Tribute To Buddy Holly* at no.5.

4 ~ Tribute To Buddy Holly by the Hep Stars

Sweden: Olga SO 04 (1965).

20.04.65: peaked at no.**5**, charted for 10 weeks

Buddy Holly, along with Ritchie Valens and J.P. 'The Big Bopper' Richardson, died in an airplane crash in February 1959.

A Tribute To Buddy Holly was originally recorded by Mike Berry with The Outlaws in 1961, and despite being banned by the BBC for being too 'morbid', it charted at no.24 in the UK. Four years later, the Hep Stars recorded a version of the tribute that gave them a no.5 hit in Sweden.

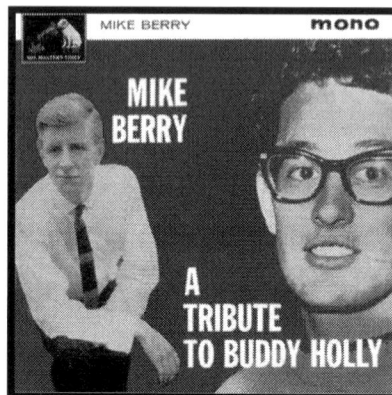

5 ~ Farmer John by the Hep Stars

Sweden: Olga SO 06 (1965).

27.04.65: peaked at no.**1** (4 weeks), charted for 19 weeks

Norway
12.06.65: 8-6-5-**4**-5-7-7-7-8-9

Farmer John, backed with a cover of Ritchie Valens's *Donna*, gave the Hep Stars their second no.1 in Sweden, and a no.4 hit in Norway.

Outside Scandinavia, *Farmer John* was released as a single in Germany, but it wasn't a hit.

6 ~ Britta by the Hootenanny Singers

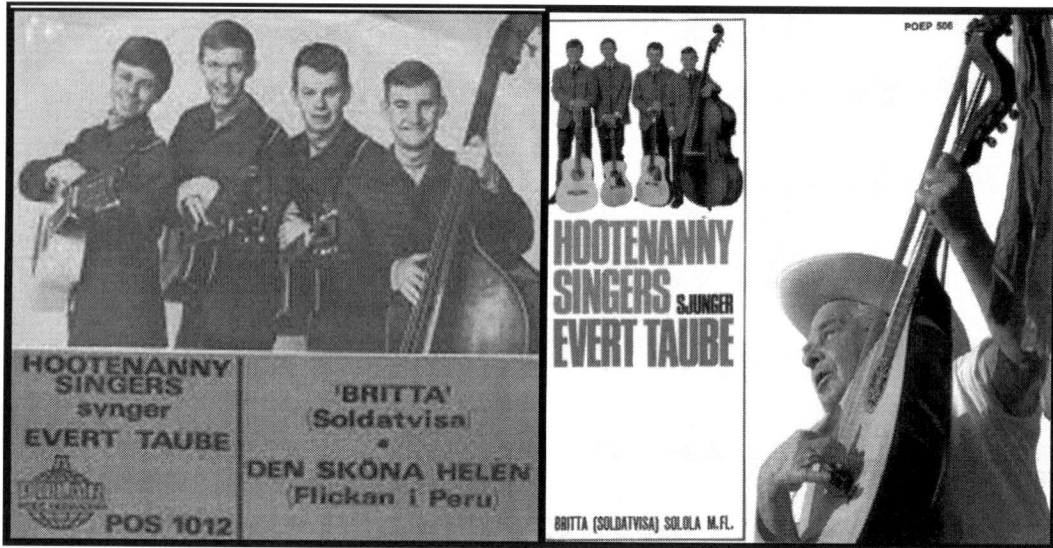

Sweden: Polar POS 1012 (1965).

29.06.65: peaked at no.**12**, charted for 10 weeks

Britta, released as a single and the lead track on an EP, was recorded by the Hootenanny Singers for their 1965 album, *HOOTENANNY SINGERS SJUNGER EVERT TAUBE* ('Hootenanny Singers Sing Evert Taube). The single achieved no.12 in Sweden, but it wasn't a hit anywhere else.

Evert Taube was a popular Swedish singer, composer and author who died in 1976.

7 ~ Bald Headed Woman by the Hep Stars

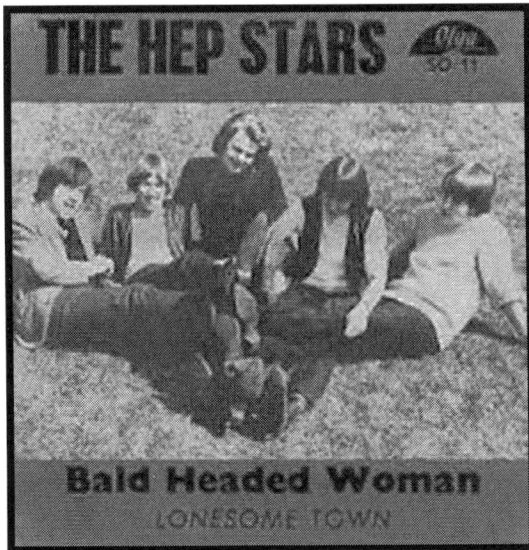

Sweden: Olga SO 11 (1965).

6.07.65: peaked at no.**1** (2 weeks), charted for 14 weeks

Finland
09.65: peaked at no.**20**, charted for 8 weeks (monthly chart)

Norway
14.08.65: 10-9-**8**-9

Composed by Shel Talmy, *Bald Headed Woman* is a traditional blues song the Kinks recorded for their self-titled debut album, released in 1964. The following year, the Who recorded a version of the song, which appeared on the B-side of their single, *I Can't Explain*.

   The Hep Stars recorded a cover of *Bald Headed Woman* for their 1965 album, *WE AND OUR CADILLAC*. Released as a single, it gave the band their third no.1 in Sweden, and charted at no.8 in Norway and no.20 in Finland.

8 ~ Donna by the Hep Stars

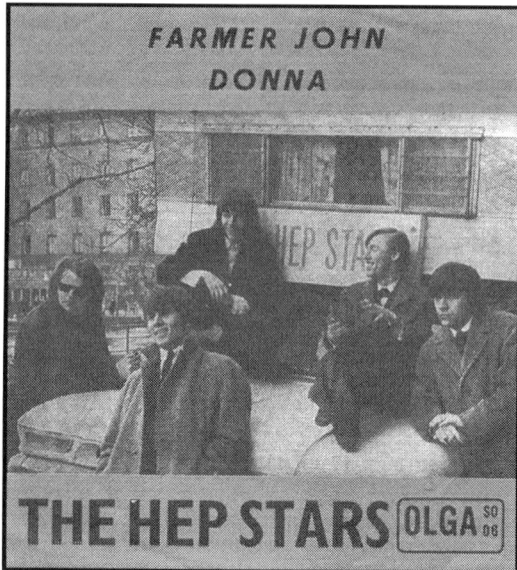

Sweden: Olga SO 06 (1965).

17.08.65: **14**

Donna was written and originally recorded by Ritchie Valens in 1958. Valens, who along with Buddy Holly died in an airplane crash in February 1959, was inspired to write *Donna* by his high school sweetheart, Donna Ludwig. *Donna*, with the more famous *La Bamba* on the B-side, gave Valens a no.2 hit in the USA and a no.29 hit in the UK.

The Hep Stars released their cover of *Donna* as the B-side of their no.1 single, *Farmer John*. However, *Donna* was popular enough to be listed as a hit in its own right, spending a week at no.14.

9 ~ No Response by the Hep Stars

Sweden: Olga SO 12 (1965).

14.09.65: peaked at no.**2**, charted for 15 weeks

Norway
9.10.65: 7-7-**6**

No Response was the third hit taken from the Hep Stars' 1965 album, *WE AND OUR CADILLAC*, achieving no.2 in Sweden and no.6 in Norway.

More significantly, *No Response* was the first hit composed by Benny Andersson.

10 ~ So Mystifying by the Hep Stars

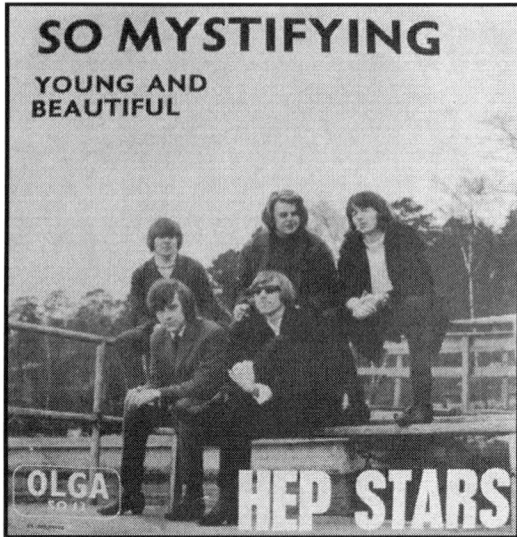

Sweden: Olga SO 13 (1965).

12.10.65: peaked at no.**5**, charted for 9 weeks

So Mystifying, like *Cadillac* and *Bald Headed Woman*, was a song the Kinks recorded for their self-titled debut album, released in 1964. Unlike *Cadillac* and *Bald Headed Woman*, however, *So Mystifying* was composed by the Kinks' front man, Ray Davies.

The Hep Stars' version of *So Mystifying* continued the band's impressive run of hits in Sweden, peaking at no.5, but it wasn't a hit in any other countries.

A live version of *So Mystifying* was featured on the Hep Stars' 1965 album, *HEP STARS ON STAGE*.

11 ~ *Den Sköna Helen* by the Hootenanny Singers

Sweden: Polar POS 1016 (1965).

16.11.65: **17**

Den Sköna Helen, which translates as 'Beautiful Helen', was another Evert Taube composition the Hootenanny Singers covered on their 1965 tribute album, *HOOTENANNY SINGERS SJUNGER EVERT TAUBE*.

Although not as successful as *Britta, Den Sköna Helen* was a hit in Sweden, spending a single week on the chart at no.17.

12 ~ Should I by the Hep Stars

Sweden: Olga SO 17 (1966).

28.12.65: peaked at no.**2**, charted for 11 weeks

Should I was the Hep Stars' eighth hit single of 1965 in Sweden, and the band were well on their way to becoming the country's most successful pop stars – more successful, in Sweden at least, than the Beatles.

    Should I peaked at no.2 in Sweden, just failing to give the Hep Stars another no.1 single.

13 ~ *Björkens Visa* by the Hootenanny Singers

Sweden: Polar POEP 509 (1965).

1.02.66: peaked at no.**7**, charted for 10 weeks

Björkens Visa ('The Bird's Song') was a non-album recording the Hootenanny Singers released as the lead song on a 4-track EP.

    Björkens Visa achieved no.7 in Sweden, but it wasn't a hit anywhere else.

14 ~ Sunny Girl by the Hep Stars

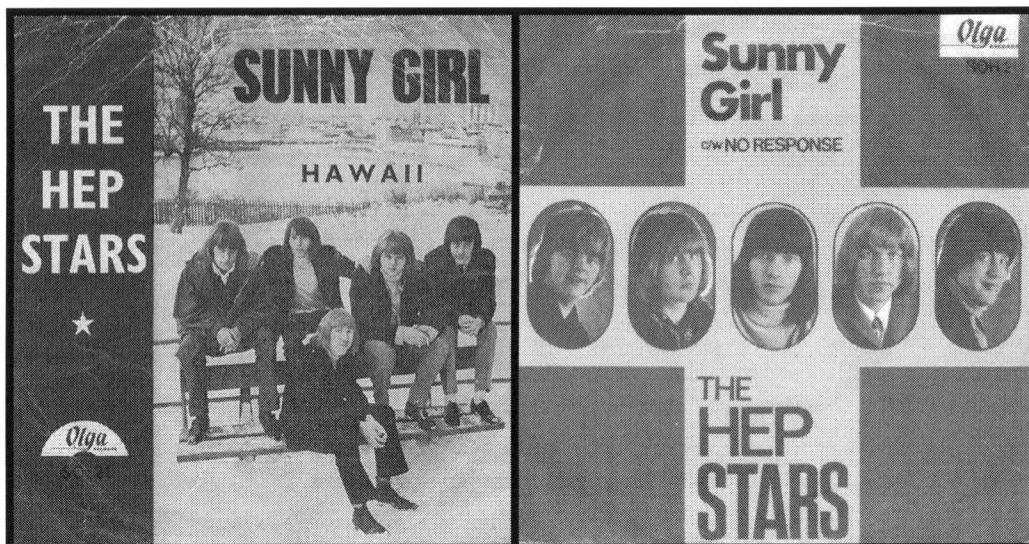

Sweden: Olga SO 21 (1966).

15.03.66: peaked at no.**1** (5 weeks), charted for 16 weeks

Finland
06.66: peaked at no.**8**, charted for 24 weeks (monthly chart)

Netherlands
13.07.68: 18-11-8-**4-4**-10-10-17

Norway
9.04.66: 9-8-8-6-**4**-5-**4**-6-6-7

Sunny Girl was composed by Benny Andersson, and was released as a single by the Hep Stars as a double A-side with *Hawaii* in Sweden. For the first two weeks, both *Hawaii* and *Sunny Girl* were listed on the chart, rising to no.7. From the third week onwards, however, only *Sunny Girl* was listed, and it went all the way to no.1.

    Sunny Girl was the Hep Stars' most successful single to date internationally, charting at no.4 in the Netherlands and Norway, and no.8 in Finland. It was also released as a single in the USA, but it wasn't a hit.

    The Hootenanny Singers recorded a cover version of *Sunny Girl*, for their 1966 album, *MÅNGA ANSIKTEN*.

15 ~ Wedding by the Hep Stars

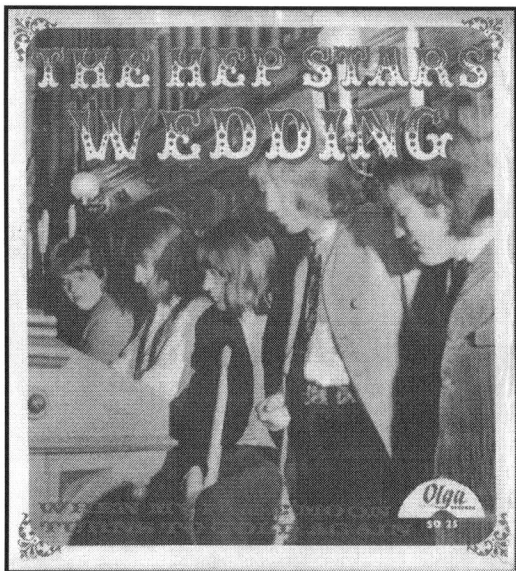

Sweden: Olga SO 25 (1966).

24.05.66: peaked at no.**1** (4 weeks), charted for 17 weeks

Finland
07.66: peaked at no.**11**, charted for 8 weeks (monthly chart)

Norway
4.06.66: 9-**8-8**

Wedding, composed by Benny Andersson and Sven Hedlund, was recorded by the Hep Stars for their self-titled 1966 album.

Wedding gave the Hep Stars their second straight no.1 in Sweden, their fifth in total, and charted at no.8 in Norway and no.11 in Finland.

16 ~ No Time by the Hootenanny Singers

Sweden: Polar 1019 (1966).

14.06.66: peaked at no.**18**, charted for 2 weeks

No Time was composed by Björn Ulvaeus and M. Dean, and featured on the Hootenanny Singers' 1965 album, *INTERNATIONAL*.

    No Time was only a hit in Sweden, spending a couple of weeks on the chart, peaking at no.18.

    When *No Time* was released in the USA, the name of the Hootenanny Singers was changed to The Northern Lights.

17 ~ Marianne by the Hootenanny Singers

Sweden: Polar POS 1022 (1966).

27.09.66: peaked at no.**3**, charted for 11 weeks

Norway
24.12.66: 10-**9**-10

The Hootenanny Singers recorded *Marianne* for their 1966 album, *MÅNGA ANSIKTEN* ('Many Faces').

Released as a single, *Marianne* rose to no.3 in Sweden, and charted at no.9 in Norway.

The Hootenanny Singers also recorded a cover of the Benny Andersson composition, *Sunny Girl*, for their *MÅNGA ANSIKTEN* album.

18 ~ *I Natt Jag Drömde* by the Hep Stars

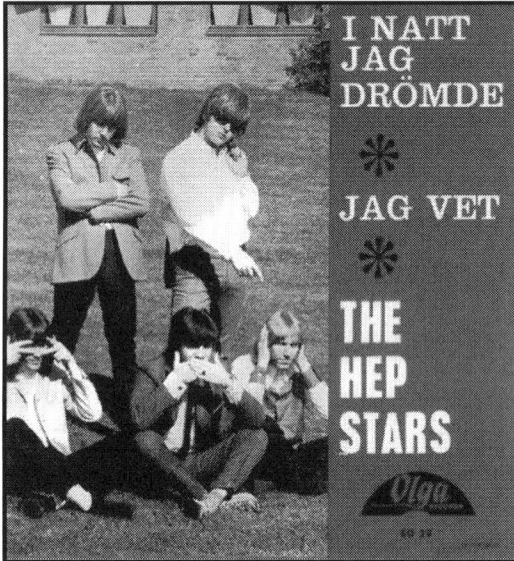

Sweden: Olga SO 29 (1966).

4.10.66: peaked at no.**2**, charted for 29 weeks

Finland
12.66: peaked at no.**12**, charted for 12 weeks (monthly chart)

Norway
22.10.66: 10-7-x-9-8-10-9-7-6-6-6-5-**4**-5-5-**4-4-4-4-4**-6-10-9-7-10-7-8-8-8

I Natt Jag Drömde ('Tonight I Dreamed') is a Swedish language cover of *Last Night I Had The Strangest Dream*, which was composed by Ed McCurdy in 1950 as an anti-war song. The Swedish lyrics were written by Cornelis Wreeswijk.

The Hep Stars recorded an English version of *Last Night I Had The Strangest Dream* for their self-titled 1966 album, while *I Natt Jag Drömde* was later included on their Swedish language album, *PÅ SVENSKA*, released in 1969.

I Natt Jag Drömde achieved no.2 in Sweden, no.4 in Norway and no.12 in Finland.

19 ~ Don't / Consolation by the Hep Stars

Sweden: Olga SO 33 (1966).

25.10.66: peaked at no.**1** (10 weeks), charted for 18 weeks

Finland
12.66: peaked at no.**9**, charted for 12 weeks (monthly chart)

Consolation was composed by Benny Andersson and, released as a double A-side with *Don't*, it gave the Hep Stars their biggest hit in Sweden, where it topped the chart for 10 weeks.

In Finland, where the single charted at no.9, only *Consolation* was listed.

Consolation, but not *Don't*, featured on the Hep Stars' self-titled 1966 album and on their first compilation album, *HEP STARS BÄSTA* ('Best Of'), released in Sweden in 1970.

20 ~ *En Sång En Gång För Längesen* by the Hootenanny Singers

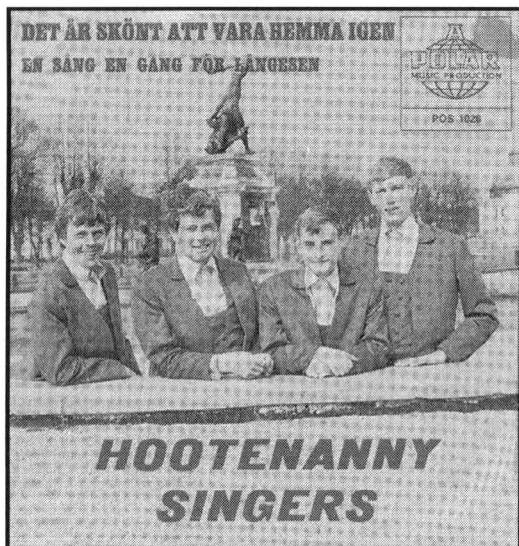

Sweden: Polar POS 1026 (1967).

14.02.67: peaked at no.**2**, charted for 11 weeks

Norway
11.03.67: 6-**3**-**3**-5-6-7-8-8

En Sång En Gång För Längesen ('A Song, Once Long Ago') is a Swedish cover of *Green, Green Grass Of Home*, which was written in 1965 by Claude 'Curly' Putman, and is best known for the version recorded in 1966 by Tom Jones.

The Swedish lyrics for *En Sång En Gång För Längesen* were written by the co-founder of the Polar record label, Stig Anderson, who went on to become the manager of ABBA.

The Hootenanny Singers never achieved a no.1 single in Sweden, but *En Sång En Gång För Längesen* came close, peaking at no.2. The single was also very successful in Norway, where it charted at no.3.

21 ~ Baby Those Are The Rules by the Hootenanny Singers

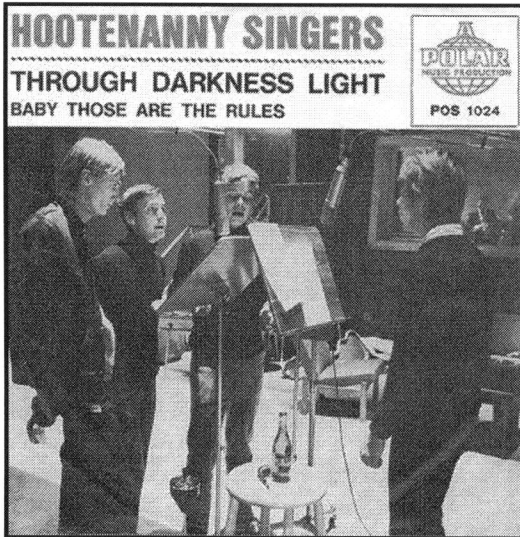

Sweden: Polar POS 1024 (1966).

7.03.67: peaked at no.**13**, charted for 3 weeks

Baby Those Are The Rules, another track featured on the Hootenanny Singers' 1966 album *MÅNGA ANSIKTEN*, was actually released before *En Sång En Gång För Längesen*, and was the B-side of *Through Darkness Light*.

The Swedish public obviously preferred *Baby Those Are The Rules* to *Through Darkness Light*, as it was the track that charted, rising to no.13 during a three week chart run.

Neither *Through Darkness Light* or *Baby Those Are The Rules* was a hit outside Sweden.

22 ~ *Malaika* by the Hep Stars

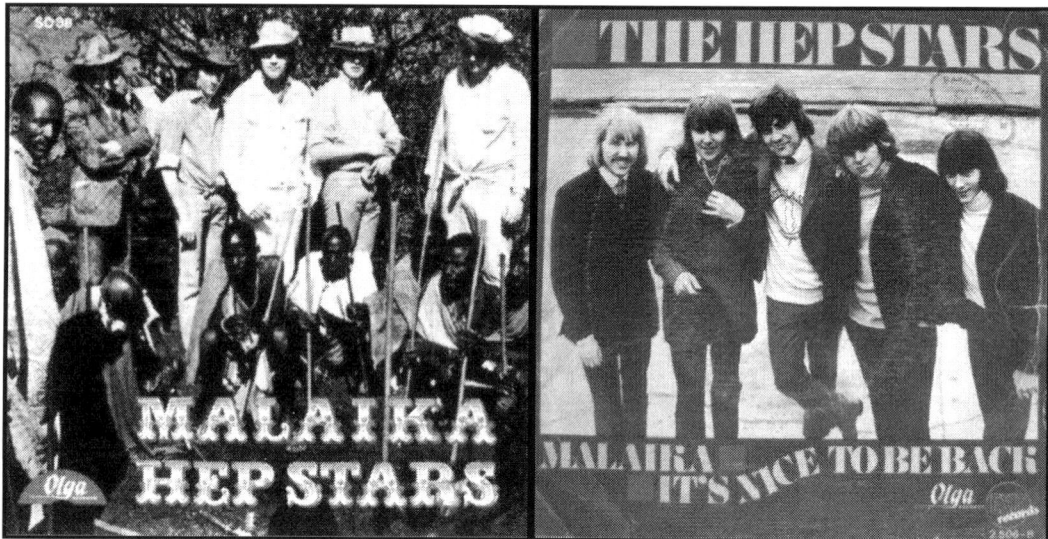

Sweden: Olga SO 38 (1967).

9.05.67: peaked at no.**1** (5 weeks), charted for 18 weeks

Malaika, which is Swahili for 'Angel', is a Swahili language song believed by many to have been composed in 1960 by the Kenyan artist, Fadhili William, who first recorded the song with his band, Jambo Boys.

The Hep Stars cover of *Malaika* gave the band another no.1 in Sweden, but it wasn't a hit anywhere else.

Boney M recorded a version of *Malaika* for their 1981 album, *BOONOONOONOOS*. Released as a single in most continental Europe countries, it achieved Top 20 status in Germany, the Netherlands, Spain and Switzerland.

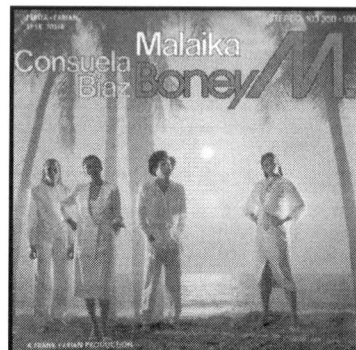

23 ~ *Mot Okänt Land* by the Hep Stars

Sweden: Olga SO 49 (1967).

3.10.67: peaked at no.**1** (3 weeks), charted for 17 weeks

Finland
11.67: **12** (monthly chart)

Mot Okänt Land ('Toward Unknown Land/Territory') gave the Hep Stars their eighth no.1 single in just three years in Sweden, but it was to prove to be their last. The single also charted at no.12 in Finland.

The Hep Stars included *Mot Okänt Land* on their 1969 album, *PÅ SVENSKA* ('In Swedish').

24 ~ She Will Love You by the Hep Stars

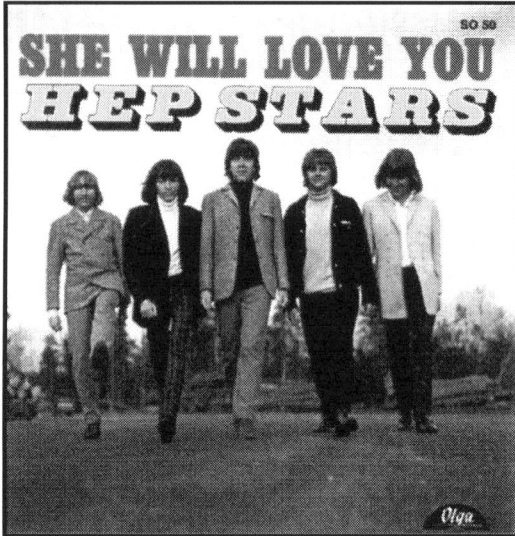

Sweden: Olga SO 50 (1967).

3.10.67: peaked at no.**7**, charted for 5 weeks

She Will Love You was composed by Benny Andersson and Svenne Hedlund, and gave the Hep Stars another Top 10 hit in Sweden, peaking at no.7.

    She Will Love You was included on the 1978 Swedish compilation, *BÄSTA 2* ('Best Of 2'), and on the Dutch compilation *GOLDEN HITS*, which was released three years earlier.

25 ~ *Början Till Slutet* by the Hootenanny Singers

Sweden: Polar POS 1040 (1967).

17.10.67: peaked at no.**4**, charted for 16 weeks

Norway
27.01.68: **10**

Början Till Slutet ('Almost Persuaded') was composed by Stig Anderson, Billy Sherrill and Glenn Sutton, and recorded by the Hootenanny Singers for their 1967 album, *CIVILA*.

    Början Till Slutet gave the Hootenanny Singers another Top 10 single in both Sweden and Norway, peaking at no.4 in Sweden and no.10 in Norway.

26 ~ *Jag Var Så Kär* by Agnetha Fältskog

Sweden: Cupol CS 211 (1968).

6.02.68: peaked at no.**1** (1 week), charted for 8 weeks

Agnetha Fältskog was singing and performing with Bernt Enghardt's dance band when she broke up with her boyfriend, Björn Lilja, which inspired her to write *Jag Var Så Kär* ('I Was So In Love').

Karl Gerhard Lundkvist, who was related to a member of Enghardt's band, was working as a producer at Cupol Records when Enghardt sent him a demo tape. Lundkvist wasn't interested in Enghardt's band, but he was interested in Agnetha's solo recording, *Jag Var Så Kär*.

Although unhappy she was being singled out, Agnetha nevertheless decided to sign with Cupol as a solo artist, and *Jag Var Så Kär* was one of the tracks she recorded for her self-titled debut album, released in Sweden in 1968.

Jag Var Så Kär was released towards the end of 1967 in Sweden, with *Följ Med Mig*, but *Jag Var Så Kär* was the track that attracted all the attention and went all the way to no.1.

27 ~ *Mårten Gås* by the Hootenanny Singers

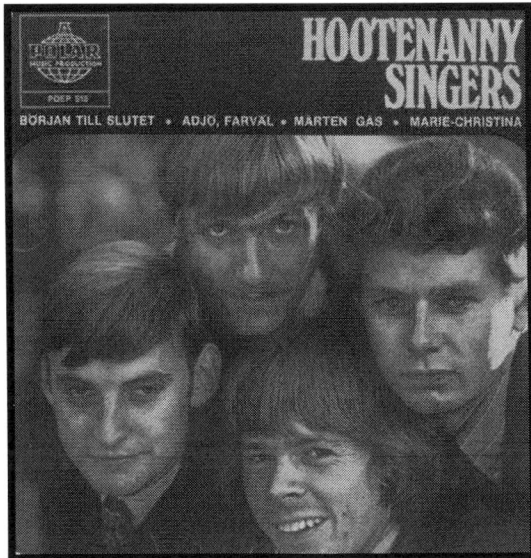

Sweden: Polar POEP 518 (1968).

20.02.68: peaked at no.**12**, charted for 4 weeks

Like *Början Till Slutet*, *Mårten Gås* ('Martin The Goose') is a song the Hootenanny Singers recorded for their 1967 album, *CIVILA* – both songs also featured on a 4-track EP released in Sweden.

Although not as successful as *Början Till Slutet*, *Mårten Gås* was still a hit, charting at no.12 in Sweden.

28 ~ It's Been A Long Long Time by the Hep Stars

Sweden: Cupol 226 (1968).

12.03.68: peaked at no.**14**, charted for 5 weeks

It's Been A Long Long Time was the title track of an album the Hep Stars released in Sweden in 1968.

The track was composed by Benny Andersson and Lars Berghagen, and was chosen as the album's lead single – it achieved no.14 in Sweden, but it wasn't a hit in any other countries.

29 ~ *Sagan Om Lilla Sofi* by the Hep Stars

Sweden: Cupol 232 (1968).

16.04.68: peaked at no.**4**, charted for 17 weeks

Sagan Om Lilla Sofi ('The Story Of Little Sophie') was composed by Benny Andersson and Lars Berghagen, and featured on the Hep Stars' 1969 album, *PÅ SVENSKA*.

   Sagan Om Lilla Sofi was released as the B-single of the single, *Det Finns En Stad*, but *Sagan Om Lilla Sofi* charted ahead of *Det Finns En Stad* and was far more successful, peaking at no.4 in Sweden.

   Sagan Om Lilla Sofi wasn't a hit outside Sweden.

30 ~ *Så Länge Du Älskar Är Du Ung* by the Hootenanny Singers

Sweden: Polar POS 1050 (1968).

30.04.68: peaked at no.**7**, charted for 9 weeks

Så Länge Du Älskar Är Du Ung ('As Long As You're In Love You Stay Young') was composed by Stig Anderson with B. Bare and C. Williams.

Released as a single, *Så Länge Du Älskar Är Du Ung* achieved no.7 in Sweden, but it wasn't a hit anywhere else.

31 ~ *Raring* by Björn Ulvaeus

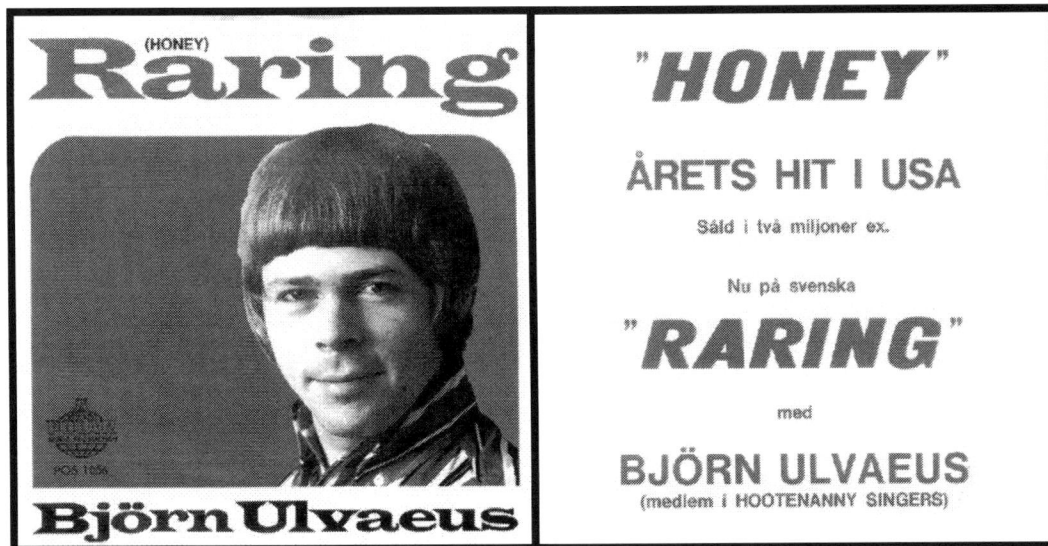

Sweden: Polar POS 1056 (1968).

9.07.68: peaked at no.**8**, charted for 6 weeks

Björn Ulvaeus's first solo hit was a Swedish cover of the Bobby Goldsboro hit, *Honey*, with Swedish lyrics written by Stig Anderson. *Honey* was composed by Bobby Russell, and Bobby Goldsboro took the song to no.1 in both Canada and the USA in 1968, and to no.2 in the UK in 1968 and again in 1975.

Raring ('Darling') charted at no.8 in Sweden but, although he went on to release a further three solo singles in Sweden before joining up with Benny Andersson, Björn didn't release a solo album.

32 ~ *Det Finns En Stad* by the Hep Stars

Sweden: Cupol 232 (1968).

13.08.68: peaked at no.**19**, charted for 2 weeks

Although it was released as the A-side, *Det Finns En Stad* ('There Is A Town') wasn't as popular as the B-side *Sagan Om Lilla Sofi*, which had charted earlier in the year and rose to no.4 in Sweden.

    Det Finns En Stad entered the chart four months after *Sagan Om Lilla Sofi*, and spent only two weeks on the chart, peaking at no.19.

33 ~ Let It Be Me by the Hep Stars

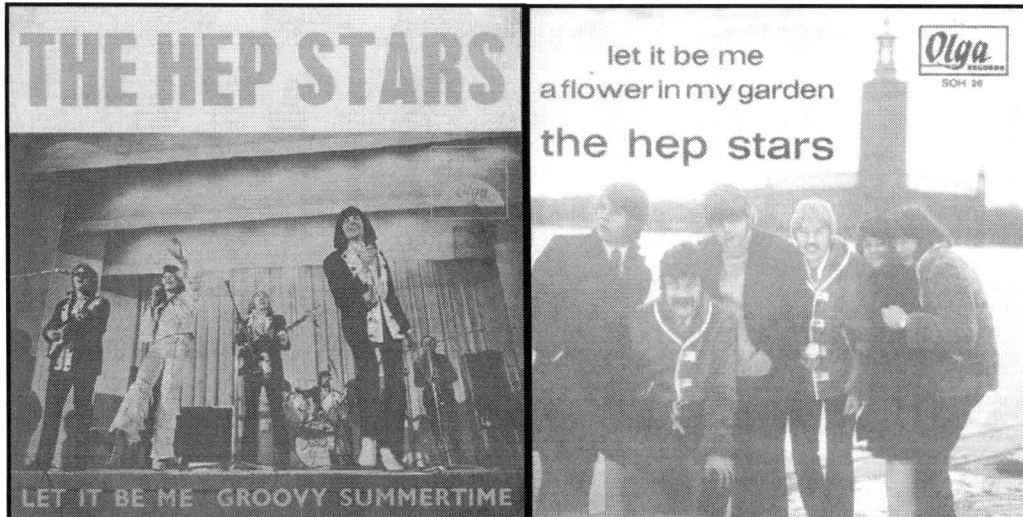

Sweden: Olga SO 64 (1968).

28.08.68: peaked at no.**4**, charted for 14 weeks

Finland
10.68: **17** (monthly chart)

Let It Be Me was composed and first recorded by Gilbert Bécaud in 1955 as *Je T'Appartiens*, with Mann Curtis writing the English lyrics two years later. The song has been a hit several times, including by the Everly Brothers in 1960, by Glenn Campbell & Bobbie Gentry in 1969, and by Willie Nelson in 1982.

The Hep Stars recorded *Let It Be Me* for their 1968 album, *SONGS WE SANG 68*, and as a single it charted at no.4 in Sweden and no.17 in Finland.

Let It Be Me was also released as a single in Germany, the Netherlands and Spain, but it wasn't a hit.

34 ~ *Måltidssång (Så Lunka Vi Så Småningom)* by the Hootenanny Singers

Sweden: Polar POS 1059 (1968).

24.09.68: peaked at no.**9**, charted for 5 weeks

Carl Michael Bellman was a famous Swedish poet and composer who was born in Stockholm in 1740, and *Måltidssång (Så Lunka Vi Så Småningom)* ('Meal Song') was one of a number of his compositions the Hootenanny Singers recorded for their 1968 tribute album, *BELLMAN PÅ VÅRT SÄTT* ('Bellman At Our Place').

    Måltidssång (Så Lunka Vi Så Småningom) achieved Top 10 status in Sweden, peaking at no.9, but it wasn't a hit anywhere else.

35 ~ *Allting Har Förändrat Sej* by Agnetha Fältskog

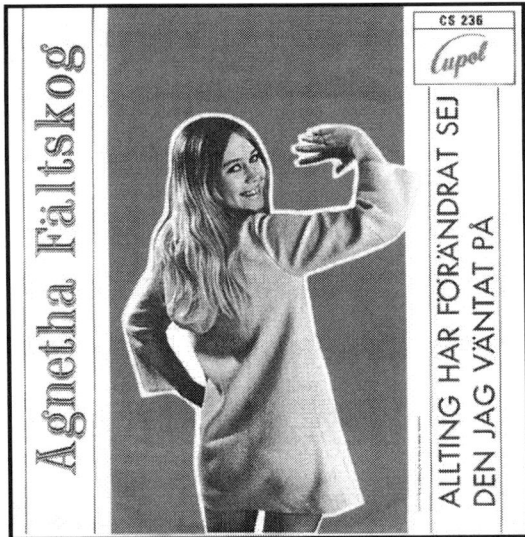

Sweden: Cupol CS 236 (1968).

1.10.68: peaked at no.**7**, charted for 7 weeks

Allting Har Förändrat Sej ('Everything Has Changed'), like Agnetha's debut hit *Jag Var Så Kär*, featured on her self-titled debut album – however, between *Allting Har Förändrat Sej* and *Jag Var Så Kär*, she released two singles that failed to chart.

    Allting Har Förändrat Sej was written by Karl Gerhard Lundkvist, and gave Agnetha her second Top 10 hit in Sweden, where it peaked at no.7. It would prove to be her final solo hit, before she joined forces with Björn Ulvaeus, Benny Andersson and Anni-Frid Lyngstad, to form the quartet that became ABBA.

36 ~ *Tända På Varann* by the Hep Stars

Sweden: Olga SO 72 (1968).

12.11.68: peaked at no.**13**, charted for 9 weeks

By 1968, in an effort to boost their waning popularity, the Hep Stars had been joined by Björn Ulvaeus, Benny Andersson's new song-writing partner, and a female vocalist, Charlotte 'Lotta' Walker.

An American, Walker met the Hep Stars' lead vocalist Sven Hedlund when her all-female trio the Sherrys were touring Sweden in 1967. Although the Sherrys returned to the United States, Walker found she missed Hedlund so much she returned to Sweden with her three children, and the pair married.

The Hep Stars recorded *Tända På Varann* ('Crazy About Each Other') for their 1969 album, *PÅ SVENSKA* – the album sleeve featured a wedding photograph of 'Svenne & Lotta', as the husband and wife duo became known.

While not as successful as many of the Hep Stars previous hits, *Tända På Varann* nevertheless charted at no.13 in Sweden.

37 ~ *Fröken Fredriksson* by Björn Ulvaeus

Sweden: Polar POS 1062 (1968).

19.11.68: peaked at no.7, charted for 6 weeks

Björn's second solo hit was a Swedish version of the country classic, *Harper Valley PTA*, which was written by Tom T. Hall and recorded by Jeannie C. Riley in 1968 – her recording topped both the Hot 100 and country chart in the USA, and charted at no.12 in the UK.

The Swedish lyrics for *Fröken Fredriksson* were written by Stikkan Andersson, and Björn's recording of the song gave him his second solo hit from two releases, when it achieved no.7 in Sweden.

38 ~ Elenore by the Hootenanny Singers

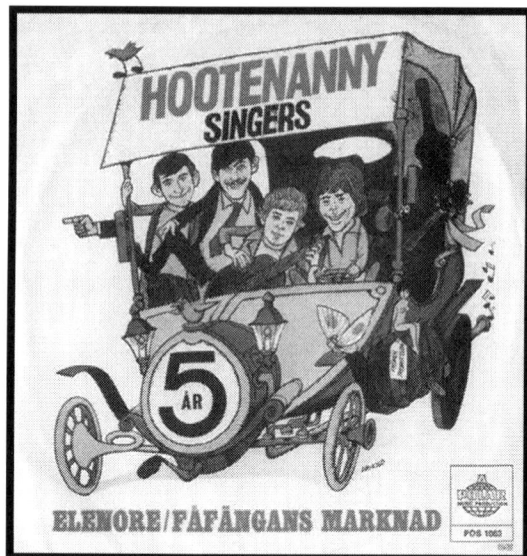

Sweden: Polar POS 1063 (1969).

11.02.69: peaked at no.**16**, charted for 3 weeks

Elenore was written by John Barbata, Howard Kaylan, Al Nichol, Jim Pons and Mark Volman, collectively known as the Turtles, who recorded the song in 1968 for their album, *THE TURLES PRESENT THE BATTLE OF THE BANDS*. Released as a single, *Elenore* achieved Top 10 status in Australia, Canada, New Zealand, the UK and the USA.

The Hootenanny Singers' cover of *Elenore* proved to be the group's penultimate hit, peaking at no.16 in Sweden but failing to chart anywhere else.

Elenore was included on the 1969 compilation, *DE BÄSTA MED* ('The Best Of With'), which was credited to the Hootenanny Singers & Björn Ulvaeus.

39 ~ *Speleman* by the Hep Stars

Sweden: Olga SO 87 (1969).

1.07.69: peaked at no.**10**, charted for 4 weeks

Speleman ('Musician') is a significant release, as it was the first hit that credited both Benny Andersson and Björn Ulvaeus as composers.

Taken from the 1969 album *PÅ SVENSKA*, *Speleman* returned the Hep Stars to the Top 10 in Sweden – it was their 17th Top 10 hit in little more than four years.

40 ~ *Saknar Du Något Min Kära?* by Björn Ulvaeus

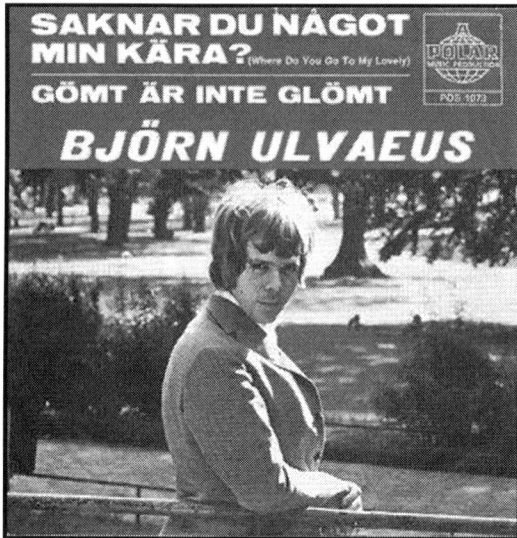

Sweden: Polar POS 1073 (1969).

1.07.69: **19**

Like his first two solo hits, Björn's third was a Swedish cover version – this time, he chose *Where Do You Go To My Lovely*, which was written and recorded by Peter Sarstedt in 1969 – Sarstedt took the song all the way to no.1 in the UK.

Saknar Du Något Min Kära? was Björn's third and final solo hit, before he formed a singer/song-writing duo with Benny Andersson.

Björn's three solo hits, *Raring*, *Fröken Fredriksson* and *Saknar Du Något Min Kära?*, were all included on the 1969 compilation, *DE BÄSTA MED* ('The Best Of With'), which was credited to the Hootenanny Singers & Björn Ulvaeus.

41 ~ Speedy Gonzales by the Hep Stars

Sweden: Olga SO 91 (1969).

19.08.69: peaked at no.**2**, charted for 10 weeks

What proved to be the final single by the Hep Stars was a cover of *Speedy Gonzales* ('the fastest mouse in all Mexico'), which was written by David Hess, Buddy Kaye and Ethel Lee, and originally recorded in 1961 by David Dante. However, the song is best known for Pat Boone's 1962 version, which was a Top 10 hit in both the UK and the USA.

The Hep Stars' cover of *Speedy Gonzales* narrowly failed to give them another no.1, peaking at no.2 in Sweden, but failing to chart anywhere else.

The B-side of *Speedy Gonzales*, *Är Det Inte Kärlek, Säg?* ('Tell Me, Isn't It Love?'), was also listed on the chart for the final four weeks of the chart run.

42 ~ *Hej Gamle Man!* by Björn Ulvaeus & Benny Andersson

Sweden: Polar POS 1110 (1970).

22.12.70: peaked at no.**5**, charted for 9 weeks

Björn and Benny composed and recorded *Hej Gamle Man!* ('Hello/Hi Old Man!') for their debut – and what proved to be their only – album as a duo, *LYCKA* ('Happiness'), released in 1970. Björn sang lead vocals on most of the tracks on the album, including *Hej Gamle Man*. More significantly, however, *Hej Gamle Man* was the first hit to feature all four members of the quartet that would become known around the world as ABBA, as Björn and Benny's respective girlfriends Agnetha Fältskog and Anni-Frid Lyngstad contributed backing vocals.

As well as Sweden, where it charted at no.5, *Hej Gamle Man* was also released as a single in Germany as *Hey, Musikant*, but it wasn't a hit.

LYCKA, which failed to chart in Sweden or anywhere else, featured a second track with backing vocals by Agnetha and Anni-Frid, *Det Där Med Kärlek* ('That With Fondness').

43 ~ *Aldrig Mer* by the Hootenanny Singers

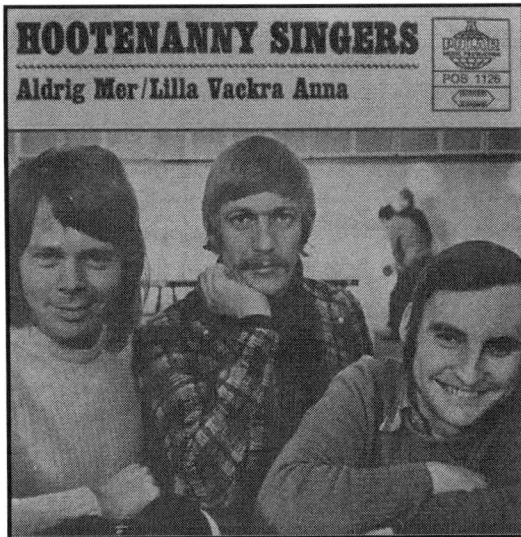

Sweden: Polar POS 1126 (1971).

29.06.71: peaked at no.**7**, charted for 8 weeks

Although it wasn't the group's final single, *Aldrig Mer* ('Never Again') was the Hootenanny Singers' final hit single – it was only released in Sweden, where it achieved no.7.

Björn Ulvaeus was one of only three members of the Hootenanny Singers pictured on the single's sleeve, confirming the group had been reduced to a trio. Björn had, of course, already formed a song-writing partnership with Benny Andersson, and recorded an album with Benny as a duo. It was the only album they would record as a duo, as their girlfriends Agnetha Fältskog and Anni-Frid Lyngstad started to play a more prominent role in the recording process.

44 ~ She's My Kind Of Girl by Benny & Björn

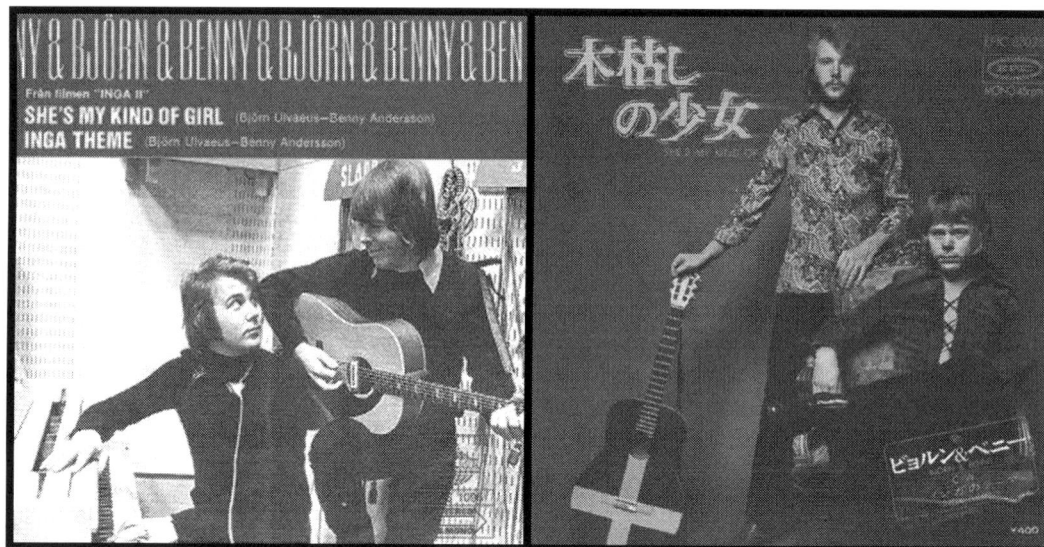

Sweden: Polar POS 1096 (1970).

She's My Kind Of Girl wasn't a hit in Sweden.

Japan
14.02.72: peaked at no.**7**, charted for 22 weeks

Björn and Benny's second hit as a duo was actually recorded and released before their first, having been composed for the Swedish film, *Inga II: The Seduction Of Inga* in November/December 1969. *She's My Kind Of Girl* was released as a single in Sweden in March 1970, but it wasn't a hit.

Two years later, *She's My Kind Of Girl* was released as a single in Japan, and gave Björn and Benny a major hit, charting at no.7 (no.1 on the International chart, which excludes Japanese artists), and reportedly selling more than half a million copies.

She's My Kind Of Girl didn't feature vocals from Agnetha Fältskog or Anni-Frid Lyngstad, which didn't prevent its release as the B-side of the English version of the 1973 single, *Ring Ring*. The track was also included on some editions of the album *RING RING*, which like the single was originally credited to Björn, Benny, Agnetha and Anni-Frid. *She's My Kind Of Girl* had also featured on several more recent ABBA compilations.

45 ~ People Need Love by Björn & Benny, Agnetha & Anni-Frid

Sweden: Polar POS 1156 (1972).

25.07.72: 20-**17-17-17**-18

People Need Love was the first single to credit all four members of the group that became ABBA. Like virtually all the group's output, the single was composed by Björn and Benny, and it gave the quartet their first hit, spending three weeks at no.17 in Sweden.

People Need Love was released as a single in the USA. It didn't enter any of Billboard's charts, but it did rise to no.114 on the sales-oriented Cashbox chart, and may have charted a lot higher if it wasn't for distribution problems and limited availability.

At the time *People Need Love* was recorded in March 1972, Björn, Benny, Agnetha and Anni-Frid had no plans to form a permanent group. They did, however, record *He Is Your Brother* as a follow-up later the same year, but although it enjoyed significant radio airplay in Sweden it wasn't a hit.

People Need Love and *He Is Your Brother* were both included on Björn, Benny, Agnetha and Anni-Frid's debut album as a quartet, *RING RING*, released in 1973.

46 ~ Ring Ring by Björn & Benny, Agnetha & Anni-Frid

Sweden: Polar POS 1171 (Swedish, 1973), Polar POS1172 (English, 1973).

27.02.73: 15-4-2-**1-1-1-1-1-1**-2-2-2-3-8-9-10-20 (Swedish version)
20.03.73: 17-4-2-2-2-4-5-12 (English version)

UK: Epic EPC 1793 (1973), Epic EPC 2452 (Remix, 1974).

13.07.74: 48-34-**32**-37-50 (remix)

Australia
12.11.73: 92-92
13.01.75: 90-90-96 (remix)
19.01.76: 56-41-34-26-14-10-**7-7**-12-11-11-10-16-17-17-18-25-32-41-51-54-68-76
                                                                                    (remix)
Austria
15.07.73: 6-**2**-4-19 (monthly chart)

Belgium
7.07.73: 11-6-3-3-3-**2-2**-4-7-11-18

France
02.74: peaked at no.**82**, charted for 2 weeks

Netherlands
16.06.73: 20-16-8-**5-5**-6-11-16

New Zealand
16.04.76: 29-29-**17**-23-**17**-20-20-x-27

Norway
14.04.73: 6-5-3-3-**2-2**-3-**2**-3-3-3-3-3-4-4-4-5-5-8

South Africa
28.12.73: 16-12-10-9-7-6-5-5-**3-3**-6-7-9-10-13

Zimbabwe
30.03.74: 29-18-17-17-16-17-13-**12-12**-15-19

Following the success of *People Need Love*, Benny and Björn were approached by the Swedish Broadcasting Company towards the end of 1972, and invited to submit a song for the Swedish heat of the forthcoming Eurovision Song Contest. Keen to gain wider recognition, the pair was happy to accept the invitation, and with their manager Stig Anderson they composed *Ring Ring (Bara Du Slog en Signal)*.

Anderson was so confident they would win the Swedish heat, he had Björn & Benny, Agnetha & Anni-Frida, as the quartet were still known, record *Ring Ring* in English, German and Spanish, as well as Swedish. Neil Sedaka and his song-writing partner Phil Cody were recruited, to help with the translation of the song into English. Björn and Benny did, however, pen the English lyrics to the B-side *Rock 'N Roll Band* themselves.

HIT OF SWEDEN

*) Courtesy Radio Sweden April 17, 1973

1. RING RING (Swedish version)
Bjorn & Benny, Anna & Frida
Polar POS 1171

2. RING RING (English version)
Bjorn & Benny, Anna & Frida
Polar POS 1172

3. RING RING (LP)
Bjorn & Benny, Anna & Frida
Polar POLS 242
Orig.publ: Union Songs AB/Sweden Music AB

The Swedish heat was staged on 10th February 1973 – around the time Agnetha was expecting her and Björn's first child. Happily, daughter Linda Elin didn't arrive until 23rd February, but although it received a rapturous reception from the audience, the panel of judges voted *Ring Ring* in third place (a row ensued, which resulted in the panel of judges being replaced with members of the public, for future heats).

The experts were proven wrong in spectacular fashion, when both the Swedish and English versions of *Ring Ring* charted in Sweden, the former at no.1 and the latter at no.2. The Swedish chart at the time was a combined singles/album chart, and remarkably for the weeks dated April 10/17, 1973, Björn & Benny, Anna & Frida (as per the printed chart) held the Top 3 positions with *Ring Ring* (Swedish Version), *Ring Ring* (English Version) and *RING RING* (LP).

As well as being a huge success in Sweden, *Ring Ring* broke the quartet that would soon become ABBA internationally, with the English version hitting no.2 in Austria, Belgium and Norway, no.3 in South Africa, no.5 in the Netherlands and no.12 in Zimbabwe. In some countries, Agnetha and Anni-Frid were billed by their nicknames, Anna and Frida (misspelled 'Frieda').

In the UK, three record companies turned down *Ring Ring*, before CBS/Epic decided to take a chance – but, first time out, *Ring Ring* failed to chart.

After Benny, Björn, Agnetha and Anni-Frid took the first letter of their names, and re-arranged them to ABBA, and after they won the Eurovision Song Contest with *Waterloo*, *Ring Ring* was remixed by Paul Atkinson and reissued in countries where it had missed out in 1973 – this time, of course, the single was credited to ABBA.

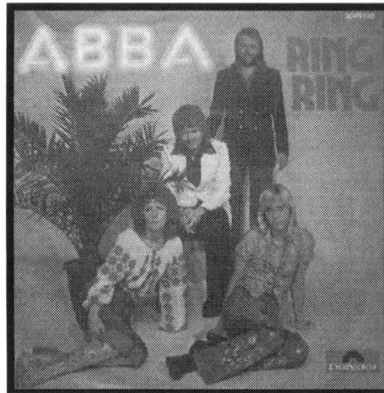

The remixed version of *Ring Ring* was only a minor in the UK, peaking at no.32, while both the original and remixed versions charted in Australia, peaking at no.92 in 1973 and no.90 in 1975, respectively. A year later, however, ABBA mania swept Australia and *Ring Ring* enjoyed a new lease of life, re-entering the chart and rising to no.7. At the same time, the single charted at no.17 in New Zealand.

In some countries, excluding Sweden and the UK, *Love Isn't Easy (But It Sure Is Hard Enough)* was released as the follow-up to *Ring Ring*. The single was credited to 'Björn Benny & Agnetha Frida', but it wasn't a hit anywhere.

An Irish band, The Others, recorded a cover of *Ring Ring* in 1974, and was rewarded with a no.12 hit in Ireland.

47 ~ Waterloo by ABBA

Sweden: Polar POS 1186 (Swedish, 1974), Polar POS 1187 (English, 1974).

12.03.74: 4-**2-2-2-2-2-2-2-2**-4-8-10 (Swedish version)
12.03.74: 9-9-8-9-4-4-3-5 (English version)

UK: Epic EPC 2240 (1974), Polydor 9820540 (2004), 9820541 (Picture Disc, 2004).

20.04.74: 17-2-**1-1**-2-6-15-23-33
29.05.04: 20-43-70

Australia
10.06.74: 70-66-41-24-16-15-14-11-7-6-**4**-5-7-9-9-9-17-25-35-45-52-63
22.03.76: 88-68-60-67-67 (EP)

Austria
15.05.74: 3-**2**-3-11-16 (monthly chart)

Belgium
13.04.74: 19-10-2-**1-1-1-1-1-1**-5-8-17-17-23

Canada
15.06.74: 64-41-26-22-16-14-**7-7-7**-39-59

Finland
05.74: peaked at no.**1**, charted for 24 weeks (monthly chart)

France
04.74: peaked at no.**3**, charted for 12 weeks

Germany
6.05.74: 28-3-2-2-2-2-**1**-2-**1**-**1**-**1**-3-3-4-4-8-10-12-11

Ireland
25.04.74: 15-**1**-**1**-2-2-3-4-9-19
20.05.04: 33-41

Netherlands
13.04.74: 19-4-2-2-**1**-**1**-4-5-9-13-24

New Zealand
14.06.74: peaked at no.**3**, charted for 13 weeks

Norway
30.03.74: 8-6-**1**-**1**-**1**-**1**-**1**-**1**-**1**-**1**-2-2-2-2-2-3-3-4-7-8-9-9-10

South Africa
31.05.74: 19-14-8-4-3-3-2-**1**-**1**-2-2-4-7-8-14

Spain
04.74: peaked at no.**3**, charted for 20 weeks

Switzerland
17.04.74: 6-**1**-**1**-**1**-**1**-**1**-**1**-**1**-**1**-**1**-2-2-3-3-5-5-6-8-9

USA
1.06.74: 76-66-52-39-30-24-18-18-15-11-7-7-**6**-24-34-43-48

Zimbabwe
8.06.74: 20-12-9-8-6-6-6-6-5-3-3-**2**-**2**-**2**-**2**-4-6-8-11-14-18

Having been unsuccessful in 1973, Benny, Björn and their manager Stig Anderson were determined to represent their country at the 1974 Eurovision Song Contest. Mindful ballads had won recent contests, they decided to go with something faster paced, and it wasn't long before Benny and Björn had composed a melody everyone agreed was strong enough. Anderson was tasked with finding a theme for the song and, after 'Honey Pie' was rejected, he settled on 'Waterloo'.

The Swedish heat for the Eurovision Song Contest took place on 9th February 1974. In the lead up to the contest, already popular thanks to the success of *Ring Ring*, Anderson often referred to Benny, Björn, Agnetha and Anni-Frid in interviews as 'ABBA', an acronym derived from the first letters of their names, and when a Swedish newspaper conducted a poll, 80% of voters agreed ABBA was a great choice of name for a pop group.

There was a problem: there was a Swedish fish canning company called Abba. But, fortunately, the canning company didn't object to a pop group sharing their name, provided members of the group didn't indulge in behaviour that might result in their good name being brought into disrepute.

Having won the Swedish heat with *Waterloo*, ABBA flew to England for the 1974 Eurovision Song Contest, which was staged at Brighton's Dome Theatre on 6th April. Determined to be noticed, they opted for colourful, glam-rock costumes, and their conductor Olof Waldoff entered into the spirit of things by dressing as Napoleon.

England's own Olivia Newton-John and the Dutch duo Mouth & McNeal provided stiff opposition, but ABBA won the contest by six votes – and took an important step on the road to superstardom.

Waterloo was recorded on 17th December 1973 at the Metronome Studios in Stockholm. In Sweden, both the Swedish and English versions charted, with the Swedish recording spending eight straight weeks at no.2, but kept out of the no.1 spot by ABBA's self-titled album. The English recording also did well, peaked at no.3.

Waterloo broke ABBA internationally, hitting no.1 in Belgium, Finland, Germany, Ireland, the Netherlands, Norway, South Africa, Switzerland and the UK. The single also achieved no.2 in Austria and Zimbabwe, no.3 in France, New Zealand and Spain, no.4 in Australia, no.6 in the USA and no.7 in Canada.

In Australia, *Waterloo* was the lead song on a 4-track EP released in 1976, which charted at no.60.

Waterloo was reissued in the UK and Ireland in 2004, to mark the 30th anniversary of the song's victory at the Eurovision Song Contest – it charted at no.20 in the UK and no.33 in Ireland.

The following year, at the 50th anniversary celebration of the Eurovision Song Contest, *Waterloo* was recognised as the best song in the competition's history.

In April 2014, to mark the 40th anniversary of ABBA winning with Eurovision Contest, *Waterloo* was reissued as a limited edition 7" single with the Swedish version on the A-side, and the English version on the B-side – to the disappointment of many fans, only 1,000 copies were pressed, thus creating an instant rarity.

48 ~ Nina, Pretty Ballerina by Björn & Benny, Agnetha & Anni-Frid

Austria: Polydor 2040 111 (1974).

15.03.74: **8**-11-13 (monthly chart)

Nina, Pretty Ballerina was only released as a single in Austria and France, to promote Björn, Benny, Agnetha and Frida's debut album, *RING RING*. The single was backed with *I Am Just A Girl* in Austria, and with *He Is Your Brother* in France.

    Nine, Pretty Ballerina made its debut on Austria's monthly chart at no.8, but rose no higher, and the single wasn't a hit in France.

    In 1975, *Nine, Pretty Ballerina* was released as a single in Kenya and the Philippines, to promote ABBA's compilation, *THE BEST OF*.

49 ~ Honey Honey by ABBA

Sweden: Polar POS 1192 (1974).

Honey Honey wasn't a hit in Sweden.

UK:

Honey Honey wasn't released as a single in the UK, however, it did enter the Top 200 on the strength of digital sales in July 2008, peaking at no.133 during a six week chart run.

Australia
4.11.74: 93-69-64-48-43-41-39-33-**30-30**-32-**30**-35-?-47-63-66-74-93

Austria
15.09.74: **4**-7 (monthly chart)

Belgium
3.08.74: **19-19-19-19**-23-20-20-24-29-30

Canada
21.09.74: 90-73-68-67-47-32-29-19-**18**-35-69

Finland
02.75: **11** (monthly chart)

Germany
8.07.74: 28-8-4-3-3-**2**-3-4-3-3-3-3-**2**-**2**-3-**2**-**2**-5-8

Netherlands
21.12.74: 25-25-**17**-**17**-23

New Zealand
8.11.74: peaked at no.**16**, charted for 3 weeks

Norway
2.08.08: **16**-20

Spain
09.74: peaked at no.**16**, charted for 2 weeks

Switzerland
7.08.74: 9-6-6-**4**-**4**-**4**-5-5-6-6-9-10

USA
14.09.74: 89-72-61-51-40-34-**27**-**27**-45-95

Composed by Benny and Björn with Stig Anderson, *Honey Honey* was the second single released from ABBA's 1974 album, *WATERLOO*, in most countries, after the title track.

Honey Honey was recorded in January 1974, and was the last song ABBA recorded in their native Swedish. Surprisingly, it wasn't a hit in Sweden, but it did chart at no.2 in Germany, no.4 in Austria and Switzerland, no.11 in Finland, no.16 in New Zealand, Norway and Spain, no.17 in the Netherlands, no.18 in Canada, no.19 in Belgium, no.27 in the USA and no.30 in Australia.

In the UK, a decision was taken to re-release *Ring Ring* instead of *Honey Honey*, but only a no.32 hit resulted. If the success of a cover version by Sweet Dreams is any guide, *Honey Honey* would have fared much, much better.

Sweet Dreams was a duo comprising Polly Brown (of Pickettywitch fame) and Tony Jackson, however, the male vocals on their cover of *Honey Honey* were actually sung by Ron Roker. The duo's cover of *Honey Honey* charted at no.9 in Zimbabwe, no.10 in the UK, no.14 in Ireland, no.38 in Australia, no.42 in Germany and no.68 in the USA.

50 ~ Another Town, Another Train by Björn & Benny, Agnetha & Anni-Frid

South Africa: Sunshine SUN 4 (1974).

Another Town, Another Train wasn't a hit in South Africa.

Zimbabwe
26.10.74: 19-**18**

Another Town, Another Train was released as a single in a small number of countries including Japan, South Africa and the USA, to promote the album, *RING RING*. In Japan, although all four members of the group featured on the picture sleeve, the single was credited to 'Björn & Benny'.

Another Town, Another Train was a no.18 hit in Zimbabwe (or Rhodesia, as the country was named at the time), but it didn't chart anywhere else. The single was first released before *Waterloo*, but it wasn't a hit until it was re-released, after the success of *Waterloo*.

A German version of *Another Town, Another Train*, with lyrics by Fred Jay, was recorded and titled *Wer Im Wartesaal Der Liebe Steht* – it featured on the B-side of the German version of the single, *Ring Ring*.

51 ~ *Hasta Mañana* by ABBA

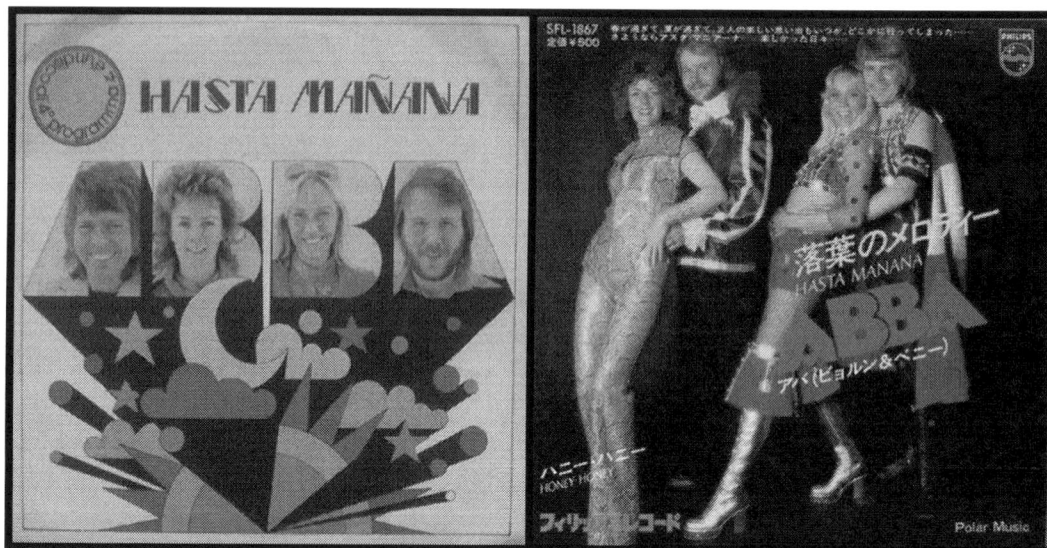

South Africa: Sunshine SUN 8 (1974).

8.11.74: 16-7-6-4-3-3-**2-2**-3-4-6-6-8-14-15

Australia: RCA 102560 (1976).

10.05.76: 95-89-68-44-35-28-22-21-20-**16**-20-21-28-30-36-52-75-93

New Zealand
16.07.76: 24-21-12-**9**-11-12-16-23-16-20-30-40

Stig Anderson was on holiday in Las Palmas, in the Canary Islands, when he wrote the lyrics to *Hasta Mañana* (Spanish for 'See you tomorrow'), after hearing the expression numerous times. Via telephone, Anderson passed on the lyrics to Benny and Björn, who composed the music.

    ABBA recorded *Hasta Mañana* on 18th December 1973, for their 1974 album, *WATERLOO* – the quartet almost gave up on the song, as none of them could think of a way to sing it the way they felt it should sound. It was Agnetha, messing around in the studio, who came up with the idea of trying to sing it like Connie Francis. 'I sang it in that really emotional way,' she said, 'and then we found that we were on the right way.'

    Originally, serious thought was given to entering *Hasta Mañana* instead of *Waterloo*, in the Swedish heat of the 1974 Eurovision Song Contest. *Waterloo*, it was felt, might be a bit too risky and *Hasta Mañana* was a safer choice. But, as Agnetha sang lead on *Hasta Mañana*, whereas Agnetha and Frida shared lead vocals on *Waterloo*, it was agreed to go with *Waterloo*.

Hasta Mañana was only released as a single in selected countries, including Australia, Italy, Japan, New Zealand, Portugal and South Africa. It charted at no.2 in South Africa, no.9 in New Zealand and no.16 in Australia.

Lena Andersson recorded two versions of *Hasta Mañana* using ABBA's original backing track. In 1974, she recorded the song in Swedish, and then two years later she recorded a German version.

In 1977, a cover of *Hasta Mañana* by the Boones (Pat Boone and his daughters) topped the Hot 100 in the USA for 10 weeks, as the B-side of Debby Boone's *You Light Up My Life*.

52 ~ So Long by ABBA

Sweden: Polar POS 1195 (1974).

28.01.75: 9-**7**-9

UK: Epic EPC 2848 (1974).

So Long wasn't a hit in the UK.

Austria
15.01.75: 7-**3** (monthly chart)

France
10.74: peaked at no.**64**, charted for 3 weeks

Germany
15.12.74: 33-24-25-**11**-25-17-16-21-20-27-19-18-20-30-34-28

As the lead single from the 1975 album, *ABBA*, *So Long* did little to suggest ABBA's career wasn't going to go downhill as fast as that of most Eurovision winners, charting at no.3 in Austria, no.7 in Sweden and no.11 in Germany, but failing to chart in most countries. In the UK, apart from the original release of *Ring Ring*, *So Long* was destined to be the only ABBA single that didn't chart.

53 ~ I Do, I Do, I Do, I Do, I Do by ABBA

Sweden: Polar POS 1207 (1975).

I Do, I Do, I Do, I Do, I Do wasn't a hit in Sweden.

UK: Epic EPC 3229 (1975).

12.07.75: 50-42-41-**38**-41-44

Australia
7.07.75: 83-76-68-67-65-52-46-32-29-22-19-9-4-2-**1-1-1**-2-5-7-7-10-15-15-18-22-25-32-
  32-42-46-50-71-78

Austria
15.05.75: 8-**4**-x-20 (monthly chart)

Belgium
29.03.75: 19-9-6-5-3-3-**2**-3-4-7-14-30

Canada
28.02.76: 89-74-64-46-45-26-23-18-17-**14**-17-19-30-36-41

France
04.75: peaked at no.**14**, charted for 14 weeks

Germany
14.04.75: 28-31-28-22-20-11-17-13-12-7-7-11-8-8-12-**6**-26-14-26-35-46-47

Netherlands
22.03.75: 19-9-7-4-**3**-6-13-26

New Zealand
11.07.75: 16-18-4-3-2-2-2-**1**-4-4-9-10-7-16-13-11-15-17-8-11-15-22-12-13-(no chart for 5 weeks)-15-14-23-33-27-x-40-x-22-26-35-22-28-12-14-19-21-17-24-23-29-31-33-34-33-39

Norway
13.09.75: 10-4-3-**2-2-2**-3-4-4-4-4-4-4-4-4-6-4-4-4-4-4-4-5-7

South Africa
9.05.75: 13-8-4-2-2-2-**1-1**-2-3-4-10

Switzerland
2.05.75: 9-5-3-**1-1-1-1-1**-2-4-4-4-6-7-8-8-10

USA
14.02.76: 86-76-69-57-46-41-36-26-23-21-17-**15-15**-39-54

Zimbabwe
28.06.75: 18-x-14-12-8-**5**-7-7-8-11-11-12-15-13-14-13-13-10-17

Although it wasn't a hit in Sweden, the second single released from the *ABBA* album returned the group to the Top 10 in many countries where it was released.

I Do, I Do, I Do, I Do, I Do, which was a tribute to the American 1950s band leader Billy Vaughan, was recorded on 21st February 1975. It is the single that is usually credited with launching ABBA mania in Australia, where it was the first of three ABBA singles to hit no.1, one after the other, during an uninterrupted 14 week reign.

I Do, I Do, I Do, I Do, I Do also hit no.1 in New Zealand, South Africa and Sweden, and charted at no.2 in Belgium and Norway, no.3 in the Netherlands, no.4 in Austria, no.5 in Zimbabwe, no.6 in Germany, no.14 in Canada and France, no.15 in the USA and no.38 in the UK.

Om Och Om Och Om Igen, a Swedish cover of *I Do, I Do, I Do, I Do, I Do* by Birgitta Wollgard & Salut, charted at no.4 in Sweden towards the end of 1975.

BANG EN BOOMERANG by Svenne & Lotta

Sweden: Polar POS 1203 (1975).

Bang En Boomerang wasn't a hit in Sweden.

Australia
15.12.75: **94**

Belgium
27.09.75: **29**

Norway
10.05.75: **11**

Towards the end of 1974, Benny and Björn were once again invited to submit a song, for the Swedish heat of the 1975 Eurovision Song Contest. Although they had no desire to see ABBA entering again, they did offer a song they had written for ABBA to two former Hep Stars, the husband and wife duo Svenne & Lotta. Stig Anderson wrote some Swedish lyrics, turning *Bang-A-Boomerang* into *Bang En Boomerang*, and although Svenne & Lotta only finished third in the Swedish heat, they did achieve Top 30 status in Norway and Belgium with the single.

Using Svenne & Lotta's backing track, ABBA re-recorded *Bang-A-Boomerang* for their self-titled 1975 album but, other than in France, it wasn't released as a single.

54 ~ S.O.S by ABBA

Sweden: Polar POS 1213 (1975).

S.O.S wasn't a hit in Sweden.

UK: Epic EPC 3576 (1975).

20.09.75: 47-31-16-13-7-**6-6**-7-21-33

Australia
10.11.75: 77-48-30-21-6-3-2-2-2-**1**-2-2-2-2-4-6-12-16-17-20-28-28-26-38-25-37-49-61-
  81

Austria
15.09.75: **2-2-2**-5-5-12 (monthly chart)

Belgium
5.07.75: 10-3-2-**1**-3-3-5-12-18

Canada
13.09.75: 98-87-83-75-53-48-37-32-27-20-**17**-19-28-36-39-39-39-56

France
10.75: peaked at no.**59**, charted for 5 weeks (b/w *Bang-A-Boomerang*)

Germany
4.08.75: 20-4-3-4-2-2-**1-1-1-1-1-1-1**-2-5-20-8-9-14-10-18-11-16-18-17-21-34-22-42-50

Ireland
22.10.75: 14-7-6-5-11-**4-4**-19

Japan
25.01.01: peaked at no.**15**, charted for 11 weeks (b/w *Chiquitita*)

Netherlands
14.06.75: 17-5-**2-2**-3-5-12-18-29

New Zealand
7.11.75: 22-12-9-6-3-2-2-(no chart for 5 weeks)-**1**-2-4-8-7-5-24-14-21-x-25-21-20-35-25-33-32-26-33

Norway
4.10.75: 8-3-3-**2-2-2-2-2-2-2-2-2-2-2-2-2-2-2-2**-3-3-4-5-7-11

South Africa
12.09.75: 18-14-8-**1-1-1-1**-2-2-3-4-5-12

Switzerland
15.08.75: 10-5-3-4-4-4-**3-3**-5-5-6-6-5-6-7-7-10

USA
9.08.75: 89-84-x-x-99-89-86-76-53-40-24-20-17-**15-15**-23-32-47-73

Zimbabwe
15.11.75: 16-9-5-3-**2-2-2-2**-3-4-6-5-6-7-12-16

S.O.S, which had the working title 'Turn Me On', was recorded on 22nd and 23rd August 1974, for ABBA's self-titled 1975 album. Stig Andersson came up with the title, and wrote the original lyrics, which Björn then re-wrote.

S.O.S was the third single released from *ABBA*, and proved to be more successful than the first two, especially in the UK where it returned ABBA to the Top 10 for the first time since *Waterloo*.

S.O.S. hit no.1 in Australia (where it deposed *Mamma Mia*), Belgium, Germany, New Zealand and South Africa, and charted at no.2 in Austria, the Netherlands, Norway (where it held the no.2 for 18 straight weeks) and Zimbabwe, no.3 in Switzerland, no.4 in Ireland, no.6 in the UK, no.15 in the USA and no.17 in Canada.

In France, the B-side *Bang-A-Boomerang* was listed alongside *S.O.S* on the chart, but the single peaked at a lowly no.59.

Lena Andersson recorded a German version of *S.O.S*, using ABBA's original backing track, but it wasn't a hit.

In 1988, Austrian trio Edelweiss sampled the chorus of *S.O.S* on their hit single *Bring Me Edelweiss*, without permission – this resulted in legal action being taken, and the payment of damages to the song's composers, Benny and Björn. *Bring Me Edelweiss* hit no.1 in Austria, Switzerland and Sweden, and charted at no.2 in Germany and the Netherlands, and no.5 in the UK.

S.O.S was recorded, in Swedish, by Agnetha for her 1975 solo album, *ELVA KVINNOR I ETT HUS* ('Eleven Women In One House') – see later entry.

S.O.S is unique, in that it is the only hit single in most countries where both the song title and the artist credit are both palindromes.

Moviestar by Harpo

Sweden: EMI 4E 006-35236 (1975).

27.11.75: 12-13-13-6-8-2-**1-1-1**-2-2-3-4-4-4-2-2-**1**-3-4-5-8-14-10 (bi-weekly)
16.05.97: 56-53-54-54-21-22-22-27-43-43-47-35-23-24-27-32-33-33-35-47-39-46-44-36

UK: DJM DJS400 (1976).

17.04.76: 45-35-27-**24**-25-34

Australia
29.03.76: peaked at no.**3**, charted for 34 weeks

Austria
15.03.76: 8-**1**-15 (monthly chart)

Belgium
20.09.75: 23-12-**3-3**-6-8-9-14-22

Germany
29.09.75: peaked at no.**1** (4 weeks), charted for 31 weeks

Ireland
13.05.76: **13**

Netherlands
30.08.75: 27-14-7-5-**3**-6-10-27

New Zealand
25.06.76: 20-18-16-10-11-**9**-11-15-13-14-12-14-25-23

Norway
21.02.76: 5-6-5-6-5-2-2-**1**-4-2-2-2-3-3-3-3-2-2-**1-1-1-1-1-1-1-1-1-1**-3-4-7

Switzerland
30.01.76: 9-8-4-**1-1-1-1-1**-3-3-4-8-9-14-15

Jan Harpo Torsten Svensson was born in Stockholm in 1950, and he was a popular singer in Sweden and continental Europe in the 1970s.

Harpo's biggest hit was *Moviestar*, which featured backing vocals from Frida and Lena Ericsson ('Moviestar, oh Moviestar…') – it hit no.1 in Austria, Germany, Norway, Sweden and Switzerland, and charted at no.3 in Australia, Belgium and the Netherlands, no.9 in New Zealand, no.13 in Ireland and no.24 in the UK.

Moviestar, which Harpo recorded in English and Swedish, returned to the Swedish singles chart in 1997, peaking at no.21.

Prior to *Moviestar*, Frida contributed backing vocals to *Pin Up Girl*, a track Harpo recorded for his 1975 album, *HARPO & BANANABAND*.

55 ~ S.O.S by Agnetha Fältskog

Sweden: Cupol CUS 303 (1975).

14.11.75: 13-15-8-5-**4**-6-8-6-10-13 (bi-weekly chart)

Although the version by ABBA is far better known, Agnetha also recorded a solo version of *S.O.S* in Swedish, for her 1975 solo album, *ELVA KVINNOR I ETT HUS* ('Eleven Women In One House'). It was the only track on the album Agnetha didn't compose herself, though she did share credits as a producer on the recording with Benny and Björn.

    S.O.S was a hit in many countries for ABBA, but their single didn't chart in Sweden, whereas Agnetha's version was released as the second single from her solo album and peaked at no.4.

56 ~ Mamma Mia by ABBA

Sweden: Polar POS 1220 (1975).

Mamma Mia wasn't a hit in Sweden.

UK: Epic EPC 3790 (1975).

13.12.75: 43-32-29-29-12-3-3-**1-1**-2-5-13-24-38
19.07.08: 86-57-56-71-68-68-83

Australia
22.09.75: 52-27-23-11-9-4-**1-1-1-1-1-1-1-1-1-1-1**-3-4-5-5-7-10-14-22-29-31-34-31-29-31-
    34-36-44-54-56-61-63-65
14.07.08: 99-48-59-70-83

Austria
15.01.76: 9-**3**-5-9 (monthly chart)

Belgium
12.75: 22-10-5-3-**2-2**-4-7-11-19

Canada
5.06.76: 96-78-72-50-42-39-33-27-24-20-**18-18**-24-28-31-35-44-51-60-89

Finland
04.76: **14** (monthly chart)

Germany
15.12.75: 40-16-24-12-4-6-9-3-**1**-2-2-3-4-4-3-8-9-20-15-22-45-38-34-39

Ireland
15.01.76: 14-3-**1-1-1-1-1**-3-9

Netherlands
6.12.75: 30-21-**12**-27

New Zealand
6.02.76: 34-**2-2**-4-3-5-4-3-6-5-7-5-3-4-9-11-23-28-26-32-29-35-39-34-x-36-40

Norway
31.01.76: 5-3-3-**2-2-2**-3-4-5-6-8

South Africa
13.03.76: 19-9-**7**-10-10-11-13-16-18

Spain
25.01.09: **48**-49

Switzerland
19.12.75: 7-6-3-2-2-**1-1**-3-3-3-3-5-7-9-14
17.08.08: 90-85-98-x-x-x-60-82-x-x-74-84-79
11.01.09: 98-93

USA
22.05.76: 83-63-53-43-39-35-**32-32**-70

Zimbabwe
17.04.76: **20-20**

ABBA recorded *Mamma Mia* on 12th March 1975 – it was the last track they recorded for their self-titled 1975 album.

There were no plans to release *Mamma Mia* as a single, before the outbreak of ABBA mania in Australia and the repeated screening of the *Mamma Mia* promo on Australian TV led to RCA – ABBA's record company in Australia – to request permission to release

Mamma Mia. Initially, the request was refused, but eventually Stig Anderson relented and gave his consent.

Mamma Mia topped the Australian chart for 10 straight weeks – it took over the top spot from *I Do, I Do, I Do, I Do, I Do*, and was deposed by *S.O.S*, giving ABBA three consecutive no.1s that dominated the chart for 14 weeks.

The success of *Mamma Mia* in Australia led to its release internationally, as the fourth single from *ABBA*. The single hit no.1 in Germany, Ireland, Switzerland and the UK, no.2 in Belgium, New Zealand and Norway, no.3 in Austria, no.7 in South Africa, no.12 in the Netherlands, no.14 in Finland, no.18 in Canada, no.20 in Zimbabwe and no.32 in the USA.

In 1999, *Mamma Mia* was one of 11 ABBA songs covered by Abba*Teens for their debut album, *THE ABBA GENERATION*. Formed the previous year, Abba*Teens were a Swedish pop group comprising Amit Paul, Dhani Lennevald, Marie Serneholt and Sara Lumholdt. *Mamma Mia* was released as the quartet's debut single – it hit no.1 in Sweden, and charted at no.3 in Norway, no.6 in Spain, no.7 in the Netherlands, no.9 in Switzerland, no.10 in Belgium and Germany, no.12 in the UK, no.13 in New Zealand, and no.14 in Austria and Finland.

To avoid any confusion, and wanting to avoid the risk of legal action, Abba*Teens wisely changed their name to A*Teens, although early pressings of *Mamma Mia* did credit Abba*Teens.

In 1999, *Mamma Mia* lent its name to a hugely successful stage musical, written around the songs of ABBA. Nine years later, the musical *Mamma Mia!* was turned into an equally successful film, which starred Meryl Streep, Pierce Brosnan, Julie Walters and Colin Firth.

57 ~ Fernando by ABBA

Sweden: Polar POS 1224 (1976).

12.04.76: 4-**2**-3-3-3-4-4-6-9-10-15 (bi-weekly chart)

UK: Epic EPC 4036 (1976).

27.03.76: 44-14-4-2-2-2-**1-1-1-1**-4-4-18-25-38

Australia
15.03.76: 75-14-2-**1-1-1-1-1-1-1-1-1-1-1-1-1-1**-2-2-2-3-3-6-7-8-9-11-16-21-29-34-39-50-
   48-58-58-70-86-88-93

Austria
15.04.76: 8-2-**1-1**-3-10 (monthly chart)

Belgium
13.03.76: 18-9-7-5-**1-1**-2-2-2-2-3-5-10-15-19-26

Canada
18.09.76: 97-69-62-52-29-15-**4-4**-11-15-19-22-23-24-24-24

Finland
05.76: peaked at no.**2**, charted for 32 weeks (monthly chart)

France
04.76: peaked at no.**1** (3 weeks), charted for 13 weeks

Germany
29.03.76: 5-5-3-3-3-**1**-3-**1-1-1-1-1-1**-2-2-4-7-3-4-10-10-8-12-21-20-22

Ireland
1.04.76: 11-9-3-**1-1-1-1-1-1**-2-2-5-10-13-17

Netherlands
13.03.76: 19-13-2-**1-1-1**-3-4-9-21

New Zealand
14.05.76: 2-2-2-**1-1-1-1-1-1-1-1**-2-2-1-2-3-3-6-4-6-5-8-7-10-17-14-13-14-13-11-20-28-
  (no chart for 7 weeks)-26-25-30-36-28

Norway
10.04.76: 9-7-4-4-3-**2-2-2-2**-3-3-3-**2-2-2**-3-3-4-4-4-4-x-x-9

South Africa
12.06.76: 19-11-5-2-**1-1-1-1-1-1**-2-2-5-8-14-18

Spain
03.76: peaked at no.**3**, charted for 26 weeks

Switzerland
19.03.76: 8-2-**1-1-1-1-1-1-1-1-1-1**-3-4-6-7-8-9-10-12-15

USA
4.09.76: 77-56-47-40-30-24-21-20-18-16-14-**13**-23-30-42-92

Zimbabwe
12.06.76: 12-9-6-5-3-**2-2-2-2-2-2**-3-3-3-4-4-5-6-9-9-11-15-17

Originally titled 'Hernandez', *Fernando* was first recorded – in Swedish – by Frida, for her 1975 album, *FRIDA ENSAM* ('Frida Alone'). The Swedish lyrics were penned by Stig Anderson and, although it wasn't released as a single, her solo version was hugely popular in Sweden and topped the *Svensktoppen* radio chart for nine straight weeks.

The success of Frida's version of *Fernando* led Benny and Björn to write English lyrics for the song, the theme being the Mexican revolution, and record it as an ABBA track. It wasn't finished in time to be included on the group's 1976 album, *ARRIVAL* (except in Australia and New Zealand, where the album was released later), so it was released as ABBA's first non-album single.

Fernando topped the chart in Australia for an impressive 14 weeks, equalling the record set by the Beatles with *Hey Jude*. It also hit no.1 in Austria, Belgium, France, Germany, Ireland, the Netherlands, New Zealand, South Africa, Switzerland and the UK, and charted at no.2 in Finland, Norway, Sweden and Zimbabwe, no.3 in Spain, no.4 in Canada and no.13 in the USA.

Fernando subsequently featured on ABBA's *GREATEST HITS* compilation, released towards the end of 1975, and was added to the CD release of *ARRIVAL* in 1997.

58 ~ I've Been Waiting For You by ABBA

Australia: RCA 102561 (1975).

14.04.75: 89-89-76-62-**49**-51-56-57-67-81
14.03.77: 98-94-96 (b/w *King Kong Song*)

New Zealand
27.03.77: 12-**8**-17-19-**8**-12-13-16-21-17-27

Recorded on 15th September 1974, *I've Been Waiting For You* was featured on ABBA's self-titled 1975 album.

In most countries, *I've Been Waiting For You* was released as the B-side of *So Long* – Benny and Björn have both said they feel the potential of *I've Been Waiting for You* was overlooked, and feel it would have fared better as a single than *So Long*.

I've Been Waiting For You was released as a single in Australia in 1975 but, despite ABBA mania sweeping the country, it failed to achieve Top 40 status.

Two years later, *I've Been Waiting For You* was released in New Zealand, and was much more successful, rising to no.8.

59 ~ Rock Me by ABBA

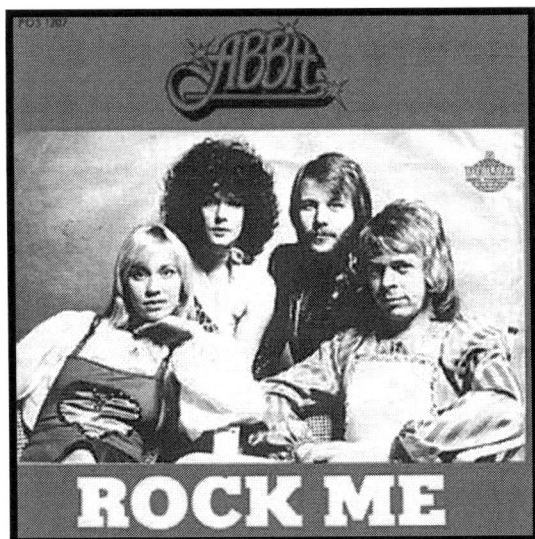

Australia: RCA 102607 (B-side of *I Do, I Do, I Do, I Do, I Do*, 1975).

12.04.76: 43-28-16-13-9-7-5-7-5-**4-4**-6-8-11-11-16-16-17-23-28-40-43-49-53-54-68

New Zealand
10.12.76: 23-23-(no chart for 7 weeks)-**2-2**-3-8-13-10-24-13-28-18-26-18-19-18-23-27-31-40

Originally recorded as 'Baby' on 18th October 1974, ABBA re-recorded the track as *Rock Me*, for their 1975 self-titled album.

   Rock Me was the B-side of *I Do, I Do, I Do, I Do, I Do* in Australia and New Zealand, where, following the success of *I Do, I Do, I Do, I Do, I Do* and to take advantage of ABBA mania, *Rock Me* was re-promoted as the A-side and became a major hit in its own right, rising to no.2 in New Zealand and no.4 in Australia.

   A short demo version of *Baby* was one of the previously unreleased rarities featured on *ABBA Undeleted*, which appeared on CD4 of the 1994 box-set, *THANK YOU FOR THE MUSIC*.

60 ~ Dancing Queen by ABBA

Sweden: Polar POS 1225 (1976).

24.08.76: **1-1-1-1-1-1-1**-2-2-2-2-4-4-7-10 (bi-weekly chart)

UK: Epic EPC 4499 (1976), Polydor PO 231 (1992).

21.08.76: 23-16-**1-1-1-1-1-1**-2-6-8-13-20-30-37
5.09.92: 21-16-19-33-50-x-x-x-96
19.07.08: 90-82-95-90-96

Australia
16.08.76: 38-8-3-**1-1-1-1-1-1-1-1**-2-4-5-6-7-10-20-25-25-27-32-46-60-73
26.10.92: 53-43-31-31-28-41-71-76-93
21.07.08: 58-63-68-84-97

Austria
15.09.76: 11-5-**4**-9-22 (monthly chart)

Belgium
21.08.76: 14-6-2-**1-1-1-1-1-1-1**-3-4-11-18

Canada
1.01.77: 97-60-53-43-32-20-14-12-9-8-6-4-3-**1**-**1**-3-3-10-15-23-28-37

Finland
09.76: peaked at no.**3**, charted for 32 weeks (monthly chart)

France
08.76: peaked at no.**5**, charted for 12 weeks

Germany
16.08.76: 21-15-5-2-2-**1**-2-2-2-3-2-3-5-5-5-8-11-14-18-22-22-28-40-38-41-42-49
12.09.92: 90-28-29-26-27-29-32-33-36-41-46-49-48-78-96-88

Ireland
27.08.76: 21-15-4-**1**-**1**-**1**-**1**-**1**-**1**-3-2-3-5-6-9-10-11-15-23-23
31.08.92: 30-12-9-17-21

Japan
25.04.77: peaked at no.**19**, charted for 55 weeks

Netherlands
7.08.76: 21-7-2-**1**-**1**-**1**-**1**-**1**-**1**-**1**-7-14-21

New Zealand
3.09.76: 4-2-2-**1**-2-2-2-2-2-2-**1**-3-**1**-2-3-5-**1**-(no chart for 7 weeks)-8-20-28-22-35-25-x-x-39

Norway
21.08.76: 6-3-**1**-**1**-**1**-**1**-**1**-**1**-**1**-**1**-**1**-**1**-**1**-**1**-2-2-2-2-3-4-4-4-8-5-6-4-10-8
26.09.92: 9-7-5-9

South Africa
30.10.76: 20-8-3-2-**1**-**1**-2-2-3-4-6-5-10-12-15-18

Spain
09.76: peaked at no.**12**, charted for 17 weeks

Switzerland
13.08.76: 14-9-6-**3**-**3**-4-**3**-**3**-**3**-4-5-6-7-10-12-13-15
11.10.92: 24-23-10-13-8-6-12-16-21-18-12-27-23-25-29-17-36

USA

11.12.76: 86-76-66-66-56-41-33-26-19-16-14-9-7-6-5-3-2-**1**-6-18-27-45

Zimbabwe

27.11.76: 18-9-8-3-3-3-**1-1-1-1**-2-2-4-4-7-9-9-15

Generally regarded as ABBA's signature song, *Dancing Queen* was originally titled 'Boogaloo', and was released as the lead single from the group's 1976 album, *ARRIVAL*.

'It's often difficult to know what will be a hit,' stated Agnetha in a TV interview. 'The exception was *Dancing Queen*. We all knew it was going to be massive.'

And so it proved: *Dancing Queen* hit no.1 in a host of countries, including Australia, Belgium, Canada, Germany, Ireland, the Netherlands, New Zealand, Norway, South Africa, the UK, the USA and Zimbabwe. Elsewhere, *Dancing Queen* charted at no.3 in Finland and Switzerland, no.4 in Austria, no.5 in France, no.12 in Spain and no.19 in Japan.

ABBA performed *Dancing Queen* at a TV Gala Tribute on 18th June 1976, to Sweden's King Carl XVI Gustaf and his future Queen, Silvia Sommerlath, who married the following day.

Dancing Queen was reissued in 1992, to promote the compilation *GOLD*, and charted at no.6 in Switzerland, no.16 in the UK, no.26 in Germany and no.28 in Australia.

In 1993, Frida recorded an *a cappella* version of *Dancing Queen* with the Swedish band, the Real Group, for their self-titled album.

There have been numerous cover versions of *Dancing Queen* over the years, with tribute acts A*Teens and Abbacadabra both enjoying chart success with their recordings.

61 ~ Money, Money, Money by ABBA

Sweden: Polar POS 1227 (1976).

Money, Money, Money wasn't a hit in Sweden.

UK: Epic EPC 4713 (1976).

20.11.76: 34-10-6-3-5-**3-3**-4-3-8-17-34

Australia
1.11.76: 53-5-**1-1-1-1-1-1**-2-4-8-11-20-20-28-64-70-82

Austria
15.12.76: 6-**3**-7-10 (monthly chart)

Belgium
20.11.76: 11-4-2-**1-1-1-1**-2-3-6-8-9-13

Canada
29.10.77: 91-72-63-54-50-**47**-53-78

Finland
01.77: peaked at no.**7**, charted for 16 weeks (monthly chart)

France
12.76: peaked at no.**1** (3 weeks), charted for 13 weeks

Germany
22.11.76: 20-7-4-3-**1-1-1-1-1**-2-2-3-7-5-9-12-12-25-20-35-37-49

Ireland
26.11.76: 15-4-**2-2-2-2**-5-4-**2**-5-10-16-25

Netherlands
13.11.76: 13-3-2-**1-1**-2-11-20

New Zealand
19.11.76: 29-24-5-**1**-2-(no chart for 7 weeks)-10-23-32

Norway
13.11.76: 7-6-6-5-3-3-**2-2-2-2-2**-4-**2**-3-3-4-7-7-7

Spain
02.77: peaked at no.**24**, charted for 11 weeks (b/w *Knowing Me, Knowing You*)

Switzerland
19.11.76: 13-6-3-**2-2-2**-3-4-6-9-10-11-13-15

USA
22.10.77: 84-82-71-64-**56**-64-96

Zimbabwe
15.05.77: 20-18-x-x-19-**16**

Money, Money, Money, which Björn thought about re-titling 'Gypsy Girl', was the second single released from ABBA's 1976 album, *ARRIVAL*.

Although it couldn't match the success of *Dancing Queen*, *Money, Money, Money* was a major hit, charting at no.1 in Australia, Belgium, France, Germany and the Netherlands, no.2 in Ireland, Norway and Switzerland, no.3 in Austria and the UK, no.7 in Finland, no.16 in Zimbabwe and no.24 in Spain.

Lasse Hallström, who directed most of ABBA's music videos, has cited *Money, Money, Money* as his favourite. 'That one turned out really well,' he said, 'it was consistent with the lyrics and the music.'

62 ~ Knowing Me, Knowing You by ABBA

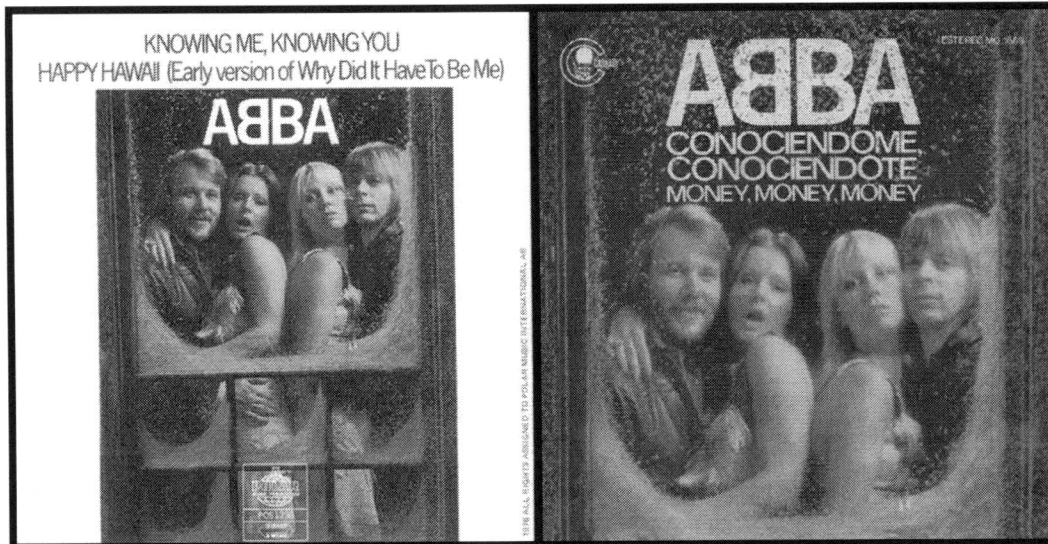

Sweden: Polar POS 1230 (1977).

Knowing Me, Knowing You wasn't a hit in Sweden.

UK: Epic EPC 4955 (1977).

26.02.77: 48-18-7-2-2-**1-1-1-1-1**-7-12-30

Australia
7.03.77: 40-18-11-**9-9**-10-15-18-24-32-33-44-62-78-83 (b/w *Happy Hawaii*)

Austria
15.03.77: 23-**2-2**-6-14 (monthly chart)

Belgium
26.02.77: 19-10-5-**2-2-2**-4-8-10-17-29

Canada
21.05.77: 91-75-63-45-41-27-17-13-11-6-**5-5**-6-8-19-28

Finland
05.77: peaked at no.**16**, charted for 8 weeks (monthly chart)

France
03.77: peaked at no.**9**, charted for 11 weeks

Germany
28.02.77: 28-13-11-3-2-2-**1-1**-2-3-2-4-4-4-5-6-7-8-12-12-31-22-36-35-43-42

Ireland
17.03.77: 15-10-2-**1-1-1-1-1-1**-4-11-17

Netherlands
26.02.77: 16-3-**2-2**-8-14-27

New Zealand
10.04.77: 24-20-17-13-12-**8**-15-21-16-17-31-28-34-35

Norway
26.02.77: 8-**6-6-6**-8-**6-6**-10-9-8-8

South Africa
21.05.77: 16-6-5-4-**1-1**-2-2-5-8-10-13-16-18

Spain
02.77: peaked at no.**24**, charted for 11 weeks (Spanish Version b/w *Money, Money, Money*)

Switzerland
16.02.77: 11-6-**3**-5-4-4-4-4-**3**-4-**3**-4-6-7-8-11-15

USA
14.05.77: 80-63-53-38-35-31-27-24-19-16-**14-14**-19-52-57

Zimbabwe
9.07.77: 16-15-12-**11-11**-14-15-14-14

Knowing Me, Knowing You, which went under the titles 'Ring It In' and 'Number One, Number One' before Stig Anderson came up with the final title and Björn wrote the lyrics, was the first track ABBA recorded for their album *ARRIVAL*, and it was released as the third single from the album in most countries.

Knowing Me, Knowing You hit no.1 in Germany, Ireland, South Africa and the UK, and charted at no.2 in Austria, Belgium and the Netherlands, no.3 in Switzerland, no.5 in Canada, no.6 in Norway, no.8 in New Zealand, no.9 in Australia and France, no.11 in Zimbabwe, no.14 in the USA, no.16 in Finland and no.24 in Spain.

63 ~ The Name Of The Game by ABBA

Sweden: Polar POS 1234 (1977).

4.11.77: **2-2-2**-3-3-4-6-14-18 (bi-weekly chart)

UK: Epic EPC 5750 (1977).

22.10.77: 20-5-**1-1-1-1**-4-11-18-35-35-29

Australia
7.11.77: 62-28-19-14-11-10-7-7-7-**6**-10-13-18-23-30-45-65-88-89

Austria
15.12.77: **12**-22-22 (monthly chart)

Belgium
22.10.77: 24-16-9-6-4-3-3-**2**-3-8-10-12-20-21

Canada
14.01.78: 87-63-48-46-38-27-26-20-19-15-15-**14-14**-27-53-55-82

Finland
12.77: peaked at no.**5**, charted for 12 weeks (monthly chart)

France
12.77: peaked at no.**12**, charted for 10 weeks

Germany
31.10.77: 30-28-8-**7**-12-10-12-18-15-19-18-26-26-28-38-46-35-41-32-50

Ireland
26.10.77: 15-8-**2-2**-5-8-**2-2-2**-11

Netherlands
29.10.77: 9-4-**2-2-2**-3-5-11-19-26-28

Norway
22.10.77: 9-4-**3-3-3-3**-4-4-4-4-4-4-4-4-4-6-9-10

South Africa
17.12.77: 17-11-10-8-4-4-**3**-5-8-11-13-18-20

Switzerland
29.10.77: 13-**6**-8-9-**6**-9-11-13-13-13

USA
24.12.77: 82-82-67-57-44-39-35-28-22-16-14-**12-12**-31-60-97

Zimbabwe
24.12.77: 14-14-13-10-11-10-8-5-**4-4**-6-5-7-9-10-12-18-x-x-20

The Name Of The Game, originally titled 'A Bit Of Myself', was the first track ABBA recorded for their 1977 album, *THE ALBUM*. It was chosen ahead of *Hole In My Soul*, as the album's lead single.

Although it went to no.1 in the UK, *The Name Of The Game* couldn't match the success of the singles from *ARRIVAL* in most other countries, peaking at no.2 in Belgium, Ireland, the Netherlands and Sweden, no.3 in Norway and South Africa, no.4 in Zimbabwe, no.5 in Finland, no.6 in Australia and Switzerland, no.7 in Germany, no.12 in Austria, France and the USA, and no.14 in Canada.

The B-side of *The Name Of The Game* was the first live recording ABBA released, *I Wonder (Departure)*, which was recorded at a concert in Sydney, Australia, in March 1977. A studio recording of *I Wonder (Departure)* featured on *THE ALBUM*.

The Name Of The Game was the first ABBA recording to be legally sampled by another act. The act in question was the Fugees, who sampled *The Name Of The Game* on their 1997 hit, *Rumble In The Jungle*, which also credited A Tribe Called Quest, Busta Rhymes and Forte.

Rumble In The Jungle was taken from the soundtrack album, *WHEN WE WERE KINGS*, the soundtrack to a 1996 documentary which told the story of the famous 'rumble in the jungle' heavyweight boxing match staged in Zaire on 30th October 1974, between Muhammad Ali and George Foreman.

    Rumble In The Jungle charted at no.3 in the UK, no.13 in New Zealand and no.36 in Sweden, but it wasn't a hit in most countries.

64 ~ Take A Chance On Me by ABBA

Sweden: Polar POS 1235 (1977).

Take A Chance On Me wasn't a hit in Sweden.

UK: Epic EPC 5950 (1978).

4.02.78: 10-2-**1-1-1**-2-3-8-15-19

Australia
30.01.78: 55-44-32-26-20-13-**12**-17-24-26-27-37-54-79

Austria
15.03.78: 5-**1**-2-8-22 (monthly chart)

Belgium
4.02.78: 22-10-4-2-2-**1**-2-5-7-10-21

Canada
6.05.78: 88-70-44-38-35-28-20-16-6-4-4-**3**-9-17-28-39-44-68-92

France
03.78: peaked at no.**10**, charted for 12 weeks

Germany
30.01.78: 41-15-5-7-5-4-**3**-7-7-7-5-7-8-10-15-15-13-12-17-19-26-29-28-40-42

Ireland
19.01.78: 17-7-16-2-2-5-**1**-2-2-3

Japan
25.01.78: peaked at no.**67**, charted for 13 weeks

Netherlands
4.02.78: 15-3-3-**2**-3-12-13-16-23

New Zealand
5.03.78: 23-21-15-**14**-15-19-22-25-32-26

Norway
11.03.78: 11-10-10-10-**8**-10

South Africa
22.04.78: 20-11-9-7-**6-6**-7-10-12-17

Switzerland
11.02.78: 14-9-4-**3-3-3-3-3**-5-5-5-5-8-10-11-14

USA
22.04.78: 69-50-30-24-17-13-9-8-6-5-4-**3-3**-9-17-24-41-81

Zimbabwe
3.06.78: 17-10-4-**2**-3-**2-2-2-2**-3-5-5-7-7-11-11-13-11-14

Originally titled 'Billy Boy', *Take A Chance On Me* was inspired by Björn's fondness for jogging – while running, he would often sing a 'tck-a-ch' style rhythm to himself over and over again, which eventually evolved into 'take-a-chance'.

Take A Chance On Me was the second single released from *THE ALBUM*, and proved more successful than *The Name Of The Game* in many countries. It gave ABBA their seventh no.1 in the UK, and it topped the chart in Austria, Belgium and Ireland as well. Elsewhere, the single charted at no.2 in New Zealand and Zimbabwe, no.3 in Canada, Germany, Switzerland and the USA, no.6 in South Africa, no.8 in Norway, no.10 in France, no.12 in Australia and no.14 in New Zealand.

65 ~ Eagle by ABBA

Sweden: Polar POS 1237 (1978).

Eagle was released as a double A-side with *Thank You For The Music* in Sweden, but it wasn't a hit.

Australia
5.06.78: 97-91-90-**85**-94-82 (b/w *Thank You For The Music*)

Austria
15.07.78: **17**-19-21 (monthly chart)

Belgium
20.05.78: 19-6-5-4-4-4-**2**-3-8-14-20 (b/w *Thank You For The Music*)

Netherlands
27.05.78: 28-**7**-**7**-11-12-10-12-21-22-27 (b/w *Thank You For The Music*)

France
05.78: peaked at no.**36**, charted for 6 weeks

Germany

22.05.78: 48-14-8-7-**6**-9-9-8-11-11-13-16-19-20-20-28-37-32-40 (b/w *Thank You For*
The Music)

Japan

25.07.78: peaked at no.**62**, charted for 8 weeks (b/w *Thank You For The Music*)

Switzerland

3.06.78: 13-8-**7-7-7**-8-8-10-12-13-15

Eagle, which was titled 'High, High' and 'The Eagle' before the final title was agreed, was the longest song ABBA recorded – at 5:51 minutes, it was one second longer than *The Day Before You Came*.

Björn, in confirming *Eagle* was inspired by Richard Bach's novel, *Jonathan Livingston Seagull*, stated, 'I was trying to capture the sense of freedom and euphoria I got from reading that book.'

Inexplicably, *Eagle* was passed over as a single in the UK and the USA, and in most countries where it was released it was treated as a double A-side with *Thank You For The Music*, although *Eagle* was the designated A-side.

Eagle was the third single released from *THE ALBUM*, and due to its length it was edited for single release, which didn't help sales. Although it was less successful than *The Name Of The Game* and *Take A Chance On Me*, *Eagle* charted at no.2 in Belgium, no.6 in Germany, no.7 in the Netherlands and Switzerland, no.17 in Austria and no.36 in France.

66 ~ Thank You For The Music by ABBA

Sweden: Polar POS 1237 (1978).

Thank You For The Music was released as a double A-side with *Eagle* in Sweden, but it wasn't a hit.

UK: Epic A 3894 (1983).

12.11.83: 64-43-**33**-34-43-57
26.12.92: 80-93

Australia
5.06.78: 97-91-90-**85**-94-82 (b/w *Eagle*)

Belgium
20.05.78: 19-6-5-4-4-4-**2**-3-8-14-20 (b/w *Eagle*)

France
09.83: peaked at no.**58**, charted for 3 weeks

Germany
2.12.92: peaked at no.**55**, charted for 2 weeks

Ireland
6.11.83: 26-**17**-20-23

Netherlands
27.05.78: 28-**7**-**7**-11-12-10-12-21-22-27 (b/w *Eagle*)
21.04.84: 29-23-36-43

Japan
25.07.78: peaked at no.**62**, charted for 8 weeks (b/w *Eagle*)

South Africa
12.08.78: 18-14-10-6-4-**2**-3-**2**-**2**-**2**-**2**-3-6-12

Zimbabwe
26.08.78: 16-12-10-6-**5**-**5**-6-7-9-9-12-13-16

Thank You For The Music was first of four songs that featured in the mini-musical 'The Girl With The Golden Hair', which ABBA performed in concert during their 1977 tour. The mini-musical also featured *I Wonder (Departure)*, *I'm A Marionette* and *Get On The Carousel* – the first two tracks, along with *Thank You For The Music*, were included on ABBA's *THE ALBUM*, but *Get On The Carousel* remains unreleased.

ABBA recorded two very different versions of *Thank You For The Music*. The first, known as the 'Doris Day' version, was recorded on 2nd June 1977, but remained unreleased until 1994, when it featured on the *THANK YOU FOR THE MUSIC* box-set. The second, recorded on 21st July 1977, is the version that was included on *THE ALBUM*.

Thank You For The Music was released as the B-side of *Eagle*, or as a double A-side with *Eagle* in countries like Belgium. The single charted at no.2 in Belgium and South Africa, no.5 in Zimbabwe and no.7 in the Netherlands.

In 1983, *Thank You For The Music* was released as a single to promote the compilation album with the same title; it was viewed, by many fans, as a kind of 'farewell' song that marked the end of ABBA as a group. The single wasn't a big hit, but achieved no.17 in Ireland, no.23 in the Netherlands and no.33 in the UK.

The Carpenters performed *Thank You For The Music* on *The Tonight Show* in June 1978, and recorded a studio version that Richard Carpenter has always refused to release. 'Nobody does ABBA like ABBA,' he stated. 'I realised Benny and Björn had done the definitive arrangement and all I'd be doing was copying it – something I just don't do, of course. It's an outtake, never completed and in storage with the rest of the stuff in Pennsylvania.'

67 ~ Summer Night City by ABBA

Sweden: Polar POS 1239 (1978).

22.09.78: 3-**1**-2-2-4-6-6-9-12-12 (bi-weekly chart)

UK: Epic EPC 6595 (1978).

16.09.78: 21-7-8-**5**-12-20-34-54-72

Australia
16.10.78: 56-37-24-20-16-16-**13**-16-19-24-24-27-34-62-73

Austria
15.11.78: **18** (monthly chart)

Belgium
23.09.78: 14-9-8-7-6-**3**-6-11-22

Canada
10.02.79: 91-**90**-99

Finland
11.78: peaked at no.**1**, charted for 20 weeks (monthly chart)

France
11.78: peaked at no.**15**, charted for 9 weeks

Germany
25.09.78: 21-13-**6-6**-10-13-14-14-19-20-25-25-26-35-32-38-42

Ireland
22.09.78: 9-**1**-3-15-x-25

Japan
5.10.78: peaked at no.**24**, charted for 26 weeks

Netherlands
23.09.78: **10**-11-11-**10**-11-13-22-32-42-44

New Zealand
26.11.78: **37**

Norway
23.09.78: 9-5-4-5-5-**3**-5-8-9-9

Switzerland
30.09.78: 13-**5**-6-6-6-8-10-12-12-14

Zimbabwe
16.12.78: 17-13-13-9-6-6-**4**-5-7-8-13-12-17-18

ABBA recorded *Summer Night City*, which had the working title '*Kalle Sändare*', in early 1978. Mixing of the track is said to have taken over a week, longer than any other ABBA recording; even then neither Benny nor Björn was happy with the result, and the decision to release it was taken reluctantly – later, Benny would admit 'we shouldn't have released that one', while Björn described the track as 'really lousy'.

Originally, *Summer Night City* was intended to be the lead single from *VOULEZ-VOUS*, but it was left off the album (though it was added, as a bonus track, to the CD reissue in 1997). The single version of the track saw the opening severely edited, and the full length version wasn't released until 1994, when it was included on the box-set, *THANK YOU FOR THE MUSIC*.

Despite Benny and Björn's reservations, *Summer Night City* continued ABBA's run of successful singles. It hit no.1 in Finland, Ireland and Sweden, and charted at no.3 in Belgium and Norway, no.4 in Zimbabwe, no.5 in Switzerland and the UK, no.6 in

Germany, no.10 in the Netherlands, no.13 in Australia, no.15 in France, no.18 in Austria, no.24 in Japan and no.37 in New Zealand.

The B-side of *Summer Night City* was unique, in that it is the only recording ABBA released which one or more members of ABBA didn't have a hand in composing. Rather, it was a medley of three traditional American songs, *Pick A Bale Of Cotton*, *On Top Of Old Smokey* and *Midnight Special*, which ABBA originally recorded in 1975 for the German charity album, *STARS IM ZEICHEN EINES GUTEN STERNS*.

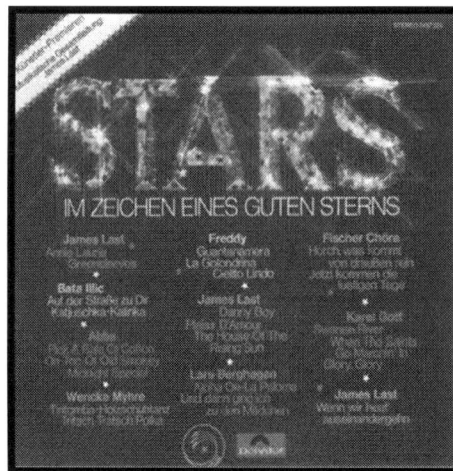

The B-side of *Summer Night City* was actually a 1978 remix of the medley, while the original 1975 mix was included on the 1994 box-set, *THANK YOU FOR THE MUSIC*, where it was mistakenly stated to be the 1978 remix.

68 ~ Chiquitita by ABBA

Sweden: Polar POS 1244 (1979).

9.02.79: 4-5-5-9-15-7-**2**-4-4-10-13-16 (bi-weekly chart)

UK: Epic EPC 7030 (1979).

3.02.79: 8-**2-2**-3-5-9-17-30-52

Australia
19.02.79: 94-31-25-13-9-5-5-**4-4**-5-11-13-20-23-28-41-56-66-99

Austria
15.03.79: 9-**6-6**-20 (monthly chart)

Belgium
27.01.79: 16-9-5-2-**1-1-1-1-1**-2-2-5-8-11-14-25

Canada
24.11.79: 94-85-71-66-57-42-42-37-**36-36**-37-50-62-74-79-90

Finland
03.79: peaked at no.**1**, charted for 16 weeks (monthly chart)

France
02.79: peaked at no.**13**, charted for 10 weeks

Germany
29.01.79: 33-15-**3-3-3-3**-4-4-**3-3**-4-6-7-9-10-8-10-15-17-22-31-34-37-43-50-49

Ireland
1.02.79: 8-**1-1-1**-3-5-14-31

Japan
25.01.79: peaked at no.19, charted for 21 weeks
25.01.01: peaked at no.**15**, charted for 11 weeks (b/w *S.O.S*)

Netherlands
3.02.79: 23-3-2-3-**1**-2-2-2-4-6-9-15-24-30-46-49

New Zealand
25.03.79: 37-18-12-5-11-**1**-2-2-3-5-5-6-12-18-19-29-31-30-42

Norway
10.02.79: 5-6-6-**4-4**-5-**4**-7-8-8-10-7-5-5-5-5-8

South Africa
7.04.79: 17-10-7-3-**1**-2-4-4-4-3-3-5-7-9-9-11-13-17-19

Spain
01.79: peaked at no.**1**, charted for 33 weeks

Switzerland
4.02.79: 12-4-4-4-2-2-**1-1**-3-4-6-8-10-11-14

USA
10.11.79: 70-60-48-46-39-35-31-31-30-**29**-65-99

Zimbabwe
21.04.79: 15-4-3-**1-1-1-1**-2-3-3-3-3-5-5-6-7-10-10-15-20-x-20

Chiquitita, which means 'little one' in Spanish, was chosen as the lead single from ABBA's 1979 album, *VOULEZ-VOUS*, ahead of *If It Wasn't For The Nights*.
    Before settling on the title, Björn's working titles included '*Kålsupare*', 'Chiquitita Angelina', 'Three Wise Guys' and 'In The Arms Of Rosalita'. The final version, which

was influenced by Simon & Garfunkel's *El Condor Pasa*, was recorded in December 1978 and released as a single the following month.

Chiquitita hit no.1 in Belgium, Finland, Ireland, the Netherlands, New Zealand, South Africa, Spain, Switzerland and Zimbabwe, and achieved no.2 in Sweden and the UK (behind Blondie's *Heart Of Glass* in both countries), no.3 in Germany, no.4 in Australia and Norway, no.6 in Austria, no.13 in France, no.19 in Japan, no.29 in the USA and no.36 in Canada.

ABBA didn't shoot a music video for *Chiquitita*, but instead used their performance of the song on their BBC TV special, *ABBA In Switzerland*, which was broadcast at Easter 1979.

ABBA first performed *Chiquitita* in New York on 8th January 1979, when they participated in the 'Music for UNICEF' charity concert. At the same time, they agreed to donate 50% of the royalties for *Chiquitita* to UNICEF, and allowed the song's inclusion on the album, *THE MUSIC FOR UNICEF CONCERT – A GIFT OF SONG*. Other acts to appear at the event included the Bee Gees, Earth, Wind & Fire, John Denver, Olivia Newton-John, Rod Stewart and Donna Summer.

The Spanish version of *Chiquitita* was hugely successful in Latin America, and topped the Mexico's Spanish singles chart for an impressive 30 weeks, and went on to sell over 1.5 million copies in Mexico alone.

69 ~ Does Your Mother Know by ABBA

Sweden: Polar POS 1251 (1979).

Does Your Mother Know wasn't a hit in Sweden.

UK: Epic EPC 7316 (1979).

5.05.79: 19-**4-4-4**-6-12-25-41-73

Australia
4.06.79: 83-43-30-21-13-9-9-**7**-8-11-18-23-34-45-59-73

Austria
15.06.79: 19-**13**-17 (monthly chart)

Belgium
12.05.79: 16-9-3-2-**1**-3-5-5-7-12-19

Canada
2.06.79: 92-78-55-43-29-19-19-18-16-16-13-13-13-**12-12**-19-19-18-27-42-46

France
05.79: peaked at no.**26**, charted for 7 weeks

Germany
21.05.79: 24-**10-10-10**-11-12-15-16-17-21-28-28-35-44

Ireland
3.05.79: 6-4-**3**-4-4-4-5-7-24

Netherlands
12.05.79: 30-8-**3**-4-4-6-8-15-20-29-41

New Zealand
15.07.79: 49-x-34-**27**-34-29-35-33

South Africa
4.08.79: 19-14-**12**-13-14-14-16

Switzerland
27.05.79: 15-9-7-7-7-**6**-9-11-13-13

USA
19.05.79: 83-63-53-37-33-28-25-22-20-**19**-21-30-29-69

Zimbabwe
18.08.79: 18-16-11-**9-9-9**-11-13-14

The working title for the song that became *Does Your Mother Know* was 'I Can Do It', and although the track was originally recorded with Agnetha and Frida on lead vocals, it didn't really work – so, for the first time since before *Waterloo*, Björn sang lead on the final version, which was recorded on 6th February 1979.

The melody of *Does Your Mother Know* evolved from another ABBA recording, *Dream World*, which failed to make the final cut for *VOULEZ-VOUS*. *Dream World* remained unreleased until 1994, when it was included on the box-set, *THANK YOU FOR THE MUSIC*.

Does Your Mother Know was chosen as the second single from ABBA's 1979 album, *VOULEZ-VOUS*, with another track from the album, *Kisses Of Fire*, on the B-side. *Kisses Of Fire*, a more typical sounding ABBA recording, could easily have been a single in its own right, but despite its rare male lead vocal *Does Your Mother Know* did well enough. It hit no.1 in Belgium, and charted at no.3 in Ireland and the Netherlands, no.4 in the UK, no.6 in Switzerland, no.7 in Australia, no.9 in Zimbabwe, no.10 in Germany, no.12 in Canada and South Africa, no.13 in Austria, no.19 in the USA, no.26 in France and no.27 in New Zealand.

70 ~ Voulez Vous by ABBA

Sweden: Polar POS 1253 (1979).

Voulez Vous was released as a double A-side with *Angeleyes* in Sweden, but it wasn't a hit.

UK: Epic EPC 7499 (1979).

14.07.79: 48-23-12-5-**3**-5-9-14-29-40-66 (b/w *Angeleyes*)
7.11.92: 76-91

Australia
27.08.79: 93-**79**-x-98-88-82-80-80-80-80-87

Belgium
21.07.79: 30-9-4-2-2-**1**-3-4-8-8-10-16-28

France
07.79: peaked at no.**9**, charted for 11 weeks

Germany
20.08.79: **14**-17-15-21-19-23-25-23-33-30-30-41-44-46-49-59

Ireland
15.07.79: 5-**3**-5-5-5-8-28-19-29-29 (b/w *Angeleyes*)

Japan
5.07.79: peaked at no.**18**, charted for 20 weeks

Netherlands
28.07.79: 13-8-5-4-**3**-9-15-19-27-46

Spain
05.79: peaked at no.**5**, charted for 17 weeks

Switzerland
26.08.79: 15-11-**9**-10-12-15

USA
1.09.79: **80-80**-93 (B-side of *Angel Eyes*)

Voulez-Vous – French for 'Will you?' – was originally titled 'Amerika', and was one of two songs Benny and Björn composed during a two week song-writing trip to the Bahamas (the other was *Kisses Of Fire*). ABBA recorded the song at the Criteria Recording Studios in Miami, Florida, on 1st February 1979, making it the only track the quartet recorded outside Sweden.

While they were in Miami, preferring to only record their own songs, Benny and Björn turned down the opportunity to record *If I Can't Have You*, which the Bee Gees had written for the film, *Saturday Night Fever*. The song was subsequently recorded by, and was a hit for, Yvonne Elliman.

Voulez-Vous was released as the third single from the album of the same title in most countries. In a few countries, including Ireland and the UK, it was released as a double A-side with another track from the same album, *Angeleyes*, while in the USA, after *Voulez-Vous* struggled to no.80, the single was flipped and *Angeleyes* promoted to the A-side.

Voulez-Vous gave ABBA another no.1 in Belgium, and charted at no.3 in Ireland, the Netherlands and the UK, no.5 in Spain, no.9 in France and Switzerland, no.14 in Germany and no.18 in Japan.

Unusually, ABBA released an extended dance remix of *Voulez-Vous* as a promo 12" single in the USA. The remix later featured on the 2001 compilation, *THE DEFINITIVE COLLECTION*.

71 ~ Angeleyes by ABBA

Sweden: Polar POS 1253 (1979).

Angeleyes was released as a double A-side with *Voulez Vous* in Sweden, but it wasn't a hit.

UK: Epic EPC 7499 (1979).

14.07.79: 48-23-12-5-**3**-5-9-14-29-40-66 (b/w *Voulez Vous*)

Canada
22.09.79: 87-75-52-51-49-44-44-**42**-48-57-61-69

Ireland
15.07.79: 5-**3**-5-5-5-8-28-19-29-29 (b/w *Voulez Vous*)

USA
22.09.79: 85-75-65-**64**-99

Angeleyes, which had the working title 'Katakusom', was recorded on 26th October 1978 for ABBA's 1979 album, *VOULEZ-VOUS*.

    Angeleyes was released as the B-side of *Voulez-Vous* in most countries, but the two tracks were issued as a double A-side in Ireland and the UK, where *Angeleyes* proved more popular, taking the single to no.3 in both countries – despite some confusion caused by Roxy Music's similarly titled *Angel Eyes* charting at the same time.

In the USA, as in most countries, *Angeleyes* was originally released as the B-side of *Voulez-Vous*. But, as *Voulez-Vous* stalled at no.80 and ABBA were due in the country for a promotional visit, the single was flipped and *Angeleyes* promoted as the A-side. However, it didn't perform much better than *Voulez-Vous*, and peaked at no.64.

72 ~ Gimme! Gimme! Gimme! (A Man After Midnight) by ABBA

Sweden: Polar POS 1256 (1979).

14.12.79: 18-18-**16** (bi-weekly chart)

UK: Epic EPC 7914 (1979).

20.10.79: 30-6-4-**3**-6-7-19-34-52-68-68-74

Australia
12.11.79: 80-58-42-27-20-17-10-9-9-**8-8**-12-13-18-25-42-60-74
21.07.08: 64

Austria
15.12.79: 5-**2**-3-3-13-19 (bi-weekly chart)

Belgium
27.10.79: 28-11-3-2-2-**1**-4-6-13-20

Finland
01.80: peaked at no.**1**, charted for 20 weeks (monthly chart)

France
10.70: peaked at no.**1** (5 weeks), charted for 18 weeks

Germany
29.10.79: 24-7-**3**-**3**-4-4-4-**3**-**3**-5-**3**-11-14-15-20-27-41-49-43-38-50-49-62-58-54-69

Ireland
21.10.79: 15-2-**1**-**1**-2-7

Japan
25.11.79: peaked at no.**17**, charted for 26 weeks

Netherlands
27.10.79: 48-3-**2**-3-4-5-8-10-19-41-34-47

New Zealand
25.11.79: 42-25-27-22-20-20-20-19-**15**-19-21-25-22-48-50

Norway
27.10.79: 8-6-3-3-**2**-**2**-**2**-**2**-**2**-**2**-**2**-**2**-**2**-3-3-4-5-8

South Africa
2.02.80: 18-17-**16**-17

Switzerland
4.11.79: 13-5-3-2-**1**-2-4-4-5-7-10-13

Gimme! Gimme! Gimme! (A Man After Midnight), which had the working title 'Been And Gone And Done It', was recorded on 2nd October 1979 – too late to feature on *VOULEZ-VOUS*, so the first album it appeared on was the 1979 compilation, *GREATEST HITS VOL.2*.

Released to promote the compilation, *Gimme! Gimme! Gimme! (A Man After Midnight)* hit no.1 in Belgium, Finland, France, Ireland and Switzerland, no.2 in Austria, the Netherlands and Norway, no.3 in Germany and the UK, no.8 in Australia, no.15 in New Zealand, no.16 in South Africa and Sweden, and no.17 in Japan.

A*Teens recorded a cover of *Gimme! Gimme! Gimme! (A Man After Midnight)*, for their 1999 album, *THE ABBA GENERATION*. Released a single, the cover charted at no.10 in Sweden, no.20 in Spain, no.24 in the Netherlands and no.33 in Germany.

Also in 1999, the Italian dance combo The Tamperer featuring Maya released *Hammer To The Heart*, which was based on *Gimme! Gimme! Gimme! (A Man After*

Midnight), although it didn't credit Benny and Björn among the song's composers. *Hammer To The Heart* charted at no.6 in the UK, and no.23 in Ireland and Sweden.

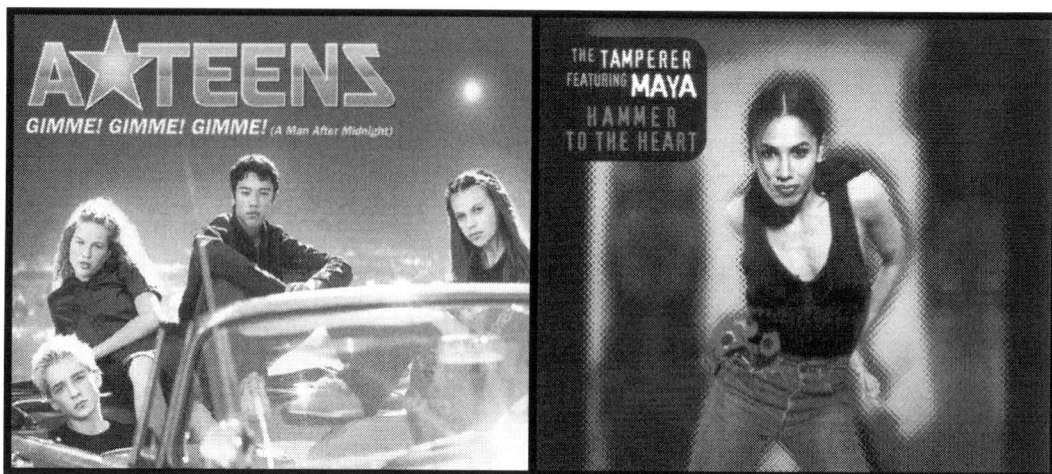

Star Academy, the French equivalent of the TV reality series *Pop Idol*, took a version of *Gimme! Gimme! Gimme! (A Man After Midnight)* to no.1 in France in 2001.

Madonna, with permission, sampled *Gimme! Gimme! Gimme! (A Man After Midnight)* on her 2005 smash, *Hung Up*, which hit no.1 in Australia, Austria, Belgium, Canada, Finland, France, Germany, the Netherlands, Norway, Spain, Sweden, Switzerland and the UK, and charted at no.2 in Ireland and New Zealand, and no.7 in the USA.

73 ~ I Have A Dream by ABBA

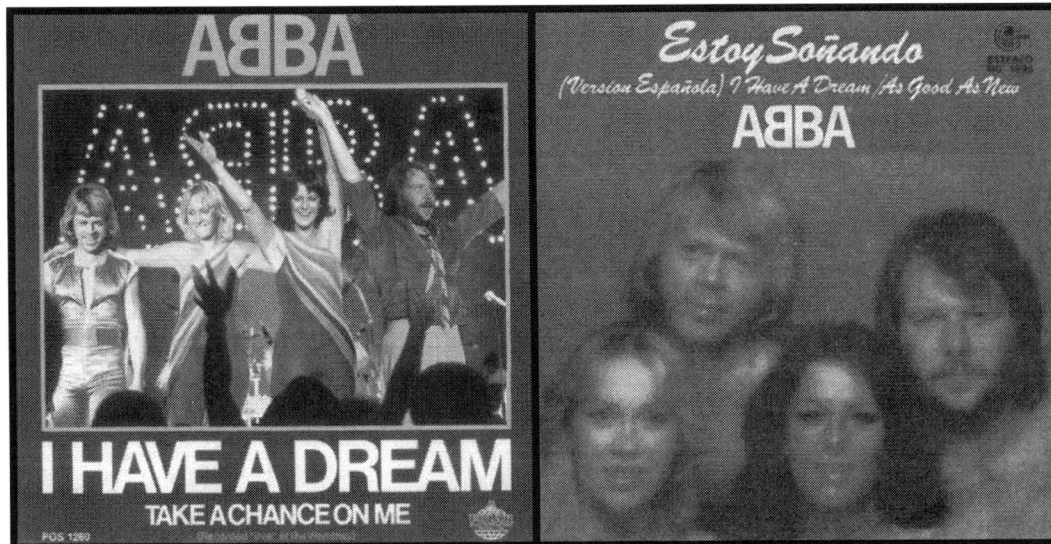

Sweden: Polar POS 1260 (1979).

I Have A Dream wasn't a hit in Sweden.

UK: Epic EPC 8088 (1979).

15.12.79: 21-**2-2-2-2**-7-13-26-43-58

Australia
3.03.80: 100-71-66-**64**-71-71-76-76-75-77-80-95-92

Austria
15.01.80: 8-2-**1**-2-3-3-4-4-11-12-15 (bi-weekly chart)

Belgium
15.12.79: 25-11-3-3-2-**1-1-1-1**-3-6-9-12

France
01.80: peaked at no.**42**, charted for 8 weeks

Germany
24.12.79: 8-39-**4**-6-**4**-5-5-7-7-10-12-13-12-13-17-14-16-14-16-28-31-36-36-47-72-67-73

Ireland
9.12.79: 19-4-4-**2-2**-3-7-10-22

Netherlands
22.12.79: 10-2-2-3-2-**1**-2-3-7-7-18-33-30

South Africa
27.10.79: 18-11-8-7-6-4-**3-3**-7-7-6-6-10-15-19

Spain
09.79: peaked at no.**15**, charted for 12 weeks (*Estoy Soñando*)

Switzerland
23.12.79: 14-4-2-**1-1**-2-2-3-7-9-14-14

Zimbabwe
22.12.79: 18-16-19-16-12-**7-7**-8-10-9-12-15

I Have A Dream was recorded on 15th March 1979, and in most countries it was the fourth single lifted from ABBA's 1979 album, *VOULEZ-VOUS*.

I Have A Dream was unusual, in that it featured voices that didn't belong to the four members of ABBA, in the form of a childrens choir – namely, the International School of Stockholm Choir. In most countries, the B-side of *I Have A Dream* was a live version of *Take A Chance On Me*, recorded at one of the group's Wembley concerts in 1979.

I Have A Dream hit no.1 in Austria, Belgium, the Netherlands and Switzerland, and charted at no.2 in Ireland and the UK, no.3 in South Africa, no.4 in Germany and no.7 in Zimbabwe, while the Spanish version of the song, *Estoy Soñando*, charted at no.15 in Spain. In the UK, *I Have A Dream* spent four weeks in the runner-up spot, behind another hit featuring a childrens choir, Pink Floyd's *Another Brick In The Wall*.

In Mexico, *I Have A Dream* was released as the B-side of another track from *VOULEZ-VOUS*, *As Good As New* – which went all the way to no.1.

Although it was certainly a strong contender, *As Good As New* wasn't released as a single in most countries.

The popular Irish quintet Westlife recorded a cover of *I Have A Dream* for their self-titled 1999 album. Their version was released as a single, as a double A-side with a version of the Terry Jacks hit, *Seasons In The Sun*. The single achieved something that ABBA's original recording failed to do, when it became the Christmas no.1 in the UK.

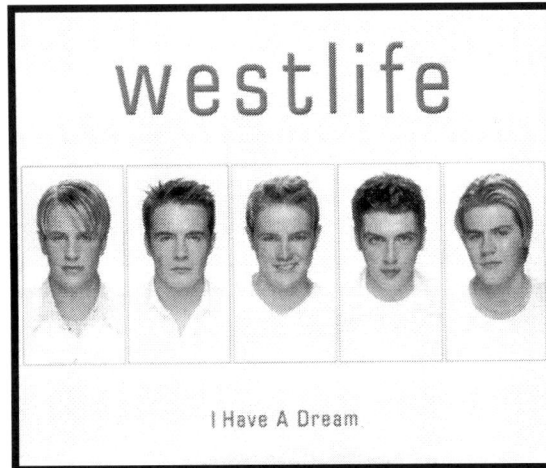

Westlife's cover of *I Have A Dream* also rose to no.1 in Ireland, and charted at no.10 in Finland and Norway, no.11 in Denmark, no.15 in Sweden, no.18 in Switzerland and no.24 in Germany.

74 ~ The Winner Takes It All by ABBA

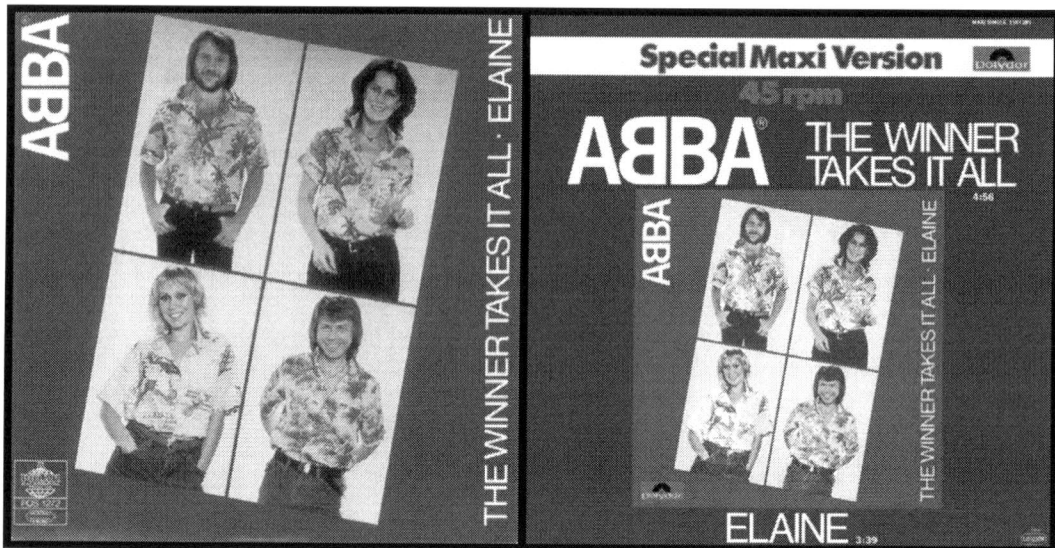

Sweden: Polar POS 1272 (1980).

8.08.80: 4-**2-2**-3-4-8-16-13 (bi-weekly chart)

UK: Epic EPC 8835 (1980).

2.08.80: 9-**1-1**-2-4-8-16-30-41-74

Australia
18.08.80: 79-57-47-42-37-33-18-13-10-**7**-10-9-12-15-21-23-30-34-44-55-55-69-70

Austria
1.09.80: **3-3**-8-7-7-11-13-19-20 (bi-weekly chart)

Belgium
2.08.80: 25-5-2-2-**1-1-1-1-1-1-1**-2-7-11-13-24

Canada
8.11.80: 98-70- (no further positions known)

Finland
09.80: peaked at no.**2**, charted for 28 weeks (monthly chart)

France
07.80: peaked at no.**5**, charted for 12 weeks

Germany
4.08.80: 14-**4**-7-**4**-6-**4**-7-10-10-13-10-11-18-17-23-21-22-39-41-38-41-39-63-42-29-46-
65-72-70

Ireland
16.08.80: 8-4-**1-1**-3-3-26

Japan
5.08.80: peaked at no.**33**, charted for 11 weeks

Netherlands
9.08.80: 11-7-**1-1-1-1-1**-5-3-3-12-16-24-43

New Zealand
28.09.80: 34-x-29-33-24-**16**-30-19-26-20-36-24-21-21-21-21-38-49

Norway
9.08.80: 7-4-**3-3**-4-5-7-8-10

South Africa
20.09.80: 11-10-3-2-2-**1-1**-2-5-5-7-9-9-14-16-20

Spain
09.80: peaked at no.**6**, charted for 24 weeks

Switzerland
3.08.80: 13-6-**3-3**-4-4-4-9-10-13-14

USA
22.11.80: 82-71-61-51-44-36-36-30-25-21-18-16-15-12-10-9-**8-8**-12-14-20-43-52-73-
92-99

Zimbabwe
25.10.80: 18-6-5-5-5-**4-4**-5-6-6-6-8-8-10-10-10-18-19

Originally titled 'The Story Of My Life', Benny and Björn have both acknowledged *The Winner Takes It All* as one of the best songs they have ever composed – even though

Björn has revealed he was drinking whisky when he wrote the lyrics. 'I was drunk,' he admitted, 'and the whole lyric came to me in a rush of emotion in one hour.'

At the same time, Björn has always denied the song was inspired by or is about his and Agnetha's divorce, instead stating the song is 'the experience of a divorce, but it's fiction. There wasn't a winner or loser in our case. A lot of people think it's straight out of reality, but it's not.'

Agnetha, who sang lead on *The Winner Takes It All*, agrees with Björn that there was no winner or loser when they divorced. Nevertheless, when she finished recording the song, tears streamed down her face. 'The lyrics are deeply personal,' she explained, 'and the music is unsurpassed. It was quite a while afterwards before I realised that we had made a small masterpiece.'

The Winner Takes It All was released as the lead single from ABBA's 1980 album, *SUPER TROUPER*, and hit no.1 in Belgium, Ireland, the Netherlands, South Africa and the UK. Elsewhere, the single charted at no.2 in Finland and Sweden, no.3 in Austria, Norway and Switzerland, no.4 in Germany and Zimbabwe, no.5 in France, no.6 in Spain, no.7 in Australia, no.8 in the USA, no.16 in New Zealand and no.33 in Japan.

Mireille Mathieu recorded a French cover of *The Winner Takes It All*, titled *Bravo Tu As Gagné*, in 1981. Benny and Björn produced her recording, and they were joined by Frida (but not Agnetha) on backing vocals. *Bravo Tu As Gagné* charted at no.14 in Sweden.

In 1999, in a poll for the UK's Channel Five, *The Winner Takes It All* was voted the nation's favourite ABBA song – as it was eleven years later, when ITV conducted a similar poll. In another Channel Five poll, held in 2006, *The Winner Takes It All* was voted Britain's favourite 'break-up' song.

75 ~ Super Trouper by ABBA

Sweden: Polar POS 1274 (1980).

28.11.80: 17-17-**11**-12 (bi-weekly chart)

UK: Epic EPC 9089 (1980).

15.11.80: 13-2-**1-1-1**-4-5-5-8-28-48-71

Australia
30.03.81: 92-92-92-**77**-91

Austria
15.12.80: 6-**3-3**-4-5-5-7-15-13-14 (bi-weekly chart)

Belgium
15.11.80: 23-14-5-2-**1-1-1**-2-2-3-4-7-14-22-32

Canada
28.03.81: 47-45-33-**32**-33-33-34

Finland
03.81: peaked at no.**5**, charted for 8 weeks (monthly chart)

France
11.80: peaked at no.**4**, charted for 14 weeks

Germany
17.11.80: 58-17-4-3-3-**1-1**-4-**1-1-1**-2-2-3-4-7-6-8-10-16-25-28-36-32-36-36-43-55-60-58

Ireland
9.11.80: 7-3-**1-1-1**-2-4-4-5-19-25

Japan
21.03.81: peaked at no.**93**, charted for 2 weeks

Netherlands
22.11.80: 29-**1**-2-2-2-4-4-5-7-21-31-47

Norway
13.12.80: 8-**2-2-2-2**-4-3-5-5-9

Spain
01.81: peaked at no.**9**, charted for 11 weeks

Switzerland
23.11.80: 12-4-**3-3-3-3**-4-4-**3**-6-12-14

USA
4.04.81: 88-78-69-59-52-46-46-**45**-56-86-95

Zimbabwe
16.05.81: 20-x-**18-18**-19-20

The working title of *Super Trouper* was '*Blinka Lilla Stjärna*', which is the Swedish title of the nursery rhyme, *Twinkle, Twinkle, Little Star*.

Super Trouper was the last song Benny and Björn composed for the album with the same title. 'We hadn't planned to call the new song *Super Trouper* as well,' Björn said, 'but strangely enough, those words just happened to fit.' A 'super trouper', of course, is the name given to the huge spotlights used for stadium concerts.

The music video for *Super Trouper*, like most of ABBA's promos, was directed by Lasse Hallström. The video featured the largest number of artists featured in any ABBA promo, and initially Hallström planned to shoot the video in London's aptly named Piccadilly Circus. UK law, however, prohibited animals and entertainers from performing in central London, so the video was filmed in Stockholm.

Super Trouper was the second single released from the album with the same title, and like *The Winner Takes It All* it was a major hit, hitting no.1 in Belgium, Germany, Ireland, the Netherlands and the UK, no.2 in Norway, no.3 in Austria and Switzerland, no.4 in France, no.5 in Finland, no.9 in Spain, no.11 in Sweden, no.18 in Zimbabwe, no.32 in Canada and no.45 in the USA.

Super Trouper was also the second single released from A*Teens' 1999 album, *THE ABBA GENERATION*, and it charted at no.2 in Sweden, no.4 in Germany, no.11 in Austria and the Netherlands, no.15 in Norway, no.18 in Switzerland and no.21 in the UK.

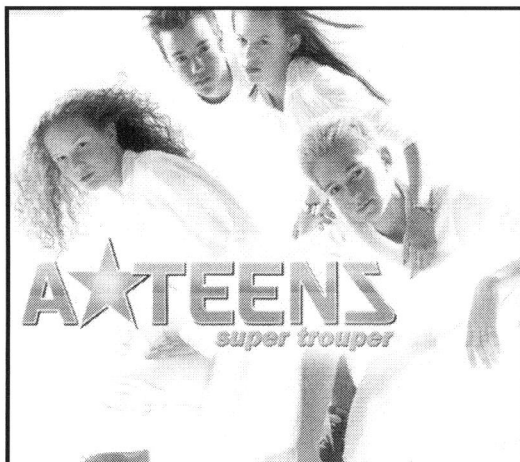

76 ~ On And On And On by ABBA

Australia: RCA Victor 103719 (1980).

15.12.80: 60-31-22-22-16-**9**-10-19-24-29-35-54

France
07.81: peaked at no.**18**, charted for 7 weeks (b/w *Lay All Your Love On Me*)

Japan
5.12.80: peaked at no.**52**, charted for 11 weeks

USA
27.06.81: 92-91-**90**-95-94-99

On And On And On, which was known by the working titles 'Til The Night Is Gone' and '*Esses Vad Det Svänger När Man Spelar Jazz*' ('God Almighty How It Swings When You're Playing Jazz'), was only released as a single in a few countries – in most other countries, it was issued as the B-side of *Lay All Your Love On Me*.

On And On And On charted at no.9 in Australia and no.18 in France, but it was only a minor hit and Japan and the USA. In the USA, however, *On And On And On* was listed alongside *Super Trouper* and *Lay All Your Love On Me* on Billboard's Hot Dance Club Play chart, and went all the way to no.1.

The music video used to promote *On And On And On* was a montage of clips, both stills and live action from concerts and previous promos, and it used an early mix of the song that featured an additional verse which was subsequently edited from the final version.

On 27th November 1980, ABBA performed *On And On And On*, together with *Super Trouper* and *The Winner Takes It All*, at the SVT TV Studios in Sweden, for a live link-up with the German TV programme, *Show Express*. Security at the TV studios was extra tight, as threats to kidnap Agnetha, Benny, Björn and Frida had been made.

Sylvie Vartan recorded a French cover of *On And On And On*, titled *Ça Va Mal* ('It Is Bad'), for her eponymous 1981 album.

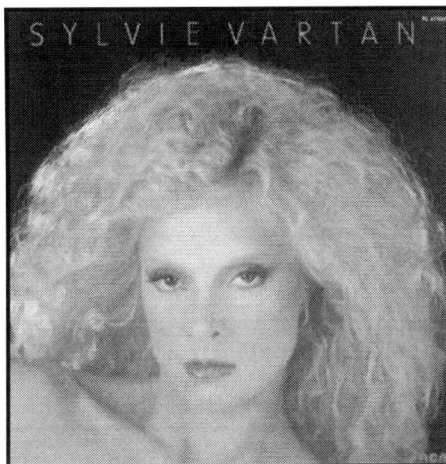

Stars On 45 Vol.2 / More Stars by Stars On 45 / Starsound

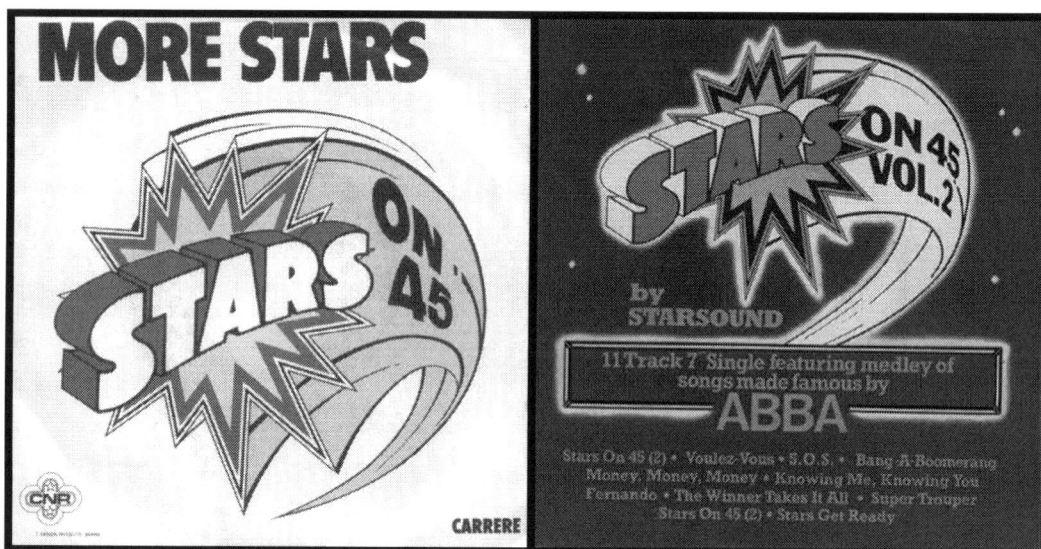

UK: Epic A1407 (1981).

4.07.81: 15-4-**2-2**-5-9-27-31-54-67

Austria
1.09.81: **4**-5-8-14-17-13-8 (bi-weekly chart)

Belgium
18.07.81: 29-16-7-5-**3-3**-4-5-7-15-23-31

Germany
13.07.81: peaked at no.**2**, charted for 18 weeks

Ireland
12.07.81: 8-4-**3**-4-8-19-26

Netherlands
25.07.81: 18-**3-3**-4-6-15-17-19-36-50

Norway
8.08.81: 6-**5**-6-**5**-10

Sweden
28.08.81: **12-12** (bi-weekly)

Switzerland
2.08.81: 15-7-3-**1**-3-4-6-7-14

Stars On 45, or Starsound or Stars On, as the group was billed in the UK and the USA, respectively, were session singers brought together by Dutch producer Jaap Eggermont. The group's debut single, also titled *Stars On 45*, featured a Beatles medley that was a huge hit in Europe especially, and started a trend for medleys.

The follow-up, titled *Stars On 45 Vol.2* in some countries and *More Stars* in others, was billed as an '11 track 7" single featuring medley of songs made famous by ABBA' on the UK release. The eight ABBA songs featured in the medley were *Voulez-Vous*, *S.O.S*, *Bang-A-Boomerang*, *Money, Money, Money*, *Knowing Me, Knowing You*, *Fernando*, *The Winner Takes It All* and *Super Trouper*.

ABBA met producer Jaap Eggermont at a CBS sales conference in September 1981 in Bournemouth, England – Benny admitted his surprise, at how accurately Eggermont had managed to re-create Agnetha and Frida's vocals on the medley.

Stars On 45 Vol.2 charted at no.1 in Switzerland, no.2 in Germany and the UK, no.3 in Belgium, Ireland and the Netherlands, no.4 in Austria, no.5 in Norway and no.12 in Sweden.

On the album, *LONGPLAY ALBUM – VOLUME II*, Stars On 45/Starsound extended their ABBA medley to over eight minutes, adding *Dum Dum Diddle, Lay All Your Love On Me, On And On And On, Summer Night City* and *Gimme! Gimme! Gimme! (A Man After Midnight)*.

Two official ABBA medleys were released in Spain only, as promo CD singles: *The Spanish Gold Medley* in October 1992 and *More ABBA Gold Spanish Medley* in June 1993 – today, both are extremely rare.

77 ~ Lay All Your Love On Me by ABBA

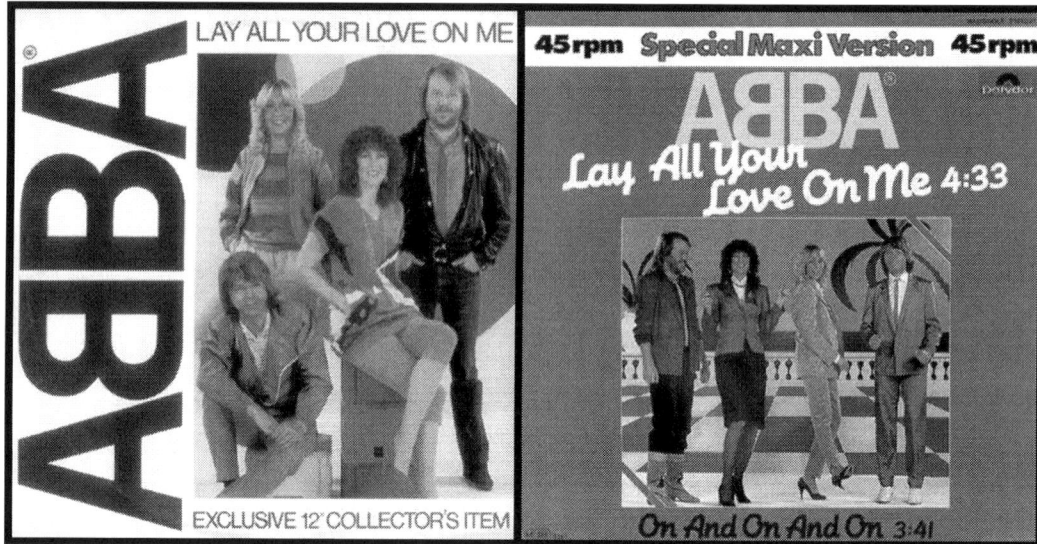

UK: Epic EPC A1456 (1981).

18.07.81: 17-**7**-9-14-24-28-66

Belgium
1.08.81: 23-15-15-**13**-29

France
07.81: peaked at no.**18**, charted for 7 weeks (b/w *On And On And On*)

Germany
17.08.81: 35-32-34-30-**26**-27-27-30-42-63-42-69-73-70

Ireland
19.07.81: 14-**8**-12

Lay All Your Love On Me was recorded in September 1980, along with *Me And I*, and before Benny and Björn had second thoughts and composed *Super Trouper*, they were supposed to be the final two songs for the album that became *SUPER TROUPER*.

There were no plans to release *Lay All Your Love On Me* as a single, until – with *On And On And On* and *Super Trouper* – a remix by Raul A. Rodriguez topped Billboard's Hot Dance Club Play chart. This prompted the track's release as a single in a few countries and, unusually, it was only issued as a 12" single. There is no doubt, had it been released as a 7" single as well, the single would have been far more successful than it was, and may even have hit no.1 in one or more countries.

As a 12" single, *Lay All Your Love On Me* charted at no.7 in the UK, no.8 in Ireland, no.13 in Belgium, no.18 in France and no.26 in Germany. In the UK, at the time, the single became the best-selling 12" release in chart history.

In the USA, *Lay All Your Love On Me* failed to enter the Hot 100, so the B-side *On And On And On* was promoted to the A-side, and became a minor hit.

The American techno-pop band Information Society recorded a cover of *Lay All Your Love On Me* in 1988, for their self-titled debut album. Released as a single, their version of the song did enter the Hot 100 in the USA, but it only rose to no.83.

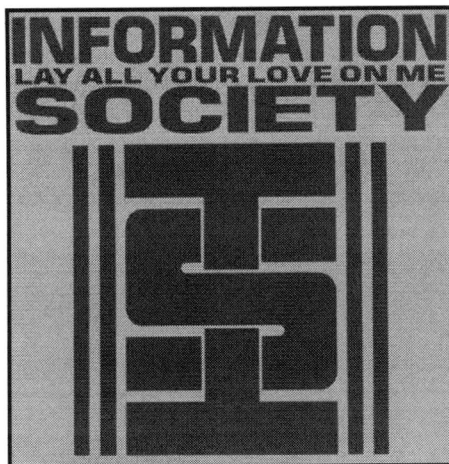

78 ~ One Of Us by ABBA

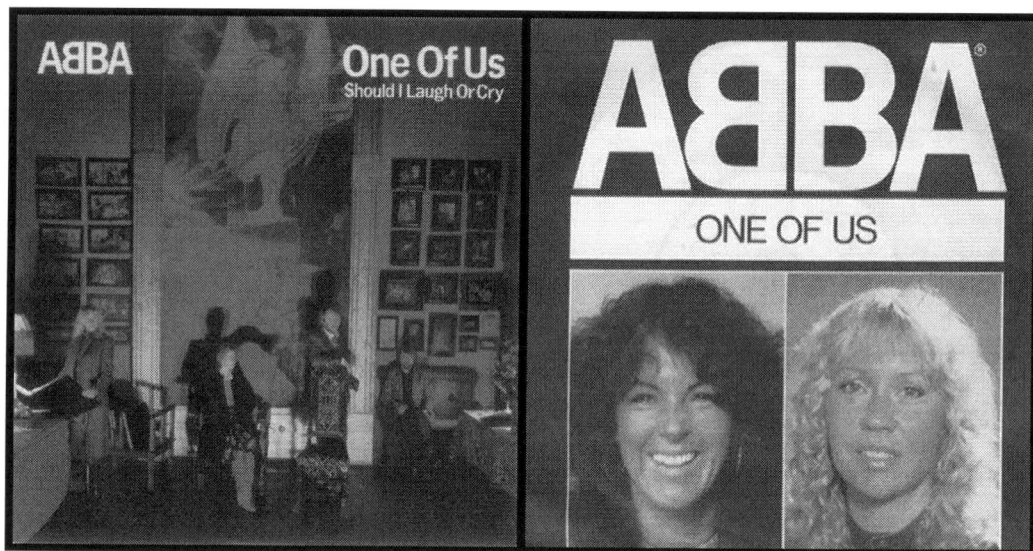

Sweden: Polar POS 1291 (1981).

22.12.81: **13** (bi-weekly chart)

UK: Epic EPC A1740 (1981).

12.12.81: 11-**3-3-3**-5-6-17-22-30-65

Australia
11.01.82: 72-61-55-56-**48**-52-61-65-70-76-85-86-98

Austria
15.01.82: 4-**3**-6-9-14-14 (bi-weekly chart)

Belgium
19.12.81: 15-2-**1-1-1-1-1**-4-9-16-21-27

Finland
01.82: **17** (monthly chart)

France
12.81: peaked at no.**8**, charted for 11 weeks

Germany
14.12.81: 33-9-3-**1**-3-4-2-5-7-7-10-10-13-17-16-27-40-46-44-54-73-73

Ireland
6.12.81: 8-2-**1**-**1**-**1**-2-4-15-27

Netherlands
12.12.81: 7-2-**1**-2-2-3-6-10-18-35-49

Norway
26.12.81: 7-7-7-**6**-10-8

South Africa
23.01.82: 17-14-8-6-**4**-**4**-5-6-10-11-13-14-18

Spain
12.81: peaked at no.**7**, charted for 12 weeks

Switzerland
20.12.81: 7-5-**3**-**3**-5-9-14

USA
One Of Us didn't enter the Hot 100 in the USA, however, it did spend four weeks on the 'Bubbling Under' section of the chart, peaking at no.7.

One Of Us, which had the working titles '*Nummer 1*' and '*Mio Amore*', was one of the last songs ABBA recorded for their eighth – and what would prove to be the group's last – studio album, *THE VISITORS*.

Initially, *When All Is Said And Done* was pencilled in as the album's lead single, but despite the somewhat depressing lyric it was felt *One Of Us* sounded more typically ABBA, and Björn and most record companies ABBA were signed with agreed *One Of Us* should be the first single.

One Of Us proved to be ABBA's last major international hit single, hitting no.1 in Belgium, Germany, Ireland and the Netherlands, no.3 in Austria, Switzerland and the UK, no.4 in South Africa, no.6 in Norway, no.7 in Spain, no.8 in France, no.13 in Sweden, no.17 in Finland and no.48 in Australia.

In most countries, *One Of Us* was released with a picture sleeve that reproduced the album's sleeve. In the UK, where *One Of Us* was the group's 18th consecutive Top 10 hit, a completely different design was chosen, with Agnetha and Frida on the front of the sleeve, and Benny and Björn on the reverse. The same photos were used for a picture disc single, with Benny and Björn on the A-side and Agnetha and Frida on the B-side.

One Of Us wasn't released as a single in the USA until February 1983 – more than a year after it had charted in most countries. Not surprisingly it struggled, and failed to enter the Hot 100, although it did spend four weeks 'bubbling under'.

Australia: RCA Victor 103955 (1982).

26.04.82: 82-86-**81**

USA
9.01.82: 87-77-59-49-39-35-32-31-28-**27-27**-36-44-99

When All Is Said And Done was recorded in March 1981, and was chosen ahead of *One Of Us*, as the lead single in the USA from ABBA's final studio album, *THE VISITORS*.

By this time, Agnetha and Björn had been divorced awhile, but Benny and Frida had only just divorced and Björn has confirmed their split was at the back of his mind when he wrote the lyrics to *When All Is said And Done*. Not wanting to cause unnecessary turmoil, Björn sought approval from Benny and Frida, before he went ahead and penned the lyrics. Frida sang lead on the track, and she later admitted, 'All my sadness was captured in that song.'

When All Is Said And Done gave ABBA their final Top 40 hit in the USA, peaking at no.27, but it was only a minor hit in Australia and wasn't released as a single in most other countries.

80 ~ Head Over Heels by ABBA

Sweden: Polar POS 1296 (1982).

Head Over Heels wasn't a hit in Sweden.

UK: Epic EPC A2037 (1982).

20.02.82: 41-34-30-26-**25**-32-52

Austria
15.04.82: **8** (bi-weekly chart)

Belgium
27.02.82: 13-11-**3**-4-6-15-22-40

France
03.82: peaked at no.**10**, charted for 10 weeks

Germany
1.03.82: 69-**19-19-19**-24-27-33-39-38-59-63-72

Ireland
14.02.82: **12**-14-18-28

Netherlands
20.02.82: 17-**1**-3-3-10-12-39

Spain
03.82: peaked at no.**12**, charted for 4 weeks (b/w *The Visitors*)

Originally titled 'Tango', *Head Over Heels* was recorded on 2nd September 1981, and was the second single released from *THE VISITORS* in most countries.

In peaking at no.25, *Head Over Heels* broke ABBA's impressive run of 18 consecutive Top 10 singles in the UK, which had equalled a record set by the Beatles. Nevertheless, although it couldn't match the success of *One Of Us*, *Head Over Heels* hit no.1 in the Netherlands, and achieved no.3 in Belgium, no.8 in Austria, no.10 in France, no.12 in Ireland and Spain, and no.19 in Germany.

In most countries, the B-side of *Head Over Heels* was *The Visitors* – arguably, a much stronger, more progressive track. In the USA, *The Visitors* was promoted to the A-side and *Head Over Heels* demoted to the B-side, but the single failed to achieve Top 40 status.

81 ~ The Visitors by ABBA

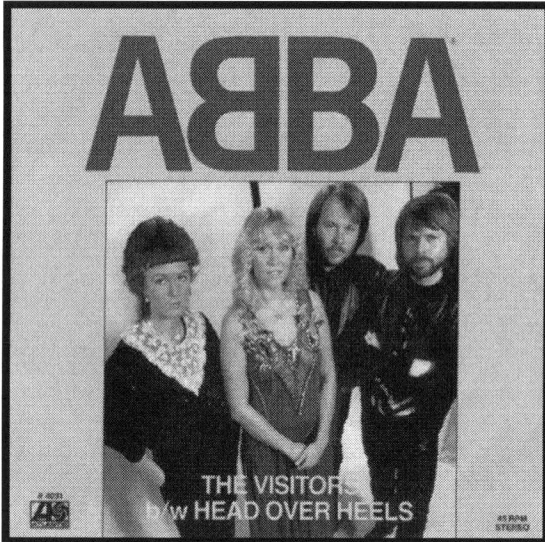

USA: Atlantic 4031 (1981).

17.04.82: 95-91-84-75-69-**63-63**-98

Spain
03.82: peaked at no.**12**, charted for 4 weeks (b/w *Head Over Heels*)

Originally titled '*Den Första*' ('The First'), *The Visitors* was recorded on 22nd October 1981, and was the second single released from the album of the same name in the USA, where it was preferred to *Head Over Heels*.

Officially, the theme of the song was the protest against the mistreatment of political dissidents in the Soviet Union – this, combined with ABBA allowing their music video for *When All Is Said And Done* to be screened on the American TV special, *Let Poland Be Poland*, led to THE VISITORS being banned in the Soviet Union.

The Visitors was only a minor hit in the USA, but it was a no.12 hit in Spain, where it was listed alongside *Head Over Heels*. On Billboard's Hot Dance Club Play chart, *The Visitors* was listed alongside *When All Is said And Done*, and peaked at no.8.

82 ~ I Know There's Something Going On by Frida

Sweden: Polar POS 1310 (1982).

31.08.82: 6-**3-3**-4-4-4-5-9-16 (bi-weekly chart)

UK: Epic EPC A2603 (1982).

21.08.82: 67-45-**43**-48-53-55-75

Australia
20.09.82: 45-29-16-13-15-10-8-7-**5**-8-13-19-25-34-44-77

Austria
15.10.82: **3**-5-9-10 (bi-weekly chart)

Belgium
4.09.82: 16-6-**1-1-1**-3-5-14-26

Canada
20.11.82: 45-39-35-**30-30**

Finland
10.82: peaked at no.**7**, charted for 16 weeks (monthly chart)

France
09.82: peaked at no.**1** (5 weeks), charted for 17 weeks

Germany
6.09.82: 72-23-16-6-8-**5-5-5**-8-10-13-16-15-22-26-30-33-46-41-58-75

Ireland
22.08.82: 26-**23**-30

Netherlands
28.08.82: 6-4-4-**3**-6-12-18-25-41

Norway
4.09.82: 7-6-5-5-4-5-**3**-4-**3**

South Africa
23.10.82: 20-19-15-11-7-**5**-7-7-9-9-9-11-13-19

Switzerland
12.09.82: 14-8-5-**1-1**-2-4-6-13

USA
6.11.82: 88-81-74-68-66-62-58-54-54-54-51-48-46-41-36-32-25-22-16-15-**13-13-13**-14-
    20-38-41-77-94

Zimbabwe
22.01.83: 20-13-10-9-8-8-**7**-8-10-13

As ABBA were supposedly between albums, Frida took the opportunity to record her first solo album in English. She chose to work with Genesis drummer and vocalist Phil Collins because she loved *In The Air Tonight* and his solo album *FACE VALUE* so much.

Frida, unlike the other members of ABBA, wasn't a song-writer, although Collins did encourage her to try her hand at composing. *I Know There's Something Going On*, the lead single from her 1982 album *SOMETHING'S GOING ON*, was written by Russ Ballard and proved far more successful than the ABBA singles *Head Over Heels*, *The Day Before You Came* and *Under Attack*.

I Know There's Something Going On, which featured Phil Collins on drums and backing vocals, hit no.1 in Belgium, France and Switzerland, and charted at no.3 in Austria, the Netherlands and Sweden, no.5 in Australia, Germany and South Africa, no.7 in Finland and Zimbabwe, no.13 in the USA, no.23 in Ireland and no.30 in Canada. More disappointingly, the single failed to enter the Top 40 in the UK, where it peaked at no.43.

83 ~ Never Again by Tomas Ledin & Agnetha Fältskog

Sweden: Polar POS 1308 (1982).

26.10.82: 8-**2-2-2**-5-4-7-10 (bi-weekly)

UK: Epic EPC A2824 (1982).

Never Again wasn't a hit in the UK.

Belgium
16.10.82: 31-15-**9**-19-39

Finland
12.82: **19** (monthly chart)

France
12.82: peaked at no.**44**, charted for 5 weeks

Germany
13.12.82: 44-**37**-42-63-49-62

Netherlands
2.10.82: 35-**19**-22-22-46

Norway
23.10.82: 9-6-6-9-6-7-8-**5**

Zimbabwe
10.09.83: 17-**12-12**-14-16-18

Tomas Ledin is popular Swedish singer who toured with ABBA in 1979 and 1980, as a backing vocalist. Like ABBA, he was signed to Polar in Sweden, and *Never Again* was a song he composed for his 1982 album, *THE HUMAN TOUCH*.

As ABBA were between albums, and Frida was recording her debut solo album in English, Stig Anderson suggested Ledin recorded *Never Again* as a duet with Agnetha in an attempt to gain wider international recognition. Ledin and Agnetha agreed, although they actually laid down their vocals at different times.

Never Again charted at no.2 in Sweden, no.5 in Norway, no.9 in Belgium, no.12 in Zimbabwe, no.19 in Finland and the Netherlands, no.37 in Germany and no.44 in France.

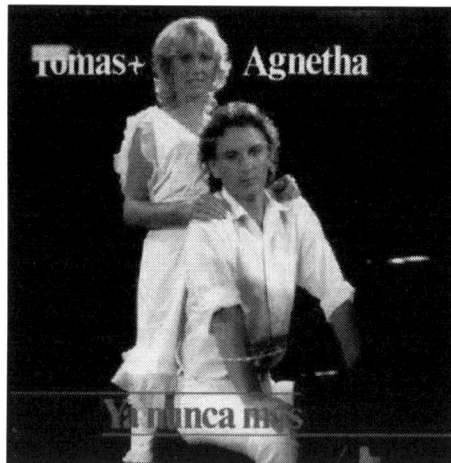

'Tomas + Agnetha', as the duo were billed, recorded a Spanish version of *Never Again*, titled *Ya Nunca Más*, which was a sizeable hit in South America.

84 ~ The Day Before You Came by ABBA

Sweden: Polar POS 1318 (1982).

9.11.82: **3-3**-4-7-15 (bi-weekly chart)

UK: Epic EPC A2847 (1982).

23.10.82: 41-**32**-35-35-37-46

Australia
15.11.82: 93-67-61-61-**48**-51-56-80

Austria
15.12.82: 19-**16**-20 (bi-weekly chart)

Belgium
30-10-82: 17-6-6-**3-3**-4-5-6-20-38

Finland
12.82: peaked at no.**2**, charted for 12 weeks (monthly chart)

France
11.82: peaked at no.**38**, charted for 6 weeks

Germany
1.11.82: 70-34-15-6-6-**5**-7-9-10-14-20-30-29-46-46-71

Ireland
10.10.82: **13**-15-27-15

Netherlands
30.10.82: 21-**3-3**-4-5-8-16-25-28-34-49

Norway
30.10.82: 7-**5**-8-8-9

Switzerland
7.11.82: 13-9-6-**4**-7-9-12-14

Zimbabwe
29.01.83: 20-17-**14**-15-20

ABBA recorded *The Day Before You Came*, which started life as '*Den Lidande Fågeln*' ('The Suffering Bird'), on 20th August 1982 – although no one knew it at the time, it would be the last song the four members of ABBA recorded as a group.

Following *THE VISITORS*, Benny and Björn started working on their first musical, *Chess*, with Tim Rice, and Agnetha and Frida took the opportunity to launch their English language solo careers. However, in May 1982 all four members of ABBA returned to Polar Studios in Sweden, aiming to record new songs for their ninth studio album. Between May and August, six new songs were recorded, including *Cassandra* and *Under Attack*, which Benny and Björn agreed were not strong enough to release as a single. This led to them composing and recording the sixth and final new song, *The Day Before You Came*.

Björn has admitted the lyrics he wrote were influenced by his divorce from Agnetha. 'Even if ninety percent of the lyrics are fiction,' he said, 'there are still feelings in songs like *(The) Winner Takes It All* and *(The) Day Before You Came* – they have something from that time in them.'

Agnetha was asked to sing *The Day Before You Came* in an 'artless' voice, in an attempt to reflect the 'ordinary' woman she was portraying in the song. With hindsight, it was a move Benny, Björn and Agnetha all questioned. 'I think perhaps it would have been better,' Benny admitted, 'to let Agnetha remain a singer, instead of making her act the part of the woman she was singing about.'

Nevertheless, although it wasn't as successful as many of ABBA's singles, *The Day Before You Came* has become a firm favourite among fans over the years. It charted at no.2 in Finland, no.3 in Belgium, the Netherlands and Sweden, no.4 in Switzerland, no.5

in Germany, no.14 in Zimbabwe, no.16 in Austria, no.32 in the UK, no.38 in France and no.48 in Australia.

ABBA promoted *The Day Before You Came* with a music video filmed in Stockholm on 21st September 1982, and directed by Kjell Sundvall and Kjell-Åke Andersson. Sundvall later commented, 'It didn't really feel like we had been working with a group, but with four individuals.'

The Day Before You Came featured on the 1982 compilation, *THE SINGLES – THE FIRST TEN YEARS*.

The British duo Blancmange, comprising Neil Arthur and Stephen Luscombe, recorded a cover of *The Day Before You Came* for their 1984 album, *MANGE TOUT*. Released as a single, their version of *The Day Before You Came* charted at no.22 in the UK – ten places higher than ABBA's original. The single also achieved no.25 in Ireland.

85 ~ To Turn The Stone by Frida

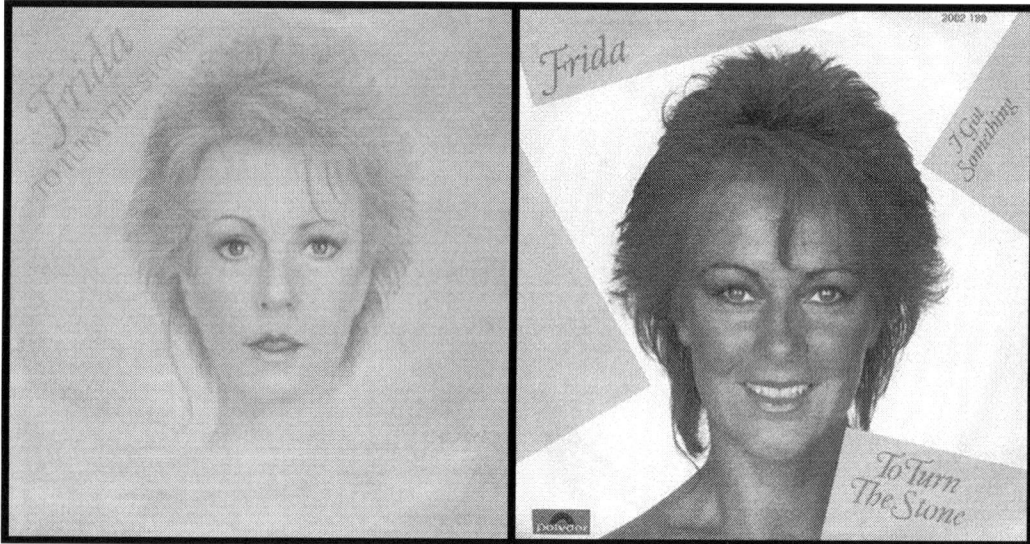

Sweden: Polydor 2002 189 (1982).

To Turn The Stone wasn't a hit in Sweden.

UK: Epic A2863 (1982).

To Turn The Stone wasn't a hit in the UK.

Belgium
23.10.82: 37-15-**9**-12-13-13-21-34

France
03.83: peaked at no.**33**, charted for 7 weeks

Germany
13.12.83: **39**-42-43-**39**-56-65-x-73

Netherlands
23.10.82: 15-**8**-11-14-22-33-50

To Turn The Stone was the second single released from Frida's 1982 album, *SOMETHING'S GOING ON.*

To Turn The Stone was written by Giorgio Moroder and Pete Bellotte for Donna Summer, who recorded the song for her 1981 album, *I'M A RAINBOW* – however, much to her dismay, the album was shelved by her record company and remained unreleased until 1996.

Frida's cover of *To Turn The Stone* was a Top 10 hit in Belgium and the Netherlands, peaking at no.8 and no.9, respectively. The single also achieved no.33 in France and no.39 in Germany, but it wasn't a hit anywhere else.

86 ~ *Belle* by Balavoine & Frida

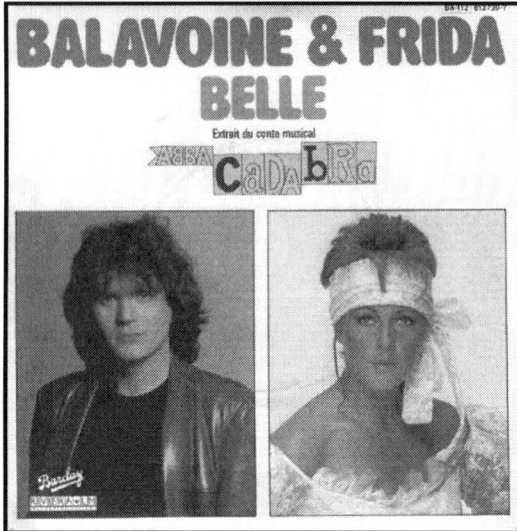

France: Barclay 813 720-7 (1982).

12.82: peaked at no.**15**, charted for 9 weeks

Only released in France, Germany and Canada, *Belle* ('Beauty') was a vocal version of ABBA's *Arrival*, with French lyrics.

Frida recorded *Belle* as a duet with Daniel Balavoine for *ABBAcadabra*, a French childrens' musical based on the songs of ABBA. Released as a non-album single, *Belle* charted at no.15 in France, but it wasn't a hit in Germany or Canada.

Frida also recorded a version of *Arrival*, titled *Time*, with English lyrics by Don Black and Mike Batt as a duet with B.A. Robertson – it charted at no.45 in the UK, but it didn't achieve Top 40 status anywhere.

87 ~ Under Attack by ABBA

Sweden: Polar POS 1321 (1983).

Under Attack wasn't a hit in Sweden.

UK: Epic EPC A2971 (1982).

11.12.82: 46-31-**26-26-26-26**-42-73

Australia
14.02.83: 98-**96**

Belgium
25.12.82: 11-5-4-4-**2**-10-19-22

Finland
04.83: **16** (monthly chart)

France
02.83: peaked at no.**43**, charted for 5 weeks

Germany
27.12.82: 37-**22**-23-23-26-35-42-51-71

Ireland
16.12.82: 17-**11**-13-22-29

Netherlands
11.12.82: 43-9-**7**-10-15-20-26-39

Spain
02.83: peaked at no.**19**, charted for 6 weeks

ABBA recorded *Under Attack* between the 2nd and 4th August 1982 and, despite Benny and Björn's initial reservations the track wasn't strong enough to be released as a single, it was issued as the follow-up to *The Day Before You Came* in most countries – and proved to be the final new single ABBA released as a group.

Under Attack includes fragments of two unreleased ABBA recordings, *Just Like That* and *Rubber Ball Man*. Like *The Day Before You Came*, it was included on the 1982 compilation, *THE SINGLES – THE FIRST TEN YEARS*.

Chart-wise, confirming Benny and Björn's fears, *Under Attack* struggled in most countries. It rose to no.2 in Belgium and no.7 in the Netherlands, but only achieved no.11 in Ireland, no.16 in Finland, no.19 in Spain, no.22 in Germany, no.26 in the UK and no.43 in France.

ABBA performed *Under Attack* and *I Have A Dream* on the BBC TV show, *Late Late Breakfast Show*, hosted by Noel Edmonds, on 11th December 1982. It proved to be Agnetha, Benny, Björn and Frida's final performance together as ABBA.

88 ~ Here We'll Stay by Frida

Sweden: Polar POS 1334 (1983).

Here Well Stay wasn't a hit in Sweden.

UK: Epic A3435 (1983).

25.06.83: **100**

Belgium
14.05.83: **36**-39

France
06.83: peaked at no.**34**, charted for 7 weeks

Netherlands
7.05.83: **34**-38-48

USA
Here We'll Stay didn't enter the Hot 100 in the USA, however, it did spend two weeks on the 'Bubbling Under' chart, peaking at no.2.

Here We'll Stay was the third single lifted from Frida's 1982 album, *SOMETHING'S GOING ON*.

Here We'll Stay was written by Tony Colton and Jean Roussel, and Frida originally recorded the song as a duet with Phil Collins, for her album. However, when it was agreed to release the track as a single, Collins declined all involvement, so Frida re-recorded the song on her own and her solo version was issued as a single.

Only a minor hit, *Here We'll Stay* nevertheless achieved Top 40 status in three countries, peaking at no.34 in France and the Netherlands, and at no.36 in Belgium.

Here We'll Stay spent a solitary week at no.100 in the UK, and narrowly failed to enter the Hot 100 in the USA.

89 ~ The Heat Is On by Agnetha Fältskog

Sweden: Polar POS 1335 (1983).

17.05.83: 6-2-**1-1**-4-6-8-18 (bi-weekly chart)

UK: Epic EPC A3436 (1983).

21.05.83: 84-47-**35**-37-36-43-53

Belgium
21.05.83: 13-11-6-5-4-**2-2**-8-11-19

France
06.83: peaked at no.**10**, charted for 10 weeks

Germany
20.06.83: 47-43-36-23-**20**-22-22-29-31-43-51-68-69-46-45-56-71

Ireland
5.06.83: **28**

Netherlands
21.05.83: 18-5-9-**8**-9-9-10-17-24-42-47

Norway
28.05.83: 7-7-6-5-2-**1**-**1**-2-4-6-6-7-8-8

Switzerland
10.07.83: **15**

Zimbabwe
17.12.83: **19-19**

The Heat Is On was composed by Florrie Palmer and Tony Ashton, and was originally recorded by Noosha Fox in 1979, but her version wasn't a hit.

Agnetha recorded a cover of *The Heat Is On* for her debut album in English, *WRAP YOUR ARMS AROUND ME*, and in most countries it was released as the lead single.

The Heat Is On gave Agnetha her first international hit as a solo artist, hitting no.1 in Norway and Sweden, and charting at no.2 in Belgium, no.8 in the Netherlands, no.10 in France, no.15 in Switzerland, no.19 in Zimbabwe, no.20 in Germany, no.28 in Ireland and no.35 in the UK.

The B-side of *The Heat Is On*, titled *Man*, was a song Agnetha composed herself.

90 ~ Wrap Your Arms Around Me by Agnetha Fältskog

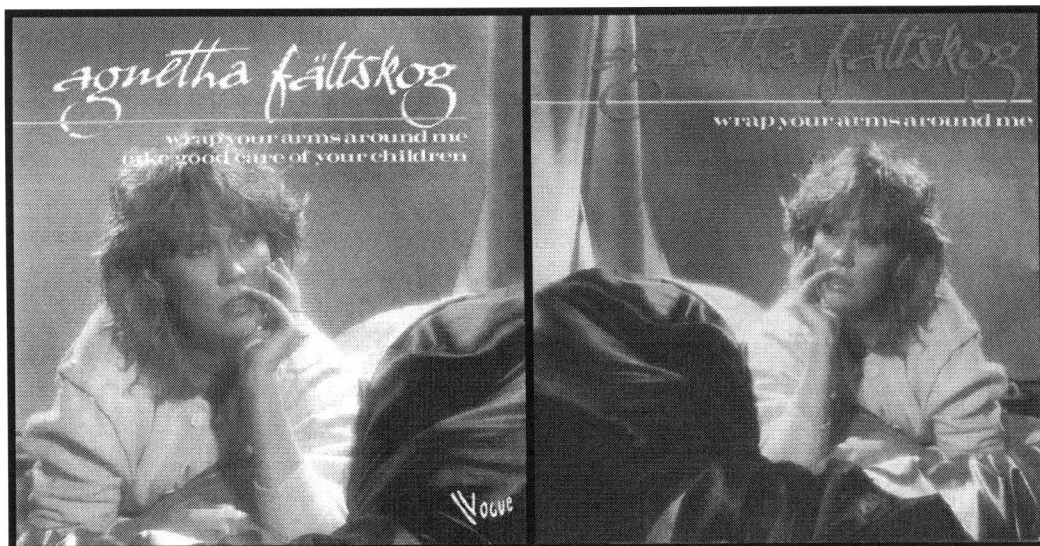

UK: Epic EPC A3622 (1983).

6.08.83: 84-61-**44**-49-58-75

Austria
15.08.83: **20** (bi-weekly chart)

Belgium
30.07.83: 17-13-6-4-2-**1-1**-5-9-15-23

France
11.83: peaked at no.**42**, charted for 6 weeks (b/w *Can't Shake Loose*)

Germany
3.10.83: 48-42-32-**30**-36-42-48-60-68-71-75

Ireland
14.08.83: **15-15**

Netherlands
30.07.83: 43-**4-4**-6-9-10-21-30-45

South Africa
29.10.83: 26-14-13-10-6-4-**2-2-2**-3-5-7-7-11-16-18-19-26

Written by Mike Chapman and Holly Knight, the ballad *Wrap Your Arms Around Me* was the second single released from the album with the same title.

Although it wasn't quite as successful as *The Heat Is On*, *Wrap Your Arms Around Me* charted at no.1 in Belgium, no.2 in South Africa, no.4 in the Netherlands, no.15 in Ireland, no.20 in Austria, no.30 in Germany, no.42 in France and no.44 in the UK.

Take Good Care Of Your Children, the B-side of *Wrap Your Arms Around Me*, was composed by Tomas Ledin.

91 ~ Can't Shake Loose by Agnetha Fältskog

UK: Epic EPC A3812 (1983).

15.10.83: 76-**63**-79

Australia
19.09.83: 86-80-**76**-79

Belgium
5.11.83: 34-**24**-30

Canada
17.09.83: 46-41-36-30-26-26-26-25-**23**-26-37

France
11.83: peaked at no.**42**, charted for 6 weeks (b/w *Wrap Your Arms Around Me*)

USA
27.08.83: 78-64-56-50-47-43-39-37-33-31-**29**-52-70-93-100

Like Frida's *I Know There's Something Going On*, *Can't Shake Loose* was composed by Russ Ballard.

In most countries, *Can't Shake Loose* was the third single released from Agnetha's album *WRAP YOUR ARMS AROUND ME*, but it was the first single in North America, where – boosted by an appearance by Agnetha on American TV – it charted at no.23 in Canada and no.29 in the USA. Elsewhere, the single was only a minor hit, rising to no.24 in Belgium, but missing the Top 40 in France, Australia and the UK.

92 ~ It's So Nice To Be Rich by Agnetha Fältskog

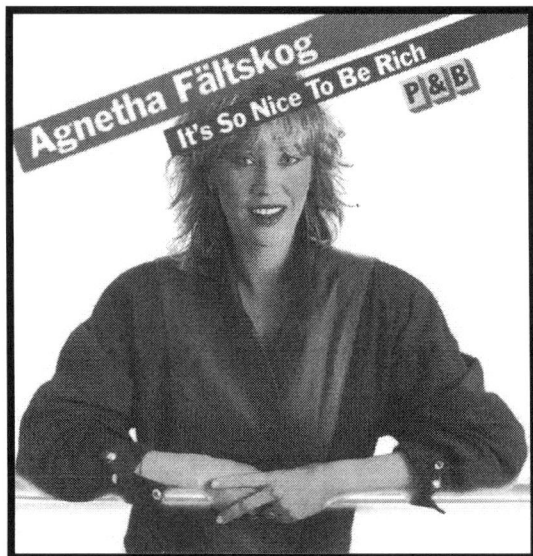

Sweden: Polar POS 1347 (1983).

10.01.84: 14-12-**8**-9 (bi-weekly chart)

Written by G. Svensson and H. Alfredson, *It's So Nice To Be Rich* is a little known song Agnetha recorded for the soundtrack of the 1983 Swedish film, *P & B*.

The track was produced and arranged by Rutger Gunnarsson, and was only released as a single in Sweden, where it charted at no.8.

93 ~ Shine by Frida

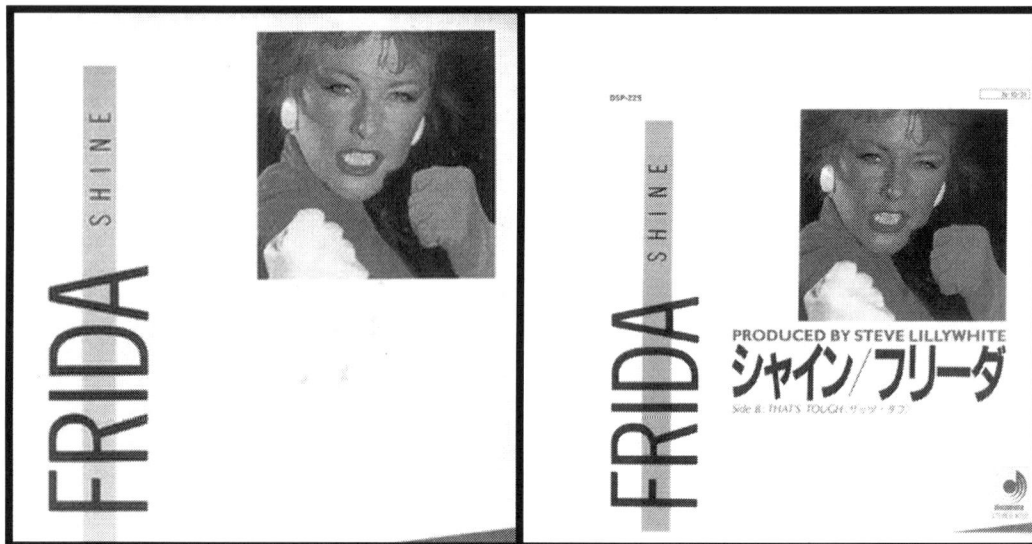

Sweden: Polar POS 1360 (1984).

31.08.84: 16-**6**-8-10-20 (bi-weekly)

UK: Epic EPC A4717 (1984).

22.09.84: 86-**82**-90

Belgium
15.09.84: 27-14-**9-9**-12-22

Germany
1.10.84: 63-62-**51**-72

Netherlands
8.09.84: **19**-27-32-47

Written by Kevin Jarvis, Guy Fletcher and Jeremy Bird, *Shine* was the title track of Frida's second English language album, released in 1984.

 Shine charted at no.6 in Sweden, no.9 in Belgium and no.19 in the Netherlands, but it was only a minor hit in Germany and the UK, and failed to chart in most countries.

One Night In Bangkok by Murray Head

Sweden: Polar CHESS 1 (1984).

9.11.84: 13-7-4-4-**3**-4-4-9-20 (bi-weekly)

UK: RCA CHESS 1 (1984).

3.11.84: 85-53-39-27-17-16-**12**-14-15-15-16-30-43-53-x-74-92

Australia
21.01.85: peaked at no.**1** (1 week), charted for 22 weeks

Austria
1.02.85: 3-**2-2**-3-7-14 (bi-weekly chart)

Belgium
8.12.84: 28-21-6-5-4-3-3-**1-1-1**-3-6-11-11-14-21-26-39

France
9.02.85: 14-11-5-4-4-**2**-3-3-5-5-6-10-16-14-17-27-31-49

Germany
17.12.84: peaked at no.**1** (2 weeks), charted for 21 weeks

Ireland
25.11.84: 20-13-15-13-12-12-**7**-**7**-18-20-16-17-12-18

Netherlands
29.12.84: 31-17-6-**1**-**1**-2-2-3-9-16-31-38-49

New Zealand
10.03.85: 39-23-4-3-**2**-3-3-**2**-5-9-11-15-18-33-40

Norway
8.12.84: 4-**3**-4-4-4-4-4-5-**3**-**3**-**3**-**3**-**3**-4-7-7

South Africa
19.01.85: 29-21-14-8-4-**1**-**1**-**1**-**1**-**1**-**1**-2-2-3-3-3-4-4-5-7-16-19-27

Switzerland
6.01.85: 7-5-**1**-**1**-**1**-**1**-**1**-2-2-3-6-10-15-15

USA
23.02.85: 81-70-57-48-35-27-19-12-9-6-5-5-**3**-7-15-23-36-58-79-87

Zimbabwe
9.03.85: 20-17-16-12-8-5-4-**3**-**3**-**3**-4-6-8-11-14-17

One Night In Bangkok was written by Benny and Björn with Tim Rice, for their 1984 musical, *Chess*.

In the musical, Murray Head played the part of 'The American', and he performed *One Night In Bangkok* at the opening of Act 2. Although uncredited, Anders Glenmark sang the chorus and backing vocals on *One Night In Bangkok*. Benny played keyboards and synthesizers on the recording.

One Night In Bangkok was a major international smash, hitting no.1 in Australia, Belgium, Germany, the Netherlands, South Africa and Switzerland. The single also charted at no.2 in Austria, France and New Zealand, no.3 in Norway, Sweden, the USA and Zimbabwe, no.7 in Ireland and no.12 in the UK.

Vinyl Shakerz, a German techno-house group, recorded a cover of *One Night In Bangkok* in 2005 – it charted at no.6 in Finland, no.14 in Belgium, no.26 in Germany and no.41 in Austria.

I Know Him So Well by Elaine Paige & Barbara Dickson

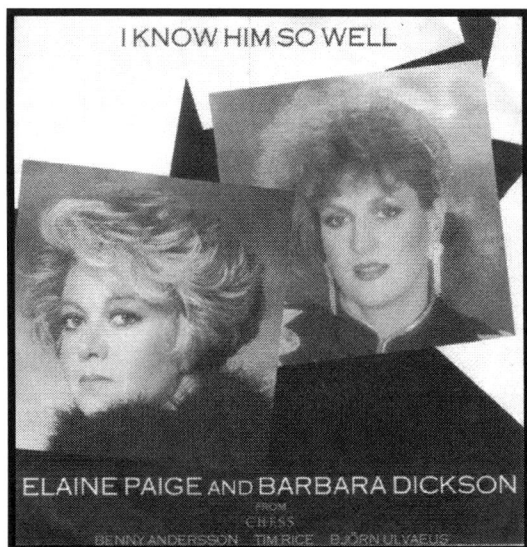

Sweden: Polar CHESS 4 (1984).

I Know Him So Well wasn't a hit in Sweden.

UK: RCA CHESS 3 (1984).

29.12.84: 79-63-34-6-3-2-**1-1-1-1**-2-8-10-28-34-41-62

Australia
11.03.85: peaked at no.**21**, charted for 26 weeks

Belgium
16.02.85: 20-14-**13-13-13**-16-17-27-37

Germany
11.03.85: peaked at no.**22**, charted for 8 weeks

Ireland
20.01.85: 7-2-**1-1-1-1-1**-10-18-22

Netherlands
16.02.85: 34-36-44-32-26-**16**-18-23-37-39

New Zealand

5.05.85: 41-47-49-41-48-44-50

21.07.85: 34-24-38-19-**9**-18-15-11-10-12-19-19-27-21-24-24-42-31-28-43-33-47

South Africa

27.04.85: 27-25-22-20-18-17-10-3-3-**2**-3-4-4-6-9-11-12-12-14-15-15-16-20-24

Switzerland

17.03.85: 19-12-8-**7**-8-10-11-22-24

Zimbabwe

2.03.85: 20-17-13-10-8-6-3-**2-2-2**-6-8-9-13-15

Like *One Night In Bangkok*, *I Know Him So Well* was written by Benny and Björn with Tim Rice, for their musical *Chess*.

The song was recorded as a duet by Elaine Paige (as Florence, the Russian chess champion's mistress) and Barbara Dickson (as Svetlana, the Russian chess champion's estranged wife), with Benny once again playing keyboards and synthesizers on the recording. Paige and Dickson never actually met during the recording of the song, as they laid down their vocals separately, but they did shoot a music video together, and appeared on numerous TV shows together to promote the single, including *Top Of The Pops*.

I Know Him So Well was hugely popular in the UK and Ireland, where it went to no.1, and in the UK the single went on to become the best-selling single by a female duo ever. In most other countries, however, *I Know Him So Well* was less popular than *One Night In Bangkok*. It charted at no.2 in South Africa and Zimbabwe, no.7 in Switzerland, no.9 in New Zealand, no.13 in Belgium, no.16 in the Netherlands, no.21 in Australia and no.22 in Germany.

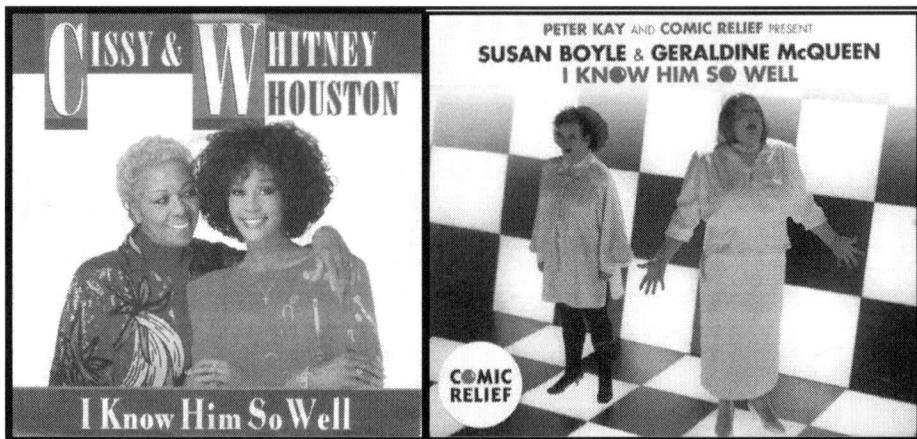

Several high profile cover versions of *I Know Him So Well* have been recorded.

Whitney Houston recorded a cover of *I Know Him So Well* with her mother Cissy, for her 1987 album, *WHITNEY*. The duet was released as a single in a limited number of countries, charting at no.16 in the Netherlands, no.19 in Belgium and no.46 in Germany.

Susan Boyle recorded *I Know Him So Well* as a duet the comedian Peter Kay, *aka* Geraldine McQueen, to raise money for the charity Comic Relief in 2011. The duet was only released in the UK, where it peaked at no.11.

Melanie C recorded *I Know Him So Well* with Emma Bunton for her 2012 album, *STAGES*. Although promoted as a single, this cover by the former Spice Girls only achieved no.153 in the UK.

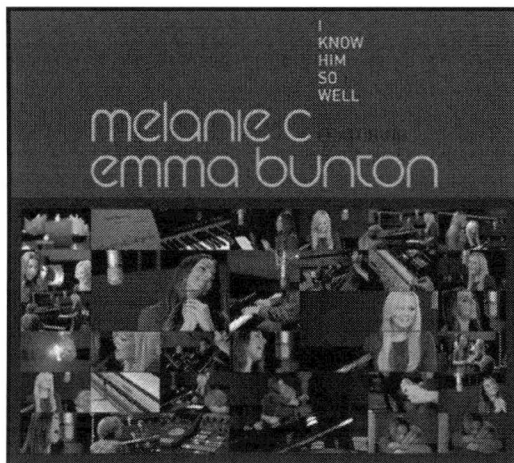

94 ~ I Won't Let You Go by Agnetha Fältskog

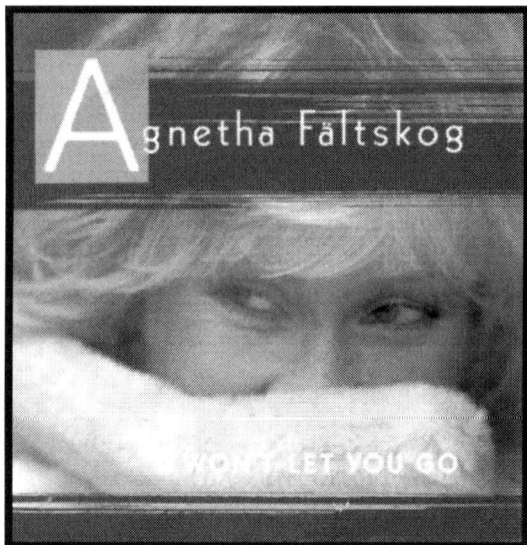

Sweden: Polar POS 1366 (1985).

8.03.85: 8-**6**-9-12 (bi-weekly chart)

UK: Epic EPC A6133 (1985).

6.04.85: 100-**84**-100-92

Belgium
23.03.85: 14-13-13-**7**-8-14-20-29

Germany
15.04.85: 66-x-44-36-**24**-31-29-42-49-56-67-72

Netherlands
16.03.85: 39-20-**17**-19-20-34-47

Agnetha composed *I Won't Let You Go* herself, with Eric Stewart (of 10cc fame) adding the lyrics. The song was released as the lead single from her 1985 album, *EYES OF A WOMAN*, but it wasn't a major hit, only charting at no.6 in Sweden, no.7 in Belgium, no.17 in the Netherlands, no.24 in Germany and a lowly no.84 in the UK.

Just Like That by Gemini

UK: Polydor POSP 782 (1986).

22.03.86: 88-**79**-86

Belgium
26.04.86: 40-**30**-35

Netherlands
12.04.86: 25-29-**24**-26-34

Just Like That is one of six songs Benny and Björn worked on, and ABBA recorded, between May and August 1982, for a new album that never materialised.

Benny and Björn re-worked the song three years later, when they co-produced a self-titled album by Gemini, a Swedish brother/sister duo comprising Anders and Karin Glenmark. Released as a single, Gemini's version of *Just Like That* charted at no.24 in the Netherlands and no.30 in Belgium, and was a minor hit in the UK.

An edited snippet of ABBA's recording of *Just Like That* featured as part of the *ABBA Undeleted* medley included on CD4 of their 1994 box-set, *THANK YOU FOR THE MUSIC*. However, ABBA's complete version of *Just Like That* has never been released, and Benny and Björn have stated that in their opinion there can't be two official versions of the same song that are so similar and yet so different.

95 ~ The Way You Are by Agnetha Fältskog & Ola Håkansson

Sweden: Sonet T-10217 (1986).

5.11.86: 4-**1-1-1**-2-7-14 (bi-weekly)

UK: Sonet SON-2317 (1986).

The Way You Are wasn't a hit in the UK.

The Way You Are was composed by Norell Oson Bard, and was recorded by Agnetha as a duet with Ola Håkansson, a member of the band Secret Service, to promote the Swedish town of Fran as a candidate for hosting the Winger Olympic Games in 1992.

Although Fran's bid was unsuccessful, *The Way You Are* was a huge hit in Sweden, where it spent six weeks at no.1. The single was also released outside Scandinavia, but it was only a hit in Sweden.

Fly Like An Eagle, the B-side of *The Way You Are*, was another song Agnetha recorded as a duet with Ola Håkansson.

96 ~ *Så Länge Vi Har Varann* by Ratata & Frida

Sweden: Record Station TATI 3 (1987).

11.02.87: 8-6-**5-5-5**-8-11 (bi-weekly chart)

Så Länge Vi Har Varann ('As Long As I Have You') was a one-off single Frida recorded in 1986 with the Swedish band, Ratata – it charted at no.5 in Sweden, but it wasn't a hit anywhere else.

Frida and Ratata also recorded an English version of *As Long As I Have You*, which was released as the B-side of Ratata's 1987 single, *Om Du Var Här* ('If You Were Here').

Mio Min Mio by Gemini

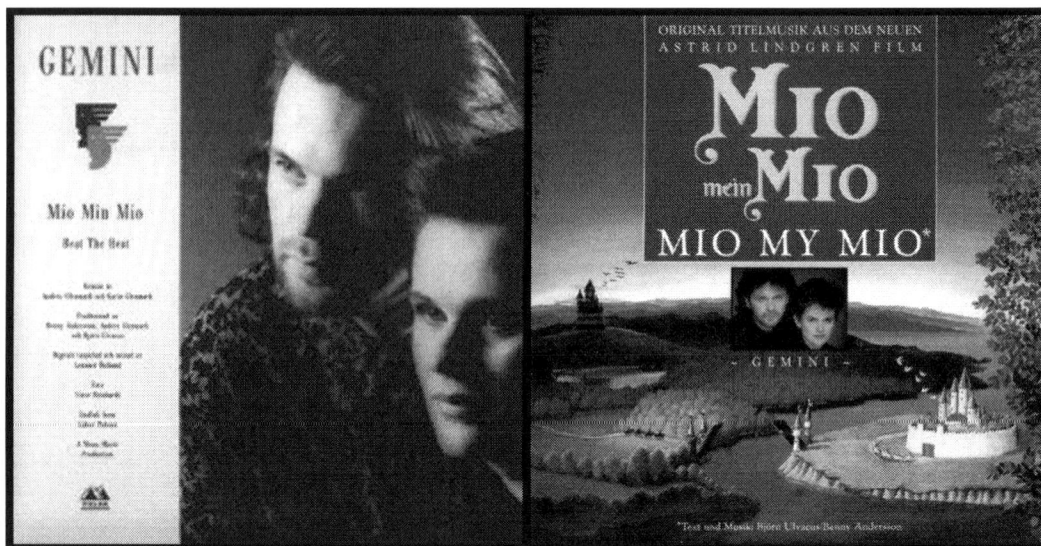

Sweden: Polar POS 1386 (1986).

11.11.87: 19-4-**3**-4-6-9 (bi-weekly chart)

Mio Min Mio ('Mio, My Mio') was composed by Benny and Björn, and was recorded by Gemini for their 1987 album, *GEMINISM* – Benny and Björn also produced the album.

 Mio Min Mio featured in the 1987 film, *Mio In The Land Of Faraway*, which was based on Astrid Lindgren's book, *Mio, My Son*.

 Mio Min Mio, which was recorded in English and Russian as well as Swedish, was only released as a single in Germany (as '*Mio Mein Mio*') and Sweden. It wasn't a hit in Germany, but it achieved Top 3 status in Sweden.

97 ~ The Last Time by Agnetha Fältskog

UK: WEA YZ170 (1988).

6.02.88: 82-**77**-88

Belgium
13.02.88: 36-**24**-34

Germany
29.02.88: 51-**49**-54-52-58-64

Netherlands
6.02.88: 93-62-49-49-**40**-47-62-79

The Last Time, composed by R. Randall, J. Randall and J. Law, was the lead single from Agnetha's 1987 album, *I STAND ALONE*.

The single achieved Top 40 status in Belgium and the Netherlands, but it wasn't a success in most countries. Even in the UK, where Agnetha made a promotional visit to London, *The Last Time* peaked at a disappointing no.77.

Agnetha recorded a Spanish version of *The Last Time*, titled *La Ultima Vez*, for the South American version of her album – today, as it sold poorly, this version of the album is a rarity.

Lassie by the Ainbusk Singers

Sweden: Mono MMS 104 (1990).

21.11.90: 17-3-**1**-3-10-19 (bi-weekly chart)

The Ainbusk Singers, who later dropped the 'Singers' part of their name, were a Swedish quartet comprising Annelie Roswall, Birgitta Jakobsson, Josefin Nilsson and Marie Milsson-Lind.

Lassie, which was only released in Sweden, was composed by Benny with lyrics by band member Marie Nilsson-Lind – the single went all the way to no.1.

As Ainbusk, the all-female quartet went on to have a further three hits in Sweden, with one of them – *Jag Saknar Dig Ibland* – achieving Top 40 status, however, neither Benny nor Björn had a hand in writing any of the songs.

Josefin Nilsson later went on a solo album, with Benny and Björn composing all the songs on the album.

Abba-esque by Erasure

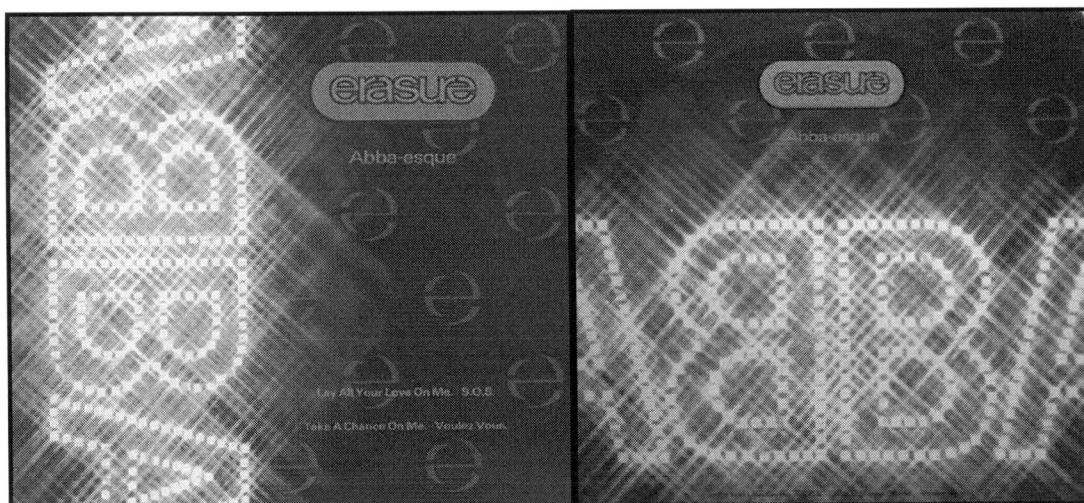

Sweden: Mute Mute 144 (1992).

24.06.92: **1-1-1-1-1-1**-2-3-8-16 (bi-weekly)

UK: Mute Mute 144 (1992).

13.06.92: **1-1-1-1-1**-4-9-12-21-37-48-73

Australia
29.06.92: peaked at np.**12**, charted for 16 weeks

Austria
5.07.92: 7-2-2-**1-1-1-1-1-1-1**-2-1-2-2-3-7-12-11-7-10-15-25

Belgium
11.07.92: 49-16-9-9-**4**-8-5-5-5-8-12-21-31-39

Germany
22.06.92: peaked at no.**2**, charted for 30 weeks

Ireland
4.06.92: 3-**1-1-1-1-1**-2-3-4-10-10-16-14-22-28

Netherlands
27.06.92: 94-63-30-13-5-5-**4**-5-7-12-21-41-67-98

New Zealand
9.08.92: **42**

Switzerland
5.07.92: 7-**3**-4-4-4-5-5-4-5-5-4-5-6-4-5-**3**-7-6-7-9-17-30-28-25-35-31-32

USA
18.07.92: 87-**85**-98-89-x-x-98-100-x-98-89-92 (album chart)

Andy Bell and Vince Clarke, as the British duo Erasure, paid tribute to ABBA in 1992 by releasing a 4-track EP titled *Abba-esque*, which featured covers of four ABBA hits: *Lay All Your Love On Me, S.O.S, Take A Chance On Me* and *Voulez-Vous*.

Take A Chance On Me was the most popular cover in many countries, especially as Erasure filmed a spoof music video that copied ABBA's original, with Bell and Clarke dressed as Agnetha and Frida.

The *Abba-esque* EP proved hugely popular, hitting no.1 in Austria, Ireland, Sweden and the UK, no.2 in Germany, no.3 in Switzerland, no.4 in Belgium and the Netherlands, no.12 in Australia and no.42 in New Zealand.

In the USA, due to the number of tracks and running time, *Abba-esque* was classed as an album for chart purposes, and did well to peak at no.85 on the Billboard 200.

HEAVEN AND HELL by Josefin Nilsson

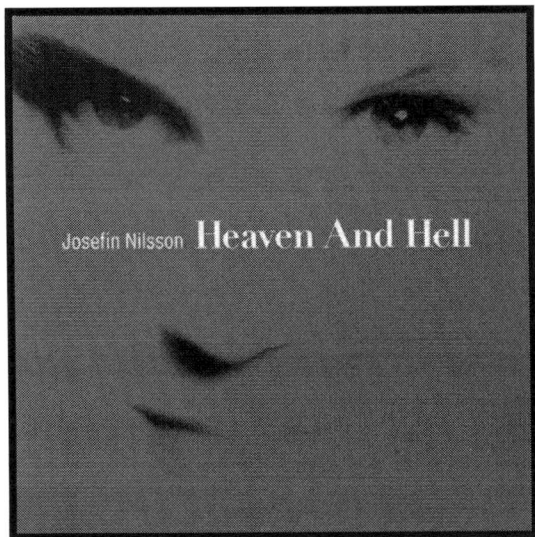

Sweden: Mono MMS 007 (1993).

10.03.93: **28**-30-35-40

Norway
3.04.93: 10-10-**9-9**

Benny and Björn composed all ten tracks on Swedish singer Josefin Nilsson's debut solo album, *SHAPES*, including the lead single, *Heaven And Hell*. Previously, as a member of the Ainbusk Singers, Nilsson had scored a Swedish no.1 with *Lassie*, which Benny composed.

Released in the Netherlands and Spain, as well as Scandinavia, *Heaven And Hell* made its debut on the Swedish chart at no.28, but it didn't climb any higher. The single spent four weeks in the Top 10 in Norway, peaking at no.9, but it wasn't a hit anywhere else.

Three further singles were released from *SHAPES*, but none was a hit anywhere.

98 ~ *Även En Blomma* by Frida

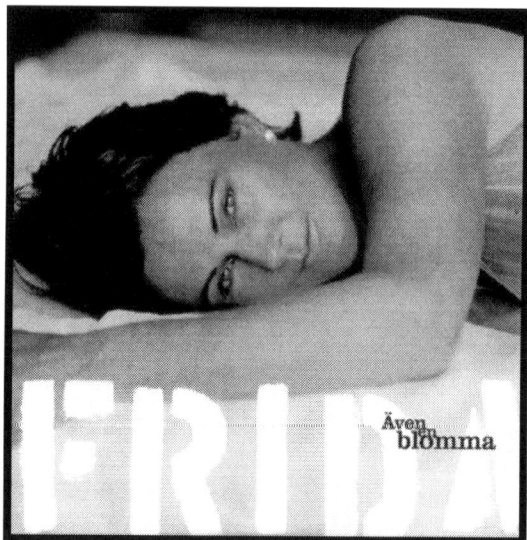

Sweden: Anderson SON 2 (1996).

30.08.96: 20-13-**11**-12-25-20-41-31-x-x-x-x-43

Även En Blomma ('Even A Flower') was the lead single from Frida's first album for more than a decade, *DJUPA ANDETAG* ('Deep Breaths'). As she didn't want to attract too much international attention, she recorded the album entirely in Swedish, and only released the album in Scandinavia.

Även En Blomma rose to no.11 in Sweden, but just missed out on achieving Top 10 status.

Du Måste Finnas by Helen Sjöholm

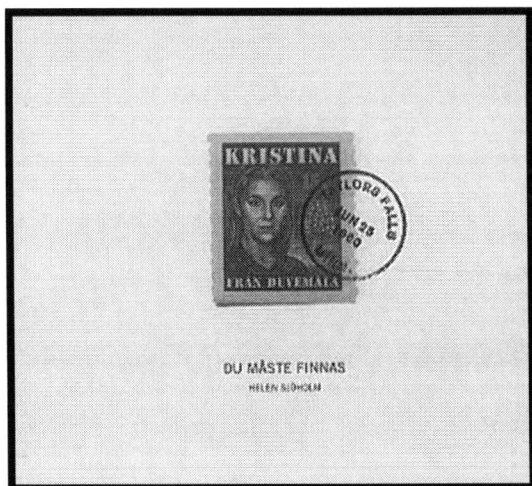

Sweden: Mono MMCD-S 116 (1996).

27.09.96: 28-17-17-**6**-19-19-28-22-37-43-42-53-38-46-46-35-32-41-x-x-53-59-x-48-55-
   x-41-54-47-44-38-37-50-40-46-41-x-x-37-x-46-x-49-55
12.12.97: 57-x-x-46-55-x-x-53

Du Måste Finnas, which translates as 'You Must Exist' and refers to God, was one of the songs Benny and Björn composed for the Swedish musical, *Kristina Från Duvemåla* ('Kristina From *Duvemåla*), which premiered at the Malmö Opera & Music Theatre in Malmö, Sweden, on 7th October 1995.

Helen Sjöholm was a member of the original cast, and played the leading role of Kristina. Her performance of *Du Måste Finnas* was only released as a single in Sweden, where it rose to no.6, charting on and off for more than a year.

99 ~ *Ögonen* by Frida

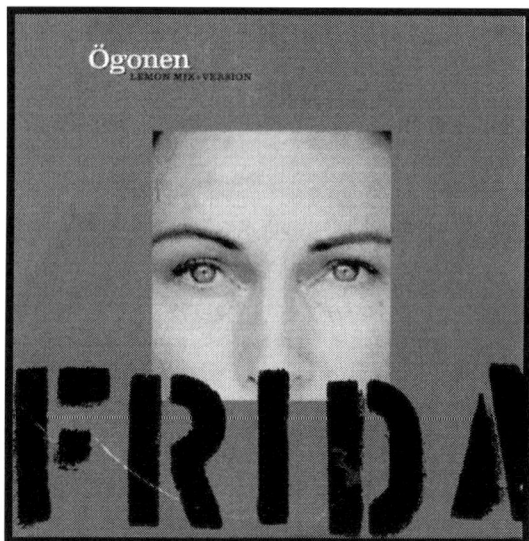

Sweden: Anderson SON 4 (1996).

29.11.96: **24**

Ögonen ('Eyes') was the second single released from Frida's 1996 album, *DJUPA ANDETAG* – it spent a solitary week at no.24 in Sweden, but wasn't a hit in any other Scandinavian countries.

The third single released from the album, *Alla Mina Bästa År* ('All My Best Years'), was a duet with Marie Fredriksson. The single spent a week at no.54 in Sweden, but it failed to achieve Top 40 status.

Guldet Blev Till Sand by Peter Jöback

Sweden: Mono MMCD-S 117 (1997).

14.02.97: 40-31-6-5-**2**-3-**2**-**2**-4-5-6-7-7-7-6-10-9-14-13-21-30-35-42-50-29-33-28-29-30-
  35-36-34-43-42
12.12.97: 51-49-49-43-50-45-36

Guldet Blev Till Sand ('Gold Turned Into Sand') was the second major hit taken from Benny and Björn's Swedish musical, *Kristina Från Duvemåla*.

This time, the performer was Peter Jöback, who like Helen Sjöholm was a member of the original cast – he played the part of Robert.

Like Helen Sjöholm's *Du Måste Finnas*, *Guldet Blev Till Sand* was only released as a single in Sweden, and like *Du Måste Finnas* it was a major hit, spending three weeks at no.2 during a lengthy chart run.

Thank ABBA For The Music by Steps, Tina Cousins, Cleopatra, B*Witched & Billie

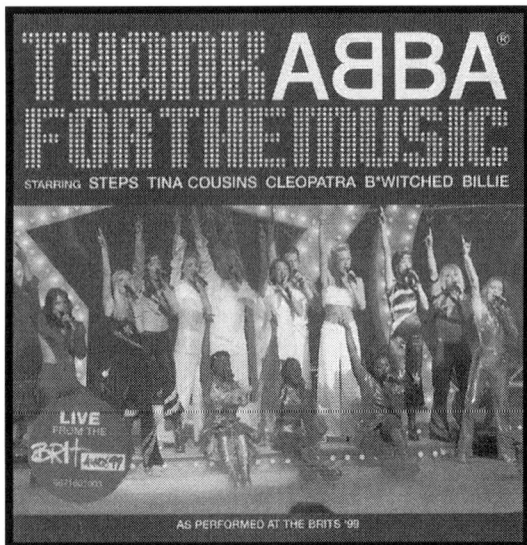

Sweden: Epic EPC 667160 1 (1999).

15.04.99: 51-28-18-14-10-**8-8**-11-15-16-24-29-35-37-x-49-52-53

UK: Epic ABCD1 (1999).

10.04.99: **4**-5-**4**-12-14-21-26-26-32-35-34-42-63

Australia
25.04.99: 29-26-16-11-10-10-**9-9**-13-14-16-16-19-28-25-29-39-43-48-49

Belgium
17.04.99: 40-34-27-**23**-25-27-30-36-41-43-46

Germany
10.05.99: **97**

Ireland
1.04.99: 9-**5**-7-6-7-7-7-9-10-14-12-18-22-26-32-39

Netherlands
17.04.99: 43-28-21-17-**14-14-14-14**-19-21-25-27-31-36-41-47-57-76

New Zealand
16.05.99: **6**-10-**6**-8-11-24-20-32-37

Thank ABBA For The Music was a medley of ABBA hits performed by Steps, Tina Cousins, Cleopatra, B*Witched and Billie Piper at The Brit Awards ceremony, staged at the London Arena on 16th February 1999.

The medley comprised four ABBA hits, namely *Take A Chance On Me*, *Dancing Queen*, *Mamma Mia* and *Thank You For The Music* (with the lyric changed to 'Thank ABBA for the music', as a tribute to ABBA).

The release of *Thank ABBA For The Music* as a single was timed to coincide with the debut of the ABBA musical, *Mamma Mia!*.

Thank ABBA For The Music charted at no.4 in the UK, no.5 in Ireland, no.6 in New Zealand, no.8 in Sweden, no.9 in Australia, no.14 in the Netherlands and no.23 in Belgium.

100 ~ Happy New Year by ABBA

Sweden: Polydor 561 462-2 (1999).

16.12.99: 52-43-34-27
4.01.07: 22
3.01.08: 18-**4**
9.01.09: 5
8.01.10: 9
7.01.11: 42
6.01.12: 51
4.01.13: 57
3.01.14: 54

Germany
27.12.99: 99-78
5.01.09: 99-77
8.01.10: 88
14.01.11: 93
13.01.12: **75**
10.01.14: 93

Netherlands
8.01.00: 15-17-39

1.01.11: 47-**8**
31.12.11: 70-11
29.12.12: 93-17
4.01.14: 24

Norway
25.12.99: 20-20
12.01.08: 11
10.01.09: **5**
2.01.10: 11
1.01.11: 18

UK
Happy New Year has never been released as a single in the UK, however, it did chart for one week at no.171 on the strength of digital sales in January 2008.

ABBA recorded *Happy New Year* for their 1980 album, *SUPER TROUPER* – the working title was the wonderfully humorous 'Daddy Don't Get Drunk On Christmas Day'.

Happy New Year wasn't released as a single until 1999, when it was issued in a limited number of countries to promote the re-release on CD of many of ABBA's singles. It was reissued in 2008, and in December 2011 a silver glitter vinyl 7" single was released – it was only available via ABBA's official website and limited to just 500 copies, which sold out inside twenty-four hours.

Thanks to the digital age, *Happy New Year* re-enters some charts on an almost annual basis – it has peaked at no.4 in Sweden, no.5 in Norway and no.8 in the Netherlands.

A*Teens recorded a cover of *Happy New Year* for their 1999 album, *THE ABBA GENERATION*, which as a single charted at no.4 in Sweden and no.12 in Finland.

101 ~ If I Thought You'd Ever Change Your Mind by Agnetha Fältskog

Sweden: WEA PR 04799 (2004).

23.04.04: **2**-7-9-11-14-24-25-29-22-26-22-40-49-60-x-60

UK: WEA 375CD1/2 (2004).

24.04.04: **11**-22-31-44-55-x-x-x-91

Belgium
1.05.04: 46-**45**

Netherlands
3.04.04: 85-39-24-**20**-21-29-40-26-88

Switzerland
2.05.04: **75**

Agnetha make a surprise comeback in 2004, when she recorded her first new album for 17 years, *MY COLOURING BOOK*.

The lead single from the album, *If I Thought You'd Ever Change Your Mind*, was composed by John Cameron and originally recorded by Cilla Black in 1969 – her version was a no.20 hit in the UK.

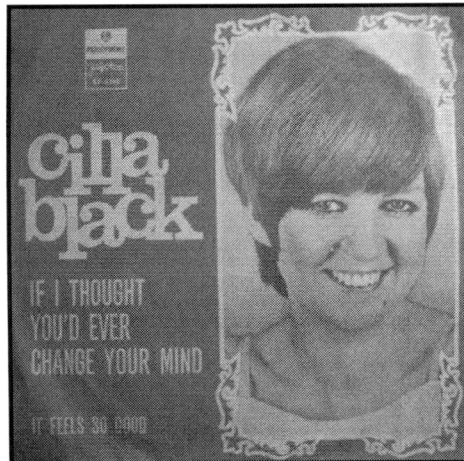

If I Thought You'd Ever Change Your Mind made its debut at no.2 in Sweden and no.11 in the UK, where it was Agnetha's most successful single to date. Elsewhere, however, the single was much less successful, charting at no.20 in the Netherlands, no.45 in Belgium and no.75 in Switzerland, but missing the charts in most countries.

102 ~ When You Walk In The Room by Agnetha Fältskog

Sweden: WEA 5050467 3834 2 5 (2004).

18.06.04: 25-**11**-12-26-35-55-48-54-47

UK: WEA 378CD1/2 (2004).

26.06.04: **34**-59

Ireland
17.06.04: **50**

When You Walk In The Room was written and originally recorded by Jackie DeShannon in 1963. The following year, the song was covered by the Searchers, who took their version to no.5 in the UK and no.35 in the USA.

Agnetha recorded *When You Walk In The Room* for her 2004 album, *MY COLOURING BOOK*, and it was released as the second single. Like the first single, *If I Thought You'd Ever Change Your Mind*, *When You Walk In The Room* only enjoyed limited success, charting at no.11 in Sweden, no.34 in the UK and no.50 in Ireland.

When You Walk In The Room has been covered by numerous other artists over the years, including Cilla Black, Paul Carrick and Child.

103 ~ *Sommaren Du Fick* by Benny Anderssons Orkester
& Helen Sjöholm

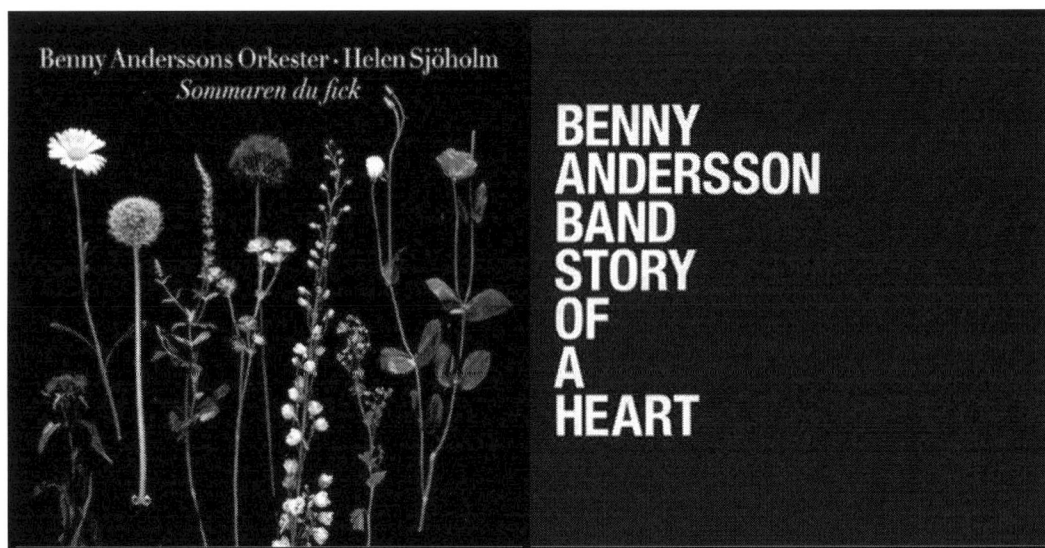

Sweden: Mono MMCD-S 134 (2009).

19.06.09: 40-35-**17**

UK: Polydor BENNYHEART2 (promo, 2009).

18.07.09: 90-**83**-100 (*Story Of A Heart*)

Sommaren Du Fick ('Summer Got You') is the Swedish version of *Story Of A Heart*, a new song Benny composed for his first internationally released album with his Benny Andersson Orkester, renamed the Benny Andersson Band for this release only.

The album, also titled *STORY OF A HEART*, featured English versions of some of the songs Benny had released in Sweden with the Benny Andersson Orkester, and included both *Sommaren Du Fick* and *Story Of A Heart*, with vocals by Helen Sjöholm on both recordings.

Sommaren Du Fick rose to no.17 in Sweden, while *Story Of A Heart* gave Benny his first hit as an artist outside of ABBA in the UK, where it spent three weeks in the Top 100.

THE ALMOST TOP 40 SINGLES

Only one ABBA or ABBA-related single has made the Top 50 in one or more countries, but failed to enter the Top 40 in any:

Time by Frida & B.A. Robertson

Time is the English version of *Belle* ('Beauty'), which Frida recorded in French as a duet with Daniel Balavoine, for the 1992 childrens' musical based on ABBA's songs, *ABBAcadabra*.

Like *Belle*, *Time* was set to the melody of ABBA's *Arrival*, and the English lyrics were penned by Don Black and Mike Batt. Frida recorded *Time* as a duet with B.A. Robertson – the single charted at no.45 in the UK, but it didn't achieve Top 40 status anywhere.

THE TOP 40 ABBA & ABBA-RELATED SINGLES

So, what is the most successful ABBA or ABBA-related single of all-time?

In this Top 40, each ABBA and ABBA-related single has been scored according to the following points system.

Points are given according to the peak position reached on the albums chart in each of the countries featured in this book:

No.1:   100 points for the first week at no.1, plus 10 points for each additional week at no.1.

No.2:   90 points for the first week at no.2, plus 5 points for each additional week at no.2.

No.3:   85 points.
No.4-6:   80 points.
No.7-10:   75 points.
No.11-15:   70 points.
No.16-20:   65 points.
No.21-30:   60 points.
No.31-40:   50 points.
No.41-50:   40 points.
No.51-60:   30 points.
No.61-70:   20 points.
No.71-80:   10 points.
No.81-100:   5 points.

Total weeks charted in each country are added, to give the final points score.

Reissues and re-entries of a single are counted together.

Rank/Album/Artist/Points

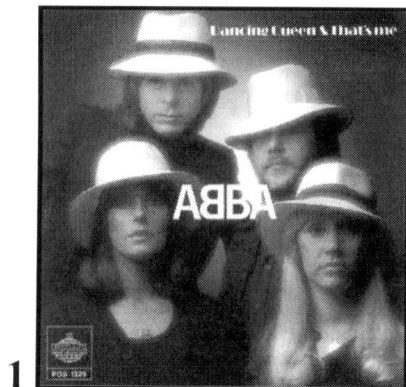

1 *Dancing Queen* | ABBA – 2874 points

2 *Fernando* | ABBA – 2793 points

3 *Waterloo* | ABBA – 2333 points

4 *Chiquitita* | ABBA – 2138 points

5 *The Winner Takes It All* | ABBA – 1915 points

6 *S.O.S* | ABBA – 1858 points

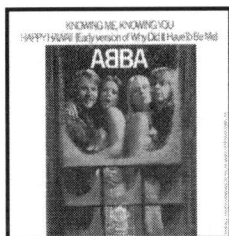

7 *Knowing Me, Knowing You* | ABBA – 1785 points

8 *Money, Money, Money* | ABBA – 1724 points

9 *Mamma Mia* | ABBA – 1695 points

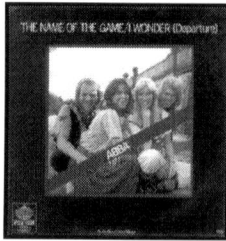

10 *The Name Of The Game* | ABBA – 1619 points

11. *Gimme! Gimme! Gimme! (A Man After Midnight)* | ABBA – 1617 points
12. *Take A Chance On Me* | ABBA – 1602 points
13. *Super Trouper* | ABBA – 1543 points
14. *I Know There's Something Going On* | Frida – 1530 points
15. *I Do, I Do, I Do, I Do, I Do* | ABBA – 1507 points
16. *Summer Night City* | ABBA – 1479 points
17. *One Of Us* | ABBA – 1344 points
18. *Does Your Mother Know* | ABBA – 1207 points
19. *I Have A Dream* | ABBA – 1186 points
20. *The Day Before You Came* | ABBA – 1052 points

21. *Ring Ring* | Benny Björn & Agnetha Anni-Frid – 1013 points
22. *Honey Honey* | ABBA – 955 points
23. *The Heat Is On* | Agnetha – 884 points
24. *Voulez-Vous* | ABBA – 869 points
25. *Head Over Heels* | ABBA – 654 points
26. *Thank You For The Music* | ABBA – 638 points
27. *Wrap Your Arms Around Me* | Agnetha – 630 points
28. *Never Again* | Agnetha – 615 points
29. *Under Attack* | ABBA – 585 points
30. *Eagle* | ABBA – 548 points

31. *Sunny Girl* | Hep Stars – 433 points
32. *Lay All Your Love On Me* | ABBA – 381 points
33. *I Won't Let You Go* | Agnetha – 323 points
34. *I Natt Jag Drömde* | Hep Stars – 309 points
35. *If I Thought You'd Ever Change Your Mind* | Agnetha – 308 points

36. *Wedding* | Hep Stars – 303 points
37. *Consolation* | Hep Stars – 295 points
38. *Shine* | Frida – 292 points
39. *Can't Shake Loose* | Agnetha – 289 points
40. *Gabrielle* | Hootenanny Singers – 285 points

Not unexpectedly, ABBA dominate the Top 40, taking the Top 13 places before Frida's *I Know There's Something Going On* appears. *Dancing Queen*, which is generally considered ABBA's signature tune, predictably emerges as the most successful ABBA single, with *Fernando* a close second.

Agnetha's highest ranked single is *The Heat Is On* at no.23, while both the Hep Stars and the Hootenanny Singers each place at least one single on the Top 40.

The make-up of the Top 40 is as follows:

27 hits	ABBA
6 hits	Agnetha
4 hits	Hep Stars
2 hits	Frida
1 hit	Hootenanny Singers

ABBA's total includes *Ring Ring*, which was originally credited to Benny Björn & Agnetha Anni-Frid.

SINGLES TRIVIA

To date, there have been 103 ABBA and ABBA-related Top 40 hits in one or more of the 19 countries featured in this book, and their success may be summarised as follows:

ABBA	39 hits
Hep Stars	22 hits
Hootenanny Singers	15 hits
Agnetha Fältskog	13 hits
Frida	8 hits
Björn Ulvaeus	3 hits
Benny & Björn	2 hits
Benny Andersson Orkester	1 hit

ABBA's total includes hits credited to Benny & Björn, Agnetha & Anni-Frid.

There follows a country-by-country look at the most successful ABBA and ABBA-related hits, starting with the group's homeland.

Note: In the past, there was often one or more weeks over Christmas and New Year when no new chart was published in some countries. In such cases, the previous week's chart has been used to complete a chart run. Similarly, where a bi-weekly or monthly chart was in place, for chart runs these are counted at two and four weeks, respectively.

ABBA IN SWEDEN

ABBA & ABBA-related No.1s

There have been 14 ABBA & ABBA-related chart toppers in Sweden, eight by the Hep Stars, three by Agnetha and three by ABBA (one as Björn & Benny, Agnetha & Anni-Frid), plus two no.1s with an ABBA connection.

1965	*Cadillac* – The Hep Stars
1965	*Farmer John* – The Hep Stars
1965	*Bald Headed Woman* – The Hep Stars
1966	*Sunny Girl* – The Hep Stars
1966	*Wedding* – The Hep Stars
1966	*Don't/Consolation* – The Hep Stars

1967	*Malaika* – The Hep Stars
1967	*Mot Okänt Land* – The Hep Stars
1968	*Jag Var Så Kär* – Agnetha Fältskog
1973	*Ring Ring (Swedish Version)* – Björn & Benny, Agnetha & Anni-Frid
1976	*Moviestar* – Harpo
1976	*Dancing Queen* – ABBA
1978	*Summer Night City* – ABBA
1985	*The Heat Is On* – Agnetha Fältskog
1986	*The Way You Are* – Agnetha Fältskog
1992	*Abba-esque* – Erasure

Most weeks at No.1

The Hep Stars have spent 34 weeks at no.1 in Sweden, ABBA 22 weeks and Agnetha 11 weeks. The singles with the most weeks at no.1 are as follows:

14 weeks	*Dancing Queen* – ABBA
10 weeks	*Don't/Consolation* – The Hep Stars
6 weeks	*Ring Ring (Swedish Version)* – Björn & Benny, Agnetha & Anni-Frid
6 weeks	*The Way You Are* – Agnetha Fältskog
5 weeks	*Sunny Girl* – The Hep Stars
5 weeks	*Malaika* – The Hep Stars
4 weeks	*Farmer John* – The Hep Stars
4 weeks	*Wedding* – The Hep Stars
4 weeks	*The Heat Is On* – Agnetha Fältskog

Most Hits

22 hits	The Hep Stars
15 hits	Hootenanny Singers
15 hits	ABBA
11 hits	Agnetha Fältskog
6 hits	Frida
3 hits	Björn Ulvaeus
1 hit	Benny Anderssons Orkester
1 hit	Björn Ulvaeus & Benny Andersson

Most Weeks

274 weeks	The Hep Stars
227 weeks	ABBA

122 weeks	Agnetha Fältskog
121 weeks	Hootenanny Singers
53 weeks	Frida
13 weeks	Björn Ulvaeus
9 weeks	Björn Ulvaeus & Benny Andersson
3 weeks	Benny Anderssons Orkester

Singles with the most weeks

30 weeks	*Dancing Queen* – ABBA
29 weeks	*I Natt Jag Drömde* – The Hep Stars
25 weeks	*Ring Ring* – Björn & Benny, Agnetha & Anni-Frid
25 weeks	*Waterloo* – ABBA
24 weeks	*The Name Of The Game* – ABBA
24 weeks	*Chiquitita* – ABBA
22 weeks	*Fernando* – ABBA
20 weeks	*S.O.S* – Agnetha Fältskog
20 weeks	*Summer Night City* – ABBA
19 weeks	*Farmer John* – The Hep Stars

ABBA IN AUSTRALIA

ABBA & ABBA-related No.1s

There have been six ABBA chart toppers in Australia, all six by ABBA, plus one no.1 with an ABBA connection:

1975	*I Do, I Do, I Do, I Do, I Do*
1975	*Mamma Mia*
1975	*S.O.S*
1976	*Fernando*
1976	*Dancing Queen*
1976	*Money, Money, Money*
1985	*One Night In Bangkok* – Murray Head

Most weeks at No.1

The ABBA singles with the most weeks at no.1 in Australia are:

| 14 weeks | *Fernando* |

10 weeks	*Mamma Mia*
8 weeks	*Dancing Queen*
6 weeks	*Money, Money, Money*

Most Hits

29 hits	ABBA
1 hit	Frida
1 hit	Agnetha Fältskog

Most Weeks

550 weeks	ABBA
16 weeks	Frida
4 weeks	Agnetha Fältskog

Singles with the most weeks

44 weeks	*Mamma Mia*
40 weeks	*Fernando*
39 weeks	*Dancing Queen*
34 weeks	*I Do, I Do, I Do, I Do, I Do*
29 weeks	*S.O.S*
28 weeks	*Ring Ring*
27 weeks	*Waterloo*
23 weeks	*The Winner Takes It All*
26 weeks	*Rock Me*
19 weeks	*Honey Honey*
19 weeks	*The Name Of The Game*
19 weeks	*Chiquitita*
19 weeks	*Gimme! Gimme! Gimme! (A Man After Midnight)*

ABBA IN AUSTRIA

ABBA & ABBA-related No.1s

There have been three ABBA chart toppers in Austria, and one no.1 with an ABBA connection:

| 1976 | *Fernando* |

1978	*Take A Chance On Me*
1980	*I Have A Dream*
1992	*Abba-esque* – Erasure

Most weeks at No.1

The ABBA singles with the most weeks at no.1 in Austria are:

8 weeks	*Fernando*
4 weeks	*Take A Chance On Me*
2 weeks	*I Have A Dream*

Abba-esque was no.1 for eight weeks.

Most Hits

25 hits	ABBA
1 hit	Frida
1 hit	Agnetha Fältskog

Most Weeks

364 weeks	ABBA
8 weeks	Frida
2 weeks	Agnetha Fältskog

Singles with the most weeks

24 weeks	*S.O.S*
24 weeks	*Fernando*
22 weeks	*I Have A Dream*
20 weeks	*Waterloo*
20 weeks	*Dancing Queen*
20 weeks	*Take A Chance On Me*
20 weeks	*Knowing Me, Knowing You*
20 weeks	*Super Trouper*
18 weeks	*The Winner Takes It All*
16 weeks	*Ring Ring*
16 weeks	*Mamma Mia*
16 weeks	*Chiquitita*
16 weeks	*Money, Money, Money*

ABBA IN BELGIUM (Wallonia)

ABBA & ABBA-related No.1s

There have been 16 ABBA and ABBA-related chart toppers in Belgium, 14 by ABBA and one each by Agnetha Fältskog and Frida, plus one no.1 with an ABBA connection:

1974	*Waterloo* – ABBA
1975	*S.O.S* – ABBA
1976	*Fernando* – ABBA
1976	*Dancing Queen* – ABBA
1976	*Money, Money, Money* – ABBA
1978	*Take A Chance On Me* – ABBA
1979	*Chiquitita* – ABBA
1979	*Does Your Mother Know* – ABBA
1979	*Voulez Vous* – ABBA
1979	*I Have A Dream* – ABBA
1979	*Gimme! Gimme! Gimme! (A Man After Midnight)* – ABBA
1980	*The Winner Takes It All* – ABBA
1980	*Super Trouper* – ABBA
1981	*One Of Us* – ABBA
1982	*I Know There's Something Going On* – Frida
1983	*Wrap Your Arms Around Me* – Agnetha Fältskog
1984	*One Night In Bangkok* – Murray Head

Most weeks at No.1

ABBA spent 48 weeks at no.1 in Belgium, Frida three weeks and Agnetha Fältskog two weeks. The singles with the most weeks at no.1 are as follows:

7 weeks	*Dancing Queen* – ABBA
7 weeks	*The Winner Takes It All* – ABBA
6 weeks	*Waterloo* – ABBA
5 weeks	*Chiquitita* – ABBA
5 weeks	*One Of Us* – ABBA
4 weeks	*Money, Money, Money* – ABBA
4 weeks	*I Have A Dream* – ABBA

Most Hits

26 hits	ABBA

7 hits	Agnetha Fältskog
4 hits	Frida

Most Weeks

311 weeks	ABBA
42 weeks	Agnetha Fältskog
25 weeks	Frida

Singles with the most weeks

22 weeks	*Dancing Queen* – ABBA
16 weeks	*Chiquitita* – ABBA
16 weeks	*Fernando* – ABBA
16 weeks	*The Winner Takes It All* – ABBA
15 weeks	*Super Trouper* – ABBA
14 weeks	*Waterloo* – ABBA
14 weeks	*The Name Of The Game* – ABBA
13 weeks	*I Have A Dream* – ABBA
13 weeks	*Money, Money, Money* – ABBA
13 weeks	*Voulez Vous* – ABBA

ABBA IN CANADA

ABBA & ABBA-related No.1s

There has only been one ABBA or ABBA-related chart topper in Canada:

1976   *Dancing Queen* – ABBA

Dancing Queen topped the chart for two weeks.

Most Hits

17 hits	ABBA
2 hits	Agnetha Fältskog
1 hit	Frida

The total for ABBA includes *The Winner Takes It All*, although complete chart action for this single is not known.

Most Weeks

234 weeks ABBA
14 weeks Agnetha Fältskog
5 weeks Frida

The total for ABBA includes two weeks for *The Winner Takes It All*.

Singles with the most weeks

22 weeks *Dancing Queen* – ABBA
21 weeks *Does Your Mother Know* – ABBA
20 weeks *Mamma Mia* – ABBA
19 weeks *Take A Chance On Me* – ABBA
18 weeks *S.O.S* – ABBA
17 weeks *The Name Of The Game* – ABBA
16 weeks *Fernando* – ABBA
16 weeks *Knowing Me, Knowing You* – ABBA
16 weeks *Chiquitita* – ABBA
15 weeks *I Do, I Do, I Do, I Do, I Do* – ABBA

ABBA IN FINLAND

ABBA & ABBA-related No.1s

There have been four ABBA and ABBA-related no.1s in Finland, all by ABBA:

1974 *Waterloo*
1978 *Summer Night City*
1979 *Chiquitita*
1980 *Gimme! Gimme! Gimme! (A Man After Midnight)*

It is not known how many months each single spent at no.1.

Most Hits

16 hits ABBA
7 hits The Hep Stars
1 hit Hootenanny Singers

1 hit	Agnetha Fältskog
1 hit	Frida

Most Weeks

244 weeks	ABBA
72 weeks	The Hep Stars
20 weeks	Hootenanny Singers
16 weeks	Frida
4 weeks	Agnetha Fältskog

Singles with the most weeks

32 weeks	*Fernando* – ABBA
32 weeks	*Dancing Queen* – ABBA
28 weeks	*The Winner Takes It All* – ABBA
24 weeks	*Sunny Girl* – The Hep Stars
24 weeks	*Waterloo* – ABBA
20 weeks	*Gabrielle* – Hootenanny Singers
20 weeks	*Summer Night City* – ABBA
20 weeks	*Gimme! Gimme! Gimme! (A Man After Midnight)* – ABBA
16 weeks	*Money, Money, Money* – ABBA
16 weeks	*Chiquitita* – ABBA

ABBA IN FRANCE

ABBA & ABBA-related No.1s

There have been four ABBA and ABBA-related chart topper in France, three by ABBA and one by Frida, plus one cover version:

1976	*Fernando* – ABBA
1976	*Money, Money, Money* – ABBA
1979	*Gimme! Gimme! Gimme! (A Man After Midnight)* – ABBA
1982	*I Know There's Something Going On* – Frida
2001	*Gimme! Gimme! Gimme! (A Man After Midnight)* – Star Academy

Most weeks at no.1

ABBA spent 11 weeks at no.1 in France, and Frida five weeks. The singles with the most weeks at no.1 are:

5 weeks   *Gimme! Gimme! Gimme! (A Man After Midnight)* – ABBA
5 weeks   *I Know There's Something Going On* – Frida
3 weeks   *Fernando* – ABBA
3 weeks   *Money, Money, Money* – ABBA

Most Hits

26 hits   ABBA
 4 hits   Frida
 3 hits   Agnetha Fältskog

Most Weeks

243 weeks   ABBA
 40 weeks   Frida
 21 weeks   Agnetha Fältskog

Singles with the most weeks

18 weeks   *Gimme! Gimme! Gimme! (A Man After Midnight)* – ABBA
17 weeks   *I Know There's Something Going On* – Frida
14 weeks   *I Do, I Do, I Do, I Do, I Do* – ABBA
14 weeks   *Super Trouper* – ABBA
13 weeks   *Fernando* – ABBA
13 weeks   *Money, Money, Money* – ABBA
12 weeks   *Waterloo* – ABBA
12 weeks   *Dancing Queen* – ABBA
12 weeks   *Take A Chance On Me* – ABBA
12 weeks   *The Winner Takes It All* – ABBA

ABBA IN GERMANY

ABBA & ABBA-related No.1s

There have been nine ABBA and ABBA-related chart topper in Germany, all by ABBA, plus one no.1 with an ABBA connection:

1974	*Waterloo*
1975	*S.O.S*
1975	*Mamma Mia*
1976	*Fernando*
1976	*Dancing Queen*
1976	*Money, Money, Money*
1977	*Knowing Me, Knowing You*
1980	*Super Trouper*
1981	*One Of Us*
1985	*One Night In Bangkok* – Murray Head

Most weeks at no.1

ABBA spent 33 weeks at no.1 in Germany. The singles with the most weeks at no.1 are:

7 weeks	*S.O.S*
7 weeks	*Fernando*
5 weeks	*Money, Money, Money*
5 weeks	*Super Trouper*
4 weeks	*Waterloo*

Most Hits

28 hits	ABBA
6 hits	Agnetha Fältskog
3 hits	Frida

Most Weeks

593 weeks	ABBA
52 weeks	Agnetha Fältskog
32 weeks	Frida

Singles with the most weeks

44 weeks	*Dancing Queen* – ABBA
30 weeks	*S.O.S* – ABBA
30 weeks	*Super Trouper* – ABBA
29 weeks	*Waterloo* – ABBA
29 weeks	*The Winner Takes It All* – ABBA
27 weeks	*I Have A Dream* – ABBA
26 weeks	*Fernando* – ABBA
26 weeks	*Knowing Me, Knowing You* – ABBA
26 weeks	*Chiquitita* – ABBA
26 weeks	*Gimme! Gimme! Gimme! (A Man After Midnight)* – ABBA

ABBA IN IRELAND

ABBA & ABBA-related No.1s

There have been 12 ABBA and ABBA-related chart toppers in Ireland, all by ABBA, plus two no.1s with an ABBA connection:

1974	*Waterloo* – ABBA
1975	*Mamma Mia* – ABBA
1976	*Fernando* – ABBA
1976	*Dancing Queen* – ABBA
1977	*Knowing Me, Knowing You* – ABBA
1978	*Take A Chance On Me*– ABBA
1978	*Summer Night City* – ABBA
1979	*Chiquitita* – ABBA
1979	*Gimme! Gimme! Gimme! (A Man After Midnight)* – ABBA
1980	*The Winner Takes It All* – ABBA
1980	*Super Trouper* – ABBA
1981	*One Of Us* – ABBA
1985	*I Know Him So Well* – Elaine Paige & Barbara Dickson
1992	*Abba-esque* – Erasure

Most weeks at no.1

ABBA spent 39 weeks at no.1 in Ireland. The singles with the most weeks at no.1 are:

6 weeks	*Fernando*

6 weeks	*Dancing Queen*
5 weeks	*Mamma Mia*
5 weeks	*Knowing Me, Knowing You*
3 weeks	*Chiquitita*
3 weeks	*Super Trouper*
3 weeks	*One Of Us*

Abba-esque and *I Know Him So Well* each spent five weeks at no.1.

Most Hits

23 hits	ABBA
3 hits	Agnetha Fältskog
1 hit	Frida

Most Weeks

203 weeks	ABBA
4 weeks	Agnetha Fältskog
3 weeks	Frida

Singles with the most weeks

23 weeks	*Dancing Queen* – ABBA
13 weeks	*Fernando* – ABBA
12 weeks	*Super Trouper* – ABBA
11 weeks	*Waterloo* – ABBA
11 weeks	*Money, Money, Money* – ABBA
10 weeks	*Knowing Me, Knowing You* – ABBA
10 weeks	*The Name Of The Game* – ABBA
10 weeks	*Take A Chance On Me* – ABBA
10 weeks	*Voulez Vous/Angeleyes* – ABBA
10 weeks	*I Have A Dream* – ABBA
10 weeks	*One Of Us* – ABBA

ABBA IN JAPAN

ABBA & ABBA-related No.1s

The highest charting ABBA or ABBA-related single in Japan, perhaps surprisingly, is Benny & Björn's *She's My Kind Of Girl*, which achieved no.7 in 1972.

Most Hits

12 hits	ABBA
1 hit	Benny & Björn

Most Weeks

219 weeks	ABBA
22 weeks	Benny & Björn

Singles with the most weeks

55 weeks	*Dancing Queen* – ABBA
32 weeks	*Chiquitita* – ABBA
26 weeks	*Summer Night City* – ABBA
26 weeks	*Gimme! Gimme! Gimme! (A Man After Midnight)* – ABBA
22 weeks	*She's My Kind Of Girl* – Benny & Björn
20 weeks	*Voulez Vous* – ABBA
15 weeks	*That's Me* – ABBA
13 weeks	*Take A Chance On Me* – ABBA
11 weeks	*The Winner Takes It All* – ABBA
11 weeks	*On And On And On* – ABBA
11 weeks	*S.O.S* – ABBA

ABBA IN THE NETHERLANDS

ABBA & ABBA-related No.1s

There have been nine ABBA and ABBA-related chart toppers in the Netherlands, all nine by ABBA, plus one no.1 with an ABBA connection:

1974	*Waterloo* – ABBA
1976	*Fernando* – ABBA

1976	*Dancing Queen* – ABBA
1976	*Money, Money, Money* – ABBA
1979	*Chiquitita* – ABBA
1979	*I Have A Dream* – ABBA
1980	*The Winner Takes It All* – ABBA
1980	*Super Trouper* – ABBA
1981	*One Of Us* – ABBA
1984	*One Night In Bangkok* – Murray Head

Most weeks at No.1

ABBA spent 23 weeks at no.1 in the Netherlands. The singles with the most weeks at no.1 are as follows:

7 weeks	*Dancing Queen*
5 weeks	*The Winner Takes It All*
3 weeks	*Fernando*
2 weeks	*Waterloo*
2 weeks	*Money, Money, Money*

Most Hits

27 hits	ABBA
7 hits	Agnetha Fältskog
4 hits	Frida
1 hit	Hep Stars

Most Weeks

276 weeks	ABBA
50 weeks	Agnetha Fältskog
23 weeks	Frida
8 weeks	Hep Stars

Singles with the most weeks

23 weeks	*Dancing Queen* – ABBA
16 weeks	*Chiquitita* – ABBA
14 weeks	*Thank You For The Music* – ABBA
14 weeks	*The Winner Takes It All* – ABBA
14 weeks	*Voulez Vous* – ABBA

13 weeks	*I Have A Dream* – ABBA
12 weeks	*Gimme! Gimme! Gimme! (A Man After Midnight)* – ABBA
12 weeks	*Super Trouper* – ABBA
11 weeks	*Waterloo* – ABBA
11 weeks	*Does Your Mother Know* – ABBA
11 weeks	*One Of Us* – ABBA
11 weeks	*The Day Before You Came* – ABBA
11 weeks	*The Heat Is On* – Agnetha Fältskog

ABBA IN THE NEW ZEALAND

ABBA & ABBA-related No.1s

There have been six ABBA and ABBA-related chart toppers in New Zealand, all six by ABBA:

1975	*I Do, I Do, I Do, I Do, I Do*
1975	*S.O.S*
1976	*Fernando*
1976	*Dancing Queen*
1976	*Money, Money, Money*
1979	*Chiquitita*

Most weeks at No.1

ABBA spent 17 weeks at no.1 in the New Zealand. The singles with the most weeks at no.1 are as follows:

9 weeks	*Fernando*
4 weeks	*Dancing Queen*

The other four chart toppers each spent one week at no.1.

Most Hits

20 hits	ABBA

Agnetha Fältskog and Frida haven't had a solo hit in New Zealand.

Most Weeks

366 weeks   ABBA

Singles with the most weeks

53 weeks   *I Do, I Do, I Do, I Do, I Do*
44 weeks   *Fernando*
37 weeks   *Dancing Queen*
31 weeks   *S.O.S*
27 weeks   *Rock Me*
26 weeks   *Mamma Mia*
19 weeks   *Chiquitita*
17 weeks   *The Winner Takes It All*
16 weeks   *Gimme! Gimme! Gimme! (A Man After Midnight)*
15 weeks   *Money, Money, Money*

ABBA IN THE NORWAY

ABBA & ABBA-related No.1s

There have been four ABBA and ABBA-related chart toppers in Norway, two by ABBA, and one each by the Hep Stars and Agnetha Fältskog, plus one no.1 with an ABBA connection:

1965   *Cadillac* – The Hep Stars
1974   *Waterloo* – ABBA
1976   *Moviestar* – Harpo
1976   *Dancing Queen* – ABBA
1983   *The Heat Is On* – Agnetha Fältskog

ABBA's *S.O.S* spent an incredible 18 weeks at no.2.

Most weeks at No.1

ABBA spent 20 weeks at no.1 in Norway, Agnetha Fältskog two weeks and the Hep Stars one week. The singles with the most weeks at no.1 are as follows:

12 weeks   *Dancing Queen* – ABBA
 8 weeks   *Waterloo* – ABBA

2 weeks   *The Heat Is On* – Agnetha Fältskog

Harpo's *Moviestar* topped the chart for 11 weeks.

Most Hits

20 hits   ABBA
 7 hits   The Hep Stars
 4 hits   Hootenanny Singers
 2 hits   Agnetha Fältskog
 1 hit   Frida

Most Weeks

294 weeks   ABBA
 74 weeks   The Hep Stars
 22 weeks   Agnetha Fältskog
 20 weeks   Hootenanny Singers
  9 weeks   Frida

Singles with the most weeks

32 weeks   *Dancing Queen* – ABBA
28 weeks   *I Natt Jag Drömde* – The Hep Stars
27 weeks   *S.O.S* – ABBA
24 weeks   *I Do, I Do, I Do, I Do, I Do* – ABBA
23 weeks   *Waterloo* – ABBA
21 weeks   *Fernando* – ABBA
19 weeks   *Ring Ring* – Björn & Benny, Agnetha & Anni-Frid
19 weeks   *Money, Money, Money* – ABBA
18 weeks   *Chiquitita* – ABBA
18 weeks   *Gimme! Gimme! Gimme! (A Man After Midnight)* – ABBA

ABBA IN THE SOUTH AFRICA

ABBA & ABBA-related No.1s

There have been eight ABBA no.1 singles in South Africa, plus one no.1 with an ABBA connection:

1974	*Waterloo*
1975	*I Do, I Do, I Do, I Do, I Do*
1975	*S.O.S*
1976	*Fernando*
1976	*Dancing Queen*
1977	*Knowing Me, Knowing You*
1979	*Chiquitita*
1980	*The Winner Takes It All*
1985	*One Night In Bangkok* – Murray Head

Most Hits

18 hits	ABBA
1 hit	Agnetha Fältskog
1 hit	Frida

Most Weeks

236 weeks	ABBA
18 weeks	Agnetha Fältskog
14 weeks	Frida

Singles with the most weeks

19 weeks	*Chiquitita* – ABBA
18 weeks	*Wrap Your Arms Around Me* – Agnetha Fältskog
16 weeks	*Fernando* – ABBA
16 weeks	*Dancing Queen* – ABBA
16 weeks	*The Winner Takes It All* – ABBA
15 weeks	*Ring Ring* – Benny & Björn, Agnetha & Anni-Frid
15 weeks	*Waterloo* – ABBA
15 weeks	*Hasta Mañana* – ABBA
15 weeks	*I Have A Dream* – ABBA
14 weeks	*Knowing Me, Knowing You* – ABBA
14 weeks	*Thank You For The Music* – ABBA
14 weeks	*I Know There's Something Going On* – Frida

ABBA IN THE SPAIN

ABBA & ABBA-related No.1s

There has only been one ABBA no.1 in Spain:

1979   *Chiquitita*

It is not known how many weeks *Chiquitita* spent at no.1.

Most Hits

14 hits   ABBA

Most Weeks

197 weeks   ABBA

Singles with the most weeks

33 weeks   *Chiquitita*
26 weeks   *Fernando*
24 weeks   *The Winner Takes It All*
20 weeks   *Waterloo*
17 weeks   *Dancing Queen*
17 weeks   *Voulez-Vous*
12 weeks   *Estoy Soñando (I Have A Dream)*
12 weeks   *One Of Us*
11 weeks   *Conociendome Conociendote (Knowing Me, Knowing You)/*
            Money, Money, Money
11 weeks   *Super Trouper*

ABBA IN THE SWITZERLAND

ABBA & ABBA-related No.1s

There have been eight ABBA and ABBA-related chart toppers in Switzerland, seven by ABBA and one by Frida, plus two no.1s with an ABBA connection:

1974   *Waterloo – ABBA*

1975	*I Do, I Do, I Do, I Do, I Do* – ABBA
1975	*Mamma Mia* – ABBA
1976	*Moviestar* – Harpo
1976	*Fernando* – ABBA
1979	*Chiquitita* – ABBA
1979	*Gimme! Gimme! Gimme! (A Man After Midnight)* – ABBA
1980	*I Have A Dream* – ABBA
1980	*I Know There's Something Going On* – Frida
1981	*Stars On 45 Vol.2* – Stars On 45

Most weeks at No.1

ABBA spent 32 weeks at no.1 in Switzerland, and Frida two weeks. The singles with the most weeks at no.1 are as follows:

11 weeks	*Fernando* – ABBA
9 weeks	*Waterloo* – ABBA
5 weeks	*I Do, I Do, I Do, I Do, I Do* – ABBA

Harpo's *Moviestar* topped the chart for 5 weeks.

Most Hits

22 hits	ABBA
2 hits	Agnetha Fältskog
1 hit	Frida

Most Weeks

318 weeks	ABBA
9 weeks	Frida
2 weeks	Agnetha Fältskog

Singles with the most weeks

34 weeks	*Dancing Queen* – ABBA
25 weeks	*Mamma Mia* – ABBA
22 weeks	*Fernando* – ABBA
19 weeks	*Waterloo* – ABBA
18 weeks	*S.O.S* – ABBA
17 weeks	*I Do, I Do, I Do, I Do, I Do* – ABBA

17 weeks	*Knowing Me, Knowing You* – ABBA
16 weeks	*Take A Chance On Me* – ABBA
15 weeks	*Chiquitita* – ABBA
14 weeks	*Money, Money, Money* – ABBA

ABBA IN THE UNITED KINGDOM

ABBA & ABBA-related No.1s

There have been nine ABBA & ABBA-related chart toppers in the UK, all by ABBA, plus two no.1s with an ABBA connection:

1974	*Waterloo* – ABBA
1975	*Mamma Mia* – ABBA
1976	*Fernando* – ABBA
1976	*Dancing Queen* – ABBA
1977	*Knowing Me, Knowing You* – ABBA
1977	*The Name Of The Game* – ABBA
1978	*Take A Chance On Me* – ABBA
1980	*The Winner Takes It All* – ABBA
1980	*Super Trouper* – ABBA
1985	*I Know Him So Well* – Elaine Paige & Barbara Dickson
1992	*Abba-esque* – Erasure

Most weeks at No.1

ABBA spent 31 weeks at no.1 in the UK. The ABBA singles with the most weeks at no.1 are as follows:

6 weeks	*Dancing Queen*
5 weeks	*Knowing Me, Knowing You*
4 weeks	*Fernando*
4 weeks	*The Name Of*
3 weeks	*Take A Chance On Me*
3 weeks	*Super Trouper*

Abba-esque was no.1 for 5 weeks, and *I Know Him So Well* for 4 weeks.

Most Hits

25 hits	ABBA
7 hits	Agnetha Fältskog
4 hits	Frida

Most Weeks

272 weeks	ABBA
31 weeks	Agnetha Fältskog
16 weeks	Frida

Singles with the most weeks

26 weeks	*Dancing Queen*
21 weeks	*Mamma Mia*
15 weeks	*Fernando*
13 weeks	*Knowing Me, Knowing You*
13 weeks	*Voulez Vous*
12 weeks	*Waterloo*
12 weeks	*Money, Money, Money*
12 weeks	*The Name Of The Game*
12 weeks	*Gimme! Gimme The Game*
12 weeks	*Super Trouper*

BPI (British Phonographic Industry) Awards

The BPI began certifying Silver, Gold & Platinum singles in 1973. From 1973 to 1988: Silver = 250,000, Gold = 500,000 & Platinum = 1 million. From 1989 onwards: Silver = 200,000, Gold = 400,000 & Platinum = 600,000. Awards are based on shipments, not sales; however, in July 2013 the BPI automated awards, based on actual sales since February 1994.

Gold	*Fernando* – ABBA (May 1976)	= 500,000
Gold	*Dancing Queen* – ABBA (September 1976)	= 500,000
Gold	*Money, Money, Money* – ABBA (February 1977)	= 500,000
Gold	*Knowing Me, Knowing You* – ABBA (April 1977)	= 500,000
Gold	*The Name Of The Game* – ABBA (November 1977)	= 500,000
Gold	*Chiquitita* – ABBA (February 1979)	= 500,000
Gold	*One Of Us* – ABBA (December 1981)	= 500,000

Gold	*I Know Him So Well* – Elaine Paige & Barbara Dickson (March 1985) = 500,000
Gold	*Abba-esque* – Erasure (July 1992) = 400,000
Silver	*Mamma Mia* – ABBA (April 1976) = 250,000
Silver	*Take A Chance On Me* – ABBA (February 1978) = 250,000
Silver	*Summer Night City* – ABBA (September 1978) = 250,000
Silver	*Does Your Mother Know* – ABBA (May 1979) = 250,000
Silver	*Angeleyes/Voulez-Vous* – ABBA (September 1979) = 250,000
Silver	*Gimme! Gimme! Gimme! (A Man After Midnight)* – ABBA (November 1979) = 250,000
Silver	*I Have A Dream* – ABBA (December 1979) =250,000
Silver	*Super Trouper* – ABBA (November 1980) = 250,000
Silver	*Thank ABBA For The Music* – Steps, Tina Cousins, Cleopatra, B*Witched & Billie (April 1999) = 200,000

ABBA IN THE UNITED STATES

ABBA & ABBA-related No.1s

The only ABBA or ABBA-related single to achieve no.1 in the USA is ABBA's *Dancing Queen* in 1976, which topped the chart for one week.

Most Hits

20 hits	ABBA
2 hits	Agnetha Fältskog
1 hit	Frida

Most Weeks

261 weeks	ABBA
29 weeks	Frida
18 weeks	Agnetha Fältskog

Singles with the most weeks

29 weeks	*I Know There's Something Going On* – Frida
26 weeks	*The Winner Takes It All* – ABBA
22 weeks	*Dancing Queen* – ABBA
18 weeks	*Take A Chance On Me* – ABBA

17 weeks	*Waterloo* – ABBA
17 weeks	*S.O.S* – ABBA
16 weeks	*Fernando* – ABBA
16 weeks	*The Name Of The Game* – ABBA
15 weeks	*I Do, I Do, I Do, I Do, I Do* – ABBA
15 weeks	*Knowing Me, Knowing You* – ABBA
15 weeks	*Can't Shake Loose* – Agnetha Fältskog

RIAA (Recording Industry Association of America) Awards

The RIAA began certifying Gold singles in 1958 and Platinum singles in 1976. From 1958 to 1988: Gold = 1 million, Platinum = 2 million. From 1988 onwards: Gold = 500,000, Platinum = 1 million. Awards are based on shipments, not sales, unless the award is for digital sales.

| Gold | *Dancing Machine* – ABBA (March 1977) = 1 million |
| Gold | *Take A Chance On Me* – ABBA (August 1978) = 1 million |

ABBA IN ZIMBABWE

ABBA & ABBA-related No.1s

There were two ABBA no.1 singles in Zimbabwe:

| 1977 | *Dancing Queen* |
| 1979 | *Chiquitita* |

Both *Dancing Queen* and *Chiquitita* topped the chart for four weeks.

Most Hits

20 hits	ABBA
2 hits	Agnetha Fältskog
1 hit	Frida

Most Weeks

258 weeks	ABBA
10 weeks	Frida
8 weeks	Agnetha Fältskog

Singles with the most weeks

23 weeks	*Fernando* – ABBA
21 weeks	*Waterloo* – ABBA
21 weeks	*Chiquitita* – ABBA
19 weeks	*Take A Chance On Me* – ABBA
18 weeks	*I Do, I Do, I Do, I Do, I Do* – ABBA
18 weeks	*Dancing Queen* – ABBA
18 weeks	*The Name Of The Game* – ABBA
18 weeks	*The Winner Takes It All* – ABBA
16 weeks	*S.O.S* – ABBA
14 weeks	*Summer Night City* – ABBA

All The Top 40 Albums

1 ~ THE HEP STARS by the Hep Stars

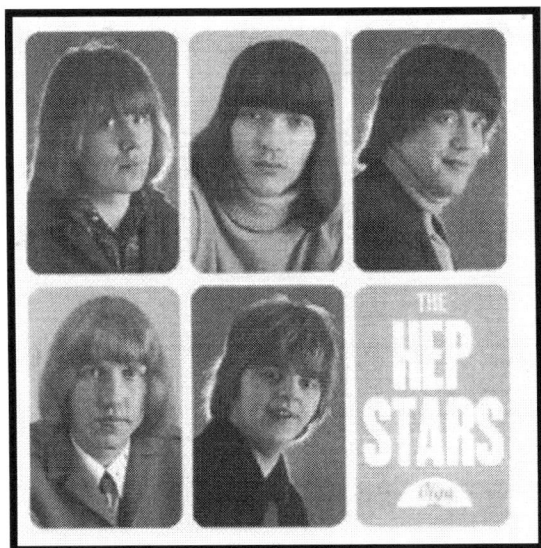

No Time/The Birds In The Sky/Consolation/Easy To Fool/Sound Of Eve/Isn't It Easy To Say/Lady Lady/Last Night I Had The Strangest Dream/Morning Comes After Night/I've Said It All Before/Wedding

Sweden: Olga LPO 04 (1966), Olga 7243 4751872 0 (CD, 1996).

27.12.66: peaked at no.**12**, charted for 5 weeks

Finland
01.67: peaked at no.**3**, charted for 8 weeks (monthly chart)

Norway
28.01.67: 12-13-11-9-**5**-6-**5**-7-9-13-13-13-14-15-15-20-15-16-16-16-14

Recorded in English, this is probably the most accessible Hep Stars album for non-Swedish speakers. Svenne Hedlund and Janne Frist provide the vocals, with Benny Andersson on keyboards.

The album is significant, as it includes *It Isn't Easy To Say*, which was the first song Benny and Björn Ulvaeus wrote together.

THE HEP STARS charted at no.3 in Finland, no.5 in Norway and no.12 in Sweden, but it wasn't released outside Scandinavia.

The Hep Stars released two albums before *THE HEP STARS*, *HEP STARS ON STAGE* (see next entry) and *WE AND OUR CADILLAC*, both issued in 1965.

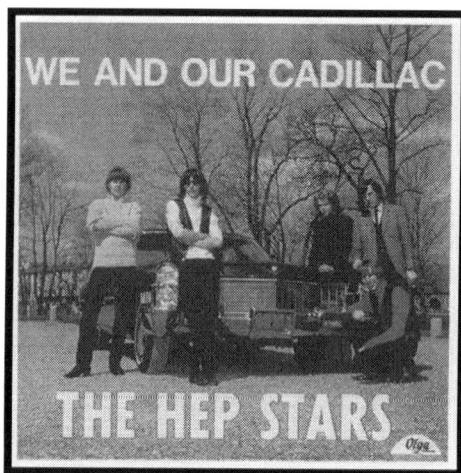

THE HEP STARS was reissued on CD in Sweden in 1996, with eight bonus tracks:

Sunny Girl/Hawaii/When My Blue Moon Turns To Gold Again/I Natt Jag Drömde/ Jag Vet/Don't/Malaika/It's Nice To Be Back

2 ~ HEP STARS ON STAGE by the Hep Stars

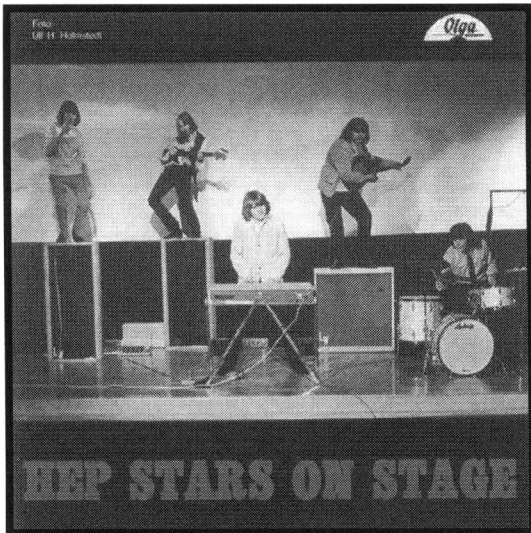

Cadillac/What'd I Say/Donna/What Do You Want To Make Those Eyes At Me For/So Mystifying/Only You/Wear My Ring Around Your Neck/Surfin' Bird/Talahassie Lassie/No Response/If You Need Me/Farmer John/Bald Headed Woman/Whole Lotta Shakin' Goin' On

Sweden: Olga LPO 02 (LP, 1965), Olga 7243 4751862 1 (CD, 1996).

HEP STARS ON STAGE wasn't a hit in Sweden.

Norway
18.02.67: **20**

This live album of the Hep Stars in concert was recorded at two different venues, Trollhättan and Västerås, Sweden, in August 1965 – it spent a solitary week at no.20 in Norway, but surprisingly it wasn't a hit in Sweden.

HEP STARS ON STAGE was released on CD in 1996, in Sweden only, with six studio recordings as bonus tracks:

Cadillac (Single Version)/Mashed Potatoes/Lonesome Town/Rented Tuxedo/So Mystifying/Should I

3 ~ RING RING by Björn Benny & Agnetha Frida / ABBA

Ring Ring (Bara Du Slog En Signal)/Another Town, Another Train/Disillusion/People Need Love/I Saw It In The Mirror/Nina, Pretty Ballerina/Love Isn't Easy/Me And Bobby And Bobby's Brother/He Is Your Brother/Ring Ring (English Version)/I Am Just A Girl/ Rock 'N Roll Band

Sweden: Polar POLS 242 (1973), Polar POLCD 242 (CD, 1988).

3.04.73: 18-3-3-**2**-3-3-4-6-9-10-16-19

Australia
19.01.76: 96-73-62-57-57-55-47-40-35-27-21-12-11-12-12-12-**10**-12-12-14-15-16-20-23-
30-36-42-43-54-68-82

New Zealand
19.03.76: 40
28.05.76: 36-**32**-x-34
2.07.76: 40-x-**32**

Norway
28.04.73: 22-18-12-14-12-**10**-**10**-13-13-11-13-12-x-17-18-20

UK

RING RING wasn't a hit in the UK, however, the deluxe edition did spend one week at no.137 on the Top 200 in October 2013.

The first song Benny, Björn, Agnetha and Frida recorded for *RING RING* was *People Need Love*, in early 1972. At the time, however, the quartet had no plans to record an album together, or even to form a permanent group. The success of *Ring Ring* changed their plans, and they completed recording their similarly titled debut album in March 1973 – as no one had coined the name 'ABBA' yet, it was released with the rather unwieldy artist credit 'Benny Björn & Agnetha Frida'.

The original Swedish released of *RING RING* opened with the Swedish version of the title track, however, outside Scandinavia this was replaced by the English version, with the English version in turn being replaced by Benny & Björn's *She's My Kind Of Girl*, which was originally released in 1969. One track on the album, *Disillusion*, was composed by Agnetha, with lyrics by Björn – it proved to be the only song she had a hand in writing that was recorded by ABBA.

In 1973, outside Scandinavia, *RING RING* was only released in a few countries including Australia, Germany, Mexico and South Africa. The album charted at no.2 in Sweden and no.10 in Norway. Two years later, the album was re-packaged and reissued in Australasia, with a new sleeve design – and with the artist credit changed to 'abba'.

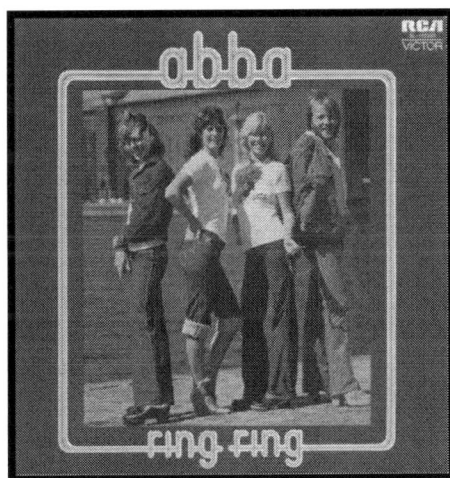

RING RING charted at no.10 in Australia and no.32 in New Zealand but, surprisingly, the album wasn't released in the UK until 1992, and in the USA until 1995.

Like all of ABBA's studio albums, *RING RING* has been reissued several times over the years. In 2001, the album was reissued with three bonus tracks: *Merry-Go-Round*, *Santa Rosa* and *Ring Ring (Bara Du Slog En Signal)*.

Four years later, as part of *THE COMPLETE STUDIO RECORDINGS* box-set, *RING RING* was reissued with the following bonus tracks:

Ring Ring (Bara Du Slog En Signal)/Åh, Vilka Tider/Merry-Go-Round/Santa Rosa, Ring Ring (Spanish Version)/Wer Im Wartesaal Der Liebe Steht (Another Town, Another Train, German Version)/Ring Ring (German Version)

Åh, Vilka Tider ('Oh, What Times') was originally released as the B-side of *Ring Ring (Bara Du Slog En Signal)* in Sweden.

Deluxe Edition

The deluxe edition of *RING RING* was released in 2013, with several bonus tracks and a DVD.

Bonus Tracks: *Ring Ring (Bara Du Slog En Signal)/Merry-Go-Round/Santa Rosa/Ring Ring (Spanish Version)/Wer Im Wartesaal Der Liebe Steht (Another Town, Another Train, German Version)/Ring Ring (German Version)/En Hälsning Till Våra Parkarrangörer*

Extra Bonus Tracks (Early Versions): *Hej Gamle Man!* (Benny & Björn)/*There's A Little Man* (Billy G-Son)/*I Saw It In The Mirror* (Billy G-Son)/*Jag Är Blott En Man* (Jarl Kulle)/*Man Vill Ju Leva Lite Dessemellan* (Anni-Frid Lyngstad)/*Välkommen Till Världen* (Lill-Babs)

En Hälsning Till Våra Parkarrangörer was a promotional single featuring excerpts of previous hits, released to coincide with Benny, Björn, Agnetha and Frida's tour of Sweden in 1973.

Benny and Björn composed *There's A Little Man* and *I Saw It In The Mirror* for Billy G-Son; Agnetha sang backing on the former, while ABBA went on to record the latter themselves. Jarl Kulle's single *Jag Är Blott En Man* ('I Am Just A Man') is the original version of the song ABBA recorded as *I Am Just A Girl*. Anni-Frid's 1972 single *Man Vill Ju Leva Lite Dessemellan* featured Agnetha, Benny and Björn on backing vocals, while all four members of ABBA sang backing vocals on *Välkommen Till Världen* by Lill-Babs.

The bonus DVD featured TV performances of *People Need Love* and *Ring Ring*, '*Ring Ring* Revealed', and an International Sleeve Gallery.

4 ~ WATERLOO by ABBA

Waterloo (Swedish Version)/Sitting In The Palmtree/King Kong Song/Hasta Mañana/My Mama Said/Dance (While The Music Still Goes On)/Honey Honey/Watch Out/What About Livingstone/Gonna Sing You My Lovesong/Suzy-Hang-Around/Waterloo (English Version)

Sweden: Polar POLS 252 (1974).

12.03.74: 2-**1-1-1-1-1-1-1-1-1-1-1-1**-2-2-4-9-7-10-9-9
23.04.04: 56-49

UK: Epic EPC 80179 (1974).

8.06.74: 46-**28**

Australia
1.07.74: 97-74-69-67-75-76-81
8.12.75: 90-84-84-87-87-87-87-82-77-74-71-76-76-79-85-67-51-43-41-32-24-**18**-20-21-
    19-21-27-26-26-30-37-50-55-69-76-99

Finland
05/74: peaked at no.**4**, charted for 24 weeks (monthly chart)

Germany
15.06.74: peaked at no.**6**, charted for 32 weeks

New Zealand
28.05.76: 39
19.02.77: **38**

Norway
30.03.74: 19-13-4-4-**1-1-1-1-1-1**-2-2-2-4-5-5-5-6-11-11-6-10-13-x-x-15

USA
WATERLOO didn't enter the Top 100 in the USA, however, it did spend eight weeks on the Billboard 200, peaking at no.145.

Zimbabwe
8.03.75: 19-13-11-8-**6**-7-8-7-9-11-14-20

Recorded between September 1973 and February 1974, *WATERLOO* was titled after the song that broke ABBA – as the group were now known – internationally, by winning the 1974 Eurovision Song Contest. The first track recorded for the album was *Dance (While The Music Still Goes On)*.

In the UK and most other countries, the album opened with the English rather than the Swedish version of *Waterloo*, and *Ring Ring* was added as the last track on the album.

WATERLOO made its chart debut in Sweden at no.2, before climbing to no.1 for twelve straight weeks – on 30th April 1974, for the third time, ABBA held the Top 3 positions on the *Kvällstoppen* combined albums/singles chart, with *WATERLOO* at no.1, the Swedish version of *Waterloo* at no.2 and the English version of *Waterloo* at no.3.

The album also hit no.1 in Norway for six weeks, and charted at no.4 in Finland, no.6 in Germany and Zimbabwe, no18 in Australia and no.28 in the UK.

When *WATERLOO* was released on CD for the first time, in Sweden in 1988, the English version of the title track was dropped from the track listing. More recently, although no deluxe edition has yet appeared, the album has been reissued several times.

In 2001, *WATERLOO* was reissued with three bonus tracks: *Ring Ring (1974 US Remix, Single Version)*, *Waterloo (Swedish Version)* and *Honey Honey (Swedish Version)*.

Three years later, a 30th anniversary edition saw *WATERLOO* reissued with the same three bonus tracks as in 2001, plus the German and French versions of *Waterloo*. This edition came with a bonus DVD featuring ABBA's Eurovision winning performance of *Waterloo*, plus TV performances of *Waterloo*, *Honey Honey* and *Hasta Mañana*.

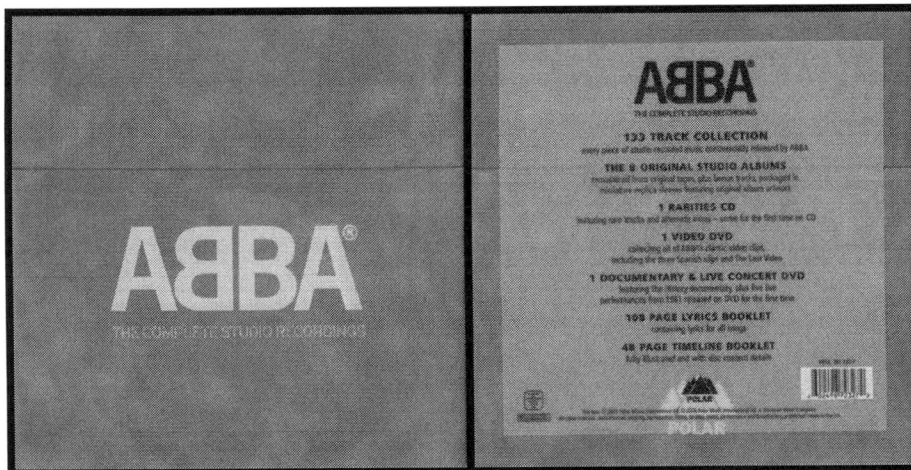

In 2005, as part of *THE COMPLETE STUDIO RECORDINGS* box-set, *WATERLOO* was reissued with the same five bonus tracks as the 2004 anniversary edition, plus *Hasta Mañana (Spanish Version)* and *Ring Ring (1974 Remix, Single Version)*.

5 ~ ABBA by ABBA

Mamma Mia/Hey Hey Helen/Tropical Loveland/S.O.S/Man In The Middle/Bang-A-Boomerang/I Do, I Do, I Do, I Do, I Do/Rock Me/Intermezzo No.1/I've Been Waiting For You/So Long

Sweden: Polar POLS 262 (1975).

29.04.75: **1-1-1-1-1-1-1-1-1-1-1-1-1-1-1-1-1**-2
14.11.75: **1**-2-4-6-8-9-17-x-38 (bi-weekly chart)
7.06.13: 39

UK: Epic EPC 80835 (1975).

31.01.76: 42-23-**13-13**-16-18-32-30-43-40

Australia
8.09.75: 67-56-50-24-19-14-13-11-9-5-4-3-3-**1-1-1-1-1-1-1-1-1-1-1**-2-4-4-7-7-7-7-6-8-8-7-8-8-8-8-7-9-9-9-13-13-13-14-16-16-20-22-22-25-28-32-34-39-50-55-61-70-73-73-83

Canada
5.06.76: 100-67-66-60-**55**

Finland
06.75: peaked at no.**6**, charted for 16 weeks (monthly chart)

Germany
15.03.76: 49-34-**31** (bi-weekly chart)

Netherlands
7.06.75: 20-15-8-9-7-**3**-4-4-5-13-13-15-16

New Zealand
12.12.75: 30-29-(no chart for 5 weeks)-5-**3**-7-14-21-27-17-25-28-21-21-24-6-5-6-14-14-15-
   17-11-32-15-14-22-28-34-35-23-29-28
10.12.76: 17-14-(no chart for 7 weeks)-11-16-24-27-18-21-17-15-26-5-9-7-10-8-13-13-16-
   29-30-32-30-34
29.07.77: 34-x-39-33

Norway
11.05.75: 4-4-4-4-4-5-5-6-6-6-8-7-13-13-7-7-6-6-7-3-2-**1-1-1-1-1-1-1-1-1-1-1-1-1-1-1-1**-2-2-
   2-2-2-2-3-3-4-5-4-5-5-6-7-16-11-11-11-8-9-14-18-x-x-x-x-14-13-13-11

USA
ABBA didn't enter the Top 100 in the USA, however, it did spend three weeks on the Billboard 200, peaking at no.174.

Zimbabwe
6.09.75: 11-8-7-2-2-2-**1-1-1-1-1-1-1-1-1-1-1-1-1-1-1-1-1-1-1**-2-2-2-3-2-4-6-7-6-7-8-10-11

ABBA's third, self-titled album was recorded between August 1974 and March 1975 and, unusually, it included an instrumental, *Intermezzo No.1*, which was originally titled 'Mama'.

Singles like *Mamma Mia, I Do, I Do, I Do, I Do, I Do* and *S.O.S* ensured *ABBA* built on the success of *RING RING* and *WATERLOO*, especially in Australia, where ABBA-mania reigned.

ABBA hit no.1 for 18 weeks in Sweden and Zimbabwe, for 14 weeks in Norway and for 11 weeks in Australia, and charted at no.3 in New Zealand and the Netherlands, no.6 in Finland, no.13 in the UK and no.31 in Germany.

In Germany, the album was titled *MAMMA MIA*, while in southern Africa it was released as *I DO, I DO, I DO, I DO, I DO*.

When *ABBA* was released on CD in 1987, five bonus tracks taken from *RING RING* and *WATERLOO* were added: *Waterloo, Hasta Mañana, Honey Honey, Ring Ring* and *Nina, Pretty Ballerina*.

Ten years on, *ABBA* was reissued, and a further two bonus tracks were added, *Crazy World* and *Medley: Pick A Bale Of Cotton/On Top Of Old Smokey/Midnight Special*.

In 2001, when *ABBA* was reissued again, the five bonus tracks from *RING RING* and *WATERLOO* were dropped, but *Crazy World* and *Medley: Pick A Bale Of Cotton/On Top Of Old Smokey/Midnight Special* were retained. The same two bonus tracks appeared on the version of *ABBA* released as part of *THE COMPLETE STUDIO RECORDINGS* box-set released in 2005, along with a third bonus track, *Mamma Mia (Spanish Version)*.

Deluxe Edition

Released in 2012, the deluxe edition of *ABBA* retained the three bonus tracks on the 2005 version, and the album came with an hour long DVD featuring the following:

- *ABBA In Australia* (1976 TV Special): *Mamma Mia/Hasta Mañana/Tropical Loveland/Waterloo/I Do, I Do, I Do, I Do, I Do/Rock Me/Dancing Queen/Honey Honey/Fernando/So Long/S.O.S*
- *Made In Sweden – For Export* (1975 TV Special): *Mamma Mia/I Do, I Do, I Do, I Do, I Do/So Long*
- *S.O.S* and *Mamma Mia* (BBC *Seaside Special* & *Top Of The Pops* performances, respectively)
- *THE BEST OF* & *GREATEST HITS* TV commercials
- International Sleeve Gallery

6 ~ GREATEST HITS by ABBA

S.O.S/He Is Your Brother/Ring Ring/Hasta Mañana/Nina, Pretty Ballerina/Honey Honey/So Long/I Do, I Do, I Do, I Do, I Do/People Need Love/Bang-A-Boomerang/ Another Town, Another Train/Mamma Mia/Dance (While The Music Still Goes On)/ Waterloo

Sweden: Polar POLS 266 (1975).

27.11.75: 4-**1-1-1-1**-3-9-18-23-27-21-25-50-x-39-18-20-25-50-45-45 (bi-weekly chart)

UK: Epic EPC 69218 (1975).

10.04.76: 38-5-5-4-**1-1-1-1-1-1-1-1-1**-2-2-4-7-6-9-7-7-7-6-4-3-2-2-**1-1**-3-4-7-12-11-9-8-
10-7-7-6-2-4-5-9-11-13-17-16-17-16-14-13-10-8-8-5-6-8-9-14-15-17-28-13-17-20-17-
26-21-19-26-27-22-25-34-43-32-46-42-47-58-9-12-17-19-20-18-17-18-22-22-19-15-
17-12-24-28-21-17-14-18-19-16-21-27-23-28-31-36-28-34-28-33-40-42-43-x-40-49-
55-58-59-50-48-36-43-39-36-46-35-47

Canada
2.10.76: 99-85-66-59-55-52-46-40-21-17-7-13-13-13-14-23-25-33-44-49-21-7-7-6-7-25-
13-8-3-**2**-3-3-4-5-3-3-8-9-15-20-28-30-31-33-39-54-52-50-45-29-24-23-22-23-23-27-
33-71

Finland
03.76: peaked at no.**3**, charted for 36 weeks (monthly chart)

France
05.76: peaked at no.**9**, charted for 12 weeks

Norway
18.01.76: 7-7-7-7-3-3-2-**1**-2-2-2-3-2-2-2-2-2-2-3-3-4-3-3-3-5-2-3-3-4-3-3-2-2-2-2-3-2-3-
5-4-6-5-6-10-10-14-15-14-13-17-14-x-9-9-9-21-13-15-11-9-14-17-20

USA
11.09.76: 97-87-80-70-59-57-53-53-49-**48**-59-59-57-57-57-57-70-72

Zimbabwe
3.07.76: 10-2-**1-1-1-1-1-1-1-1-1-1**-2-2-2-3-3-4-4-5-5-9-10-11-12-x-x-13-14-14-14-19

GREATEST HITS was rush-released in Scandinavia in November 1975, amid fears of imports of other ABBA compilations released by licensees across Europe, particularly *THE BEST OF.*

The album was originally released with a gatefold sleeve that reproduced a strange painting by Hans Arnold, which had been awarded as a prize by a magazine that voted ABBA as Artists of the Year. The four members of ABBA loved the painting so much, they sought and were granted permission to use it.

In most countries, *GREATEST HITS* was released with a more conventional gatefold sleeve, with Agnetha and Björn on one side, and Benny and Frida kissing on the other.

In some countries, *Fernando* was added to the track listing of *GREATEST HITS* in early 1976.

GREATEST HITS gave ABBA their first no.1 album in the UK – it topped the chart for 11 weeks, and went on to become the no.1 best-selling album of 1976. The compilation also hit no.1 in Norway, Sweden and Zimbabwe, and charted at no.2 in Canada, no.3 in Finland, no.9 in France and no.48 in the USA, where the track listing was slightly different:

S.O.S/He Is Your Brother/Ring Ring/Another Town, Another Train/Honey Honey/So Long/Mamma Mia/I Do, I Do, I Do, I Do, I Do/People Need Love/Waterloo/Nina, Pretty Ballerina/Bang-A-Boomerang/Dance (While The Music Still Goes On)/ Fernando

To mark its 30th anniversary, *GREATEST HITS* was released on CD in 2006, with a miniature replica gatefold sleeve – the outer sleeve featured the design based on the Hans Arnold painting, while the inner sleeve featured the international 'park bench' design. The track listing was as per the original release, but with *Fernando* added as the opening track.

7 ~ *FRIDA ENSAM* by Anni-Frid Lyngstad

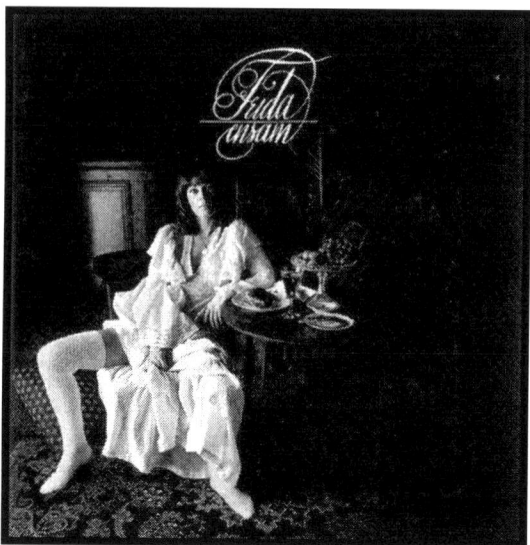

Fernando/Jag Är Mej Själv Nu/Som En Sparv/Vill Du Lana En Man/Liv Par Mars/ Syrtaki/Aldrig Mej/Guld Och Gröna Ängar/Ett Liv I Solen/Skulle De Va Skönt/Var Är Min Clown

Sweden: Polar POLS 265 (LP, 1975), Polar 986 876-4 (CD, 2005).

27.11.75: 9-8-9-4-2-**1-1-1**-2-2-3-5-4-7-10-11-14-41-38-x-37 (bi-weekly chart)

Anni-Frid Lyngstad released her debut album, titled simply *FRIDA*, in Sweden in 1971 but it wasn't a hit.

Frida's second solo album, *FRIDA ENSAM* ('Frida Alone'), was recorded entirely in Swedish between February 1974 and October 1975 – it took so long because she had to work around her commitments with ABBA. The album was produced by Benny and Björn and, one song apart, it featured Swedish cover versions of well-known songs, including Gary Puckett & The Union Gap's *Young Girl*, David Bowie's *Life On Mars*, 10cc's *The Wall Street Shuffle*, the Beach Boys' *Wouldn't It Be Nice*, Charlie Rich's *The Most Beautiful Girl* and Judy Collins' *Send In The Clowns*.

The one original song on *FRIDA ENSAM*, which Benny and Björn composed, was *Fernando*. The song topped the *Svensktoppen* radio chart for nine weeks, but it wasn't released as a single in Sweden, as Polar wanted people to buy the album instead. The ploy worked, with *FRIDA ENSAM* giving Frida her first no.1 album as a solo artist – the album it deposed was ABBA's *GREATEST HITS*.

Fernando was released a single in neighboring Norway, but it wasn't a hit. However, such was the popularity of *Fernando* in Sweden, Benny and Björn decided to record an English version, with ABBA – which went on to become one of ABBA's biggest and best loved hits.

FRIDA ENSAM was remastered and reissued in 2005, with two bonus tracks: *Man Vill Ju Leva Lite Dessemellan* and *Ska Man Skratta Eller Gråta*. Both were cover versions of Italian hits, with Swedish lyrics by Stig Anderson, with Benny and Björn producing.

Man Vill Ju Leva Lite Dessemellan ('One Wants To Live A Little In Between') had given Frida her second no.1 on the *Svensktoppen* radio chart in 1972, after *Min Egen Stad* ('My Own Town'), which Benny composed.

8 ~ *ELVA KVINNOR I ETT HUS* by **Agnetha Fältskog**

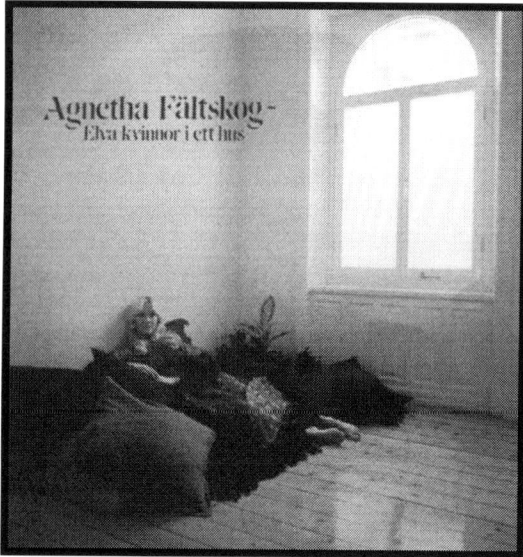

S.O.S/En Egen Trädgård/Tack För En Underbar, Vanlig Dag/Gulleplutt/Är Du Som Han?/Och Han Väntar På Mej/Doktorn!/Mina Ögon/Dom Har Glömt/Var Det Med Dej?/ Visa I Åttonde Månaden

Sweden: Cupol CLPS 351 (1975).

11.12.75: 26-18-15-20-26-35-x-32-29-x-19-12-**11**-13-21 (bi-weekly)

Agnetha released her first, self-titled album in Sweden in 1968, and a further three albums followed before her fifth became her first hit.

Agnetha started work on '*Tolv Kvinnor I Ett Hus*' ('Twelve Women In One House'), as the project was originally titled, in 1973, when she planned to write twelve songs about twelve different women who live under the same roof. However, pregnancy and her commitments with ABBA meant the project dragged on into 1975, by which time Agnetha had only composed ten songs, with Bosse Carlgren penning the Swedish lyrics. The songs included *Mina Ögon* ('My Eyes'), which ABBA (as Björn Benny & Agnetha Frida) recorded for their *RING RING* album as *Disillusion*.

Although it didn't really fit the album's theme, Agnetha recorded a Swedish cover of ABBA's *S.O.S*, and released the eleven songs she had as *ELVA KVINNOR I ETT HUS* ('Eleven Women In One House'). Agnetha produced the whole album herself, and she was rewarded with a no.11 hit, but sensibly she decided to put her solo career on hold as ABBA found greater and greater success.

9 ~ THE BEST OF by ABBA

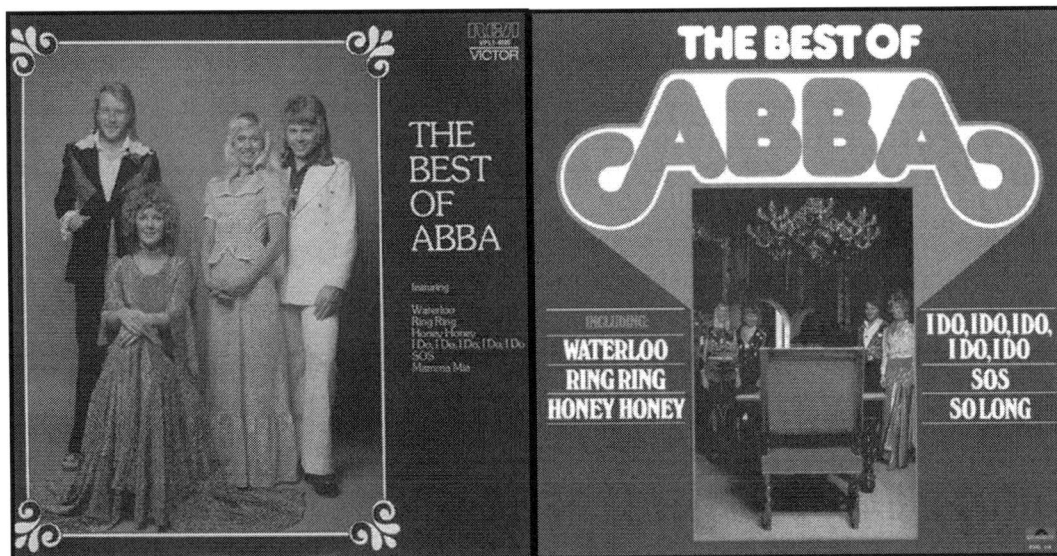

Waterloo/Ring Ring/Honey Honey/Mamma Mia/People Need Love/Nina, Pretty Ballerina/I Do, I Do, I Do, I Do, I Do/S.O.S/Dance (While The Music Still Goes On)/ Bang-A-Boomerang/Hasta Mañana/So Long

Australia: RCA VPL1-4020 (1975).

22.12.75: 72-61-54-46-43-42-34-32-31-31-24-12-3-2-**1-1-1-1-1-1-1-1-1-1-1-1-1-1-1-1**-2-3-4-5-5-5-5-6-5-6-7-7-7-6-7-9-6-9-10-11-13-22-27-31-32-35-35-37-39-48-56-62-67-73-75-67-76-83-94-95

Germany: Polydor 2459 301 (1975).

15.10.75: peaked at no.**1** (4 weeks), charted for 84 weeks

Austria
15.04.76: 10-6-4-6-**1-1**-2-4-7-8-13-17-21 (monthly chart)

Netherlands
30.08.75: 20-8-7-8-12-18
1.01.77: 3-**2**-3-6-10
2.04.77: 9

New Zealand

6.02.76: 19-2-**1**-3-5-4-3-4-2-4-4-**1-1-1-1-1-1-1-1-1-1-1-1-1-1-1**-2-3-2-2-2-2-3-**1**-2-2-2-2-
2-**1**-2-3-2-3-2-(no chart for 7 weeks)-5-5-6-8-8-9-13-10-8-11-13-13-12-16-12-17-13-20-23-
27-27-20-32-16-22-26-17-35-30-32-35-x-35

Norway

7.12.75: **14**-19

Switzerland

1.02.76: peaked at no.**2**, charted for 48 weeks

While *GREATEST HITS* was released globally, *THE BEST OF* compilation was only issued in a limited number of countries. In 1975, it was released in Australasia, Germany, the Netherlands and Norway, with Austria and India having to wait until the following year.

In the countries where it was released, *THE BEST OF* was just as successful as *GREATEST HITS*, hitting no.1 in Australia (for 16 weeks), Austria, Germany and New Zealand (for 18 weeks), and charted at no.2 in the Netherlands and Switzerland, and no.14 in Norway. In Australia, the album has sold more than a million copies, and has been certified 22 x Platinum.

THE BEST OF was released on CD in 1988, but only for a limited time period.

10 ~ GOLDEN DOUBLE ALBUM by ABBA

LP1: *Fernando/My Mama Said/What About Livingstone/Hey, Hey Helen/Honey Honey/ Bang-A-Boomerang/Mamma Mia/Tropical Loveland/Rock Me/Love Isn't Easy (But It Sure Is Hard Enough)/People Need Love/Intermezzo No.1*

LP2: *I Do, I Do, I Do, I Do, I Do/Nina, Pretty Ballerina/Dance (While The Music Still Goes On)/Gonna Sing You My Lovesong/I've Been Waiting For You/Waterloo/Ring Ring/ So Long/Sitting In The Palmtree/Suzy Hang Around/Hasta Mañana/S.O.S*

France: Vogue SLVLX 685 (1976).

05.76: peaked at no.**2**, charted for 27 weeks

This double album was released exclusively in France, where it peaked at no.2, and spent over six months on the chart.

11 ~ THE VERY BEST OF by ABBA

LP1: *Ring Ring/So Long/Sitting In A Palm Tree/Suzy-Hang-Around/Hasta Mañana/ S.O.S/Mamma Mia/Tropical Loveland/Rock Me/Love Isn't Easy/People Need Love/ Intermezzo No.1*

LP2: *Fernando/My Mama Said/What About Livingstone/Hey Hey Helen/Honey Honey/ Bang-A-Boomerang/I Do, I Do, I Do, I Do, I Do/Nina, Pretty Ballerina/Dance (While The Music Still Goes On)/Gonna Sing You My Lovesong/I've Been Waiting For You/Waterloo*

Germany: Polydor 2612 032 (1976).

15.09.76: 33-3-4-8-3-3-**2**-4-4-5-17-8-8-9-31-19-20-22-33-25-37-50-50-x-x-x-50-x-x-x-49-48-x-x-x-42-x-48-36-40-48-x-40-39-43-38-42-48-45-35-46 (bi-weekly chart)

Austria
15.10.77: **19** (monthly chart)

Switzerland
15.09.76: peaked at no.**3**, charted for 18 weeks

This compilation was released in Germany and the Netherlands only, peaking at no.2 in Germany. It also charted at no.3 in Switzerland and no.19 in Austria.

12 ~ ARRIVAL by ABBA

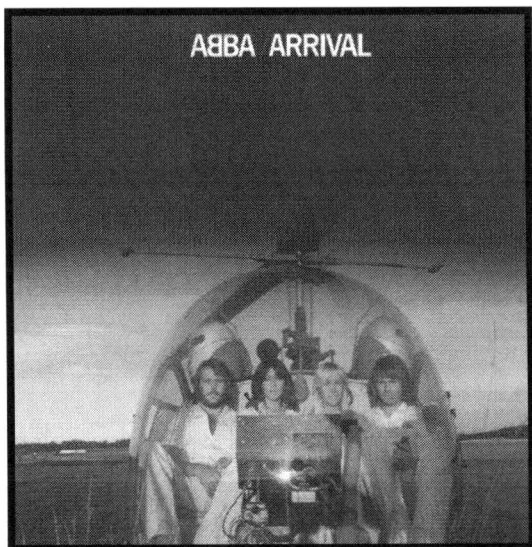

When I Kissed The Teacher/Dancing Queen/My Love, My Life/Dum Dum Diddle/ Knowing Me, Knowing You/Money, Money, Money/That's Me/Why Did It Have To Be Me/Tiger/Arrival

Sweden: Polar POLS 272 (1976).

19.10.76: **1-1-1-1-1-1**-2-2-5-9-16-13-23-35-33-45 (bi-weekly chart)

UK: Epic EPC 86018 (1976).

27.11.76: 6-3-2-2-2-2-3-**1**-2-2-5-10-11-14-9-11-9-3-3-2-**1-1-1-1-1-1-1-1-1-1**-3-3-5-5-6-9-
14-13-13-12- 10-13-18- 9-17-25-37-34-33-39-25-31-30-25-30-21-19-21-21-20-21-12-
22-25-30-23-19-13-15-17-19-29-22-25-38-35-37-47-32-38-58-44-49-40-x-54-x-46-x-
52-x-56-x-58-x-60-52-53
13.01.01: 73

Australia
22.11.76: **1-1-1-1-1-1-1-1**-2-1-2-3-5-6-9-14-16-16-17-17-21-27-35-39-48-58-67-68-72-72-
67-70-72-79-90

Austria
15.01.77: 18-17-20-**12**-23-20-20-25 (monthly chart)

Canada
26.02.77: 85-53-20-20-35-10-**4-4-4-4-4**-9-25-62-69-65-82-90
10.09.77: 77-67-64-61-66-50-42-42-80

Finland
11.76: peaked at no.**2**, charted for 56 weeks (monthly chart)
18.04.09: 24

France
11.76: peaked at no.**15**, charted for 10 weeks

Germany
15.12.76: 9-5-**1-1-1-1-1-1**-2-**1**-2-2-3-2-4-4-5-9-14-18-31-29-36-43-49-40-42-43-46-46-
45-47-39-20-x-46-49-46-48 (bi-weekly chart)

Japan
25.05.77: 21-17-14-12-12-14-12-14-14-15-16-19-17-19-22-20-20-24-23-28-28-22-23-46-
47-53-64-76-82-84-89-87-84-60-58-64-56-68-80-85-71-52-81-62-70-65-78-84-95-70-
68-67-79-70-58-56-33-32-23-12-13-12-17-14-17-18-23-22-21-27-33-33-33-48-47-42-
29-19-10-10-8-7-5-4-4-**3-3**-5-7-7-7-8-8-9-10-19-22-22-23-24-25-29-40-56-63-61-67-
67-68-69-83-85-84-81-86-90-97-94-100-94 (LP chart)

Netherlands
6.11.76: 9-2-**1-1-1-1-1-1-1**-2-3-4-5-5-9-8-9-12-12-9-6-5-6-6-6-7-7-10-14-14
3.12.77: 17
7.01.78: 25
21.10.06: 85

New Zealand
26.11.76: **1-1-1-1**-(no chart for 7 weeks)-**1**-2-5-6-7-8-10-7-9-10-10-9-8-9-11-12-12-14-16-
22-13-19-21-15-20-23-20-32-23-29-34-x-37-35-34-x-35-x-33-39-x-x-37

Norway
17.10.76: 2-**1-1-1-1-1-1-1-1-1-1-1-1-1-1-1-1-1-1-1-1-1**-2-3-3-3-3-4-4-4-5-9-9-9-14-15

Switzerland
15.11.76: peaked at no.**2**, charted for 46 weeks

USA
29.01.77: 61-51-46-42-38-35-35-31-26-24-22-**20-20**-47-76-74
23.07.77: 93-90-90-88-90-94-92-92-x-100-100

Zimbabwe
10.12.76: 10-3-3-3-**1-1-1-1-1-1-1-1-1-1-1-1-1**-3-3-4-5-8-12-17-19

ABBA's fourth studio album was recorded between August 1975 and September 1976 – *Fernando* didn't appear on most editions, but it was slotted into the track listing between *Why Did It Have To Be Me* and *Tiger* in Australia, New Zealand and South Africa

One track ABBA recorded for *ARRIVAL*, but chose not to include, was titled *Funky Feet.*; it was left off the album because it was felt it was too similar to *Dancing Queen Funky Feet* was later recorded by Svenne and Lotta, but ABBA's version has never been released.

Two further recordings known to have been made during the *ARRIVAL* sessions are *Monsieur Monsieur*, an early version of *My Love, My Life*, and *National Song*. The latter was a short track, made over the backing track of *Fernando*, recorded for an Australian TV commercial for National appliances. *Monsieur Monsieur* and *National Song* have never been released.

Boosted by three of ABBA's biggest hits, *Dancing Queen*, *Money, Money, Money* and *Knowing Me, Knowing You*, *ARRIVAL* was ABBA's most successful studio album to date. It hit no.1 in Australia, Germany, the Netherlands, New Zealand, Norway (for 20 weeks), the UK (for 10 weeks) and Zimbabwe, and charted at no.2 in Finland and Switzerland, no.3 in Japan, no.4 in Canada, no.12 in Austria, no.15 in France and no.20 in the USA.

ARRIVAL was the no.1 best-selling album of 1977 in the UK.

When *ARRIVAL* was reissued on CD in 1997, *Fernando* was added to the track listing as a bonus track. Four years later, another reissue saw *Happy Hawaii*, an early version of *Why Did It Have To Be Me* released as the B-side of *Knowing Me, Knowing You*, added as well.

In 2005, as part of *THE COMPLETE STUDIO RECORDINGS*, *ARRIVAL* was reissued with five bonus tracks. As well as *Fernando* and *Happy Hawaii*, three Spanish recordings from the 1980 album, *GRACIAS POR LA MUSICA* were added: *La Reina Del Baile* (*Dancing Queen*), *Conociendome Conociendote* (*Knowing Me, Knowing You*) and *Fernando*.

Deluxe Edition

The deluxe edition of *ARRIVAL* was released in 2006. As well as the five bonus tracks featured on the 2005 version, a sixth was added, Frida's solo recording of *Fernando*. Additionally, the deluxe edition came with an hour long DVD that featured:

- *ABBA-DABBA-DOOO!* – TV Special featuring interviews with ABBA, *Dancing Queen* music video, ABBA's performance of *Waterloo* at the Eurovision Song

Contest, plus seven filmed/live performances: *Knowing Me, Knowing You, When I Kissed The Teacher, Dum Dum Diddle, My Love, My Life, Money, Money, Money, Tiger* and *Why Did It Have To Be Me*

- *Dancing Queen* & *Fernando* (from *Musikladen* & *Top Of The Pops*, respectively)
- *Happy Hawaii* (cartoon)
- *Dancing Queen* recording sessions, including the 'lost verse'
- ABBA in London (British news report)
- ABBA's 1976 Success (Swedish news report)
- *ARRIVAL* – two different TV commercials
- International Sleeve Gallery

13 ~ GREATEST HITS 24 by ABBA

LP1: *Dancing Queen/What About Livingstone/Hey Hey Helen/Honey Honey/Mamma Mia/Waterloo/Gonna Sing You My Lovesong/Another Town, Another Train/Nina, Pretty Ballerina/Ring Ring/Suzy-Hang-Around/Bang-A-Boomerang*

LP2: *That's Me/Hasta Mañana/My Mama Said/I Am Just a Girl/Dance (While The Music Still Goes On)/Intermezzo No.1/Fernando/S.O.S/Rock Me/I Do, I Do, I Do, I Do, I Do/ People Need Love/I've Been Waiting For You*

Japan: Discomate DSP-3012/3 (1977).

25.10.77: 66-52-53-51-59-66-71-86-94-76-92-89-69-73-38-31-26-14-14-16-19-16-19-23-32-25-32-39-47-49-49-66-76-57-71-26-17-18-11-8-9-5-5-**4**-6-6-8-9-8-9-9-11-17-22-28-25-28-28-34-34-50-51-76-76-84-94-97-84-91-100 (LP chart)

This double album was released exclusively in Japan, where it enjoyed a lengthy chart run, and peaked at no.4 on the LP chart.

14 ~ THE ALBUM by ABBA

Eagle/Take A Chance On Me/One Man, One Woman/The Name Of The Game/Move On/
Hole In Your Soul/The Girl With The Golden Hair (Three Scenes From A Mini-Musical):
Thank You For the Music/I Wonder (Departure)/I'm A Marionette

Sweden: Polar POLS 282 (1977).

30.12.77: **1-1**-3-4-10-17-47 (bi-weekly chart)

UK: Epic EPC 86052 (1977).

4.02.78: **1-1-1-1-1-1-1**-2-2-2-3-5-5-5-6-5-5-4-5-2-4-5-7-6-9-14-14-15-18-22-27-20-20-
20-22-24-38-36-49-59-53-61-62-50-57-54-69-42-51-58-55-56-72-69-x-x-66-70-69-71-
65-57-62

Australia
23.01.78: 24-10-5-5-**4-4-4**-6-7-10-13-20-21-27-34-40-61-66-83-93

Austria
15.02.78: 21-6-**2**-3-**2**-3-11-21-15-23 (monthly chart)

Canada
4.03.78: 88-58-49-40-39-30-30-28-20-20-21-21-21-20-20-29-27-24-16-12-12-12-**8-8**-20-

22-33-33-55-75

Finland
01.78: peaked at no.**2**, charted for 24 weeks (monthly chart)

France
01.78: peaked at no.**13**, charted for 10 weeks

Germany
1.02.78: 24-3-3-4-4-**2-2-2-2**-3-3-6-6-9-9-9-7-7-9-9-6-6-9-9-11-12-12-19-15-17-20-14-26-
  27-27-38-44-41-42-45-40-39-40-40-40-45
24.01.79: 50
4.04.79: 46-x-39
30.05.79: 37-18-x-41-x-49

Japan
5.02.78: 28-**9-9**-11-14-13-21-17-18-21-27-25-29-36-41-45-45-65-37-51-37-21-20-19-26-
  22-26-26-35-30-35-44-46-56-48-56-66-62-57-53-37-35-29-24-21-24-15-17-19-22-22-
  24-29-37-38-40-74-62-55-69-85-66-80-93-99 (LP chart)

Netherlands
14.01.78: 2-**1-1-1-1-1**-2-3-5-6-7-8-9-11-14-14-16-19-19-13-8-16-11-11-14-20-14-14-18-
  26-31-26-30-31-33-40-37

New Zealand
3.02.78: 12-**1-1-1-1-1**-5-6-6-8-9-9-16-24-25-25-x-39

Norway
18.12.77: 5-2-**1-1-1-1-1**-2-2-2-2-2-2-2-5-7-11-11-13-14-17

Switzerland
1.02.78: peaked at no.**1**, charted for 36 weeks

USA
18.02.78: 80-64-56-49-45-40-38-37-36-47-46-51-48-45-43-40-36-36-30-24-19-16-**14-14**-
  23-31-34-34-65-65-67-62-83

Zimbabwe
11.02.78: 10-6-3-**2-2-2**-4-3-**2**-5-5-7-8-8-11-11-13-14-10-7-6-5-4-3-3-3-3-4-5-7-7-7-7-8-
  6-6-4-4-4-4-4-5-5-7-7-5-4-4-4-5-7-9-9-13-19-20-20

ABBA's fifth album, released to coincide with the film *ABBA: The Movie*, which featured several of the songs on the album, was recorded between May and November 1977. The album was released the following month in Sweden but, due to UK pressing plants being unable to meet demand for pre-orders, the UK release was put back to January.

During *THE ALBUM* sessions ABBA worked on several songs that didn't feature as part of the final track listing. The mini-musical, *The Girl With The Golden Hair*, actually comprised four songs, as performed in concert by ABBA. Three of the songs featured on *THE ALBUM*, but *Get On The Carousel* was omitted, as Benny and Björn didn't feel it was strong enough to merit inclusion. The chorus of *Get On The Carousel* later surfaced in another ABBA track, *Hole In Your Soul*.

A snippet of *Scaramouche* featured on the *ABBA Undeleted* melody, which was released on the 1994 box-set, *THANK YOU FOR THE MUSIC*. *ABBA Undeleted* also featured an excerpt of *Billy Boy*, an early version of *Take A Chance On Me*. *Love For Me Is Love Forever*, an early version of *Move On*, remains unreleased.

In most countries, the sleeve of *THE ALBUM* had a pure white background but, in a rare departure from the usual conformity of design, the UK release came with a sky blue background at the top, which faded to white toward the bottom of the sleeve.

THE ALBUM was the first ABBA album to debut at no.1 in the UK, where it went on to become the no.3 best-selling album of 1978, behind two soundtracks, *GREASE* and *SATURDAY NIGHT FEVER*.

THE ALBUM also hit no.1 in the Netherlands, New Zealand, Norway, Sweden and Switzerland, no.2 in Austria, Finland, Germany and Zimbabwe, no.4 in Australia, no.8 in Canada, no.9 in Japan, no.13 in France and no.14 in the USA.

THE ALBUM was reissued on CD in 2001 with one bonus track, the so-called Doris Day version of *Thank You For The Music*, which had previously been included on the 1994 box-set, *THANK YOU FOR THE MUSIC*.

Four years later, as part of *THE COMPLETE STUDIO RECORDINGS* box-set, *THE ALBUM* was reissued with two bonus tracks, *Al Andar (Move On, Spanish Version)* and *Gracias Por La Musica (Thank You For The Music, Spanish Version)*.

Deluxe Edition

The deluxe edition of *THE ALBUM* was released in 2007, to commemorate the album's 30th anniversary. The album came with a DVD and six bonus tracks:

Eagle (Single Edit)/Take A Chance On Me (Live Version)/Thank You For The Music (Doris Day Version)/Al Andar (Move On, Spanish Version)/I Wonder (Departure) (Live Version)/Gracias Por La Musica (Thank You For The Music, Spanish Version)

The DVD included with the deluxe edition featured a host of TV performances and interviews:

- *Eagle/Thank You For The Music* (from ZDF's *Star Parade*)
- *Take A Chance On Me* (from Radio Bremen's *Am Laufenden Band*)
- *The Name Of The Game* (from TBS's *ABBA Special*)
- *Thank You For The Music* (from the BBC's *Mike Yarwood's Christmas Show*)
- *Take A Chance On Me* (from ZDF's *Star Parade*)
- ABBA On Tour in 1977 (from SVT's *Rapport*)
- Recording *ABBA – THE ALBUM* (from SVT's *Gomorron Sverige*)
- ABBA in London, February 1978 (from the BBC's *Blue Peter*)
- ABBA in America, May 1978 (from SVT's *Rapport*)
- *THE ALBUM* – two different TV commercials (Australia & UK)
- International Sleeve Gallery

15 ~ VOULEZ-VOUS by ABBA

As Good As New/Voulez-Vous/I Have A Dream/Angeleyes/The King Has Lost His Crown/ Does Your Mother Know/If It Wasn't For The Nights/Chiquitita/Lovers (Live A Little Longer)/Kisses Of Fire

Sweden: Polar POLS 292 (1979).

4.05.79: **1-1-1-1-1**-2-4-7-10-16-25-26-34 (bi-weekly chart)

UK: Epic EPC 86086 (1979).

19.05.79: **1-1-1-1**-2-2-4-6-8-12-10-7-7-4-4-4-5-7-10-12-24-24-20-38-25-36-53-43-43-69-70-47-35-35-33-37-35-33-40-51-57-74-65

Australia
21.05.79: 42-11-9-**5-5-5**-7-7-8-11-14-15-17-18-23-26-28-31-33-40-42-49-54-60-59-72

Austria
15.06.79: 5-3-**2**-6-13 (monthly chart)
1.03.80: 16-9-10-6-12-19-x-11-16-8-20 (bi-weekly chart)

Canada
7.07.79: 87-72-51-47-43-25-25-25-24-19-13-7-7-**6**-9-11-9-13-13-13-8-8-7-7-7-7-7-8-8-8-

13-13-13-21-25-35-35-29-30-25-28-28-40-44-48-40-40-35-37-60-64-76

Finland
06.79: peaked at no.**1**, charted for 20 weeks (monthly chart)

France
05.79: peaked at no.**6**, charted for 16 weeks

Germany
21.05.79: **1-1-1-1**-2-2-2-4-4-4-6-5-6-5-6-6-7-8-9-14-14-15-16-17-21-22-19-23-26-42-49-35-40-38-39-39-41-37-41-58-34-28-47-45-62-40-33-38-36-42-50-48-54-55-65-x-44-x-x-51

Japan
1.05.79: 34-3-**1-1**-2-3-5-5-6-8-6-6-5-7-4-4-6-6-10-6-7-7-11-18-13-15-15-23-34-33-79-85-60-56-82-84-90 (LP chart)

Netherlands
19.05.79: **1-1-1-1**-2-2-2-2-3-7-3-5-2-**1**-2-2-8-10-14-11-23-28-35-31-28-24-31-30-33-41-33-25-39-17-8-12-7-10-9-9-12-10-22-20-31-24-30-46-45

New Zealand
25.05.79: 3-**2-2-2**-4-7-12-15-20-19-21-22-24-25-24-32-32-43-43-42

Norway
29.04.79: 11-5-**1-1-1-1-1-1**-2-3-3-4-4-4-6-8-9-12-17-18-20

Spain
04.79: peaked at no.**3**, charted for 21 weeks

Switzerland
13.05.79: peaked at no.**1**, charted for 26 weeks

USA
7.07.79: 97-71-41-36-29-27-25-23-**19-19**-31-30-29-27-27-47-61-61-59

Zimbabwe
30.06.79: 2-2-**1-1-1-1-1**-2-3-3-4-4-3-2-4-4-4-5-4-4-5-8-7-9-11-12-15-x-16-x-13

ABBA recorded their sixth studio album between March 1978 and March 1979, mostly at the new Polar Studios in Stockholm. A few tracks were composed by Benny and Björn during a break in Nassau, Bahamas, and one – what would become the album's title track – was recorded at the Criteria Studios in Miami, Florida. This was the first and last time ABBA released a song they had recorded outside Sweden.

ABBA worked on numerous songs that, for one reason or another, didn't make the final track listing of *VOULEZ-VOUS*. Snippets of several of them later appeared as part of *ABBA Undeleted*, which was released on the 1994 box-set, *THANK YOU FOR THE MUSIC*. These included *Burning My Bridges, Crying Over You, Free As A Bumble Bee, Hamlet III Parts 1 & 2, Just A Notion* and *Rubber Ball Man*.

Part of the melody of *Rubber Ball Man* was reused in what proved to be ABBA's final single, *Under Attack*, while the chorus of *Free As A Bumble Bee* was later reused in *I Know Him So Well*, which featured in Benny, Björn and Tim Rice's musical, *Chess*. *Hamlet III Parts1 & 2* later featured on Benny's debut solo album, *KLINGA MINA KLOCKER*, an instrumental folk album released in 1987. On the album, Benny retitled the track *Lottis Schottis*, a 'schottis' being a primitive Swedish dance.

Another track that failed to make the final track listing of *VOULEZ-VOUS*, but was included on the *THANK YOU FOR THE MUSIC* box-set in its final version was *Dream World*. *Dream World* was also released as the lead song on a 4-track promo CD single in Australia, Germany and Sweden, to promote the box-set. The other three tracks on the promo were *Put On Your White Sombrero, Just Like That (2:05 Edit)* and *Thank You For The Music (Doris Day Version)*.

VOULEZ-VOUS hit no.1 in Finland, Germany, Japan, the Netherlands, Norway, Sweden, Switzerland, the UK and Zimbabwe, and charted at no.2 in Austria and New Zealand, no.3 in Spain, no.5 in Australia, no.6 in Canada and France, and no.19 in the USA.

VOULEZ-VOUS was reissued on CD in 1997 with two bonus tracks, *Summer Night City* and *Lovelight*. Four years later, another reissue saw a third bonus track added, *Gimme! Gimme! Gimme! (A Man After Midnight)*.

In 2005, as part of *THE COMPLETE STUDIO RECORDINGS* box-set, *VOULEZ-VOUS* was reissued with six bonus tracks:

Summer Night City/Lovelight/Gimme! Gimme! Gimme! (A Man After Midnight)/ Estoy Soñando (I Have A Dream, Spanish Version)/Chiquitita (Spanish Version)/ Dame! Dame! Dame! (Gimme! Gimme! Gimme! (A Man After Midnight), Spanish Version)

Deluxe Edition

The deluxe edition of *VOULEZ-VOUS* was released is 2010, and came with five bonus tracks and a DVD. The five bonus tracks were:

Summer Night City (Full Length Version)/Lovelight/Gimme! Gimme! Gimme! (A Man After Midnight)/Dream World/Voulez-Vous (Extended Remix, 1979 US Promo)

The DVD featured a TV special, TV performances and interviews, plus two TV commercials and an international sleeve gallery:

- *ABBA in Switzerland* (BBC TV Special): *Take A Chance On Me, The King Has Lost His Crown, The Name Of The Game/Mamma Mia/Hole In Your Soul* (skiing/winter sports montage), *Kisses Of Fire, Lovers (Live A Little Longer), Chiquitita, Does Your Mother Know & Thank You For The Music*
- *Chiquitita* (from the Music for UNICEF concert)
- *I Have A Dream* (extended concert promo)
- *If It Wasn't For The Nights* (from the BBC's *Mike Yarwood's Christmas Show*)
- *Chiquitita* (from the BBC's *Christmas Snowtime Special*)
- Björn & Benny Interview & Viewer Phone-In (from the BBC's *Multi-Coloured Swap Shop*)
- *GREATEST HITS VOL.2* – two different TV commercials
- International Sleeve Gallery

16 ~ *TIO ÅR MED AGNETHA* by Agnetha Fältskog

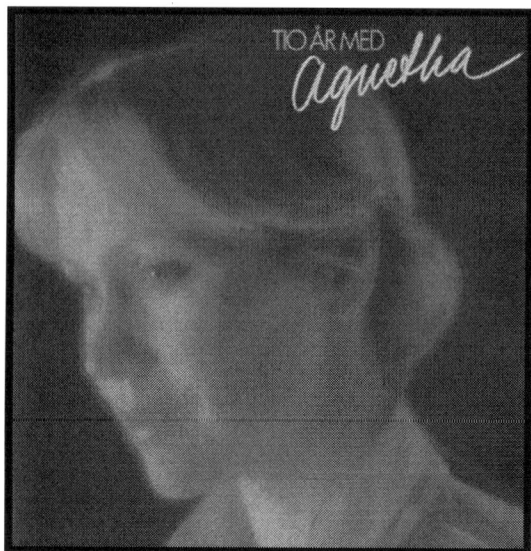

Jag Var Så Kär/Utan Dej Mitt Liv Går Vidare/Allting Har Förändrat Sej/Fram För Svenska Sommaren/Zigenarvän/Om Tårar Vore Guld/En Sång Och En Saga/Många Gånger Än/Dröm Är Dröm Och Saga Saga/Vart Ska Min Kärlek Föra/Så Glad Som Dina Ögon/En Sång Om Sorg Och Glädje/S.O.S/Doktorn/Tack För En Underbar Vanlig Dag/ När Du Tar Mej I Din Famn

Sweden: Cupol CLPS 352 (1979).

5.10.79: 39-**32**-49 (bi-weekly chart)

This compilation, the title of which translates as 'Ten Years With Agnetha', brought together some of Agnetha's Swedish hits, including her first no.1 *Jag Var Så Kär* and her solo version of *S.O.S.*

The album included one new song, *När Du Tar Mej I Din Famn* (When You Take Me In Your Arms'), which Agnetha composed herself, with lyrics by Ingela 'Pling' Forsman.

TIO ÅR MED AGNETHA was only released in Sweden, where it rose to no.32 on the album chart.

17 ~ GREATEST HITS VOL.2 by ABBA

Gimme! Gimme! Gimme! (A Man After Midnight)/Knowing Me, Knowing You/Take A Chance On Me/Money, Money, Money/Rock Me/Eagle/Angeleyes/Dancing Queen/Does Your Mother Know/Chiquitita/Summer Night City/I Wonder (Departure)/The Name Of The Game/Thank You For The Music

Sweden: Polar POLS 312 (1979).

16.11.79: 21-**20**-27-28-25 (bi-weekly chart)

UK: Epic EPC 10017 (1979).

10.11.79: 8-**1-1-1**-2-2-2-2-2-**1**-2-4-5-11-11-17-19-25-35-33-41-31-43-55-64-72-x-x-63-71-55-x-67-60
16.08.80: 75-32-39-61-40-37-43-48-53-x-64-x-x-x-x-72-62-60-49-44-44-59-62-69-65-71-x-68-x-x-x-74-45-46-53-55
25.07.81: 71-x-90-76-64-94

Australia
12.11.79: 46-34-29-28-22-23-21-**20-20**-23-23-24-32-34-46-62-72-85-96-97

Austria
15.12.79: 21-9-5-3-3-**2-2**-5-5-3-6-5-12-13-9-16-19 (bi-weekly chart)

Canada
15.12.79: 77-51-34-34-16-12-10-**8-8-8**-13-13-13-14-10-14-14-18-19-23-23-27-19-20-18-18-18-22-30-34-52-53-70

Finland
12.79: peaked at no.**5**, charted for 16 weeks (monthly chart)

France
11.79: peaked at no.**5**, charted for 9 weeks

Germany
26.11.79: 11-14-14-11-13-14-15-11-12-12-8-**6**-9-9-16-20-14-18-18-14-13-14-15-20-24-28-18-24-26-26-24-29-43-50-47-45-38-37-22-24-30-21-19-24-20-22-25-36-37-51-48-39-34-34-39-41-38-33-40-45-27-38-36-48-42-x-47-x-56-45-56-63-57

Japan
5.11.79: 19-**2-2**-5-5-5-4-4-4-3-3-3-3-3-**2-2**-3-6-3-**2**-3-3-4-5-9-12-16-14-14-17-22-21-24-30-36-39-50-58-59-54-70-65-74-83-64-65-84-95-97-96 (LP chart)

Netherlands
17.11.79: 3-**2**-3-4-6-5-11-8-11-10-8-7-12-22-25-22-35-24-33-44-42-50

New Zealand
30.11.79: 31-31-20-9-9-9-9-**3-3**-9-9-18-17-24-36-27-46

Norway
18.11.79: 28-28-**25**-37

Spain
11.79: peaked at no.**25**, charted for 3 weeks

Switzerland
11.11.79: peaked at no.**2**, charted for 23 weeks

USA
22.12.79: 95-95-56-50-**46-46**-66-84

Zimbabwe
16.02.80: 16-4-**2**-3-4-4-4-4-5-6-8-12-11-12-13-13-20-18

Just four years after releasing *GREATEST HITS*, ABBA had accumulated enough new hit singles to justify a second volume.

GREATEST HITS VOL.2 was released to coincide with ABBA's tour of North America and Europe, and included two recent non-album singles, *Summer Night City* and *Gimme! Gimme! Gimme! (A Man After Midnight)*.

As is often the case, this second greatest hits compilation wasn't as successful as the first in terms of sales, but it was still a major hit in most countries. *GREATEST HITS VOL.2* went all the way to no.1 in the UK, and charted at no.2 in Austria, Japan, the Netherlands, Switzerland and Zimbabwe, no.3 in New Zealand, no.5 in Finland and France, no.6 in Germany, no.8 in Canada, no.20 in Australia and Sweden, no.25 in Norway and Spain, and no.46 in the USA.

The Spanish edition of *GREATEST HITS VOL.2*, titled *GRANDES ÉXITOS VOL.2*, featured the Spanish versions of *I Have A Dream* (*Estoy Soñando*) and *Chiquitita*.

GREATEST HITS VOL.2 was deleted in 1992, as a major new compilation was released, titled *GOLD*.

18 ~ *GRACIAS POR LA MUSICA* by ABBA

Gracias Por La Musica/Reina Danzante/Al Andar/Dame! Dame! Dame!/Fernando/Estoy Soñando/Mamma Mia/Hasta Mañana/Conociendome Conociendote/Chiquitita

Sweden: Septima SRLM1 (1980).

GRACIAS POR LA MUSICA wasn't a hit in Sweden.

Japan
21.07.80: 31-34-**26-26**-49-47-58-74-78-78-92-96-99 (LP chart)

Spain
04.80: peaked at no.**2**, charted for 21 weeks

Following the success of the Spanish versions of *Chiquitita* and *I Have A Dream* in Latin America in 1979, particularly in Argentina and Mexico, ABBA decided to record Spanish versions of some of their other hits, for an album that was titled *GRACIAS POR LA MUSICA* ('Thank You For The Music').

Agnetha and Frida recorded a further eight of ABBA's hits in Spanish, with the lyrics being translated by Buddy and Mary McCluskey, in Sweden in January 1980. Benny and Björn didn't play an active role in the new recordings, happy to leave their engineer Michael B. Tretow in charge, which resulted in some of the Spanish mixes being noticeably different from the original English recordings.

GRACIAS POR LA MUSICA was a success in Latin America, and charted at no.2 in Spain and no.26 in Japan.

In 1992, *GRACIAS POR LA MUSICA* was deleted, and replaced with a Spanish edition of *GOLD*, titled *ORO* (Spanish for 'Gold').

There are plans to reissue *GRACIAS POR LA MUSICA* towards the end of 2014 or in 2015, as a deluxe edition, with a bonus DVD.

19 ~ SUPER TROUPER by ABBA

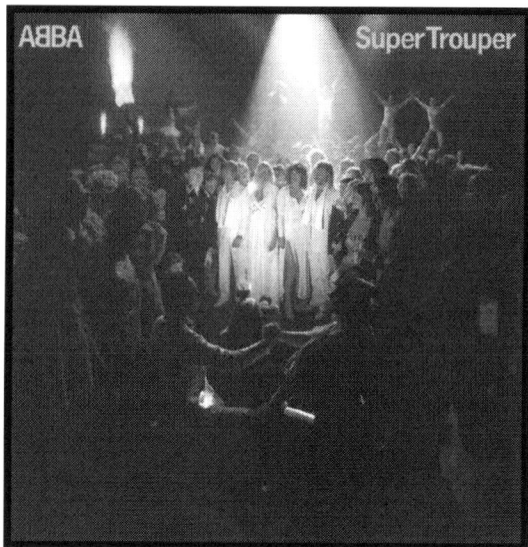

Super Trouper/The Winner Takes It All/On And On And On/Andante, Andante/Me And I/
Happy New Year/Our Last Summer/The Piper/Lay All Your Love On Me/The Way Old
Friends Do

Sweden: Polar POLS 322 (1980).

14.11.80: 2-**1-1-1-1**-3-4-10-25-37-48 (bi-weekly chart)

UK: Epic EPC 10022 (1980).

22.11.80: **1-1-1-1-1-1-1-1-1-1**-5-10-13-24-22-23-36-36-43-38-41-44-49-37-41-42-50-x-
   68-70-x-x-x-65-65-55-51-36-41-52-38-55-58-72
26.12.81: 90-90-85-79

Australia
1.12.80: 63-16-14-8-**5-5-5-5**-6-7-11-12-12-16-17-19-23-26-33-54-77-90-92-87

Austria
1.12.80: 17-**3**-4-5-**3**-7-7-13-6-6-8-6-7-13-8-8-20 (bi-weekly chart)

Canada
6.12.80: 31-19-13-9-8-**7-7**-12-12-11-10-13-13-12-12-21-21-23-22-23-34-36-36-48

Finland
12.80: peaked at no.**2**, charted for 20 weeks (monthly chart)

France
11.80: peaked at no.**8**, charted for 12 weeks

Germany
24.11.80: 14-6-**1**-2-**1**-2-3-3-2-2-2-2-4-3-4-2-2-5-6-6-9-8-12-15-17-16-26-26-23-24-34-
38-39-40-52-47-40-52

Japan
5.12.80: 12-**8**-9-**8**-**8**-12-11-10-13-13-13-15-27-32-32-41-42-47-58-79-96-100 (LP chart)

Netherlands
22.11.80: 2-**1-1-1-1-1-1-1-1-1**-2-3-6-12-19-23-22-30-24-29-47-46

New Zealand
5.12.80: 16-11-**5-5-5-5**-7-16-15-14-19-17-25-30-25-33-47

Norway
16.11.80: 3-**1-1-1**-2-2-2-2-2-2-2-3-3-3-3-5-6-9-7-11-11-14-23-18-15-15-21-21-23-28

Spain
11.80: peaked at no.**3**, charted for 23 weeks

Switzerland
16.11.80: peaked at no.**1**, charted for 26 weeks

USA
13.12.80: 64-52-32-32-28-23-22-22-20-19-18-**17-17-17**-22-27-37-40-55-54-54-53-51-66-
64-69-73-72-94

Zimbabwe
11.01.81: 14-4-2-**1-1-1-1-1-1**-2- (chart discontinued)

SUPER TROUPER was recorded the year after Agnetha and Björn divorced, between February and October 1980, and saw the group starting to explore more mature themes on songs like *The Winner Takes It All* – a song both Agnetha and Björn have denied is about their failed marriage, stating there was no winner when they split.

Unusually, ABBA chose to close the album with a live recording of *The Way Old Friends Do*, a song they regularly performed in concert during 1979.

Two songs that didn't make the final track listing of *SUPER TROUPER* were *Elaine* and *Put On Your White Sombrero*. *Elaine* was released as the B-side of *The Winner Takes It All*, but *Put On Your White Sombrero* – which was replaced by *Super Trouper* on the album – remained unreleased until 1994, when it was included on the box-set, *THANK YOU FOR THE MUSIC*.

SUPER TROUPER continued ABBA's impressive run of success in most countries, hitting no.1 in Germany, the Netherlands, Norway, Sweden, Switzerland, the UK and Zimbabwe, no.2 in Finland, no.3 in Austria and Spain, no.5 in Australia and New Zealand, no.7 in Canada, no.8 in France and Japan, and no.17 in the USA.

SUPER TROUPER was the no.1 best-selling album of 1980 in the UK.

Like all ABBA's studio albums, *SUPER TROUPER* has been reissued several times. In 1997, it was released on CD with three bonus tracks, *Gimme! Gimme! Gimme! (A Man After Midnight)*, *Elaine* and *Put On Your White Sombrero*. Four years later, *Gimme! Gimme! Gimme! (A Man After Midnight)* was dropped, and the album reissued with only *Elaine* and *Put On Your White Sombrero* as bonus tracks.

The version of *SUPER TROUPER* released as part of *THE COMPLETE STUDIO RECORDINGS* in 2005 featured three bonus tracks: *Elaine, Andante, Andante (Spanish Version)* and *Felicidad (Happy New Year, Spanish Version)*.

Deluxe Edition

The deluxe edition of *SUPER TROUPER* was released in 2011, and came with a DVD and five bonus tracks:

Elaine/On And On And On (Full Length Version, Stereo Mix)/Put On Your White Sombrero/Andante Andante (Spanish Version)/Felicidad (Happy New Year, Spanish Version)

The DVD featured:

- ABBA on German TV (ZDF's *Show Express*): *The Winner Takes It All, Super Trouper & On And On And On*
- *Happy New Year* (SVT)
- *Words & Music* (documentary)
- *Somewhere In The Crowd There's You – On Location With ABBA*
- *Super Trouper* (remastered music video)
- *Happy New Year* (remastered music video)
- *SUPER TROUPER* – two different UK TV commercials
- International Sleeve Gallery

20 ~ THE MUST OF ABBA by ABBA

Fernando/Money, Money, Money/Voulez-Vous/I Have A Dream/Gimme! Gimme! Gimme! (A Man After Midnight)/Waterloo/The Name Of The Game/I Do, I Do, I Do, I Do, I Do/ Chiquitita/Ring Ring/Dancing Queen/Take A Chance On Me/Knowing Me, Knowing You/ Does Your Mother Know/Super Trouper/The Winner Takes It All

France: Vogue VBTV.08 (1981).

02.81: peaked at no.**13**, charted for 5 weeks

This compilation was only released in France and Belgium, and rose to no.13 in France, but it didn't quite sell well enough to achieve Top 10 status.

21 ~ *A WIE ABBA* / *A VAN ABBA* by ABBA

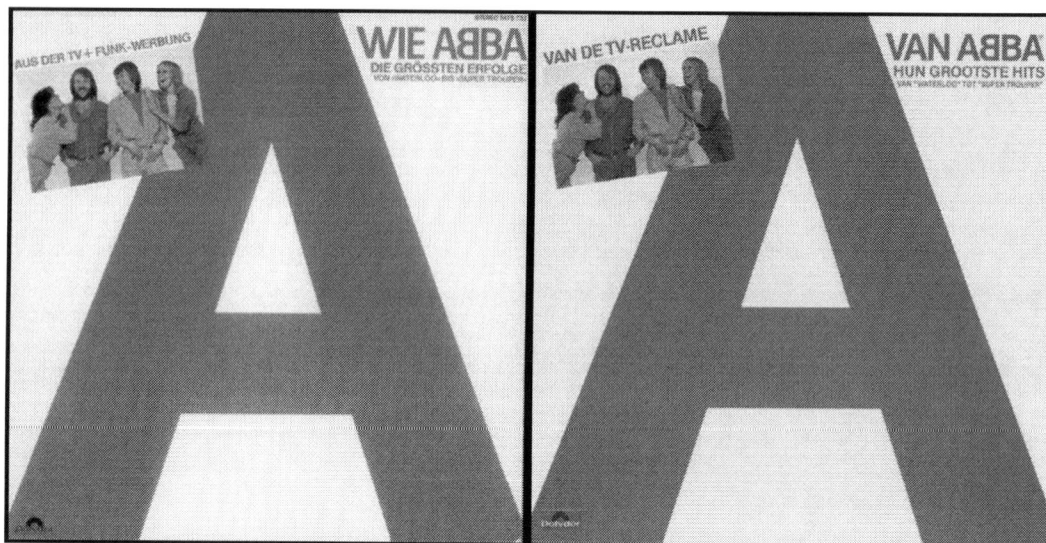

Super Trouper/Knowing Me, Knowing You/Waterloo/Take A Chance On Me/Mamma Mia/I Have A Dream/The Name Of The Game/Fernando/The Winner Takes It All/ Dancing Queen/S.O.S/Gimme! Gimme! Gimme! (A Man After Midnight)/I Do, I Do, I Do, I Do, I Do/Money, Money, Money/Summer Night City/Chiquitita

Germany: Polydor 2475 732 (1981).

11.05.81: 60-5-4-3-**1-1-1-1-1**-2-2-7-8-8-12-15-17-16-26-26-23-30-23-32-38-35-32-34- 33-32-29-23-24-34-38-39-40-52-47-40-52

Austria
1.06.81: 2-**1-1-1-1**-5-7-9-12-14-17-20 (bi-weekly chart)

Netherlands
20.06.81: 2-**1-1-1-1-1-1-1-1**-3-2-7-7-8-8-10-24-20-30
12.12.81: 47-48-x-x-x-19

Switzerland
1.06.81: peaked at no.**3**, charted for 8 weeks

Only released in a few countries, this compilation hit no.1 in Austria, Germany and the Netherlands, and charted at no.3 in Switzerland.

22 ~ *NU TÄNDAS TUSEN JULELIJUS* by Agnetha & Linda

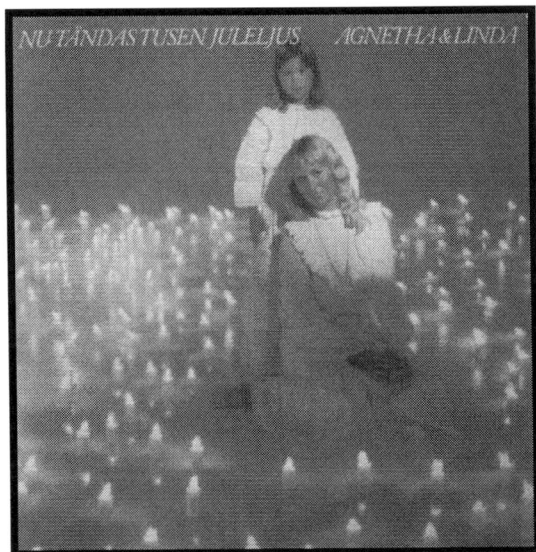

Nej Se Det Snöar/Bjällerklang/Nu Tändas Tusen Juleljus/Två Små Röda Luvor/Nu Står Julen Vid Snöig Port/Jag Såg Mamma Kyssa Tomten/När Juldagsmorgon Glimmar/ Medley (Nu Har Vi Ljus Här I Vårt Hus/Tre Små Pepparkaksgubbar/Räven Raskar Över Isen/Vi Äro Musikanter/Hej Tomtegubbar/Jungfru Jungfru Kär/Nu Är Det Jul Igen)/Hej Mitt Vinterland/Så Milt Lyser Stjärnan/Mössens Julafton/När Det Lider Mot Jul

Sweden: Polar POLS 328 (1981).

8.12.81: 38-10-**6**-31 (bi-weekly chart)

Titled after a popular Swedish Christmas carol, *NU TÄNDAS TUSEN JULELIJUS* ('Now A Thousand Christmas Candles Are Lit'), is a festive album Agnetha recorded with her and Björn's daughter, Linda.

The album, which Agnetha co-produced with Michael B. Tretow, ABBA's sound engineer, was recorded in November 1980, when Linda was just seven years old. As it was too late to release the album that year, it was postponed, and issued the following October.

NU TÄNDAS TUSEN JULELIJUS included Swedish versions of Christmas classics like *Jingle Bells* and *Santa Claus Is Comin' To Town*, and it gave Agnetha and her daughter a no.6 hit in Sweden, where it went on to become one of the country's best-selling Swedish Christmas albums.

Although it wasn't a hit, Agnetha recorded a children's album titled *KOM FÖLJ MED I VÅR KARUSELL* ('Come Join Us On Our Carousel') with her and Björn's son, Christian, in 1987 – Christian was nine years old at the time.

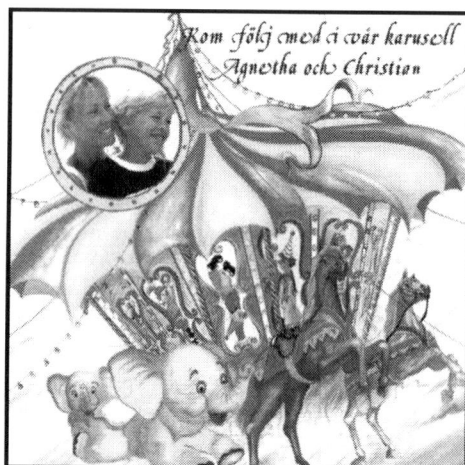

23 ~ THE VISITORS by ABBA

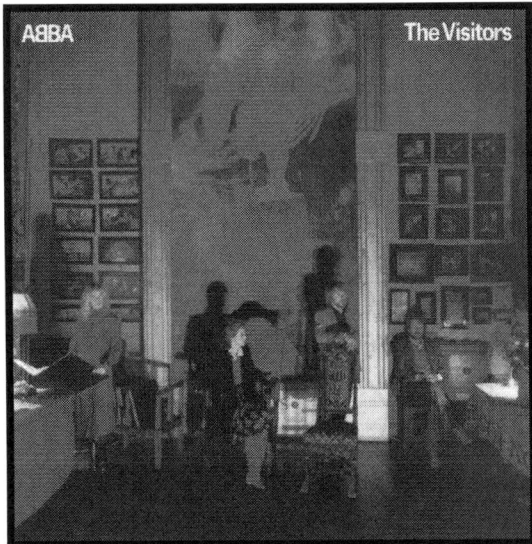

The Visitors/Head Over Heels/When All Is Said And Done/Soldiers/I Let The Music Speak/One Of Us/Two For The Price Of One/Slipping Through My Fingers/Like An Angel Passing Through My Room

Sweden: Polar POLS 342 (1981).

22.12.81: **1-1-1-1**-4-10-33 (bi-weekly chart)
27.04.12: 18-55 (Deluxe Edition)

UK: Epic EPC 10032 (1981).

19.12.81: **1-1-1**-2-3-4-6-11-15-21-19-26-25-28-28-37-77-64-87-88-94
5.05.12: 62 (Deluxe Edition)

Australia
28.12.81: 37-37-26-**22**-29-36-39-56-63-66-75-99

Austria
1.01.82: 19-6-**3**-5-9-11-18-9-16 (bi-weekly chart)

Canada
26.12.81: 41-19-**18-18**-19-20-20-25-26-34-42

Finland
01.82: peaked at no.**3**, charted for 16 weeks (monthly chart)

France
12.81: peaked at no.**12**, charted for 9 weeks

Germany
21.12.81: 11-**1-1-1-1-1**-2-3-7-7-8-8-9-6-8-15-20-20-25-26-37-39-49-46-53-53-55-51-46-57
7.05.12: 75 (Deluxe Edition)

Japan
20.12.81: 40-13-**12-12-12**-16-18-21-19-33-36-40-64-66-79-66-82 (LP chart)

Netherlands
12.12.81: 2-**1**-2-2-2-2-2-3-2-3-4-4-5-7-7-10-12-15-24-35-31-48-36
28.04.12: 55 (Deluxe Edition)

New Zealand
15.01.82: 23-**19**-29-29-44

Norway
6.12.81: 15-**1-1-1-1-1-1-1**-6-6-7-9-13-16

South Africa
9.01.82: 11-9-11-9-7-11-8-**3**-6-7-10-10-12-14-16-17-18-20

Spain
11.81: peaked at no.**3**, charted for 15 weeks
29.04.12: 94 (Deluxe Edition)

Switzerland
13.12.81: peaked at no.**1**, charted for 17 weeks
6.05.12: 93 (Deluxe Edition)

USA
9.01.82: 75-45-37-35-31-**29-29**-36-43-48-80

Zimbabwe
23.01.82: 2-3-**1**-3-5-6-14-13-17-13-20-17-16-15-11-18-18-x-14-20-14-13-x-x-15

The four members of ABBA entered the recording studio, to work on what would prove to be their final studio album as a group, in March 1981 – just a month after Benny and Frida formally announced, like Agnetha and Björn, they were splitting up and filing for divorce. Understandably, the sessions didn't progress quite as smoothly as they did when Agnetha/Björn and Frida/Benny were happily married couples, with Björn later admitting, 'It could be frosty sometimes'.

Nevertheless, the quartet tried to put their differences aside, and by November 1981 *THE VISITORS* was completed. The album had a noticeably more mature sound than previous ABBA albums and, almost inevitably, included a couple of songs that explored troubled relationships, *One Of Us* and *When All Is Said And Done*.

THE VISITORS, although not as successful as some of ABBA's previous albums, hit no.1 in Germany, the Netherlands, Norway, Sweden, Switzerland, the UK and Zimbabwe, and charted at no.3 in Finland, South Africa and Spain, no.12 in France and Japan, no.18 in Canada, no.19 in New Zealand, no.22 in Australia and no.29 in the USA.

THE VISITORS was reissued on CD in 1997 with four bonus tracks: *Should I Laugh Or Cry*, *The Day Before You Came*, *Under Attack* and *You Owe Me One*. Four years later, the album was reissued again, with *Cassandra* replacing *You Owe Me One* as one of the four bonus tracks.

In 2005, when it was reissued as part of *THE COMPLETE STUDIO RECORDINGS* box-set, *THE VISITORS* featured seven bonus tracks:

Should I Laugh Or Cry/No Hay A Quien Culpar (When All Is said And Done, Spanish Version)/Se Me Está Escapando (Slipping Through My Fingers, Spanish Version)/The Day Before You Came/Cassandra/Under Attack/You Owe Me One

Deluxe Edition

The deluxe edition of *THE VISITORS*, released in 2012, came with a DVD and seven bonus tracks:

Should I Laugh Or Cry/I Am The City/You Owe Me One/Cassandra/Under Attack/The Day Before You Came/From A Twinkling Star To A Passing Angel (Demos)

The demo medley, *From A Twinkling Star To A Passing Angel*, was the first previously unheard ABBA recording to be released since 1994.

The DVD featured the usual mix of TV appearances, TV commercials and an international sleeve gallery:

- *Two For The Price Of One* (from *Dick Cavett Meets ABBA*)
- *Slipping Through My Fingers* (from *Dick Cavett Meets ABBA*)
- *When All Is Said And Done* (Original Promo Clip)

- ABBA in London, November 1982 (from the BBC's *The Late Late Breakfast Show*)
- ABBA in Stockholm, November 1982 (from SVT's *Nöjesmaskinen*)
- *THE VISITORS* – Australia & UK TV commercials
- *THE SINGLES – THE FIRST TEN YEARS* – Australia & UK TV commercials
- International Sleeve Gallery

Sales-wise, *THE VISITORS* is the most successful of the deluxe editions – it charted at no.18 in Sweden, no.55 in the Netherlands, no.62 in the UK, no.75 in Germany, no.93 in Switzerland and no.94 in Spain.

24 ~ SOMETHING'S GOING ON by Frida

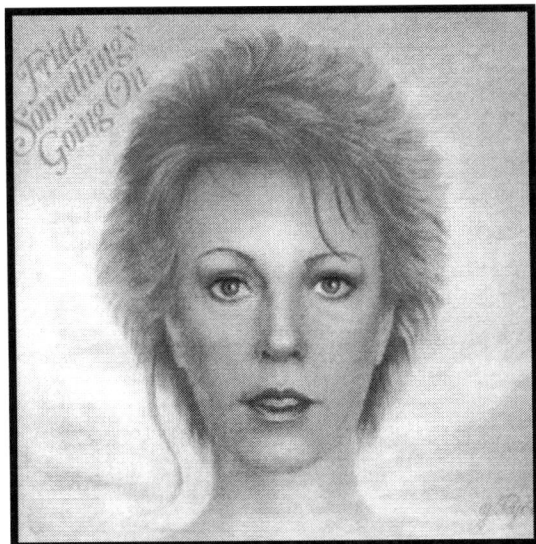

Tell Me It's Over/I See Red/I Got Something/Strangers/To Turn The Stone/I Know There's Something Going On/Threnody/Baby Don't You Cry No More/The Way You Do/You Know What I Mean/Here We'll Stay

Sweden: Polar POLS 355 (1982).

28.09.82: **1-1**-2-3-4-9-9-9-19-37 (bi-weekly chart)

UK: Epic EPC 85966 (1982).

18.09.82: **18**-20-19-40-60-85-95

Australia
11.10.82: 50-55-57-50-41-**40**-42-63-72-90-100

Austria
15.10.82: **10** (bi-weekly chart)

Finland
10.82: peaked at no.**3**, charted for 16 weeks (monthly chart)

France
12.82: peaked at no.**22** (number of weeks unknown)

Germany
27.09.82: 57-30-13-**12**-16-16-30-21-26-36-32-27-43-34-55-58

Netherlands
18.09.82: 12-**2**-4-13-6-5-9-13-14-18-33-x-46-36

Norway
19.09.82: 7-**2-2-2**-4-7-3-4-8-7-7-15-23-27

Switzerland
26.09.82: peaked at no.**3**, charted for 14 weeks

USA
12.02.83: 95-77-68-59-51-47-43-43-**41-41**-56-78-83

Frida recorded her third solo album – her first in English – in February and March 1982, around the time she and Benny filed for divorce.

Having heard *In The Air Tonight* by Phil Collins, and fallen in love with his 1981 album, *FACE VALUE*, Frida was keen to work with him on her new album. Collins agreed, and in one TV interview he commented, 'Frida and I had something in common as far as our divorces were concerned – we were both the injured party.'

Over 500 songs were submitted, for consideration, when Polar sent out invitations to publishing companies worldwide. Among the songs to make the final selection were Bryan Ferry's *The Way You Do*, Rod Argent's *Baby Don't You Cry No More*, Tomas Ledin's *I Got Something* and Pete Bellotte & Giorgio Moroder's *To Turn The Stone*, which they had originally recorded with Donna Summer. Frida also recorded a re-worked version of *You Know What I Mean*, a track Collins had composed and recorded for his *FACE VALUE* album.

Boosted by the success of the lead single, *I Know There's Something Going On*, which featured Collins on drums, *SOMETHING'S GOING ON* hit no.1 in Sweden, no.2 in the Netherlands and Norway, no.3 in Finland and Switzerland, no.10 in Austria, no.12 in Germany, no.18 in the UK, no.22 in France, no.40 in Australia and no.41 in the USA.

SOMETHING'S GOING ON went on to sell around 1.5 million copies worldwide, making it the most successful solo album released by any member of ABBA.

SOMETHING'S GOING ON was remastered and reissued in 2005 with two bonus tracks: *I Know There's Something Going On (Single Edit)* and *Here We'll Stay (Solo Version)*.

25 ~ THE SINGLES – THE FIRST TEN YEARS by ABBA

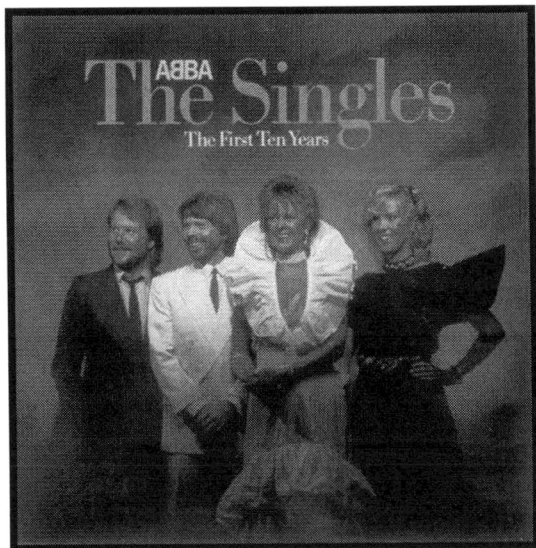

LP1: *Ring Ring/Waterloo/So Long/I Do, I Do, I Do, I Do, I Do/S.O.S/Mamma Mia/ Fernando/Dancing Queen/Money, Money, Money/Knowing Me, Knowing You/The Name Of The Game/Take A Chance On Me/Summer Night City*

LP2: *Chiquitita/Does Your Mother Know/Voulez-Vous/Gimme! Gimme! Gimme! (A Man After Midnight)/I Have A Dream/The Winner Takes It All/Super Trouper/One Of Us/The Day Before You Came/Under Attack*

Sweden: Polar POLMD 400/1 (1982).

7.12.82: 42-**29**-30 (bi-weekly chart)

UK: Epic ABBA 10 (1982).

20.11.82: 6-**1**-2-2-3-2-2-2-9-14-21-22-27-46-51-60-51-64-81-91-66-x-76

Australia
20.12.82: 71-78-25-**18**-25-41-59-67-74-69-63-58-55-48-47-60-62-59-62-69-80-93
19.09.83: 91-73-72-60-60-67-90

Canada
4.12.82: 94-69-52-33-25-**24-24**-34-40-38-43-48-50-48-48-68-76-78-83

Finland
01.83: peaked at no.**11**, charted for 8 weeks (monthly chart)

France
11.82: peaked at no.**6**, charted for 10 weeks

Germany
29.11.82: 52-10-**5**-7-8-10-9-9-10-13-20-24-30-50-53-64-57-62

Netherlands
20.11.82: 14-**5**-6-8-8-6-**5**-**5**-6-8-15-21-42-42-40

New Zealand
21.01.83: 49
4.03.83: 22-**5**-6-9-15-39-45

Norway
5.12.82: **33**

South Africa
4.12.82: 19-5-3-3-**1**-**1**-**1**-3-4-5-6-8-9-9-11-12-16-20

Spain
03.83: peaked at no.**10**, charted for 14 weeks

Switzerland
28.11.82: peaked at no.**4**, charted for 12 weeks

USA
25.12.82: 94-94-87-80-75-68-**62**-**62**-**62**-**62**-**62**-**62**-79-91

In May and June 1982, the four members of ABBA came together, to start work on a new album with the working title 'Opus 10'. Three new songs – *I Am The City*, *Just Like That* and *You Owe Me One* – were recorded, but Benny and Björn weren't happy with the way the sessions were progressing, and everyone agreed to take a summer break.

ABBA returned to the studio in early August, and it wasn't long before all four members agreed to shelve plans for a new album, and to release a compilation to target the Christmas market instead. A further three new songs were recorded, with two of them – *The Day Before You Came* and *Under Attack* – being released as singles, as well as featuring on the compilation, *THE SINGLES – THE FIRST TEN YEARS*. The third new song, *Cassandra*, was released as the B-side of *The Day Before You Came*.

The track listing of *THE SINGLES – THE FIRST TEN YEARS* featured 23 ABBA hits in chronological order of release, from *Ring Ring* to *Under Attack*. ABBA promoted the double album with appearances on several TV shows, including *Saturday Superstore* and *The Late Late Breakfast Show* in the UK, *Show Express* in Germany and *Nöjesmaskinen* in Sweden.

Although no one knew it at the time, ABBA made their final TV appearance as a group on 11th December 1982, when they appeared on *The Late Late Breakfast Show* via a live TV link with a studio in Stockholm.

ABBA never officially announced their split as a group and throughout 1983 and 1984, even though both Agnetha and Frida were working on solo projects and Benny and Björn were involved with their first musical, *Chess*, there was talk of a reunion and a new ABBA album. It didn't happen. Thirty years on, it still hasn't happened, and all four members of ABBA have made it clear it is unlikely ever to happen.

26 ~ WRAP YOUR ARMS AROUND ME by Agnetha Fältskog

The Heat Is On/Can't Shake Loose/Shame/Stay/Once Burned, Twice Shy/Mr Persuasion/ Wrap Your Arms Around Me/To Love/I Wish Tonight Could Last For Ever/Man/Take Good Care Of Your Children/Stand By My Side

Sweden: Polar POLS 365 (1983).

14.06.83: **1-1**-2-2-3-4-9-16-26-33 (bi-weekly chart)
10.01.84: 45 (bi-weekly chart)

UK: Epic EPC 25505 (1983).

11.06.83: 23-**18**-21-38-49-61-79-99-70-86-52-88-98

Australia
19.09.83: 84-65-**49**-82

Finland
07.83: peaked at no.**4**, charted for 12 weeks (monthly chart)

France
12.83: peaked at no.**47** (number of weeks unknown)

Germany
27.06.83: 34-18-21-17-16-23-27-27-29-35-29-31-36-**13**-16-17-19-19-25-31-34-37-52-56-55-61

Netherlands
11.06.83: 25-**4**-10-11-14-28-21-10-6-6-5-6-8-18-17-15-22-37

Norway
12.06.83: 7-4-3-2-**1-1-1-1-1**-2-2-4-4-7-6-7-13-16

South Africa
14.01.84: 18-**15-15**-18

Switzerland
19.06.83: peaked at no.**9**, charted for 7 weeks

USA
WRAP YOUR ARMS AROUND ME didn't enter the Top 100 in the USA, however, it did spend 11 weeks on the Billboard 200, peaking at no.102.

Agnetha recorded her first English album between January and March 1983 at the Polar Studios in Stockholm, working with producer Mike Chapman, who had previously enjoyed success with acts including Mud, Suzi Quatro and Sweet.

In contrast to her Swedish albums, which she mostly composed herself, *WRAP YOUR ARMS AROUND ME* included just one track Agnetha wrote, *Man*. The album hit no.1 in Norway and Sweden, and boosted by the hit singles *Can't Shake Loose*, *The Heat Is On* and *Wrap Your Arms Around Me*, it gave Agnetha her first taste of international success as a solo artist. The album charted at no.4 in Finland and the Netherlands, no.9 in Switzerland, no.13 in Germany, no.15 in South Africa, no.18 in the UK, no.47 in France and no.49 in Australia.

WRAP YOUR ARMS AROUND ME was remastered and reissued in 2005 with five bonus tracks:

Never Again/It's So Nice To Be Rich/P & B/The Heat Is On (Super Dance Music Mix)/ Ya Nunca Más (Never Again, Spanish Version)

27 ~ I LOVE ABBA by ABBA

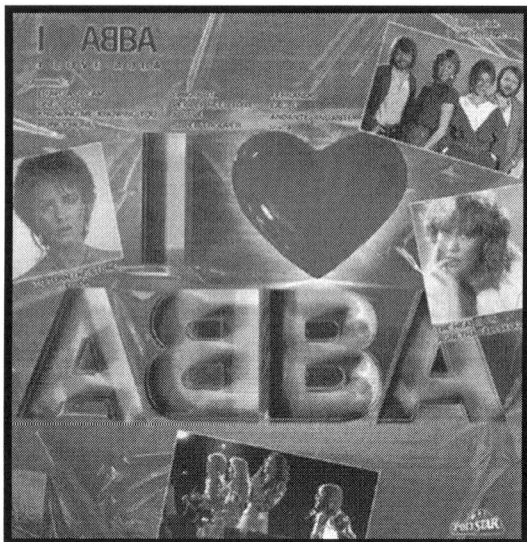

I Have A Dream/One Of Us/Knowing Me, Knowing You/Andante, Andante/Honey Honey/ People Need Love/Chiquitita/To Turn The Stone/Arrival/Super Trouper/Move On/ Fernando/When I Kissed The Teacher/Eagle/When All Is Said And Done/The Heat It On

Germany: Polystar 815 601-2 (1983).

17.10.83: 59-18-11-13-**10**-17-28-36-33-43-57-64

Austria
1.12.83: **5**-16 (bi-weekly chart)

France
12.83: peaked at no.**12**, charted for 3 weeks

Switzerland
6.11.83: **14**-20-28

This compilation was only released in France, Germany and the Benelux countries and, as well as the usual ABBA hits, it featured Frida's *To Turn The Stone* and Agnetha's *The Heat Is On*.

 I LOVE ABBA charted at no.5 in Austria, no.10 in Germany, no.12 in France and no.14 in Switzerland.

28 ~ THANK YOU FOR THE MUSIC by ABBA

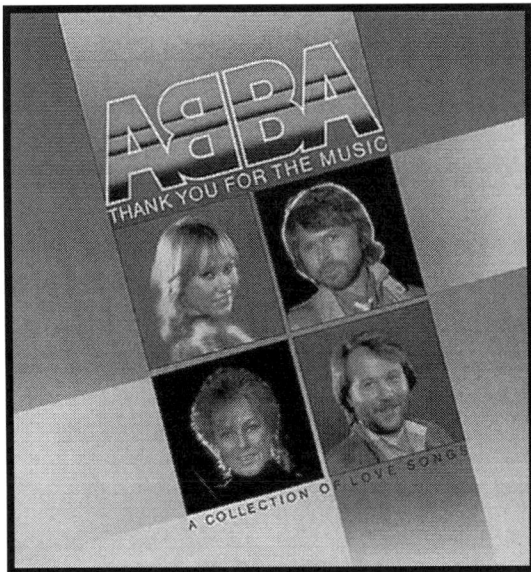

I Have A Dream/Our Last Summer/The Day Before You Came/Chiquitita/Should I Laugh Or Cry/The Way Old Friends Do/Thank You For The Music/My Love, My Life/I Wonder (Departure)/Happy New Year/Slipping Through My Fingers/Fernando (Spanish Version)/One Man, One Woman/Eagle

UK: Epic EPC 10043 (1983).

19.11.83: 44-28-**17**-19-21-28-28-38-45-73-73-100

Sub-titled 'A Collection Of Love Songs', *THANK YOU FOR THE MUSIC*, which included the Spanish version of *Fernando*, was only released in the UK, where it charted at no.17 – thus ending ABBA's run of eight consecutive no.1 albums.

To promote the album, the title track was released as a single for the first time in the UK, but it only rose to no.33 on the chart.

29 ~ FROM ABBA WITH LOVE by ABBA

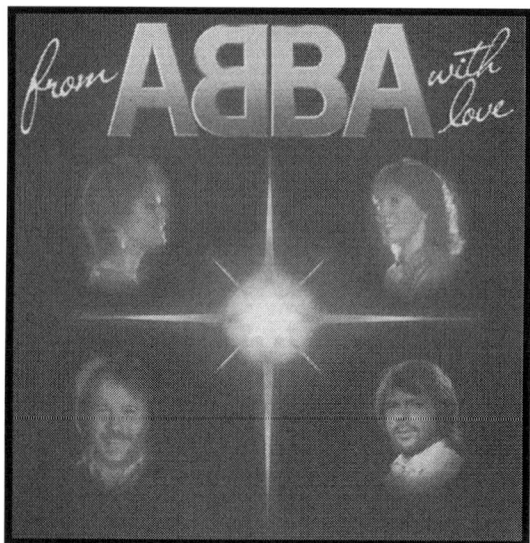

One Of Us/Lay All Your Love On Me/Eagle/The Winner Takes It All/Head Over Heels/To Turn The Stone/Voulez-Vous/My Love, My Life/Wrap Your Arms Around Me/Cassandra/ The Day Before You Came/Elaine/Slipping Through My Fingers/Thank You For The Music

Netherlands: Polydor 817 466-1 (1984).

21.04.84: 10-9-9-**6**-10-10-13-28-32-36-50

This Dutch compilation, like *I LOVE ABBA*, featured a solo track by both Agnetha and Frida, alongside a selection of ABBA hits, album tracks and B-sides. Once again, Frida's *To Turn The Stone* was included, but this time Agnetha's *Wrap Your Arms Around Me* was chosen ahead of *The Heat Is On*.

    FROM ABBA WITH LOVE achieved no.6 in the Netherlands.

30 ~ SHINE by Frida

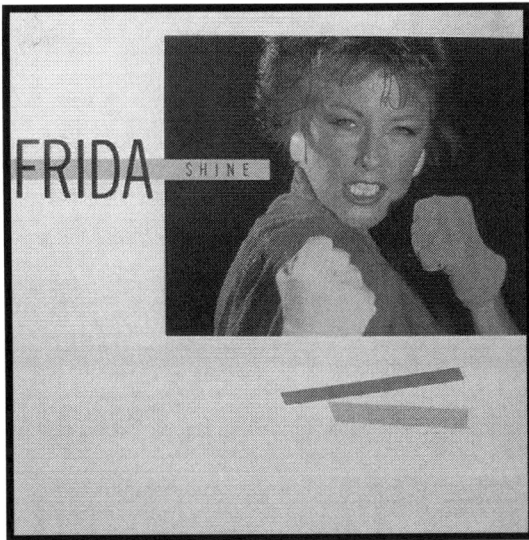

Shine/One Little Lie/The Face/Twist In the Dark/Slowly/Heart Of The Country/Come To Me (I Am Woman)/Chemistry Tonight/Don't Do It/Comfort Me

Sweden: Polar POLS 390 (1984).

28.09.84: **6-6**-12-33-46 (bi-weekly chart)

UK: Epic EPC 26178 (1984).

20.10.84: **67**

Germany
1.10.84: 65-x-**49**

Netherlands
29.09.84: **21**-25-34

Norway
19.09.84: 12-12-**10**-12

Switzerland
7.10.84: **29**

Frida's fourth solo album, and what is her most recent in English, was recorded in Paris in February and March 1984. Originally, following the success of *SOMETHING'S GOING ON*, Frida had wanted to work with Phil Collins again, but due to his Genesis commitments he was unavailable, so she teamed up with producer Steve Lillywhite instead.

The resultant album, titled *SHINE*, included *Don't Do It*, a track Frida composed herself – a first, as she wasn't known as a song-writer, and had never released one of her own songs before. Another track, *Slowly*, was written by Benny and Björn, and this remains the most recent recording of one of their compositions by either Agnetha or Frida.

One Little Lie, *The Face* and *Chemistry Tonight* were all co-written by the late Kirsty MacColl, who also sang backing vocals on the album.

SHINE, with only the title track achieving Top 40 status as a single, couldn't match the success of *SOMETHING'S GOING ON*, but the album charted at no.6 in Sweden, no.10 in Norway, no.21 in the Netherlands and no.29 in Switzerland.

Come To Me (I Am Woman), *Heart Of The Country* and *Twist In The Dark* were all released as singles, in one or more countries, but neither was more than a minor hit anywhere.

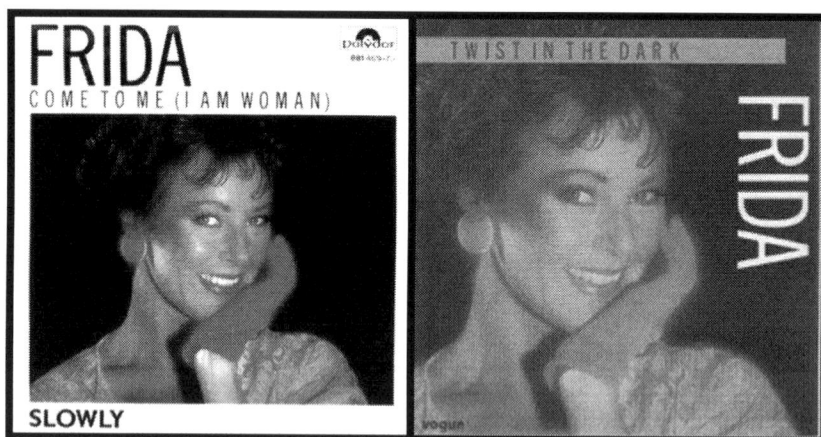

Frida admitted, keen as she was to distance herself from the 'pop' sound associated with ABBA, her album *SHINE* was perhaps 'a bit too modern' for its time.

SHINE was remastered and reissued in 2005, with two bonus tracks: *That's Tough* and *Shine (Extended Mix)*.

Frida co-wrote *That's Touch* with her son, Hans Fredriksson, and Kirsty MacColl.

31 ~ CHESS by Benny Andersson, Tim Rice & Björn Ulvaeus

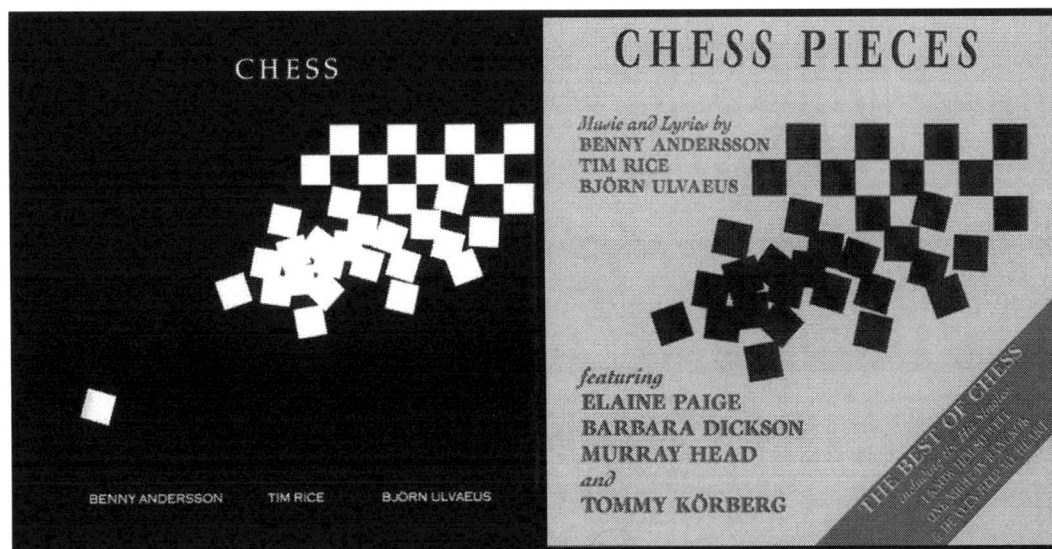

Act 1: *Merano/The Russian And Molokov/Where I Want To Be/Opening Ceremony/ Quartet (A Model Of Decorum And Tranquillity)/The American And Florence/Nobody's Side/Chess/Mountain Duet/Florence Quits/Embassy Lament/Anthem*

Act 2: *Bangkok/One Night In Bangkok/Heaven Help My Heart/Argument/I Know Him So Well/The Deal (No Deal)/Pity The Child/Endgame/Epilogue: You And I/The Story Of Chess*

Sweden: Polydor 847 445-2 (1984).

9.11.84: 4-**1-1-1**-2-2-4-6-13-22-42-46-x-43-46-27 (bi-weekly chart)

UK: RCA PL 70500 (1984).

10.11.84: 89
19.01.85: 54-35-27-21-11-12-**10**-17-20-22-28-49-43-x-x-99
22.06.85: 99
2.11.85: 100-x-87-100 (*CHESS PIECES*)

Australia
4.03.85: peaked at no.**35**, charted for 27 weeks

Austria
15.02.85: 21-**17**-24-29 (bi-weekly chart)

Germany
3.12.84: peaked at no.**6**, charted for 27 weeks

Netherlands
17.11.84: 42-**30**-40
19.01.85: 45-36-39-43-44-42-46-31-43-37-36-43-48-47

New Zealand
31.03.85: 49-47-44-x-21-**20**-48-43-24-21-**20**-27-27-32-26-33-32-x-32-31-31-28-23-29-
    32-32-44-42-38-37-34-36

Norway
25.12.84: 17-17-15-8-10-7-5-5-5-5-5-7-**3**-5-4-7-6-5-8-8-13-20-20-20-19
30.11.96: 35-22-22-36-29-36

South Africa
23.02.85: 19-17-8-7-5-5-**4-4-4-4-4-4-4-4-4-4-4**-5-6-7-11-16-18

Switzerland
20.01.85: 17-8-5-**3**-5-5-6-6-7-9-10-10-11-13-20-28

Zimbabwe
12.05.85: **8**

Having released what would prove to be the final ABBA studio album, *THE VISITORS*, Benny and Björn were eager to expand their horizons and write a musical. However, as neither had any experience in the field, they recognised they couldn't do it on their own. At the same time Tim Rice, who had enjoyed success with *Joseph And The Amazing Technicolor Dreamcoat*, *Jesus Christ Superstar* and *Evita*, was looking for a new project.

Benny and Björn first met with Tim Rice in Stockholm on 15th December 1981, and the trio quickly agreed to work together, but it was another year before the project really got started. Set during the Cold War, the musical that became *Chess* focussed on two chess grandmasters, one American and one Russian.

Benny and Björn composed the music, with Björn often coming up with 'dummy' lyrics (one, 'one night in Bangkok makes a hard man humble', was used in the final version of *One Night In Bangkok*), and Tim Rice writing the lyrics. Benny and Björn weren't afraid to use elements of ABBA songs, for example, the chorus of *I Know Him So Well* was borrowed from *I Am An A*, a song ABBA performed in concert in 1977 but never released. Another song, *Heaven Help My Heart*, was originally recorded by Agnetha as *Every Good Man*, although the lyrics were completely re-written for the final version.

CHESS, which is generally described as a concept album, was released in 1984. The principal vocalists on the album included Murray Head (the American), Tommy Körberg (the Russian), Elaine Paige (the Russian's mistress), Barbara Dickson (the Russian's estranged wife) and Björn Skifs (the Arbiter).

The album produced two major hit singles, Murray Head's *One Night In Bangkok* and *I Know Him So Well*, by Elaine Paige and Barbara Dickson. *Nobody's Side* and *Heaven Help My Heart*, both by Elaine Paige, and Björn Skifs's *The Arbiter* were all released as singles as well, but weren't hits.

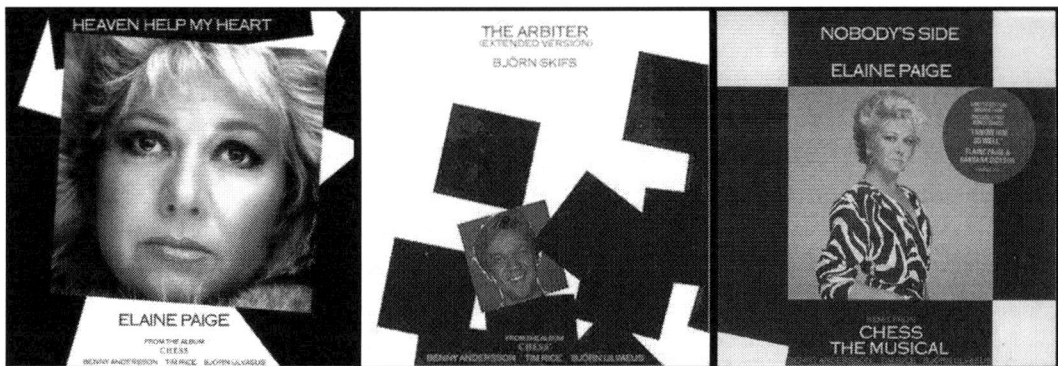

CHESS went to no.1 in Sweden, and charted at no.3 in Norway and Switzerland, no.4 in South Africa, no.6 in Germany, no.8 in Zimbabwe, no.10 in the UK, no.17 in Austria, no.20 in New Zealand, no.30 in the Netherlands and no.35 in Australia.

The musical *Chess* premiered on 14th May 1986 at the Prince Edward Theatre in London, and the production ran for three years. Murray Head, Elaine Paige and Tommy Körberg reprised their roles on stage, but due to prior commitments Barbara Dickson was replaced by Siobhan McCarthy.

A much changed version of *Chess* was previewed on Broadway on 11th April 1988, and opened on 28th April, but disappointing ticket sales meant it only ran for two months.

CHESS PIECES, a 'best of' version of *CHESS*, was released in 1985 in the UK and continental Europe, with the following track listing:

Merano/The Arbiter/Nobody's Side/Chess/Mountain Duet/Embassy Lament/Anthem/ One Night In Bangkok/Heaven Help My Heart/I Know Him So Well/Pity The Child/ You And I/The Story Of Chess

32 ~ EYES OF A WOMAN by Agnetha Fältskog

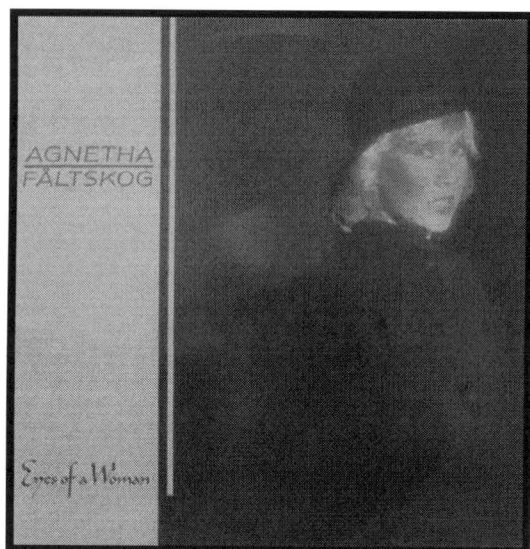

One Way Love/Eyes Of A Woman/Just One Heart/I Won't Let You Go/The Angels Cry/ Click Track/We Should Be Together/I Won't Be Leaving You/Save Me (Why Don't Ya)/I Keep Turning Off Lights/We Move As One

Sweden: Polar POLS 385 (1985).

5.04.85: **2**-3-7-7-11-16-21-34 (bi-weekly chart)

UK: Epic EPC 26446 (1985).

4.05.85: **38**-63-99

Germany
15.04.85: 43-52-41-**30**-31-33-40-38-52-49-62

Netherlands
6.04.85: 25-**19**-21-39

Norway
15.04.85: 15-15-15-**14**

Agnetha recorded her second English album in October and November 1984 – again, the album was recorded at Polar Studios in Stockholm, but this time Agnetha worked with 10cc's Eric Stewart.

Like *WRAP YOUR ARMS AROUND ME* before it, *EYES OF A WOMAN* included only one song Agnetha had composed herself, the hit single *I Won't Let You Go*, which Eric Stewart penned the lyrics for.

Agnetha also composed *You're There*, one of two songs that didn't make the final track listing. The second, *Turn The World Around*, was composed by Randy Edelman. Although they failed to make the album, both tracks were released as B-sides.

With only one hit single, *EYES OF A WOMAN* struggled to match the success of *WRAP YOUR ARMS AROUND ME* – it charted at no.2 in Sweden, no.14 in Norway, no.19 in the Netherlands, no.30 in Germany and no.38 in the UK, but it wasn't a hit in most countries.

EYES OF A WOMAN was remastered and reissued in 2005, with five bonus tracks:

You're There/Turn The World Around/I Won't Let You Go (Extended Version)/The Way You Are/Fly Like An Eagle

The Way You Are and *Fly Like An Eagle* are both duets Agnetha recorded with Ola Håkansson.

GEMINI by Gemini

Slowly/Too Much Love Is Wasted/Slow Emotion/Just Like That/Falling/Have Mercy/Live On The Love/In The Middle Of Nowhere/Another You, Another Me

Sweden: Polar POLS 400 (1985).

29.11.85: **9-9**-12-14-27-42 (bi-weekly chart)

UK: Polydor POLD 5189 (1985).

GEMINI wasn't a hit in the UK.

As well as producing the self-titled debut album by Gemini, the brother/sister duo Anders and Karin Glenmark, Benny and Björn wrote six of the nine tracks on the album; Björn also co-wrote *Live On The Love* with Anders Glenmark.

The Benny/Björn tracks included a cover of *Slowly*, which Frida had recorded for her *SOMETHING'S GOING ON* album, and *Just Like That*, a re-worked version of one of six tracks ABBA recorded between May and August 1982 for a follow-up to *THE VISITORS*, before the project was shelved.

GEMINI achieved Top 10 status in Sweden, but it wasn't a hit anywhere else.

GEMINISM by Gemini

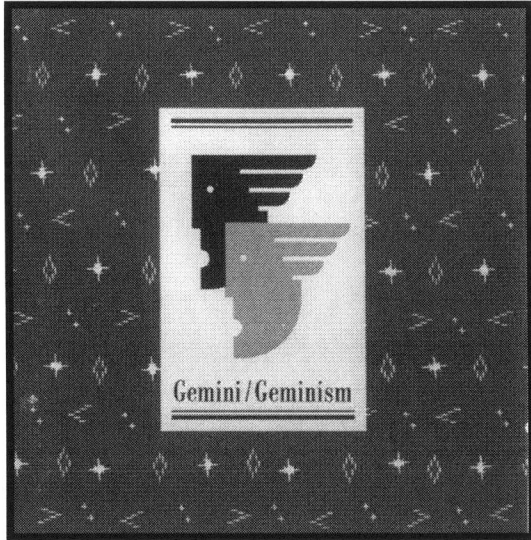

T.L.C./Beat The Heat/Mio My Mio/Ghost Town/I Am The Universe/Sniffin' Out The Snakes/I'm A Bitch When I See Red/There's No Way To Fool A Heart/Wild About That Girl/Nearly There

Sweden: 22.04.87: 33-17-**13**-15-16-16-17-29-37-x-x-x-42-38-41-37-45-41 (bi-weekly chart)

The second album by the duo Gemini, like the first, was produced by Benny and Björn. Benny and Björn composed six of the ten tracks on the album, and Björn co-wrote *Wild About That Girl* with Anders Glenmark and Dan Sundqvist.

   GEMINISM, which was only released in Scandinavia and the Soviet Union, charted at no.13 in Sweden but it wasn't a hit anywhere else.

33 ~ *KLINGA MINA KLOCKOR* by Benny Andersson

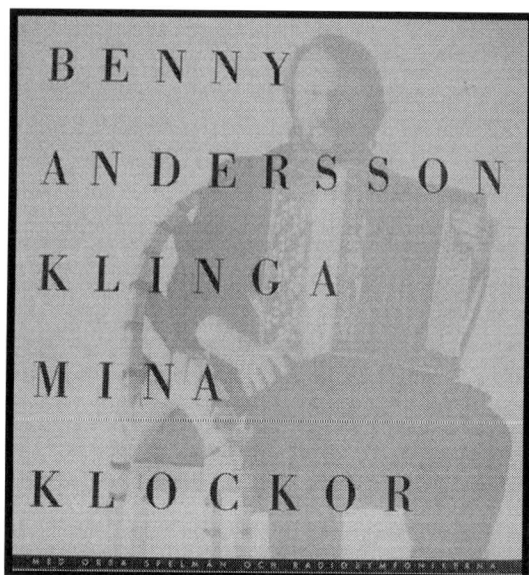

Inledningsvisa/Lottis Schottis/Födelsedagsvals Till Mona/Om Min Syster/Efter Regnet/ Ludvigs Leksakspolka/Gladan/Långsammazurkan/Tittis Sång/Trolskan/Klinga Mina Klockor

Sweden: Mono MML 001 (1987).

25.11.87: 28-20-8-**6**-8-18-20-24-36-50 (bi-weekly chart)

Benny's debut solo album *KLINGA MINA KLOCKOR* ('Ring My Bell') was released in Sweden in 1987, and featured mostly instrumental folk music composed by Benny himself. Björn wrote the lyrics to the four tracks that did feature vocals, namely *Lottis Schottis*, *Födelsedagsvals Till Mona*, *Trolskan* and *Klinga Mina Klockor*.
 Frida, Benny's ex-wife, was part of the choir who sang on the title track.
 KLINGA MINA KLOCKOR rose to no.6 in Sweden – the album was also issued in the Netherlands in 1988, but it wasn't a hit.

34 ~ I STAND ALONE by **Agnetha Fältskog**

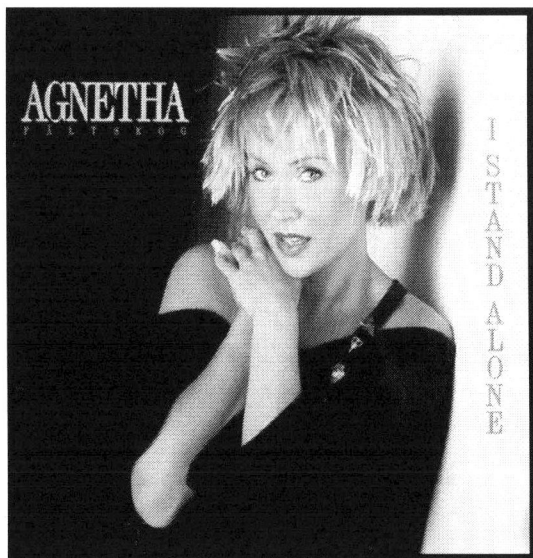

The Last Time/Little White Secrets/I Wasn't The One (Who Said Goodbye)/Love In A World Gone Mad/Maybe It Was Magic/Let It Shine/We Got A Way/I Stand Alone/Are You Gonna Throw It All Away/If You Need Somebody Tonight

Sweden: WEA 242 231-2 (1987).

9.12.87: **1-1-1-1**-4-11-19-32 (bi-weekly chart)

UK: WEA 242 231-1 (1987).

12.03.88: **72**

Australia
13.06.88: **96**

Germany
12.03.88: **47-47**-62

Netherlands
6.02.88: 54-**19**-23-38-32-36-35

Norway

Agnetha overcame her fear of flying, to cross the Atlantic and record her third English album in Los Angeles, with Chicago's Peter Cetera and Bruce Gaitsch.

This time, Agnetha didn't compose a single track herself, and the only hit single lifted from the album to achieve Top 40 status anywhere was *The Last Time*.

I Wasn't The One (Who Said Goodbye), a duet with Peter Cetera, and *Let It Shine* were both released as singles. *I Wasn't The One (Who Said Goodbye)* was a minor hit in the USA, but neither single charted anywhere else.

Despite the lack of success with singles, *I STAND ALONE* was a huge success in Sweden, where it topped the chart for two months and went on to become the no.1 best-selling album of 1988.

In other countries, success was more limited, but *I STAND ALONE* did chart at no.15 in Norway and no.19 in the Netherlands, and the album was a minor hit in Germany and the UK.

Although no one knew it at the time, Agnetha wouldn't release another solo studio album for 17 years.

35 ~ THE LOVE SONGS by ABBA

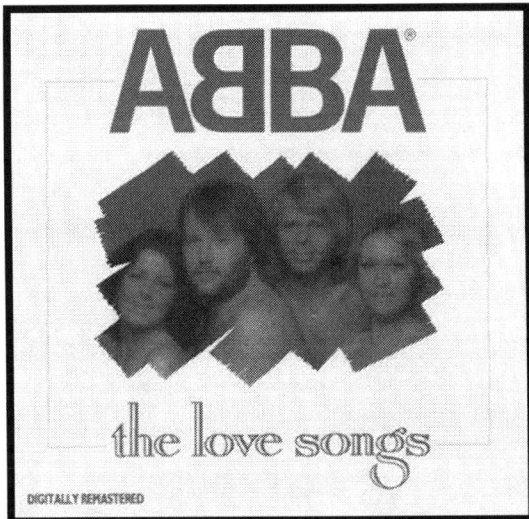

Under Attack/Slipping Through My Fingers/Should I Laugh Or Cry/Gonna Sing You My Lovesong/Lovers (Live A Little Longer)/Lovelight/I've Been Waiting For You/My Love, My Life/One Man, One Woman/Tropical Loveland/Another Town, Another Train/When All Is Said And Done/If It Wasn't For The Nights/So Long

UK: Pickwick PWKS 564 (1989).

THE LOVE SONGS, as a budget priced album, was ineligible to chart in the UK.

Netherlands
28.10.89: 76-41-31-27-25-24-21-19-**18**-21-23-27-39-41-53-72-94-100

This budget-priced collection of lesser known ABBA recordings was only released in the UK and continental Europe. In the UK, budget-priced albums are excluded from the albums chart, but *THE LOVE SONGS* did rise to no.18 in the Netherlands.

36 ~ NOVEMBER 1989 by Benny Andersson

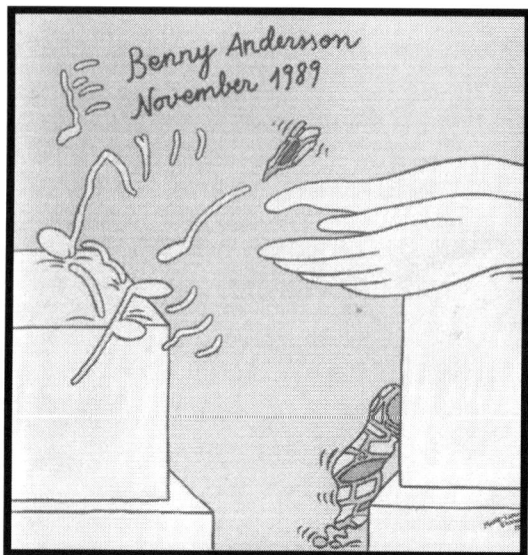

Skallgång/Machopolska/Vals Efter Efraim Andersson/Sekelskiftesidyll/Dans På Vindbryggan/Stjuls/Tröstevisa/Målarskolan/Novell #1/The Conducator/Stockholm By Night

Sweden: Mono MML 003 (1989).

29.11.89: 21-**13**-18-17-26-41-41

Benny's second solo album, titled after its release date, followed much the same pattern as his first, in that it largely comprised Swedish instrumental folk music composed and produced by Benny himself.

This time, Björn only wrote the lyrics for one track, *The Conductator*.

NOVEMBER 1989, which was only released in Sweden, wasn't quite as successful as Benny's first album but still charted at a respectable no.13.

This was the last solo album Benny released, before he formed the Benny Anderson Orkester in 2001.

37 ~ ABBA STORY by ABBA

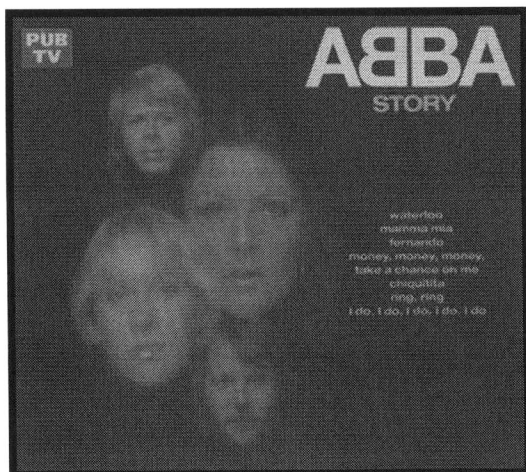

CD1: *Waterloo/Mamma Mia/Fernando/Dancing Queen/Money, Money, Money/Knowing Me, Knowing You/The Name Of The Game/Take A Chance On Me/Chiquitita/Voulez-Vous/I Have A Dream/The Winner Takes It All/Thank You For The Music*

CD2: *Ring Ring/Super Trouper/I Do, I Do, I Do, I Do, I Do/S.O.S/Gimme! Gimme! Gimme! (A Man After Midnight)/Happy New Year/Rock Me/Summer Night City/Eagle/One Of Us/One Man, One Woman/So Long*

France: Polydor 849 443-2 (1990).

09.90: peaked at no.**1**, charted for 13 weeks
21.06.91: **2-2** (Compilations chart)

This compilation was released exclusively in France, where it hit no.1 in 1990, before it spent two weeks at no.2 on the compilations chart the following year.

38 ~ CHESS – Original Broadway Cast Recording

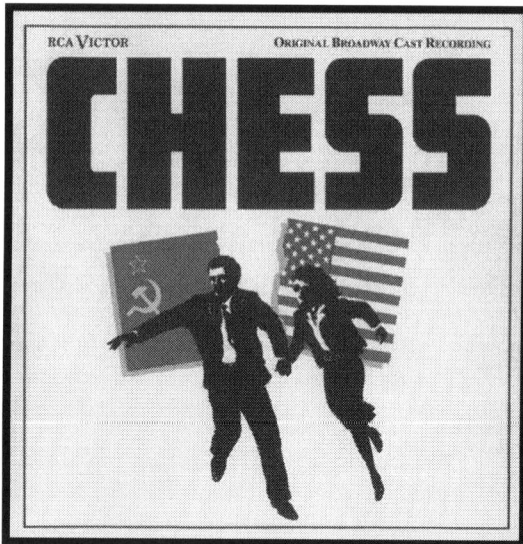

Prologue/The Story Of Chess/Where I Want To Be/How Many Women/Chess Hymn/ Quartet (A Model Of Decorum And Tranquility)/You Want To Lose Your Only Friend/ Someone Else's Story/Bangkok/Terrace Duet/Nobody's Side/Anthem/Hungarian Folk Song/Heaven Help My Heart/No Contest/You And I/I Know Him So Well/Pity The Child/Lullaby (Apukád Erős Kezén)/Endgame/You And I (Reprise)

Sweden: Polar POLCD 419 (1988).

The Original Broadway Cast Recording of *CHESS* wasn't a hit in Sweden.

UK: RCA BD87700 (1988).

The Original Broadway Cast Recording of *CHESS* wasn't a hit in the UK.

New Zealand
26.01.92: 44-31-26-**14**-17-16-17-24-42-48-35-46

The musical *Chess*, in a much altered form, opened on Broadway on 28th April 1988, but closed just two months later following poor ticket sales.

The Original Cast Recording of *CHESS* charted at no.14 in New Zealand, but it wasn't a hit in most countries, including the USA.

39 ~ GOLD by ABBA

Dancing Queen/Knowing Me, Knowing You/Take A Chance On Me/Mamma Mia/Lay All Your Love On Me/Super Trouper/I Have A Dream/The Winner Takes It All/Money, Money, Money/S.O.S/Chiquitita/Fernando/Voulez-Vous/Gimme! Gimme! Gimme! (A Man After Midnight)/Does Your Mother Know/One Of Us/The Name Of The Game/Thank You For The Music/Waterloo

Sweden: Polydor 517 007-2 (1992).

30.09.92: 10-**1-1**-2-2-2-2-3-3-5-13-26-29-44 (bi-weekly chart)
29.04.99: 44-10-5-4-3-**1-1-1-1-1-1-1-1-1**-2-3-3-5-5-12-10-10-11-16-20-28-24-34-54-51-33-
   53-50-35-35-32-35-39-37-33-45-x-x-52
28.06.01: 44
12.09.01: 33-31-35-35
19.05.05: 42-51
27.10.05: 10-16-25-53-x-53
5.07.07: 58
7.08.08: 37-23-29-28-37-37-37-38-27-47-37-22-33-45-37-49-38-56-57-47-x-54-44-46-
   51-x-x-60-52
8.05.09: 43
5.06.09: 55
21.08.09: 43
23.04.10: 51

14.10.11: 21-20
10.02.12: 31
15.06.12: 57
7.06.13: 12-13-5-11-14-13-14-8-10-8-9-6-7-11-18-11-23-40-37

UK: Polydor 517 007-2 (1992).

3.10.92: **1**-3-3-5-4-4-5-7-8-8-7-8-10-10-10-9-13-13-18-21-30-37-46-32-39-37-43-56-57-
51-55-73-58-77-74-53-33-31-26-29-32-36-38-8-14-11-16-18-20-30-36-55-53-46-45-
52-58-63-67-70-66-62-61-65-57-56-70-58-52-57-77-74-91-86-75-93-80-x-x-x-x-x-24-
11-10-22-22-26-26-39-53-x-x-x-x-x-97-x-95-88-x-x-81-59-52-52-48-47-48-47-53-75-
87-86-86-83-80-78-60-73-69-76-67-75-91-x-x-x-x-x-94-x-x-x-x-98-71-13-17-21-33-
37-45-62-68-55-59-71-75-79-75-54-58-67-79-78-63-69-65-62-83-89-83-89-82-88-88-
83-82-79-85-74-74-72-70-65-70-68-x-x-x-85-87-80-90-x-97-82-75-72-73-73-94-83-
85-74-73-69-61-75-69-69-65-61-63-65-71-31-29-39-55-46-55-64-60-93-97-94-97-93-
89-80-94-x-87-74-70-64-74-71-91-99-94-86-92-91-x-82-85-81-88-88-88-80-86-88-77-
77-82-74-73-72-72-65-66-72-82-88-65-48-49-58-60-71-76-85-66-59-71-69-76-85-83-
82-76-82-81-64-76-x-x-89-x-x-x-21-15-21-27-34-39-46-39-19-26-25-28-30-29-26-27-
35-38-39-37-39-37-41-44-44-49-47-52-56-71-78-71-84-74-77-74-79-76-69-63-66-67-
x-84-79-64-68-53-44-13-12-16-13-18-11-8-**1**-2-**1-1**-2-2-**1-1**-2-2-3-5-6-6-5-5-4-7-8-7-7-
11-10-16-20-25-18-10-15-17-21-10-14-13-14-15-16-12-8-10-10-11-14-14-11-7-11-26-
29-32-30-23-31-29-40-40-39-39-41-36-45-40-36-35-35-32-36-37-37-29-37-37-36-33-
29-38-41-40-44-48-59-57-47-46-51-51-52-55-54-51-75-77-67-61-72-74-69-64-86-89-
93-91-71-92-92-94-100-73-83-80-79-89-x-x-72-64-88-87-66-77-75-69-67-68-83-87-
99-90-96
5.10.02: 96-93
23.08.03: 30-28-45-57-63-84
17.04.04: 4-8-15-19-17-21-32-37-47-74-81 (30th Anniversary Edition)
28.08.04: 85-81-79-80-x-51-84-x-86-86-77-83-84-78-29-39-38-43-44-71-63-55-63-75-
83-87-92
10.09.05: 83
26.11.05: 65-64-82-83-81-50-97-82-87-84-95-88-85-90-98
2.09.07: 84-64-79-x-x-x-x-x-78-61-49-57-68-74-88-89-89-91
10.05.08: 85-63-79-79-78-62-77-84-92-43-12-5-2-**1-1**-2-2-6-6-9-14-20-25-27-33-37-51-
59-67-67-63-60-57-52-53-34-34-31-28-31-36-37-34-30-28-31-39-37-38-34-25-30-37-
41-40-39-42-47-50-57-50-56-49-55-41-38-37-36-35-36-33-55-57-67-76-53-59-72-92-
x-x-x-x-x-97-94-93-78-81-90-87-97
3.04.10: 91-95-83-85-89-x-x-100
7.08.10: 99-70-55-63-73-85-75-92-81-80-83-82-87
18.12.10: 31-42-42-66-68-74-77-93
23.04.11: 57-98

30.07.11: 93-83-79-68-65-65-78-74-78-90-x-x-97-92
24.12.11: 98-89-71-45-56-67-89-73-89-89-89
5.05.12: 90-x-x-x-100-x-x-x-x-x-67
17.11.12: 94-88-84-73-93-x-99-x-53-51-55-68-63-84-x-x-x-82-67-90
18.05.13: 88-76-71-x-x-95
31.08.13: 97-86
16.11.13: 93-99-x-x-x-94-69-64-49-55-61-49-65-69-84

Australia
2.11.92: 6-4-2-2-3-**1-1-1-1**-3-6-7-11-14-16-20-23-32-39-43-44-20-41
30.10.94: 50-30-5-5-4-4-3-9-7-7-8-11-12-18-24-30-29-35-42-47
2.05.99: 40-45-12-14-8-7-2-3-7-8-10-10-7-8-9-21-28-23-19-27-33-37-39-42-x-x-x-x-49-
   x-34-30-28-40-31-32-35-46-50-47-32-25-28-33-46-47
21.07.08: 4-4-4-5-6-9-13-19-24-30-37-44-38-54-48-58-41-44-51-49-54-48-46-42-39-38-
   31-32-41-41-48-46-52-50-48-54-53-67-66-64-73-81-85-80-96-90
13.03.11: 95-83-73-81
13.05.13: 45-65-84
8.07.13: 63-91-68-x-100-96-86-99
14.10.13: 11-x-x-x-69-69-66-66-84-97-81-78-57-57-71-60-64-88

Austria
18.10.92: 32-4-6-**1-1-1-1-1**-2-**1-1**-2-4-4-4-4-10-6-12-11-14-14-15-11-15-5-17-16-13-18-
   20-23-13-24-16-18-19-22-15-27-23
11.11.05: 56-48-44-62-63-37-36-36-38-27-28-34-27-19-18-17-27-36-44-45-67-58-39-59-
   62
1.08.08: 30-30-27-14-9-14-15-15-17-22-26-26-28-35-44-45-61-57-70-72-72-68-63-40-
   30-23-19-21-24-20-22-30-34-30-39-58-52-68-71
7.01.11: 49-27-45-55-59-71
6.01.12: 65-19-23-33-33-37-39-51-37-46-66-62-53-x-72-64-65-65-72-61-75-x-63-21-31-
   47-53-x-74-31-51-69-52-59-67-x-x-x-x-63-49-55-52-57-58-54-61-60-54-x-64-64-71-
   26-23-36-34-42-43-61-53-70-66-67-74
24.05.13: 74-70
19.07.13: 29-63-57-52-50-51
18.10.13: 73-44-47-40-60-69-53-52-49-39-35-20-14-21-36-27-40-43-58-57-64-57-*

Belgium
8.04.95: 43
1.07.95: 41
30.03.96: 50-27-32-30-48-x-x-33-48
31.08.96: 40-43
22.08.98: 50-46

8.05.99: 29-22-22-26-25-22-19-**16**-20-22-24-25-22-19-**16**-**16**-26-25-23-32-25-25-36-30-
   29-26-30-44-x-x-x-45-48-46-40-40-36-40
4.03.00: 50
13.09.00: 90-38-21-43-44-32-34-48-49-65-64-71-75-83-93-79-x-100-x-89-x-x-90

Canada
6.03.93: 34-16-**4**-5-7-11-12-10-15-17-19-20-23-26-31-31-43-54-54-51-48-54-58-56-52-
   56-70-70-72-75-90
24.07.00: peaked at no.22, charted for 64 weeks
10.07.08: peaked at no.13, charted for ?? weeks

Finland
10.92: peaked at no.**1**, charted for 96 weeks (monthly chart)
1.11.97: 30
24.04.99: 37-11-2-**1**-2-3-3-5-5-5-5-5-6-8-5-7-8-7-13-9-28-17-16-30-20-21-32-36
1.01.00: 28-38-34-35-x-x-x-x-40-x-x-38-x-38-37
23.08.08: 8-7-14-14-15-20-21-26-37-30-26
17.01.09: 38-4-4-7-8-8-11-17-24-31-20-37-x-31
9.10.10: 29

France
10.92: peaked at no.**1**, charted for 48 weeks
12.09.93: 5-13-14-15-21-28-28-28-21-15-6-9-18-19-20-37
3.03.96: 5-**1-1-1-1-1-1**-2-3-5-7-9-6-12-21 (Compilations chart)
10.05.98: 20 (Compilations chart)
13.10.06: 39-46-44 (Compilations chart)
7.09.08: 2-**1-1**-2-3-4-4-7-9-10-12-13-12-12-14-16-23-22-20-22-27-x-27-38-22-17-12-19-
   21-11-17-18-27-38-x-x-14-23-16-32 (Compilation chart)
4.05.09: 45-38
3.08.09: 36-49-42-42-x-45
16.11.09: 35
23.11.09: 34 (Compilation chart)
4.01.10: 37
4.06.11: 75
7.01.12: 95

Germany
5.10.92: 98-54-5-2-**1-1-1-1-1-1-1-1-1-1-1**-2-4-5-5-11-11-11-11-12-13-14-13-14-13-13-
   14-16-24-25-22-29-23-26-26-28-30-36-29-40-38-40-39-42-41-43-50-61-60-57-60-76-
   80-71-76-81
10.05.99: 63-69-63-73-72-59-56-42-61-49-52-52-53-52-49-52-55-67-68-74-72-92-96-99-

95
28.04.03: 63-69-63-73-72-59-56-42-61-49-52-52-53-52-49-52-55-67-68-74-72-92-96-99-
95
22.09.03: 64-90
27.10.03: 53-68-95-82
12.01.04: 65-82-87-79-79-82-89-91
19.04.04: 39-18-27-43-48-60-72-81-95
22.08.04: 66-75-78-81-81-88-86
3.01.05: 67-64-77-58-69-84-75-72-87-89-94-76-91-95-86-91-95-77
9.12.05: 63-57-52-48-43-38-25-39-40-61-46-53-65-63-77-85-92-80-73-70-85-89-81-77-
87-85-92-95-88-80-81-99-92-78-75-86-98
5.08.08: 44-43-38-31-24-28-42-40-45-62-73-72-85-90-99
7.01.11: 39-47-60-73-85-93-99
5.08.11: 72
28.10.11: 96
6.01.12: 75-58-66-84-96-x-86-94-80
15.06.12: 34-57-100-x-x-74-40-69-86-85-95
10.01.14: 72-86-85

Japan
21.04.99: peaked at no.**13**, charted for 14 weeks (CD chart)

Netherlands
3.10.92: 54-13-7-5-5-4-5-7-7-8-8-9-9-7-**3**-5-6-7-6-5-6-9-10-15-19-20-16-17-17-22-23-
22-24-30-23-23-21-19-30-32-30-43-45-45-41-37-31-35-39-41-43-77-80-83-94-79-73-
70-82
26.02.94: 92-82-66-61-82
2.08.08: 45-16-9-9-12-13-21-28-33-45-50-58-75-91-96-x-x-x-100-x-x-x-x-90-98

New Zealand
8.11.92: 4-**3**-4-4-4-9-9-9-9-9-25-31-39-42-46
2.04.95: 37-7-**3-3**-6-6-5-5-6-8-8-9-17-26-36
13.08.95: 50-39-36-33-30-x-42-x-29-41-38-44
6.06.99: 19-45-44-32-32-30-38
14.03.04: 42-30-23-21-24-19-23-x-33-28-x-x-36
21.07.08: 25-19-9-10-13-15-22-21-28-33
22.12.08: 17-17-12-13-13-19-20-17-21-20-25-27-30-29-32-32-37

Norway
26.09.92: 20-4-4-2-3-3-2-2-**1-1-1**-2-2-4-2-2-3-5-x-13-14-18-20
10.04.99: 31-x-x-x-x-29-28-23-10-5-5-6-6-5-6-7-6-6-8-11-13-14-14-16-20-25-26-28-38

22.01.00: 32-31
22.04.00: 38
3.06.00: 31
29.07.00: 29
2.04.05: 40
19.07.08:30-20-17-13-11-6-4-7-6-8-10-11-19-25-31-33-29-29-14-22-25-31-31-32-33-x-x-33-x-36
18.07.09: 30-27-28-38-38-30-32-26
12.01.13: 22
18.05.13: 39-30-36-18-32-35-32-34-31-29-x-37-26-40
11.01.14: 28

Spain
10.92: peaked at no.**1** (1 week), charted for 23 weeks
04.99: peaked at no.**1** (4 weeks), charted for 48 weeks
8.10.06: 99-92
17.08.08: 52-24-24-26-29-40-40-51-58-64-76-56-38-41-46-81-86-83-80-75-66-72-82-94-97

Switzerland
4.10.92: 31-15-4-2-2-**1-1-1-1-1-1-1-1-1-1**-2-2-2-3-4-5-7-8-12-12-12-14-15-15-18-15-14-19-24-31-31-20
25.04.99: 50
20.06.99: 50-47-45-x-45-42-33-37-37-39-41-40-48-45-49
19.12.99: 83-83
16.01.00: 78-x-79-82-87-81-82-67-81-80-100
23.07.00: 86-x-x-x-100-x-94
7.01.01: 95-53-86-80-96-61-62-73-x-x-68-x-72-x-44-25-19-19-26-24-37-52-57-62-x-68
19.08.01: 69-92-79
19.10.03: 89-x-92
5.12.04: 81-91-x-92-88-x-x-96
14.08.05: 90-96-93
1.01.06: 77-61-47-57-63-67-97-87-81-86-83-x-x-x-x-78
21.05.06: 99-x-x-x-96-x-97-x-x-83
28.11.04: 81-91-x-92-88-x-96-81-91-92-88-96
3.08.08: 25-22-20-14-11-17-23-26-21-29-35-31-23-35-47-55-57-66-55-50-50-50-46-38-39-34-48-44-45-47-54-48-48-62-54-48-47-48-46-57-54-67-32-41-66-84-59-58-70-77-64-66-59-70-51-56-58-64-79-94
8.11.09: 85-85-95
10.01.10: 83-62-82-78-68-68-59-76-92-86-90-90-x-96-92-89-74-83-75-75-95-95-74-95-84-97-x-x-99-x-85-78-75-81-71-89-92-x-43-61-76-99

5.12.10: 66-96-67-79-79-61-38-52-59-72-78-78-66-67-91-x-91-77-x-x-x-84-84-96-94-
  66-91-71-56-78-73-x-93-76-86-67-72-91-87-72-81
6.11.11: 98-84
8.01.12: 91-34-37-43-72-92-67-71-75-92-98
6.05.12: 97-x-x-91-x-58-33-60-96-x-98-74-70-95-91-68-85
13.01.13: 47-33-37-32-52-62-x-98-x-x-83-95
2.06.13: 65-88
11.08.13: 84-75-90-x-x-x-86
22.12.13: 96-77-59-29-21-26-29-62-89-91

USA
9.10.93: 63-70-68-81-79-87-85-97
6.05.95: 93-86-82-84-90-94-95-96-100
26.07.08: 98-33-19-17-**11-11**-19-29-35-44-56-71-84-91-87-96-x-x-x-x-73-x-x-85-67-44-
  55-48-61-70-76-73-64-69-62-65-69-86-95-x-76-65-81-74-88
27.06.09: 78-72-75-78-85
12.01.13: 36

Zimbabwe
5.04.93: 6-6-7-**3**-6-x-x-x-9-9 (bi-weekly chart)

* = charting at cut-off date for publication

GOLD is far and away the most successful album ABBA ever released.

Sub-titled 'Greatest Hits', the compilation brought together 19 of ABBA's biggest hits – prior to its release, all other ABBA compilations were deleted. The original Australian edition of *GOLD* had a slightly different track listing:

Dancing Queen/Knowing Me Knowing You/Take A Chance On Me/Mamma Mia/Lay All Your Love On Me/Ring Ring/I Do, I Do, I Do, I Do, I Do/The Winner Takes It All/Money, Money, Money/S.O.S/Chiquitita/Fernando/Voulez-Vous/Gimme! Gimme! Gimme! (A Man After Midnight)/Does Your Mother Know/One Of Us/The Name Of The Game/Rock Me/Waterloo

In Spain, the English versions of *Chiquitita* and *Fernando* were replaced with the Spanish versions.

In 1992, or early 1993 in some cases, *GOLD* hit no.1 in a host of countries including Australia, Austria, Finland, France, Germany, Norway, Spain, Sweden, Switzerland and the UK, and charted at no.3 in the Netherlands, New Zealand and Zimbabwe, and no.4 in Canada.

GOLD was reissued in 1999, with the full length versions of *The Name Of The Game* and *Voulez-Vous* replacing the edited versions on the original release. This release coincided with the premiere of the *Mamma Mia!* musical, and saw *GOLD* returning to no.1 in Finland, Spain, Sweden and the UK. The compilation also charted at no.2 in Australia, no.5 in Norway, no.13 in Japan, no.16 in Belgium, no.19 in New Zealand, no.22 in Canada and no.33 in Switzerland.

A 10th anniversary edition of *GOLD* was released in Europe and New Zealand in 2002, with an up-dated sleeve design and revised liner notes. The following year, in continental Europe only, the compilation was reissued with a bonus CD featuring the following tracks:

Summer Night City/Angeleyes/The Day Before You Came/Eagle/I Do, I Do, I Do, I Do, I Do/So Long/Honey Honey/The Visitors/Ring Ring/When I Kissed The Teacher/The Way Old Friends Do

30th Anniversary Edition

This edition of *GOLD*, released in the UK in 2004, saw the usual black sleeve replaced with a gold sleeve, and the compilation was released as a single CD and a CD/DVD package. The DVD featured the music videos for 18 of the 19 songs included on *GOLD*, with only *The Name Of The Game* omitted. The release of this edition saw *GOLD* re-entering the UK chart at no.4.

In 2008, when the film *Mamma Mia!* premiered, *GOLD* was reissued again, with up-dated liner notes and all the tracks remastered. This time, the same track listing was released in Australia as was usual for the rest of the world. *GOLD* returned to no.1 in the UK for a third different year, and topped the chart in France as well. Elsewhere, the compilation charted at no.4 in Australia and Norway, no.7 in Finland, no.9 in Austria, the Netherlands, and New Zealand, no.11 in Switzerland and the USA, no.13 in Canada, no.23 in Sweden, and no.24 in Germany and Spain.

Two years later, *GOLD* was reissued as a combined CD/DVD package; the CD was unchanged, but the DVD featured a rare cartoon video for *Money, Money, Money* that had been screened in Australia in the 1970s. Additionally, all the music videos were remastered, with five of the videos being able to be viewed with a split screen, to show the difference between the original and remastered versions.

40th Anniversary Edition

To mark the 40th anniversary of ABBA's victory at the Eurovision Song Contest in 1974 with *Waterloo*, a 3CD edition of *GOLD* was released in April 2014. The two bonus CDs were *MORE GOLD* and 'Golden B-Sides', with the latter bringing together 20 ABBA B-sides:

She's My Kind Of Girl/I Am Just A Girl/Gonna Sing You My Lovesong/King Kong Song/I've Been Waiting For You/Rock Me/Man In The Middle/Intermezzo No.1/That's Me/Crazy World/Happy Hawaii/I'm A Marionette/Medley (Pick A Bale Of Cotton/On Top Of Old Smokey/Midnight Special)/Kisses of Fire/The King Has Lost His Crown/ Elaine/The Piper/Andante Andante/Should I Laugh Or Cry/Soldiers

GOLD, with global sales fast approaching 30 million, is easily ABBA's biggest selling album. It is the no.1 best-selling album ever in Switzerland, the no.2 best-selling album ever in the UK (behind Queen's *GREATEST HITS*), and the no.3 best-selling album ever in Germany.

GOLD is certified 6 x Platinum in the USA, denoting a shipment of six million copies, and the compilation has sold over five million copies in the UK – where, in January 2014, the album chalked up its 1,000[th] week on the Top 200. *GOLD* was only the third album to achieve this milestone, after Queen's *GREATEST HITS* and Bob Marley's *LEGEND*.

GOLD has enjoyed astonishingly long chart runs in many countries and, while other ABBA compilations have come and gone, *GOLD* keeps on selling.

SHAPES by Josefin Nilsson

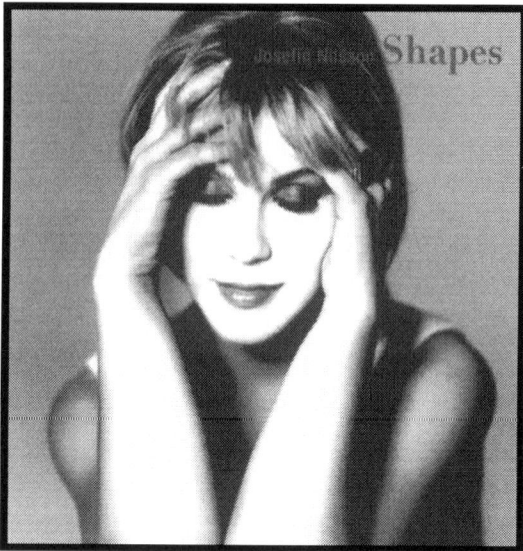

Surprise, Surprise/Heaven And Hell/We Won't Be Going Anywhere/Where The Whales Have Ceased To Sing/High Hopes And Heartaches/Midnight Dancer/Leave It To Love/ When I Watched You In Your Sleep/Now You See Him, Now You Don't/The Film I'd Like To See

Sweden: Mono MMCD 008 (1993).

7.04.93: **14**-20-30-47-45-41
11.08.93: 49

All ten tracks on Josefin Nilsson's debut solo album were composed by Benny and Björn, and Benny produced the whole album as well.

SHAPES was released in Scandinavia and continental Europe, but it was only a hit in Sweden, where it peaked at its debut position of no.14.

Heaven And Hell, the lead single from *SHAPES*, was a hit in Norway and Sweden, but three further singles – *Surprise, Surprise*, *High Hopes And Heartaches* and *Where The Whales Have Ceased To Sing* – all missed the chart.

Summer Night City/Angeleyes/The Day Before You Came/Eagle/I Do, I Do, I Do, I Do, I Do/So Long/Honey Honey/The Visitors/Our Last Summer/On And On And On/Ring Ring/ I Wonder (Departure)/Lovelight/Head Over Heels/When I Kissed The Teacher/I Am The City/Cassandra/Under Attack/When All Is Said And Done/The Way Old Friends Do

Sweden: Polydor 519 353-2 (1993).

16.06.93: 14-7-18-27 (bi-weekly chart)
30.09.99: 48-43-51-x-**3**-50
13.11.08: 56
5.06.09: 50
21.08.09: 21-24
21.05.10: 59
7.06.13: 19-19-19-18-23-24-20-20-21-23-26-30-27-40

UK: Polydor 519 353-2 (1993).

5.06.93: 14-14-17-23-33-46-63-69-16-25-29-35-50-73-95
7.08.99: **13**-17-25-32-32-39-53-65-90
20.11.99: 69-78-84-95
6.09.08: 63-86-99-63-75-97-82-71-85-85-90-97-x-x-99

Australia
2.08.93: peaked at no.65, charted for 8 weeks
13.09.99: peaked at no.80, charted for 13 weeks
21.07.08: 54-**38**-40-51-56-96

Austria
20.06.93: 13-13-14-18-**7**-26-21-28-33-35-31-31-33-28-32-32

Belgium
29.09.08: **60**-86-81-x-92

Canada
22.11.93: peaked at no.**48**, charted for 6 weeks

Finland
9.10.10: **33**

France
08.93: peaked at no.**10**, charted for 21 weeks
7.09.08: **35** (Compilations chart)

Germany
7.06.93: 98-27-10-**9**-10-13-17-18-20-29-38-38-46-42-51-54-65-76-82-79

Netherlands
5.06.93: 68-19-**10-10**-16-17-23-25-26-26-24-28-29-34-34-34-59-98

Norway
19.06.93: **16**-18
28.08.99: 25-26-18-26-34

Switzerland
6.06.93: 33-34-**13**-14-24-20-25-21-29-26-30-27-34-26-40
24.08.08: 80-66-56-82-x-91

Zimbabwe
1.11.93: **2** (bi-weekly chart)

The success of *GOLD*, given ABBA had achieved more than the 19 hits it featured, almost guaranteed there would be a follow-up and, just one year on, *MORE GOLD* – sub-titled 'More ABBA Hits' – duly appeared.

MORE GOLD brought together some of ABBA's lesser hits, a few albums tracks and one previously unreleased song, *I Am The City*, which was one of six new songs ABBA recorded during their final studio sessions in 1982.

ABBA's live recording of *The Way Old Friends Do* was released as a promo CD single in some countries, to promote *MORE GOLD*, which charted at no.2 in Zimbabwe, no.7 in Austria and Sweden, no.10 in France and the Netherlands, no.13 in Switzerland, no.14 in the UK and no.16 in Norway.

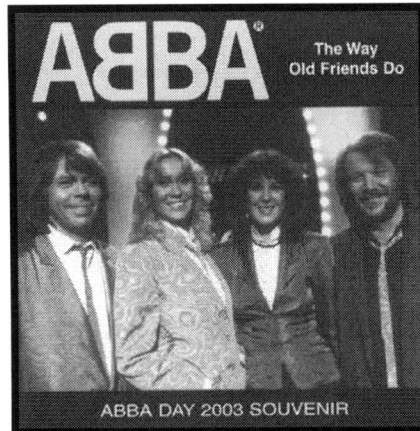

25th Anniversary Edition

MORE GOLD was reissued in 1999 and, benefitting from the publicity attracted by the *Mamma Mia!* musical, the compilation returned to the chart in some countries, peaking at no.3 in Sweden, no.13 in the UK and no.18 in Norway.

In Australia, where *Ring Ring* and *I Do, I Do, I Do, I Do, I Do* had been added to the local version of *GOLD*, the opportunity was taken to revise the track listing:

Summer Night City/Angeleyes/The Day Before You Come/Eagle/Super Trouper/So Long/Honey Honey/The Visitors/Our Last Summer/On And On And On/I Have A Dream/I Wonder (Departure)/Head Over Heels/When I Kissed The Teacher/I Am The City/Under Attack/When All Is Said And Done/The Way Old Friends Do/Thank You For The Music

Although nowhere near as successful as *GOLD*, *MORE GOLD* had sold an estimated three million copies worldwide.

41 ~ THANK YOU FOR THE MUSIC by ABBA

CD1: *People Need Love/Another Town, Another Train/He Is Your Brother/Love Isn't Easy/Ring Ring/Waterloo/Hasta Mañana/Honey Honey/Dance (While The Music Still Goes On)/So Long/I've Been Waiting For You/I Do, I Do, I Do I Do, I Do/S.O.S/Mamma Mia/Fernando/Dancing Queen/That's Me/When I Kissed A Teacher/Money, Money, Money/ Crazy World/My Love, My Life*

CD2: *Knowing Me, Knowing You/Happy Hawaii/The Name Of The Game/I Wonder (Departure) (Live Version)/Eagle/Take A Chance On Me/Thank You For The Music/ Summer City Night/Chiquitita/Lovelight/Does Your Mother Know/Voulez-Vous/ Angeleyes/Gimme! Gimme! Gimme! (Man After Midnight)/I Have A Dream*

CD3: *The Winner Takes It All/Elaine/Super Trouper/Lay All Your Love On Me/On And On And On/Our Last Summer/The Way Old Friends Do/The Visitors/One Of Us/Should I Laugh Or Cry/Head Over Heels/When All Is Said And Done/Like An Angel Passing Though My Room/The Day Before You Came/Cassandra/Under Attack*

CD4: *Put On Your White Sombrero/Dream World/Thank You For The Music (Doris Day Version)/Hej Gamle Man/Merry-Go-Round/Santa Rosa/She's My Kinda Girl/Medley (Pick A Bale Of Cotton/On Top Of Old Smokey/Midnight Special)/You Owe Me*

One/Slipping Through My Fingers/Me And I/ABBA Undeleted/Waterloo (French/Swedish Version)/Ring Ring (Swedish/Spanish/German Version)/Honey Honey (Swedish Version)

ABBA Undeleted: *Scaramouche/Summer Night City/Take a Chance on Me/Baby (Early Version of Rock Me)/Just A Notion/Rikky Rock 'N' Roller/Burning My Bridges/Fernando (Frida's Swedish Solo Version)/Here Comes Rubie Jamie/Hamlet III Part 1 & 2/Free As A Bumble Bee/Rubber Ball Man/Crying Over You/Just Like That (Saxophone Version)/ Givin' A Little Bit More*

Sweden: Polydor 523 472-2 (1994).

11.11.94: **17**-27-41
21.08.08: 47

UK: Polydor 523 472-2 (1994).

THANK YOU FOR THE MUSIC wasn't a hit in the UK.

Australia
28.11.94: peaked at no.**76**, charted for 2 weeks

This comprehensive, 4CD box-set brought together all ABBA's big hits, selected B-sides and album tracks, plus a whole CD of rarities, including the previously unreleased *Dream World* and *Put On Your White Sombrero*, the very different Doris Day version of *Thank You For The Music* and a live recording of *Slipping Through My Fingers/Me And I*.

The fourth CD also included *ABBA Undeleted*, a 23 minutes medley of snippets of previously unheard ABBA demos and songs, and including Frida's solo version of *Fernando*. Rounding off the fourth CD were a French/Swedish version of *Waterloo*, a Swedish/Spanish/German version of *Ring Ring* and the Swedish version of *Honey Honey*.

The relatively high price of *THANK YOU FOR THE MUSIC*, compared with the average album, meant the box-set didn't chart in most countries. It did, however, achieve no.17 in Sweden, and it was a minor hit in Australia.

42 ~ *DJUPA ANDETAG* by Frida

Älska Mig Alltid/Ögonen/Även En Blomma/Sovrum/Hon Fick Som Hon Ville/Alla Mina Bästa År/Lugna Vatten/Vem Kommer Såra Vem Ikväll/Sista Valsen Med Dig/Kvinnor Som Springer

Sweden: Anderson AND 1 (1996).

27.09.96: 2-**1**-**1**-2-5-11-18-12-16-24-11-10-12-17-17-13-17-19-30-31-44-52

Finland
28.09.96: 37-34
16.11.96: **32**

Norway
5.10.96: **17**-38-x-x-x-x-39-27

For her fifth, and most recent, solo album Frida wanted to keep it low profile, and to avoid the attention an international release would surely bring. Having recorded two albums in English in the 1980s, she decided to record her first new album for twelve years in Swedish.

DJUPA ANDETAG ('Deep Breaths') was recorded at Polar Studios in Stockholm, with Anders Glenmark of the duo Gemini producing. Frida wrote the lyrics to one track,

Kvinnor Som Springer ('Women Who Run'), herself, after reading and being inspired by Clarissa Pinkola Estes's book, *Women Who Run With The Wolves*.

Originally, Frida wanted to record *Alla Mina Bästa År* ('All My Best Year') with Agnetha but, fearing the two of them singing together again would incite rumours of an ABBA reunion, Agnetha declined. Instead, Frida recorded the track as a duet with Roxette's Marie Fredriksson.

DJUPA ANDETAG was only released in Scandinavia – it hit no.1 in Sweden, and charted at no.17 in Norway and no.32 in Finland.

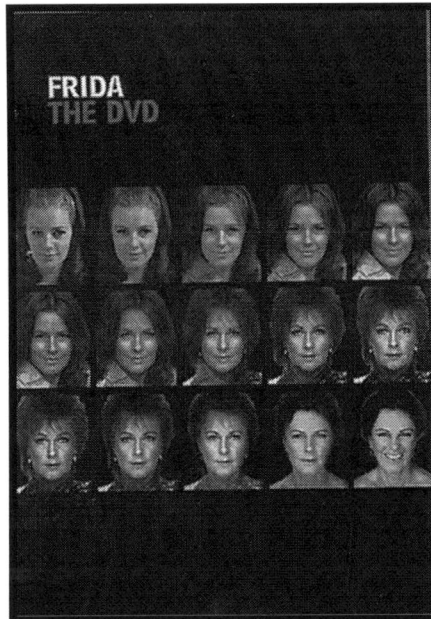

Frida made a one hour documentary of the making of *DJUPA ANDETAG* which, together with the music videos she filmed for this and previous albums, was included on *Frida – The DVD*, a three hour long DVD released in Sweden in 2005. In the DVD, Frida speaks candidly about her life and career, from 1967 right up to the summer of 2005, when she filmed her lengthy contribution in Zermatt, Switzerland.

43 ~ FOREVER GOLD by ABBA

This two CD package brought together two recent compilations, ABBA's *GOLD* and *MORE GOLD*.

Europe: Polydor 533 355-2 (1996), Polydor 533 083-2 (with free CD single, 1996).

Belgium
26.10.96: 31-**20**-23-24-25-39
8.02.97: 42

France
29.09.96: 9-**4**-6-9-16-24 (Compilations chart)
5.12.99: 19-6-6-7-**4**-6-6-7-10-11-15-20-24 (Compilations chart)
3.06.05: 24-19-24-21-28-36-39-33-x-39 (Compilations chart)
30.12.05: 15-15-14-8-9-12-15-19-24-23-56-x-60-x-x-39-16-26-23-27-27-40-50-53-59-
    26-21-23-23-28-31-34-38-38-50-58-59-66-35-34-40 (Compilations chart)

Germany
25.11.96: 68-85-70-84-67-67-**50**-54-56-56-54-66-60-69-78
24.03.97: 98-98

UK
FOREVER GOLD didn't enter the Top 100 in the UK, however, it did spend 18 weeks on the Top 200, peaking at no.151.

A limited edition of *FOREVER GOLD* came with a free CD single, *Put On Your White Sombrero*, a track recorded during the *SUPER TROUPER* sessions, but failed to make the album's final track listing.

Put On Your White Sombrero remained unreleased until 1994, when it was included on the box-set, *THANK YOU FOR THE MUSIC*. As well as *Put On Your White Sombrero*, the CD single featured two more tracks, *Dream World* and *Dame! Dame! Dame!*, the Spanish version of *Gimme! Gimme! Gimme! (A Man After Midnight)*.

In some South American countries, including Chile, *FOREVER GOLD* was re-packaged and re-titled, *SERIE TOTAL*.

FOREVER GOLD wasn't as successful as the two compilations it included, but it charted at no.4 in France in 1996 and 1999, no.20 in Belgium and no.50 in Germany.

44 ~ MY LOVE MY LIFE by **Agnetha Fältskog**

CD1: *Introduktion/Jag Var Så Kär/Utan Dej Mitt Liv Går Vidare/Sonny Boy/Allting Har Förändrat Sig/En Gång Fanns Bara Vi Två/Så Här Börjar Kärlek/Om Tårar Vore Guld/ En Sång Och En Saga/Jag Ska Göra Allt/Tänk Va' Skönt/Många Gånger Än/Tågen Kan Gå Igen/Jag Ska Inte Fälla Några Tårar/Dröm Är Dröm Och Saga Saga/Kanske Var Min Kind Lite Het/Vart Ska Min Kärlek Föra/Så Glad Som Dina Ögon/Tio Mil Kvar Till Korpilombolo*

CD2: *En Sång Om Sorg Och Glädje/S.O.S/Dom Har Glömt/Visa I Åttonde Månaden/ Tack För En Underbar, Vanlig Dag/När Du Tar Mej I Din Famn/Disillusion/My Love, My Life/The Winner Takes It All/Never Again/The Day Before You Came/Wrap Your Arms Around Me/It's So Nice To Be Rich/I Won't Let You Go/The Way You Are/Let It Shine/Nu Tändas Tusen Juleljus/På Söndag*

Sweden: Columbia COL 483 910-2 (1996).

4.10.96: **21**-47-41

This compilation was only released in Sweden and, as well as a selection of Agnetha's solo recordings in Swedish and English, featured four ABBA tracks: *Disillusion* (which Agnetha co-wrote with Björn), *My Love, My Life*, *The Winner Takes It All* and *The Day Before You Came*. The album made its chart debut at no.21, but it didn't rise any higher.

45 ~ KRISTINA FRÅN DUVEMÅLA

CD1: *Prolog/Duvemåla Hage/Min Lust Till Dej/Ut Mot Ett Hav/Missväxt/Nej/Lilla Skara/Aldrig/Kom Till Mig Alla/Vi Öppnar Alla Grindar*

CD2: *Bönder På Havet/Löss/Stanna/Begravning Till Sjöss/A Sunday In Battery Park/ Hemma/Från New York Till Stillwater/Tänk Att Män Som Han Kan Finnas/Kamfer Och Lavendel/Drömmen Om Guld/Min Astrakan*

CD3: *Överheten/Ljusa Kvällar Om Våren/Präriens Drottning/Vildgräs/Jag Har Förlikat Mej Till Slut/Gildet Blev Till Sand/Wild Cat Money/Ut Mot Ett Hav/Vill Du Inte Gifta Dej Med Mej/Ett Herrans Underverk/Down To The Sacred Wave/Missfall/Du Måste Finnas/ Skördefest/Här Har Du Mej Igen/Red Iron/Hjälp Mej Trösta/Var Hör Vi Hemma/I Gott Bevar*

Sweden: Mono MMCD 011 (1996).

1.11.96: **2**-3-4-10-6-**2**-5-**2**-4-7-11-7-5-6-8-11-5-3-6-6-4-6-9-9-9-11-10-13-16-9-13-11-17-
    17-20-21-22-19-20-17-15-16-16-22-21-24-21-34-36-34-35-42-27-25-24-28-26-22-13-
    13-20-28-28-40-43-39-34-35-43-49-52-51
17.12.98: 46-x-x-55
18.11.99: 32-22-35-31-31-33-31-37-43-37 (*SEXTON FAVORITER UR KRISTINA FRÅN*
3.08.00: 54 (*SEXTON FAVORITER UR KRISTINA FRÅN DUVEMÅLA*)   *DUVEMÅLA*)

Finland
28.04.12: **27**

Kristina Från Duvemåla ('Kristina From Duvemåla') is a musical Benny and Björn wrote, based on four novels by the Swedish author Vilhelm Moberg: *The Emigrants*, *Unto A Good Land*, *The Settlers* and *The Last Letter Home*. The musical told the story of Kristina and her family, as they are driven by poverty to migrate from Sweden to the USA in the mid-1800s.

The musical premiered at the Malmö Opera & Music Theatre in Sweden on 7th October 1995, with Helen Sjöholm as Kristina, Anders Ekborg as Karl, Peter Jöback as Robert and Åsa Bergh as Ulrika.

The accompanying cast album, which was only released in Scandinavia, was a huge success, spending three weeks at no.2 and logging well over a year on the chart. The album also charted in Finland, peaking at no.27.

KRISTINA FRÅN DUVEMÅLA picked up a *Grammis* award – the Swedish equivalent of a Grammy – for the Best Album of 1996.

In 1999, a single disc 'best of' compilation was released in Sweden, titled *SEXTON FAVORITER UR KRISTINA FRÅN DUVEMÅLA* ('Sixteen Favourites From Kristina From Duvemåla'). The track listing was as follows:

Prolog/Duvemåla Hage/Ut Mot Ett Hav/Lilla Skara/Aldrig/Vi Öppnar Alla Grindar/ Stanna/Hemma/Tänk Att Män Som Han Kan Finnas/Min Astrakan/Vildgräs/Guldet Blev Till Sand/Du Måste Finnas/Här Har Du Mej Igen/Var Hör Vi Hemma/I Gott Bevar

SEXTON FAVORITER UR KRISTINA FRÅN DUVEMÅLA charted at no.22 in Sweden.

In the mid-2000s, Björn and Herbert Kretzmer translated *Kristina Från Duvemåla* into English.

46 ~ LOVE STORIES by ABBA

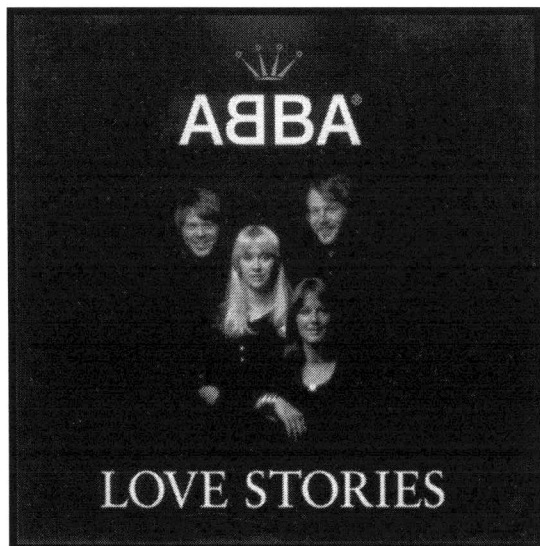

*Fernando/The Name Of The Game/Chiquitita/The Winner Takes It All/I Have A Dream/
The Day Before You Came/One Of Us/Andante, Andante/One Man One Woman/Eagle/
Slipping Through My Fingers/My Love, My Life/Our Last Summer/Like An Angel Passing
Through My Room/I Wonder (Departure)/I Let The Music Speak/The Way Old Friends*

Europe: Polar 559 221-2 (1998).

UK
7.11.98: **51**-66

Austria
22.11.98: 15-24-30-38-39-42-42-43-50-26-44-**14**-29-31-45-43

Belgium
21.11.98: **36-36**-41-48-50-x-x-x-x-47

Finland
28.11.98: 32-33-28-**23**-24-30-32-36-36-30-40-31
10.04.99: 40-40-40

France
4.04.99: 11-**3**-6-12-9-11-17-16-x-21 (Compilations chart)

Germany
9.11.98: 86-**82**-96

New Zealand
14.02.99: 45-**24**-43-49

Norway
28.11.98: **30**-32-34-39
24.04.99: 35

Switzerland
10.01.99: **47**-48

This compilation, a mix of hits and album tracks, was released to replace two previous ABBA compilations that had been deleted, *I LOVE ABBA* and *FROM ABBA WITH LOVE*.

Although not a major hit, *LOVE STORIES* sold reasonably well, charting at no.3 in France, no.14 in Austria, no.23 in Finland, no.24 in New Zealand, no.30 in Norway, no.36 in Belgium, no.47 in Switzerland and no.51 in the UK.

47 ~ *DE GROOTSTE HITS IN NEDERLAND* by ABBA

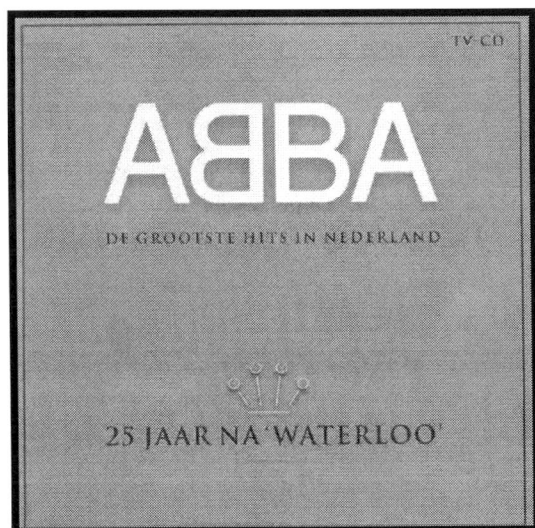

Waterloo/I Do, I Do, I Do, I Do, I Do/S.O.S/Fernando/Dancing Queen/Money, Money, Money/Knowing Me, Knowing You/The Name Of The Game/Take A Chance On Me/ Thank You For The Music/Summer Night City/Chiquitita/Gimme! Gimme! Gimme! (A Man After Midnight)/I Have A Dream/The Winner Takes It All/Happy New Year/Super Trouper/One Of Us/The Day Before You Came

Netherlands: Polydor 547 486-2 (1999).

17.04.99: 16-5-3-2-2-2-4-4-4-4-2-**1-1**-2-3-3-2-2-2-2-4-5-5-5-7-16-11-13-13-14-16-21-28-
30-25-28-27-15-15-17-23-26-25-31-46-52-68-79-78-84-81

Subtitled '*25 Jaar Na 'Waterloo*'' ('*25 Years After 'Waterloo*''), this TV-advertised Dutch compilation celebrated the 25th anniversary of ABBA winning the Eurovision Song Contest with *Waterloo*, and brought together some of the group's biggest hits.

The compilation was a huge success in the Netherlands, spending two weeks at no.1 during a lengthy chart run.

THE ABBA GENERATION by A*Teens

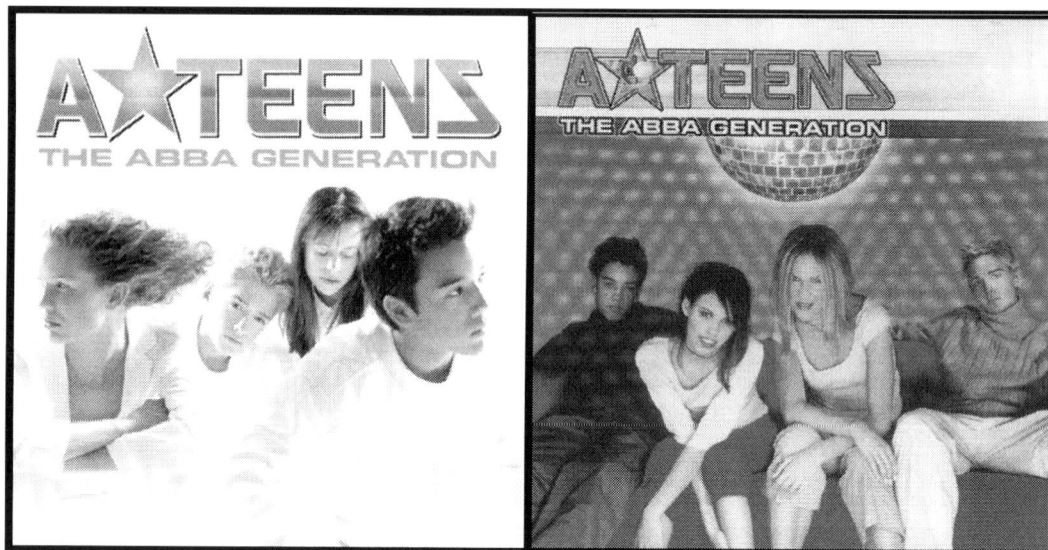

Mamma Mia/Gimme! Gimme! Gimme! (A Man After Midnight)/Super Trouper/One Of Us/Voulez-Vous/S.O.S/Dancing Queen/Take A Chance On Me/Lay All Your Love On Me/The Name Of The Game/Our Last Summer

Sweden: Stockholm 547 666-2 (1999).

2.09.99: **1-1-1-1-1**-2-5-11-12-13-10-16-14-17-118-6-6-10-20-24-29-34-35-38-44-55-x-58
13.04.00: 58-54-55

UK: Stockholm 547 666-2 (1999).

THE ABBA GENERATION wasn't a hit in the UK.

Austria
6.02.00: 4-**2**-3-**2**-4-13-7-12-7-11-9-11-12-22-23-37-47

Finland
21.08.99: 13-5-3-**2-2**-3-4-7-8-13-23-27-34-27-20-20-24-28-38-24-25-40

France
18.09.99: 52-48-**39**-47-48

Germany

7.02.00: peaked at no.**2**, charted for 24 weeks

Japan

25.10.99: 19-**18**-24-34-39-55-64-87

Netherlands

4.09.99: 26-4-3-**2**-3-5-6-10-8-6-10-14-12-13-15-16-23-25-25-24-31-46-48-48-56-68-82-88-89-100-97

Norway

4.09.99: **2**-3-**2**-**2**-3-7-12-9-33-37

Switzerland

5.12.99: 34-31-27-25-25-22-16-20-13-17-13-**12**-15-21-27-29-27-23-27-30-29-33-34-41-56-62-71-72

USA

3.06.00: 100-x-x-x-97-77-80-**71**-76-95-86-83-77-91-100-x-98-92-79-72

A*Teens, who originally called themselves Abba*Teens before changing their name for obvious reasons, formed in Stockholm, Sweden, in 1998 as an ABBA tribute band. The quartet comprised Amit Paul, Dhani Lennevald, Marie Serneholt and Sara Lumholdt.

The debut album by A*Teens, as the title suggests, was an album of ABBA cover versions. Released in 1999, *THE ABBA GENERATION* hit no.1 in Sweden, and charted at no.2 in Austria, Finland, Germany, the Netherlands and Norway, no.12 in Switzerland, no.18 in Japan and no.39 in France.

For the Latin American market, A*Teens recorded Spanish versions of *Gimme! Gimme! Gimme! (A Man After Midnight)* and *Mamma Mia*, which were added to *THE ABBA GENERATION* as bonus tracks.

A*Teens enjoyed several hit singles with covers of ABBA songs, but struggled when they moved on to non-ABBA material, and the quartet announced they had split in April 2006.

48 ~ *DE GROOTSTE HITS IN NEDERLAND DEEL 2* by ABBA

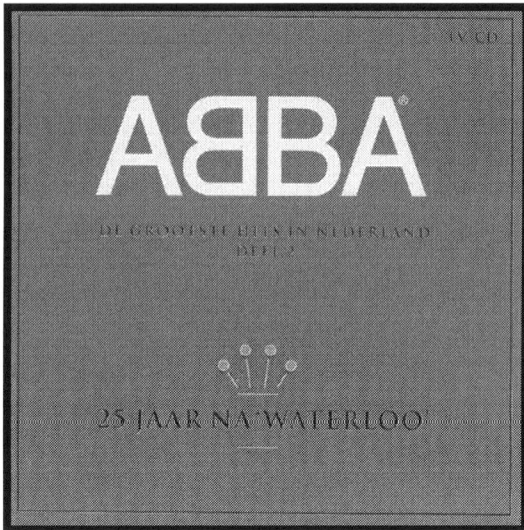

Mamma Mia/Does Your Mother Know/Voulez-Vous/Head Over Heels/Slipping Through My Fingers/Angeleyes/That's Me/Cassandra/Honey Honey/Eagle/Ring Ring/People Need Love/Lay All Your Love On Me/When I Kissed The Teacher/I Am The City/Our Last Summer/Under Attack/And On And On And On/When All Is Said And Done/The Way Old Friends Do

Netherlands: Polydor 543 065-2 (1999).

2.10.99: 60-14-**7**-8-9-8-13-19-30-33-27-30-31-28-22-23-27-32-31-42-60-63-94

The success of *DE GROOTSTE HITS IN NEDERLAND* saw the release, just six months later, of a second volume of ABBA hits – this time, with a few albums tracks and rarities like *I Am The City* featured as well.

Although not as successful as the first release, *DE GROOTSTE HITS IN NEDERLAND DEEL 2* rose to no.7 in the Netherlands, and spent nearly six months on the chart.

49 ~ MAMMA MIA! – Original Cast Recording

Act 1: *Overture-Prologue/Honey Honey/Money, Money, Money/Thank You For The Music/Mamma Mia/Chiquitita/Dancing Queen/Lay All Your Love On Me/Super Trouper/Gimme! Gimme! Gimme! (A Man After Midnight)/The Name Of The Game/ Voulez-Vous*

Act 2: *Entr'Acte/Under Attack/One Of Us/S.O.S/Does Your Mother Know/Knowing Me, Knowing You/Our Last Summer/Slipping Through My Fingers/The Winner Takes It All/Take A Chance On Me/I Do, I Do, I Do, I Do, I Do/I Have A Dream*

Sweden: Polydor 543 115-2 (1999).

18.11.99: **26**-48-31-29-29-31-34-44 (bi-weekly chart)

UK: Polydor 543 115-2 (1999).

13.11.99: 56-75
17.04.04: 98
12.07.08: 66-35-19-20-24-16-18-13-16-**12**-13-21-26-34-33-35-38-45-51-55-54-62-72-85-
   84-82-64-51-56-59-66-70-71-69-81-87-89-80
5.09.09: 96

Austria

17.02.06: **68**-70

Belgium

11.06.05: 99-**75**-78-83-99

Canada

9.09.05: **89**

Finland

26.05.07: 40-**23**-30

Germany

25.11.02: peaked at no.**63**, charted for 8 weeks

New Zealand

14.03.04: 38-50-43-38-32-33-x-37-**31**

The idea of *Mamma Mia!*, a musical written around ABBA songs, was dreamt up by producer Judy Craymer, who met with Benny and Björn in 1983 to discuss her vision. At the time, Benny and Björn were busy working with Tim Rice on another musical, *Chess*, and while they didn't dismiss Craymer's proposal out of hand, nor were they wildly enthusiastic about it.

It wasn't until 1997 that Craymer commissioned playwright Catherine Johnson to write the book for the musical, with Phyllida Lloyd as the musical's director. The musical was set on the Greek island of Kalokairi where, with her wedding fast approaching, Sophie is keen to have her father walk her down the aisle. However, from her mother's old diary, she discovers her father could be any one of three men – so, without telling her mother, she invites all three to her wedding.

With Benny and Björn now on board, and actively involved with the project, *Mamma Mia!* opened at London's Prince Edward Theatre on 6th April 1999. The cast included Lisa Stokke as Sophie, Siobhan McCarthy as her mother Donna, Hilton McRae, Paul Clarkson and Nicolas Colicos.

Mamma Mia! made its debut on Broadway the following year, on 17th November, at the Orpheum Theater in San Francisco.

Since it opened in 1999, *Mamma Mia!* has been seen by more than 54 million people in over forty countries, grossing in excess of $2 billion. The musical also served to re-ignite interest in ABBA's music, with the compilation *GOLD* especially benefitting in terms of sales.

Benny and Björn produced the original cast album, which over the years has charted at no.12 in the UK, no.23 in Finland, no.26 in Sweden and no.31 in New Zealand.

5th Anniversary Edition

A 5th anniversary edition of *Mamma Mia!* was released in 2004, with three bonus tracks: *Mamma Mia (Reprise)*, *Dancing Queen (Reprise)* and *Waterloo*.

A second 5th anniversary release commemorated the Broadway production – it came with a deluxe souvenir booklet and a bonus DVD, which gave a behind-the-scenes glimpse of international productions of *Mamma Mia!*.

ABBAMANIA by Various Artists

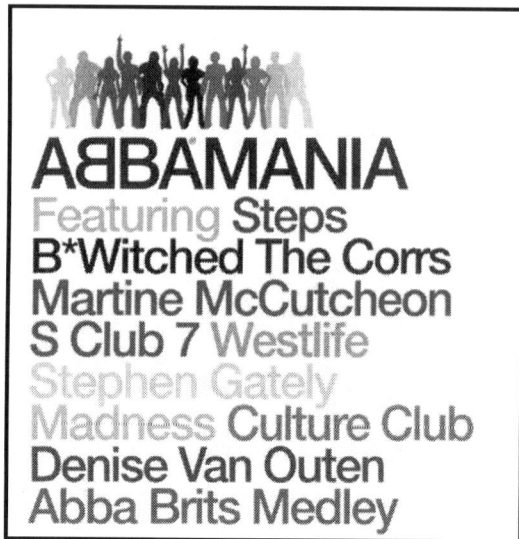

Money, Money, Money (Madness)/*Lay All Your Love On Me* (Steps)/*I Have A Dream* (Westlife)/*Chiquitita* (Stephen Gately)/*Gimme! Gimme! Gimme! (A Man After Midnight)* (Denise Van Outen)/*Voulez-Vous* (Culture Club)/*Mamma Mia* (Martine McCutcheon)/ *Dancing Queen* (S Club 7)/*I Know Him So Well* (Steps)/*Does Your Mother Know* (B*Witched)/*The Winner Takes It All* (The Corrs)/*Thank ABBA For The Music* (Steps, Cleopatra, B*Witched, Billie & Tina Cousins)

UK: Polydor 543 359-2 (1999).

20.11.99: peaked at no.**2**, charted for 14 weeks (Compilations chart)

This tribute album, which featured a cover of *I Know Him So Well* alongside versions of well-known ABBA hits by British and Irish artists, followed an ITV TV programme with the same title.

Westlife's cover of *I Have A Dream* and *Thank ABBA For The Music*, as performed at The Brits awards ceremony, were both hit singles in the UK.

50 ~ THE COMPLETE SINGLES COLLECTION by ABBA

CD1: *People Need Love/Ring Ring/Waterloo/Waterloo (German Version)/Honey Honey/ So Long/I Do, I Do, I Do, I Do, I Do/S.O.S/Mamma Mia/Fernando/Dancing Queen/ Money, Money, Money/Knowing Me, Knowing You/The Name Of The Game/Take A Chance On Me/Eagle/Thank You For The Music/Summer Night City*

CD2: *Chiquitita/Does Your Mother Know/Voulez-Vous/Gimme! Gimme! Gimme! (A Man After Midnight)/I Have A Dream/The Winner Takes It All/Super Trouper/Lay All Your Love On Me/One Of Us/Head Over Heels/The Day Before You Came/Under Attack/Ring Ring (German Version)/Happy New Year/Wer Im Wartesaal Der Liebe Steht (Another Town, Another Train, German Version)*

Germany: Polydor 543 231-2 (1999).

6.12.99: 39-23-11-**10-10**-11-14-15-18-18-18-18-18-25-23-31-31-37-38-51-39-50-55-60-
   62-72-93
26.06.00: 87-91-99
18.12.00: 54-76-81-79-98-78-87

Austria
12.12.99: 25-21-18-18-21-**11**-13-15-19-20-20-23-30-28-36-40

Switzerland
19.12.99: 43-17-**6-6-6**-9-11-15-17-21-24-33-36-42-42-51-55-60-66-68-91
21.01.01: 76
4.03.01: 77-x-89

This compilation was only released in Germany and, as well as the usual selection of ABBA hits, also included the German versions of *Waterloo*, *Ring Ring* and *Another Town, Another Train*.

THE COMPLETE SINGLES COLLECTION was a Top 10 hit in Germany, but was also made available in neighbouring countries, where it charted at no.6 in Switzerland and no.11 in Austria.

51 ~ THE COMPLETE GOLD COLLECTION by ABBA

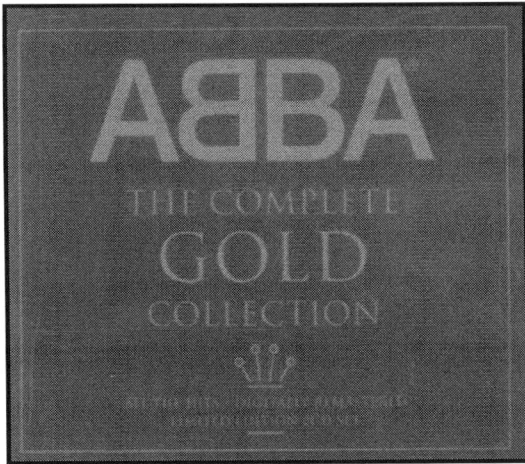

This is a limited edition 2 x CD release, comprising the Australian editions of ABBA's *GOLD* and *MORE GOLD*.

Australia: Polydor 543 710-2 (2000).

21.05.00: 16-12-20-26-34-43-44-x-50
3.12.00: 46-x-47-41-38-45-42-50
14.05.01: 83-x-x-22-**6**-9-9-8-10-15-21-23-24-40-44-42-42-62-60-69-64-75-59-89

THE COMPLETE GOLD COLLECTON was essentially a reissue of *FOREVER GOLD*, however, the original editions of *GOLD* and *MORE GOLD* released in Australia did feature slightly different track listings, and this was the first time those editions had been brought together.

THE COMPLETE GOLD COLLECTION was only released in Australia, where it peaked at no.6 more than a year after it was released.

52 ~ S.O.S. by ABBA

S.O.S/Chiquitita/Dancing Queen/That's Me/Take A Chance On Me/Eagle/Summer Night City/Voulez-Vous/Gimme! Gimme! Gimme! (A Man After Midnight)/The Winner Takes It All/On And On And On/Super Trouper/Mamma Mia/Money, Money, Money/Knowing Me, Knowing You/The Name Of The Game/Fernando/Lay All Your Love On Me/Waterloo

Japan: Polar/Universal UICY-1040 (2001).

7.02.01: peaked at no.**3**, charted for 35 weeks

This compilation, sub-titled 'The Best Of', was released exclusively in Japan, where it rose to no.3 on the Oricon chart during a lengthy chart run.

53 ~ THE BEST OF – THE MILLENNIUM COLLECTION by ABBA

*Waterloo/S.O.S/I Do, I Do, I Do, I Do, I Do/Mamma Mia/Fernando/Dancing Queen/
Knowing Me, Knowing You/The Name Of The Game/Take A Chance On Me/Chiquitita/
The Winner Takes It All*

USA: Polydor 314 543 948-2 (2000).

THE BEST OF – THE MILLENNIUM COLLECTION didn't enter the Top 100 in the
USA, however, the album did spend 10 weeks on the Billboard 200 in 2008-9, peaking at
no.114.

Europe: Polar 5329716 (as *ICON*, 2010).

Canada
06.01: peaked at no.**19**, charted for 102 weeks
05.04: 99
08.07: peaked at no.32, charted for 10 weeks
06.08: peaked at no.32, charted for 7 weeks

New Zealand
21.02.11: 31-**24** (*ICON*)

This mid-price compilation was one of numerous 'best of' albums released in North America in the 20th Century Masters series, all issued around the start of the new millennium.

Only a minor hit in the USA, *THE BEST OF – THE MILLENNIUM COLLECTION* rose to no.19 in Canada, where it has spent over two years on the chart.

THE BEST OF – THE MILLENNIUM COLLECTION was repackaged and retitled *ICON*, and released in Europe and Australasia in 2010. It charted at no.24 in New Zealand, but it wasn't a hit in most countries.

54 ~ BENNY ANDERSSONS ORKESTER by Benny Anderssons Orkester

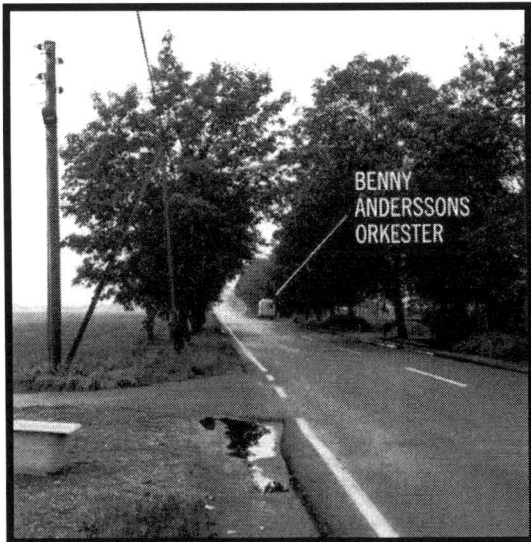

Hardangervidda/Snedseglarn/Cirkus Finemang/Vår Sista Dans/Briggens Blåögda Blonda Kapten/Knasluvan/Anitas Polska/Schottis I Tyrolen/Sång Från Andra Våningen/Laureen/Tösabiten/Nya Månvalsen/Lätt Som En Sommarfjäril/P.S.

Sweden: Mono MMCD 017 (2001).

5.07.01: 51-30-43-57-x-x-5-4-5-5-**1**-3-4-11-9-14-22-29-38-34-43-36-23-27-21-21-9-3-4
   4-11-15-15-15-19-28-25-26-34-45-x-44
30.05.02: 55-x-55-36-40-40-39-32-49-33
12.09.02: 41-53-53
6.02.03: 52
15.08.03: 30-46-53

Following two solo albums, Benny formed the Benny Andersson Orkester, a group of 15 or so musicians including himself, in early 2001.

The group's self-titled debut album was recorded over just two weekends, in Stockholm, and was recorded 'live' in the studio. All but two of the tracks on the album were instrumental, the exceptions being *Vår Sista Dans* and *Lätt Som En Sommarfjäril*, for which Björn penned the lyrics and Helen Sjöholm was the vocalist.

BENNY ANDERSSONS ORKESTER was only released in Sweden, where it gave Benny his first no.1 outside ABBA, and spent more than a year on the chart.

55 ~ THE DEFINITIVE COLLECTION by ABBA

CD1: *People Need Love/He Is Your Brother/Ring Ring/Love Isn't Easy (But It Sure Is Hard Enough)/Waterloo/Honey Honey/So Long/I Do, I Do, I Do, I Do, I Do/S.O.S/ Mamma Mia/Fernando/Dancing Queen/Money, Money, Money/Knowing Me, Knowing You/The Name Of The Game/Take A Chance On Me/Eagle/Summer Night City/ Chiquitita/Does Your Mother Know*

CD2: *Voulez-Vous/Angeleyes/Gimme! Gimme! Gimme! (A Man After Midnight)/I Have A Dream/The Winner Takes It All/Super Trouper/On And On And On/Lay All Your Love On Me/One Of Us/When All Is Said And Done/Head Over Heels/The Visitors/The Day Before You Came/Under Attack/Thank You For The Music/Ring Ring (1974 Remix/Single Version)/Voulez-Vous (Extended Remix)*

Australia Bonus Tracks: *Rock Me & Hasta Mañana*

Sweden: Polydor 549 974-2 (2001).

16.11.01: 28-40-46-47-42-43-49-36-42-45-52
21.05.04: 27-**26**-32-31-36-38-50-x-53
27.08.04: 60
9.04.10: 45
14.05.10: 50
9.07.10: 57-x-60-47-52-56-x-52-55

UK: Polydor 549 974-2 (2001).

10.11.01: **17**-25-41-56-68-70-68-66-79-x-x-85-x-x-x-x-x-83-88
1.06.02: 99-89-100-100

Australia
16.09.02: 24-14-**10**-14-12-18-22-43-45-43-60-47-50-51-35-40-49-51-56-55-67-72-77-93-
    93-93-94-100
12.05.03: 91-x-x-x-86-62-71-78-65-90-71-74-93-65-24-23-23-18-22-30-33-45-47-46-37-
    36-43-34-45-52-48-45-46-51-44-57-49-68-87-94-96-100
4.10.04: 67-29-50-51-38-45-50-37-37-50-43-44-44-43-32-45-55-68-95-x-100
23.01.06: 98
28.07.08: 40-52-38-42-52-44-64-87-83-94-96

Austria
18.11.01: 45-**38**-40-54-66-72-72-52-53-67-67-53-48-54-51-61-68

Belgium
4.06.05: **81**
11.02.06: 100-98

Finland
22.05.10: 34-x-x-x-50-46-x-**28**-30-32-32-44

France
14.10.01: 27-**12**-15-30 (Compilation chart)
21.04.06: 39-76-56 (Compilations chart)
9.04.11: 92-91-90
4.06.11: 35-43-65-87-x-97
3.09.11: 67

Germany
25.02.02: 35-42-44-57-69-74-91
29.07.02: 50-46-48-54-38-40-54-53-61-75-78-94-100-95-68-46-23-26-23-29-29-24-26-
    28-32-29-27-34-42-46-55-70-48-57-34-47-66-40-36-33-41-41-50-35-40-50-53-51-60-
    69-73-74-76-80-71-75-77-88-97-82
19.04.04: 38-**14**-18-22-32-36-39-56-58-69-72-77-85-77-74-67-72-76-68-67-73-91-78-83-
    92
10.01.05: 63-68-92-77-93
18.11.05: 67-72-76-61-58-54-62-73-77

Netherlands
22.03.03: 77-60-66-69-51-**39**-67-74-46-44-52-60-74-74-76-91-93-88-96-97-89-99
7.02.04: 96-75-61-67-63-61-63-75-100

New Zealand
10.03.02: 14-**9**-11-13-11-29-37-44-47-41

Norway
10.07.04: 21-12-**8**-13-13-13-22-26-28
11.03.06: 35

Switzerland
25.11.01: 100-85
13.01.02: 93-x-100
20.04.03: 86-89
4.04.04: 98-97-63-**34**-40-50-56-40-61-82-88-99-x-98
12.02.06: 66-84-89
3.02.08: 86

USA
THE DEFINITIVE COLLECTION didn't enter the Top 100 in the USA, however, it did spend one week on the Billboard 200 at no.186.

THE DEFINITIVE COLLECTION was the natural successor to ABBA's *THE SINGLE – THE FIRST TEN YEARS* compilation, and featured the group's hit singles spread over two CDs in chronological order, with the first disc covering 1972-79 and the second disc 1979-82. The second disc also included two bonus tracks, the 1974 Single Remix of *Ring Ring* and the Extended Remix of *Voulez-Vous*.

The Australian edition included *Rock Me* and *Hasta Mañana*, which had been sizeable hits in that country.

Given how many ABBA compilations had been released, coupled with the ongoing success of *GOLD*, it is not surprising *THE DEFINITIVE COLLECTION* wasn't a major hit. However, it did chart at no.9 in New Zealand, no.10 in Australia, no.12 in France, no.14 in Germany, no.17 in the UK, no.26 in Sweden, no.28 in Finland, no.34 in Switzerland, no.38 in Austria and no.39 in the Netherlands.

56 ~ CHESS – *PÅ SVENSKA*

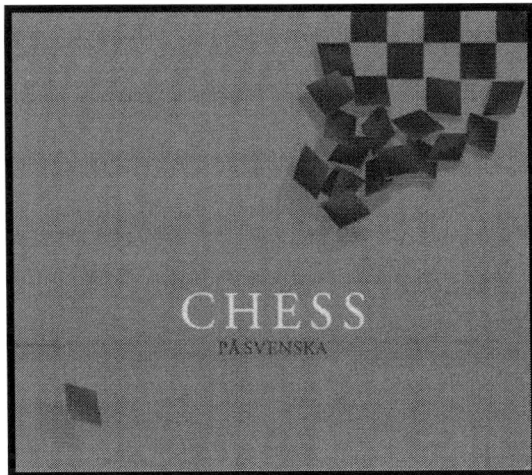

Ouvertyr/Historien Om Schack/Där Jag Ville Vara/Merano/Anatolij Och Molokov/ Ungern '56/Lämna Inga Dörrar På Glänt/Jag Vill Se Schack/Chess/Kvartett (En Förebild För Dygd Och Högsta Ambition)/Inte Jag/Möte På En Bro/I Mitt Hjärtas Land/ Florence Lämnar Freddie/Vem Ser Ett Barn/Ni Dömer Mig/Om Han Var Här/Han Är En Man, Han Är Ett Barn/Vem Kunde Ana/Drömmar Av Glas/Jag Vill Se Schack/Jag Vet Vad Han Vill/Glöm Mig Om Du Kan/Capablanca/Drömmar Av Glas/Historien Om Schack

Sweden: Mono MMCD 019 (2002).

7.11.02: **2**-13-11-24-21-7-11-11-15-27-51-60

The Swedish version of Benny and Björn's musical *Chess* premiered in Stockholm in 2002, and the accompanying cast album *CHESS – PÅ SVENSKA* ('*Chess* – In Swedish') made its chart debut in Sweden at no.2, but it rose no higher.

57 ~ CADILLAC MADNESS by the Hep Stars

CD1: *Intro/Cadillac/Kana Kapila/Tribute To Buddy Holly/Farmer John/Donna/Bald Headed Woman/No Response/Rented Tuxedo/So Mystifying/Young And Beautiful/Should I/Sunny Girl/Hawaii/Wedding/Don't/It Isn't Easy To Say/When My Blue Moon Turns To Gold Again/Tallahassee Lassie/Surfin' Bird/Wear My Ring Around Your Neck*

CD2: *Love Is Coming Back/I Natt Jag Drömde/Consolation/It's Nice To Be Back/ Malakia/Mot Okänt Land/She Will Love You/Like You Used To Do/It's Been A Long Long Time/Sagan Om Lilla Sofi/Det Finns En Sad/Groovy Summertime/Let It Be Me/Tända På Varann/The Music Box/Holiday For Clowns/Speleman/Är Det Inte Kärlek Säg?/Speedy Gonzales/Cadillac 2004*

Sweden: Olga 7243 5 97344 2 2 (2004).

9.04.04: 13-11-**9**-11-18-33-46-55

This double CD of Hep Stars hits and album tracks was sub-titled '40 Years * 40 Hits * 1964-2004', and was only released in Sweden. Two versions of *Cadillac* were included, the original 1965 recording and an up-dated 2004 mix.
   CADILLAC MADNESS charted at no.9 in Sweden.

58 ~ THE ABBA STORY by ABBA

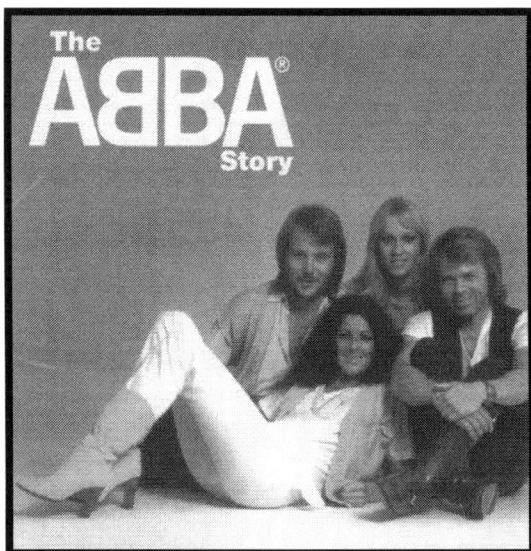

Ring Ring/Waterloo/I Do, I Do, I Do, I Do, I Do/S.O.S/Mamma Mia/Fernando/Dancing Queen/Money, Money, Money/Knowing Me, Knowing You/The Name Of The Game/Take A Chance On Me/Thank You For The Music/Summer Night City/Voulez-Vous/Gimme! Gimme! Gimme! (A Man After Midnight)/I Have A Dream/The Winner Takes It All/Super Trouper/One Of Us/When All Is Said And Done

Europe: Polar 0602498664537 (2004).

Austria
2.05.04: 44-**21**-29-45-59-72

Belgium
20.03.04: 78-56-51-**44**-60-69-62-82
19.06.04: 83-64-69-81-93

France
20.02.04: 5-**2**-4-7-9-14-13-12-14-20-27-37-40-39-x-17-14-26-x-39-x-27-33-36-37-38-x-
x-37-40 (Compilation chart)

Germany
10.05.04: **31**-50-47-55-75-89

Switzerland
2.05.04: 19-**14**-22-18-27-35-50-77-88-77-85-98

This compilation was released exclusively in Europe, and it only achieved Top 40 status in a few countries, charting at no.2 on the compilations chart in France, no.14 in Switzerland, no.21 in Austria, no.31 in Germany and no.44 in Belgium.

59 ~ MY COLOURING BOOK by Agnetha Fältskog

My Colouring Book/When You Walk In The Room/If I Thought You'd Ever Change Your Mind/Sealed With A Kiss/Love Me With All Your Heart/Fly Me To The Moon/Past, Present And Future/A Fool Am I/I Can't Reach Your Heart/Sometimes When I'm Dreaming/The End Of The World/Remember Me/What Now My Love

Sweden: WEA 5050467 3122 2 7 (2004).

30.04.04: **1-1**-3-6-5-5-3-4-4-5-6-7-7-11-15-10-18-15-23-31-35-43
6.01.05: 33-53-x-55

UK: WEA 5050467 3122 2 7 (2004).

1.05.04: **12**-25-46-62-98

Australia
31.05.04: **50**-82

Austria
9.05.04: **25**-60-65

Finland
1.05.04: 5-4-**2**-4-7-10-4-5-9-13-8-7-6-8-9-21-20-28-35

Germany
10.05.04: **6**-16-19-26-40-37-59-73-90-96

Netherlands
24.04.04: 31-15-**11**-17-26-32-47-61-75-85
7.08.04: 94

Norway
4.05.04: 32-**25**-27

Switzerland
2.05.04: 53-**17**-32-57-75-91

Agnetha returned to the studio in February 2003, to record what would be her first new album for 17 years. The album took a year to complete, with Agnetha recording her own versions of songs she had listened to and fallen in love with then she was growing up in the 1960s, including classics like *Fly Me To The Moon*, *Sealed With A Kiss* and *What Now My Love*.

Agnetha co-produced *MY COLOURING BOOK* with Anders Neglin and Dan Strömkvist, and the album produced two hit singles, *If I Thought You'd Ever Change Your Mind* and *When You Walk In The Room*. A third single, *Sometimes When I'm Dreaming*, was released as a promo CD single in Sweden only, but its full release was cancelled as *MY COLOURING BOOK* had slipped out of the charts in most countries, and Agnetha herself was refusing to do any promotion.

MY COLOURING BOOK returned Agnetha to no.1 in Sweden, and the album charted at no.2 in Finland, no.6 in Germany, no.11 in the Netherlands, no.12 in the UK, no.17 in Switzerland, no.25 in Austria and Norway, and no.50 in Australia.

60 ~ *BAO!* by Benny Anderssons Orkester with Helen Sjöholm

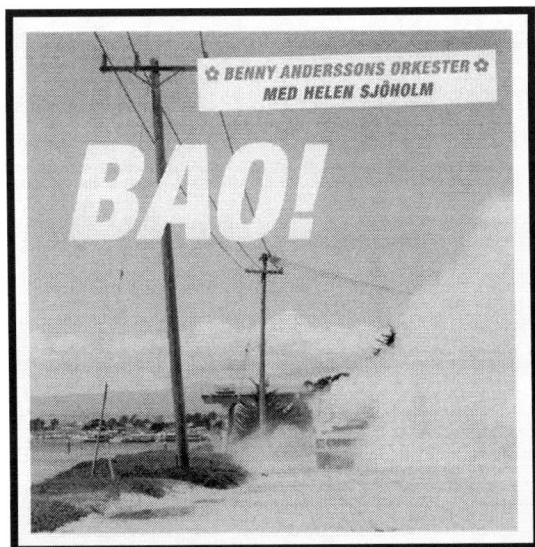

Glasgow Boogie/En Dans På Rosor/Du Är Min Man/Vitalins Vals/På En Solskens-promenad/Jehu/Midnattsdans/Riks 1:an/Julvals/Skenbart/Trettondagspolkan/Stora Skuggan/Saknadens Rum/Kärlekens Tid

Sweden: Mono MMCD 012 (2004).

2.07.04: 2-3-3-3-4-3-3-2-3-3-2-**1**-2-4-5-11-14-10-19-19-19-30-31-25-24-20-27-26-24-24-
   21-30-28-23-31-28-43-48-18-x-x-34-36-35-54-44-x-56-x-46
4.08.05: 45-12-16-16-30-37-38-50
20.10.05: 58

The second album by the Benny Andersson Orkester credited Helen Sjöholm as well, as she was the featured vocalist on five tracks. Benny composed all the tracks, with Björn writing the lyrics for *Midnattsdans*, which Helen Sjöholm sang as a duet with Kalle Moraeus, and *Du Är Min Man*, which Björn also sang backing vocals on.

    Du Är Min Man ('You Are My Man') topped the Svensktoppen radio chart for an record shattering 65 weeks, and remained on the chart for a mighty 278 weeks – another record. An English version of *Du Är Min Man* was included on the 2009 album, *STORY OF A HEART*, credited to the Benny Andersson Band.

    BAO! gave the Benny Andersson Orkester their second consecutive no.1 album in Sweden, and spent more than a year on the chart.

61 ~ MAMMA MIA! – *Originalversion Des Deutschen Musicals*

Act 1: *Prologue/Mich Trägt Mein Traum (I Have A Dream)/Honey Honey/Money, Money, Money/Danke Für Die Lieder (Thank You For The Music)/Mamma Mia/ Chiquitita/ Dancing Queen/Leg Dein Herz An Eine Leine (Lay All Your Love On Me)/ Super Trouper/ Gib Mir, Gib Mir, Gib Mie! (Gimme, Gimme, Gimme!)/Was Ist Das Für Ein Spiel? (The Name Of The Game)/Voulez-Vous*

Act 2: *Unter Beschuss (Under Attack)/Einer Von Uns (One Of Us)/S.O.S/Wenn Das Mami Wüsst (Does Your Mother Know)/Ich Bin Ich, Du Bist Du (Knowing Me, Knowing You)/ Unser Sommer (Our Last Summer)/Durch Meine Finger Rinnt Die Zeit (Slipping Through My Fingers)/Komm Und Wag's Mit Mir (Take A Chance On Me)/Ich Will, Ich Will, Ich Will, Ich Will, Ich Will (I Do, I Do, I Do, I Do, I Do)/Mich Trägt Mein Traum (I Have A Dream)*

Germany: Polydor 986 7013 (2004).

5.07.04: peaked at no.**3**, charted for 56 weeks

The first non-English production of the musical *Mamma Mia!* opened in Hamburg, Germany, on 3rd November 2002. A second German production, in Stuttgart, coincided with the release of a German cast recording, which charted at no.3 in Germany and spent more than a year on the chart.

62 ~ MAMMA MIA! – *Nederlands Cast Album*

Act 1: *Ouverture/Proloog/Honey Honey/Money, Money, Money/Dank Je Voor De Liedjes/Mamma Mia/Chiquitita/Dancing Queen/Spaar Al Je Liefs Voor Mij/Super Trouper/Geef Me! Geef Me! Geef Me!/Als'k Maar Weet Hoe Het Heet/Voulez-Vous*

Act 2: *Entr'Acte/Een Offensief/Een Van Ons/S.O.S/Weet Je Moeder Dat/Zo Ben Ik, Zo Ben Jij/Onze Zomer/'T Glipt Me Door M'n Vingers/De Winnaar Krijgt De Macht/Pak Je Kans/Ik Wil, Ik Wil, Ik Wil/Ik Heb Een Droom*

Netherlands: Polydor 981 372-1 (2004).

21.08.04: 13-2-7-**6**-16-14-18-18-21-24-46-29-32-36-37-32-43-39-60-14-16-28-25-68-22-
    27-23-85-45-39-27-27-71-50-29-29-20-19-25-x-27-35-17-18-55-27-29-21-66
17.09.05: 80-84
18.03.06: 79-x-x-x-82-83

The first Dutch production of *Mamma Mia!* opened in Utrecht in 2003, and the following year a Dutch cast recording was released. It rose to no.6 in the Netherlands, and like the German cast recording issued around the same time, it enjoyed a lengthy chart run.

63 ~ *TODO ABBA* by ABBA

CD: *Waterloo/Take A Chance On Me/Mamma Mia/Dancing Queen/S.O.S/Super Trouper/ Chiquitita (Español)/Conociéndome, Conociéndote (Knowing Me, Knowing You)/I Do, I Do, I Do, I Do, I Do/Voulez-Vous/Does Your Mother Know/Estoy Soñando (I Have A Dream)/Gimme! Gimme! Gimme! (A Man After Midnight)/The Winner Takes It All/No Hay A Quién Culpar (When All Is Said And Done)/One Of Us/Fernando/Felicidad (Happy New Year)/Thank You For The Music*

DVD: *Waterloo/Take A Chance On Me/Mamma Mia/Dancing Queen/S.O.S/Super Trouper/Chiquitita (Inglés)/Knowing Me, Knowing You/I Do, I Do, I Do, I Do, I Do/ Voulez-Vous/Does Your Mother Know/Estoy Soñando (I Have A Dream)/Gimme! Gimme! Gimme! (A Man After Midnight)/The Winner Takes It All/No Hay A Quién Culpar (When All Is Said And Done)/One Of Us/Fernando/Felicidad (Happy New Year)/Thank You For The Music*

Spain: Polar 0602498248270 (2004).

9.01.05: 36-44-39-45-61-64-60-79-82-87-94-86-87-73-93-94-84-94-x-68-x-x-100
21.01.06: 74-67-67-61-45-48-34-21-31-24-23-24-14-19-28-44-69-95-94
14.01.07: 11-18-17-**4**-10-10-5-7-9-18-20-14-18-60
17.08.08: 42-12-7-9-12-14-15-20-22-25-30-35-46-50-68-64-64-71-59-57-63-87-77-80

Sub-titled '*Sus Grandes Éxitos*' ('The Greatest Hits'), this compilation comprised one CD and one DVD, and was released exclusively in Spain – naturally, both the CD and DVD featured the Spanish versions of several ABBA hits.

TODO ABBA was released towards the end of 2004, but it didn't enter the chart until January 2005, when it made its debut at no.36 and rose no higher. The following January, the compilation re-entered the chart, this time climbing to no.14, however, it wasn't until the following year the compilation finally achieved its peak position of no.4.

64 ~ *BAO PÅ TURNÉ* by Benny Anderssons Orkester with Helen Sjöholm & Tommy Körberg

Glasgow Boogie/Vitalins Vals/När Tvenne Hjärtan Slå/För Dig/Klinga Mina Klockor/ Födelsedagsvals Till Mona/Tobakshandlarna/Lätt Som En Sommarfjäril/Det Är Vi Ändå/Aj Aj Aj Vilken Röd Liten Ros/Gamle Svarten/Slängpolska Efter Bysskalle/ Hjortingen/Bälter Svens Paradpolkett/Moon River/Badinerie/O Sole Mio/Jehu/Du Är Min Man/True Love/Vår Sista Dans/Finalpotpurri

Sweden: Mono MMCD 022 (2006).

18.05.06: **6**-9-12-14-13-13-12-16-9-14-20-22-21-20-19-20-22-24-25-26-36-37-39-41-x-x-43
29.03.07: 30-46-42

As the title suggests, *BAO PÅ TURNÉ* ('BAO On Tour') is a live album the Benny Andersson Orkester recorded during their summer 2005 tour, with the album featuring a selection of tracks recorded in the Swedish towns of Leksand and Örebro.

As well as Benny's own compositions, BAO performed traditional Swedish folk songs and classics like *Moon River*, *O Sole Mio* and *True Love*. The album also featured two new songs, *För Dig* and *Det Är Vi Ändå*, both composed by Benny with lyrics by Björn, and performed as duets by Helen Sjöholm and Tommy Körberg.

Only released in Sweden, *BAO PÅ TURNÉ* made its chart debut at no.6, but it didn't climb any higher.

65 ~ 18 HITS by ABBA

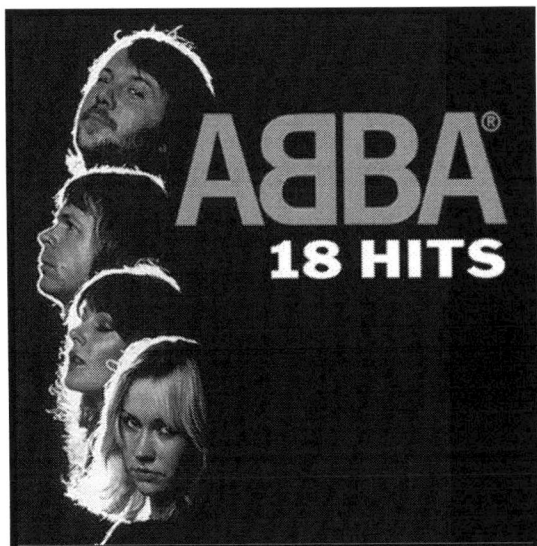

The Winner Takes It All/Super Trouper/Waterloo/Gimme! Gimme! Gimme! (A Man After Midnight)/The Name Of The Game/Ring Ring/I Do, I Do, I Do, I Do, I Do/S.O.S/Fernando/Hasta Mañana/Mamma Mia/Lay All Your Love On Me/Thank You For The Music/Happy New Year/Waterloo (French Version)/Honey Honey (Swedish Version)/Ring Ring (German Version)/Dame! Dame! Dame! (Gimme! Gimme! Gimme! (A Man After Midnight), Spanish Version)

UK

27.05.06: 79-82-99-x-x-x-95
27.01.07: 46-64
19.07.08: 54-48-54-58-51-54-27-24-28-30-**15**-17-24-32-36-43-56-67-72-86
29.08.09: 64-63-71-87
11.02.12: 96-x-x-x-74-58-58-63-75-96-98-83-83-78-82-53-71-79-99-92-65-78-65-75-79-88-98-100

Australia
21.11.05: 41-75-94
12.06.06: 52-33-**32**-36-43-67-93
28.08.06: 90-70-82-54-55-59-65-68-90-40-66-x-86
9.06.08: 36-53-61-61-47-45-43-67-71-72
9.02.09: 61-61-82-81-84-92

20.04.09: 97
20.07.09: 88-96-93
31.08.09: 96
28.09.09: 98-95
9.11.09: 59-37-53-78-77-91-87-x-95-83-72-64-85-90-92-x-x-99-x-95-x-x-98
10.05.10: 94
7.06.10: 77-49-49-46-53
8.11.10: 91-56-66
13.05.13: 42-41-63-57-55-58-61-62-56-45-45-50-66-75-80-97-98-92-90-95-x-81-85-78-
88
23.12.13: 100-99

France
30.12.05: 43-41-40-25-31-58 (Compilations chart)
31.12.06: 30-15-19-29-30 (Compilations chart)
3.06.07: 28-26-14-17-31-32-33-x-39 (Compilations chart)
30.12.07: 14-12-16-16-24-39 (Compilations chart)
8.06.08: 11-13-18-19-18-27-37 (Compilations chart)
25.05.09: 17-7-**5**-6-8-11-13-19-18-40 (Compilations chart)
21.09.09: 29 (Compilations chart)
23.04.11: 100-96
16.06.12: 93-82-96-92-83-99-97
19.01.13: 87-81-80-89
18.05.13: 96-96-94-x-x-94-x-x-x-79

Germany
5.08.08: 62-74-80-62-**58**-76

Spain
10.09.06: 76-26-24-40-56-53-73-75-78
8.04.07: 62-**17**-24-46-53-63-56-58-61-85
30.03.08: 83
21.09.08: 69-65-83
15.03.09: 49-48-40-43-37

The compilation *18 HITS* was released as a mid-price alternative to *GOLD* – it included 14 of ABBA's hits, followed by the French version of *Waterloo*, the Swedish version of *Honey Honey*, the German version of *Ring Ring* and the Spanish version of *Gimme! Gimme! Gimme! (A Man After Midnight)*. At the same time, the compilation deliberately omitted some of ABBA's biggest hits, including *Dancing Queen* and *Chiquitita*.

The Swedish edition of *18 HITS* came with a slightly different track listing:

The Winner Takes It All/Super Trouper/Waterloo/Gimme! Gimme! Gimme! (A Man After Midnight)/The Name Of The Game/Ring Ring/I Do, I Do, I Do, I Do, I Do/S.O.S/ Fernando/Hasta Mañana/Mamma Mia/Lay All Your Love On Me/Thank You For The Music/Happy New Year/Waterloo (Swedish Version)/Honey Honey (Swedish Version)/ Ring Ring (Bara Du Slog En Signal)/Åh, Vilka Tider

Åh, Vilka Tider ('Oh, What Times') was originally released as the B-side of *Ring Ring (Bara Du Slog En Signal)* in Sweden.

18 HITS wasn't especially successful when it was originally released, but over the years it has sold steadily and continues to re-enter some national charts occasionally. The compilation has peaked at no.5 in France, no.15 in the UK, no.17 in Spain, no.32 in Australia and no.58 in Germany.

A budget-priced DVD, *16 HITS*, was released at the same time as *18 HITS* – it included the following music videos:

The Winner Takes It All/Gimme! Gimme! Gimme! (A Man After Midnight)/The Name Of The Game/I Do, I Do, I Do, I Do, I Do/Thank You For The Music/Dancing Queen/ Chiquitita/The Day Before You Came/On And On And On/Voulez-Vous/Does Your Mother Know/Happy New Year/Waterloo/Knowing Me, Knowing You/When All Is Said And Done

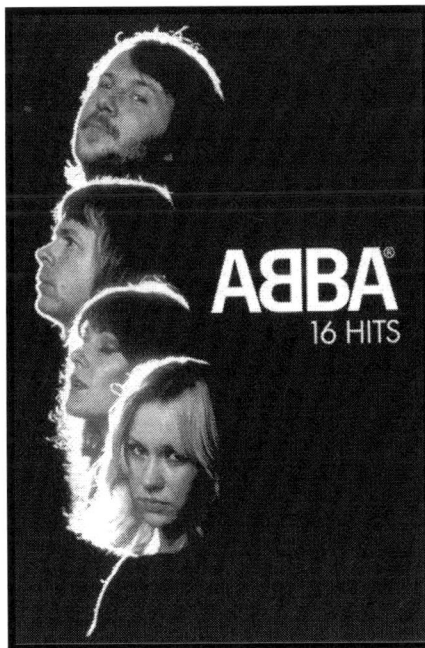

66 ~ MAMMA MIA! – *PÅ SVENSKA*

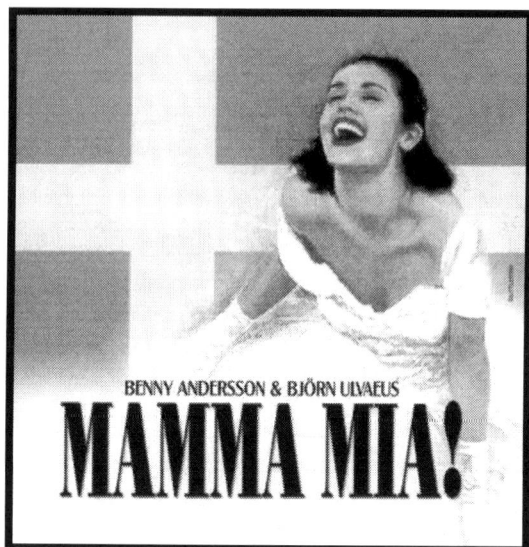

Act 1: *Overture/Jag Har En Dröm (I Have A Dream)/Honey Honey/Money. Money, Money/Tack För Alla Sånger (Thank You For The Music)/Mamma Mia/Chiquitita/ Dancing Queen/I Tryggt Förvar Hos Mig (Lay All Your Love On Me)/Super Trouper/Säg OK Eller Nej (The Name Of The Game)/Voulez-Vous*

Act 2: *Entracte/Under Attack/En Av Oss (One Of Us)/S.O.S/Väntar Inte Mamma På Dig (Does Your Mother Know)/Jag Är Jag, Du Är Du (Knowing Me, Knowing You)/Sista Sommarn (Our Last Summer)/Kan Man Ha En Solkatt I En Bur (Slipping Through My Fingers)/Vinnaren Tar Allt (The Winner Takes It All)/Tänk, Det Känns Som Vi (Take A Chance On Me)/Jag Vill, Jag Vill, Jag Vill (I Do, I Do, I Do, I Do, I Do)/Jag Har En Dröm (I Have A Dream)/Waterloo*

Sweden: Mono 987 202-5 (2005).

16.06.05: **2**-5-12-18-10-14-22-20-9-10-10-15-21-15-22-22-26-38-35-57
1.12.05: 59-52-58-x-58-x-53-x-x-46-50-55-58-55-53-52
27.04.06: 56-x-x-57-42-29

The first Swedish production of the hit musical *Mamma Mia!* opened in the capital, Stockholm, in 2005. The Swedish cast album made its chart debut at no.2, and charted on and off for nearly a year.

RAJATON SINGS ABBA by Rajaton with Lahti Symphony Orchestra

Dancing Queen/Chiquitita/Money, Money Money/One Of Us/Voulez-Vous/Does Your Mother Know/Head Over Heels/Mamma Mia/Gimme! Gimme! Gimme! (A Man After Midnight)/The Winner Takes It All/Thank You For The Music/Fernando/Waterloo

Finland: Plastinka PLACD043 (2006).

11.11.06: **1**-3-4-7-9-10-8-5-12-12-x-x-x-x-40

This tribute album, which was only released in Finland, was largely orchestral – the three exceptions are *Voulez-Vous*, *Head Over Heels* and *Fernando*, which are all *a cappella*.

   RAJATON SINGS ABBA made its debut on the Finnish chart at no.1, but it only spent one week at the top.

67 ~ NUMBER ONES by ABBA

Gimme! Gimme! Gimme! (A Man After Midnight)/Mamma Mia (Album Version)/Dancing Queen/Super Trouper/S.O.S (Album Version)/Summer Night City (Long Version)/Money, Money, Money/The Winner Takes It All (Album Version)/Chiquitita/One Of Us/Knowing Me, Knowing You/Voulez-Vous/Fernando/Waterloo/Ring Ring/The Name Of The Game/I Do, I Do, I Do, I Do, I Do/Take A Chance On Me/I Have A Dream

CD2 (UK Special Edition): *When I Kissed The Teacher/Hole In Your Soul/ Dance (While The Music Still Goes On)/Me And I/The King Has Lost His Crown/Rock Me/Tiger/I Wonder (Departure)/Another Town, Another Train/Our Last Summer/Kisses Of Fire/ Slipping Through My Fingers*

Sweden: Polydor 171 931-9 (2006), Polydor 170 931-8 (2CD, 2006).

30.11.06: 46-43-27-27-22-37-30-**20**-23-31-44-x-x-51
24.05.07: 57

UK: Polydor 171 931-9 (2006), Polydor 170 931-8 (2CD, 2006).

18.11.06: **15**-30-47-55-66-68-64-91-x-x-x-x-x-x-95

Australia
20.11.06: 77-94-68-83-87-81-97

26.02.07: 100-90-x-90-x-77-97
14.07.08: 95-49-**36**-45-83-100

Austria
1.12.06: 27-30-44-36-36-24-**22**-27-45-50-70-56-57-49-65

Belgium
16.12.06: **100**

Finland
2.12.06: 38-17-20-25-18-**11**-14
26.05.07: 25-40

Germany
11.12.06: 33-37-39-32-**24**-34-44-36-45-54-57-63-70-81

Netherlands
9.12.06: 87-88-100-87-**57**-63-63-88-87-99
26.05.07: 47

New Zealand
8.01.07: **1-1-1**-6-10-14-16-25-24-34-34-34-34

Norway
10.05.08: 39
2.08.08: **25**

Switzerland
3.12.06: 57-66-x-x-82-65-**53-53**-57-74-88-93-91-x-96

USA
NUMBER ONES didn't enter the Top 100 in the USA, however, it did spend seven weeks on the Billboard 200, peaking at no.139.

This compilation, as the title suggests, was a collection of ABBA hits that achieved no.1 in one or more countries.

Ring Ring and the extended version of *Summer Night City* were only included on the UK edition; all other editions omitted *Ring Ring* and featured the originally released edited version of *Summer Night City*.

A special edition of *NUMBER ONES* was issued in the UK that came with a bonus CD of selected tracks from ABBA's no.1 albums – some of which, like *When I Kissed The*

Teacher, *Hole In Your Soul*, *Our Last Summer* and *Kisses Of Fire*, were strong enough to have been successful singles, had they been released.

In Taiwan only, *NUMBER ONES* featured a 'hidden' track after *I Have A Dream*, titled *ABBA Remix*. This was a previously unreleased three and a half minute medley of the choruses of the 18 hits featured on the compilation.

Inevitably, *NUMBER ONES* included many of the same hits as *GOLD* – only three hits featured on *GOLD* didn't appear on *NUMBER ONES* as well, namely *Does Your Mother Know* (which was a no.1 in Belgium), *Lay All Your Love On Me* and *Thank You For The Music*.

NUMBER ONES was most successful in New Zealand, where it topped the chart for three weeks. The compilation was less successful in other countries, charting at no.11 in Finland, no.15 in the UK, no.20 in Sweden, no.22 in Austria, no.24 in Germany, no.25 in Norway, no.36 in Australia, no.53 in Switzerland and no.57 in the Netherlands.

68 ~ BAO 3 by Benny Anderssons Orkester with Helen Sjöholm & Tommy Körberg

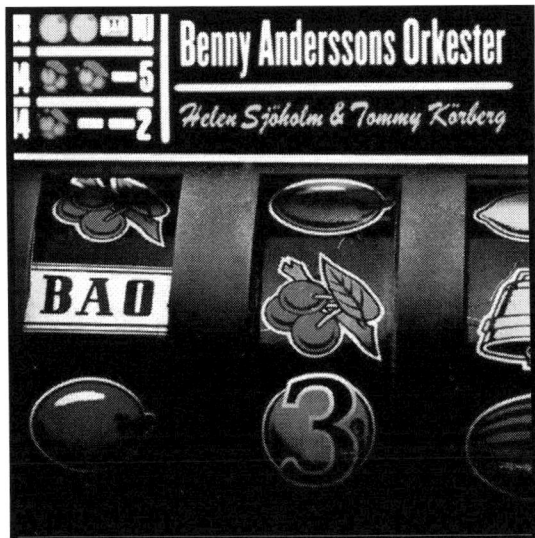

Marsch Pannkaka/För Dig/Du Frälste Mig I Sista Stund/Fait Accomplit/Crush On You/ Calle J:S Vals/Helens Brudvals/Upp Till Dig/Bonde Söker Fru/Nu Mår Jag Mycket Bättre/Wienerbrot/Godnattvisa

Sweden: Mono MMCD 023 (2007).

1.11.07: **3**-9-20-32-32-40-34-23-22-18-20-24-21-42-40-47-56-53-46-x-50-18-29-34-44
14.08.08: 38-57-52-52-47-51-57
13.11.08: 57
3.07.09: 41-x-55

The third studio album by the Benny Andersson Orkester credited both Helen Sjöholm and Tommy Körberg, as seven of the twelve tracks were vocal – two by Helen, two by Tommy and three duets.

Benny, as usual, composed and produced all twelve tracks, while Björn penned the lyrics for six of the seven vocal tracks, including BAO's first English recording, *Crush On You*. This song actually dated back to 1979 and the *VOULEZ-VOUS* sessions, although no demo is believed to exist with vocals by Agnetha and Frida.

The instrumental track, *Helens Brudvals*, was written for Helen Sjöholm's wedding in 2006.

The first two BAO albums hit no.1 in Sweden, but *BAO 3* peaked at its debut position of no.3.

69 ~ MAMMA MIA! – THE MOVIE SOUNDTRACK

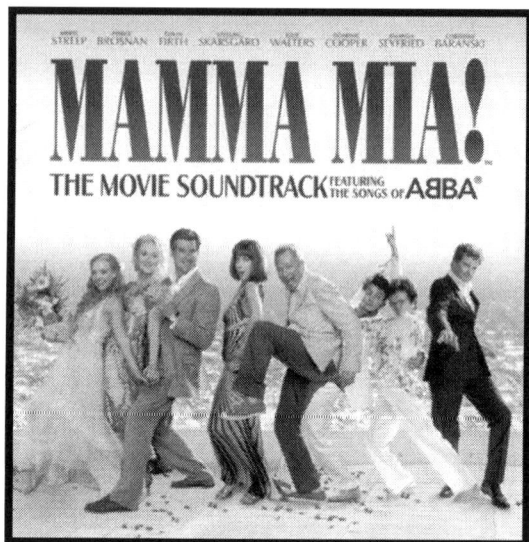

Honey, Honey (Amanda Seyfried, Ashley Lilley & Rachel McDowall)/*Money, Money, Money* (Meryl Streep, Julie Walters & Christine Baranski)/*Mamma Mia* (Meryl Streep)/*Dancing Queen* (Meryl Streep, Julie Walters & Christine Baranski)/*Our Last Summer* (Colin Firth, Pierce Brosnan, Stellan Skarsgård, Amanda Seyfried & Meryl Streep)/*Lay All Your Love On Me* (Dominic Cooper & Amanda Seyfried)/*Super Trouper* (Meryl Streep, Julie Walters & Christine Baranski)/*Gimme! Gimme! Gimme! (A Man After Midnight)* (Amanda Seyfried, Ashley Lilley & Rachel McDowall)/*The Name Of The Game* (Amanda Seyfried)/*Voulez-Vous* (Full Cast)/*S.O.S* (Pierce Brosnan & Meryl Streep)/*Does Your Mother Know* (Christine Baranski)/*Slipping Through My Fingers* (Meryl Streep & Amanda Seyfried)/*The Winner Takes It All* (Meryl Streep)/*When All Is Said And Done* (Pierce Brosnan & Meryl Streep)/*Take A Chance On Me* (Julie Walters, Stellan Skarsgård & Colin Firth)/*I Have A Dream/Thank You For The Music* (Amanda Seyfried)

iTunes Edition Bonus Tracks: *I Have A Dream* (Amanda Seyfried)/*Thank You For The Music* (Amanda Seyfried)

Sweden: Polydor 1774184 (2008).

MAMMA MIA! – THE MOVIE SOUNDTRACK wasn't a hit in Sweden.

UK: Polydor 1774184 (2008).

19.07.08: **1-1**-2-2-2-**1-1-1-1-1-1-1-1-1**-3-2-4-6-7-7-2-4-4-5-2-2-**1**-2-3-3-6-7-4-4-6-8-8-7-10-14-13-15-16-13-15-14-15-16-13-16-20-28-18-15-14-17-23-18-15-11-12-15-17-15-14-13-10-15-27-28-31-36-42-50-43-42-40-43-44-47-40-45-43-48-44-37-35-33-35-39-42-36-38-44-47-46-49 (Compilations chart)

Australia
14.07.08: 4-**1-1-1-1-1**-2-2-3-2-6-11-15-13-17-24-21-18-12-16-22-26-23-26-25-25-22-19-20-25-29-32-38-42-41-52-58-62-86-83-86-79-76-76-76

Austria
1.08.08: **1-1-1-1-1-1**-2-2-2-5-10-10-11-15-21-18-28-28-17-15-14-9-10-14-12-11-13-13-15-19-18-22-26-27-41-45-47-53-62-62-52-55-64-x-x-41-35-31-48-45-48-54-59-39-38-35-36-39-41-56-69
4.12.09: 63-72-61-72-72-70-53
14.01.11: 45-51-56-54-70-60-69
19.07.13: 28-64-x-43-62

Belgium
13.09.08: 43-21-12-8-**7**-9-19-12-27-24-31-39-50-56-56-56-60-70-80-83-54-86-94-73-77-x-73-x-x-89-98-80-74-x-x-84

Finland
26.07.08: 4-**1-1-1**-2-3-8-9-7-6-5-10-15-16-16-31-34-38-x-36-x-38-32-26-19-5-5-6-9-9-15-15-18-23-27

France
6.09.08: 77-20-**8**-11-15-18-18-22-27-40-45-63-79-92-83-89-98
14.03.09: 70-42-15-29-33-39-51-67-35-29-33-59-97-x-x-x-51-58-62-70-78-91
2.01.10: 62-69-64-91-87
29.01.11: 91-x-87-92-31-79-60-x-89-x-x-85-x-80
4.06.11: 93
27.08.11: 93-72
9.03.13: 74

Germany
22.07.08: peaked at no.**2**, charted for 46 weeks

Netherlands
19.07.08: 20-9-8-7-**5**-7-7-10-14-17-21-22-29-34-44-52-62-70-83-83-71-70-74-74-70-58-

75-78-77-76-80-100-94
4.04.09: 59-54-56-54-30

New Zealand
14.07.08: **44**

Norway
19.07.08: 6-**1-1-1-1-1-1-1-1**-2-3-2-2-**1**-2-5-5-8-5-6-5-11-11-12-10-16-10-11-10-11-12-
19-38-30-31-26-20-18-21-23-19-33-40-14-15-21-25
26.09.09: 32

Spain
3.08.08: 60-25-2-**1**-2-3-5-8-7-11-15-16-20-16-8-10-21-30-34-32-29-29-25-25-22-30-44-
47-60-28-25-21-21-14-14-15-x-x-96
14.06.09: 69-88-92-x-x-84-x-x-x-95
8.11.09: 99-89

Switzerland
20.07.08: 30-27-3-3-**1-1-1**-3-2-2-3-6-8-8-11-9-14-14-19-27-27-31-26-26-21-28-24-21-
29-31-36-39-46-45-46-46-50-41-47-56-82-73-92-94
3.10.10: 93

USA
26.07.08: 7-3-3-3-**1**-2-4-5-7-10-13-16-24-25-26-29-42-39-46-67-50-44-37-19-18-12-11-
15-21-23-30-40-43-38-42-51-46-63-80-71-97-97-x-71
8.08.09: 74-68-80-80-88

Mamma Mia!, following its global success as a musical, was even more successful as a major film.

Mamma Mia! was largely shot on location, on the Greek island of Skopelos, during August and September 2007. The film was directed by Phyllida Lloyd, and the cast included:

- Meryl Streep as Donna
- Amanda Seyfried as Sophie
- Pierce Brosnan as Sam
- Colin Firth as Harry
- Stellan Skarsgård as Bill
- Julie Walters as Rosie
- Christine Baranski as Tanya

- Dominic Cooper as Sky

Mamma Mia! premiered on 30th June 2008 in London. More significantly, four days later saw the Swedish premiere, at Stockholm's Rival Theatre. As well as the principal cast members, the Swedish premiere was attended by all four members of ABBA – the first time Benny, Björn, Agnetha and Frida had been photographed together since 1986.

Mamma Mia! was the 5th highest grossing film of 2008 – it went on to become the no.1 musical of all-time, grossing over $600 million. The film picked up two Golden Globe nominations, for Best Motion Picture: Comedy or Musical and Best Actress in a Motion Picture: Comedy or Musical (for Meryl Streep), but it failed to win either.

Benny and Björn produced the accompanying soundtrack album which, like the film, was hugely successful, hitting no.1 in Australia, Austria, Finland, Norway, Spain, Switzerland and the USA, no.2 in Germany, no.5 in the Netherlands, no.7 in Belgium and no.8 in France. In the UK, the soundtrack album was ineligible to enter the main album chart, but it spent 11 weeks at no.1 on the compilations chart.

Three songs from the film were omitted from *MAMMA MIA! – THE MOVIE SOUNDTRACK*: *Chiquitita* (Christine Baranski & Julie Walters), *I Do, I Do, I Do, I Do, I Do* (Full Cast) and *Waterloo* (Full Cast).

The soundtrack has sold over a million copies in the UK alone, and nearly two million copies in the USA, where it has been certified 3 x Platinum.

MAMMA MIA! – THE MOVIE SOUNDTRACK was nominated for a Grammy, for Best Compilation Soundtrack Album for Motion Picture, Television or Other Visual Media, but it didn't win.

70 ~ MY VERY BEST by **Agnetha Fältskog**

CD1: *S.O.S (Swedish version)/Var Det Med Dej?/När Du Tar Mig I Din Famn/Många Gånger Än/En Sång Om Sorg Och Glädje/Dröm Är Dröm, Och Saga Saga/Doktorn!/ Tack För En Underbar, Vanlig Dag/Så Glad Som Dina Ögon/Vart Ska Min Kärlek Föra/Tio Mil Kvar Till Korpilombolo/Så Här Börjar Kärlek/Sången Föder Dig Tillbaka/Dom Har Glömt/Om Tårar Vore Guld/Allting Har Förändrat Sig/Fram För Svenska Sommaren/Jag Var Så Kär*

CD2: *Wrap Your Arms Around Me/Little White Secrets/Can't Shake Loose/The Heat Is On/If I Thought You'd Ever Change Your Mind/I Stand Alone/Mr Persuasion/I Won't Let You Go/If You Need Somebody Tonight/Never Again/Let It Shine/Take Good Care Of Your Children/Sometimes When I'm Dreaming/The Way You Are/I Won't Be Leaving You/When You Walk In The Room/The Winner Takes It All*

Sweden: Sony 88697389442 (2008).

16.10.08: **4-4**-7-11-12-21-34-43-51-57
9.01.09: 54

This compilation, which was only issued in Sweden, saw the release of Agnetha's Swedish recordings on one CD, and her English recordings on another CD, including ABBA's *The Winner Takes It All*. The compilation made its chart debut at no.4, but it didn't climb any higher.

71 ~ THE ALBUMS by ABBA

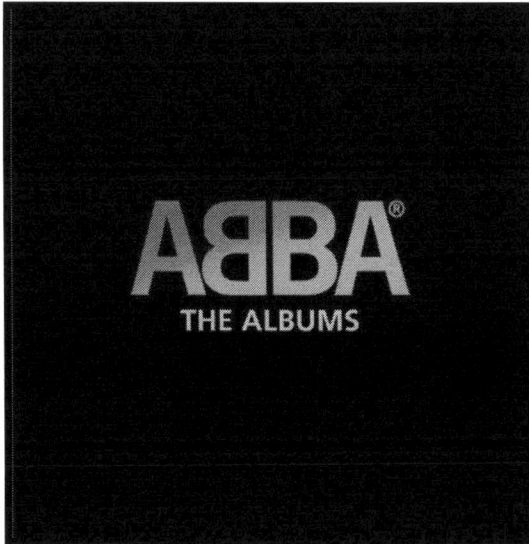

THE ALBUMS is a box-set of ABBA's eight studio albums on CD, plus one bonus CD:

- *RING RING*
- *WATERLOO*
- *ABBA*
- *ARRIVAL*
- *THE ALBUM*
- *VOULEZ-VOUS*
- *SUPER TROUPER*
- *THE VISITORS*
- *BONUS TRACKS*

Bonus Tracks: *Merry-Go-Round/Santa Rosa/Ring Ring (Bara Du Slog En Signal)/ Waterloo (Swedish Version)/Fernando/Crazy World/Happy Hawaii/Summer Night City/ Medley (Pick A Bale Of Cotton/On Top Of Old Smokey/Midnight Special)/Lovelight (Original Version)/Gimme! Gimme! Gimme! (A Man After Midnight)/Elaine/Should I Laugh Or Cry/You Owe Me One/Cassandra/Under Attack/The Day Before You Came*

Sweden: Polydor 177 485-2 (2008).

30.10.08: 12-**4**-7-8-12-13-7-7-5-6-6-12-14-20-31-38-54-54

3.02.12: 36-34
19.10.12: 58-59
1.03.13: 24

UK: Polydor 177 485-2 (2008).

6.12.08: **89-89**-95
18.04.09: 94

Finland
8.11.08: 38-40-x-39-19-14-**11**-13-14-12-15-37-37-x-36-36

France
2.11.08: 77-**57**-73-89-93-97

Germany
18.11.11: **61**-99-91-x-96-88-91-82-73-80

Netherlands
11.04.09: 88-**37**-41-55-61-83

Norway
8.11.08: 14-12-**7**-10-15-23-23-11-8-14-33

Switzerland
9.11.08: **68**-75-70-x-90-92

Given its high price, compared with the average album, this box-set of ABBA's eight studio albums, plus a Bonus Tracks compilation, sold remarkably well in Scandinavia especially, where it charted at no.4 in Sweden, no.7 in Norway and no.11 in Finland.

THE ALBUMS also charted at no.37 in the Netherlands, and was a minor hit in France, Germany, Switzerland and the UK.

72 ~ STORY OF A HEART by the **Benny Andersson Band**

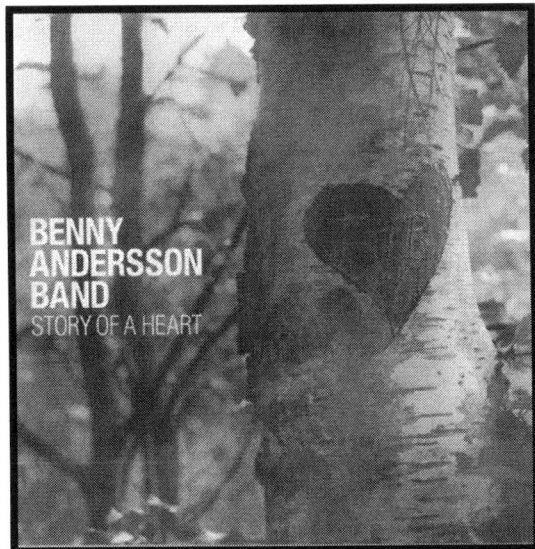

Glasgow Boogie/Trolska/Story Of A Heart/Bed Of Roses/You Are My Man/Cirkus Finemang/Fait Accompli/Sång Från Andra Våningen (Song From The Second Floor)/ Födelsedagsvals Till Mona (Birthday Waltz For Mona)/(If This Is) Our Last Dance/ Jehu/Tyrolean Schottische/The Stars/P.S.

Sweden Bonus Track: *Sommaren Du Fick*

Sweden: Mono MMCD 025 (2009).

3.07.09: **5**-13-7-33-28-31-27-27-28-41-40

UK: Polydor 270 912-4 (2009).

18.07.09: **29**-45-60

Norway
15.08.09: 11-**10**-13-15-19

In an effort to appeal to a wider audience, the Benny Andersson Orkester – renamed the Benny Andersson Band for one release only – released a compilation album featuring nine instrumental and six vocal tracks.

Four of BAO's most popular songs were re-recorded with English lyrics, which Björn wrote, namely *You Are My Man*, *Fait Accompli*, *(If This Is) Our Last Dance* and *The Stars*. Benny and Björn also composed one new song for the album, which became the title track, *Story Of A Heart*. As well as English, a Swedish version titled *Sommaren Du Fick* was recorded, however, the Swedish version only featured on the Swedish release of the album.

STORY OF A HEART was released throughout Europe and in the USA. In Sweden, where most of the songs had already been heard before, albeit not in their English versions for the vocal tracks, the album was promoted as a 'greatest hits' collection, and charted at no.5.

Outside Sweden, *STORY OF A HEART* charted at no.10 in Norway and no.29 in the UK, but it wasn't a hit anywhere else.

The success of the album in the UK was a direct result of a concert the Benny Andersson Band played on London's Hampstead Heath on 4th July 2009, just five days before the album was released. The publicity surrounding the concert led to generally favourable reviews for the album, and significant airplay for the title track, which became a minor hit on the singles chart.

73 ~ *LES NO.1 DE ABBA* by ABBA

CD1: *People Need Love/He Is Your Brother/Ring Ring/Love Isn't Easy (But It Sure Is Hard Enough)/Waterloo/Honey Honey/So Long/I Do, I Do, I Do, I Do, I Do/S.O.S/ Mamma Mia/Fernando/Dancing Queen/Money, Money, Money/Knowing Me, Knowing You/The Name Of The Game/Take A Chance On Me/Eagle/Summer Night City/ Chiquitita/Does Your Mother Know*

CD2: *Voulez-Vous/Angeleyes/Gimme! Gimme! Gimme! (A Man After Midnight)/I Have A Dream/The Winner Takes It All/Super Trouper/On And On And On/Lay All Your Love On Me/One Of Us/When All Is Said And Done/Head Over Heels/The Visitors/The Day Before You Came/Under Attack/Thank You For The Music/Ring Ring (1974 Remix, Single Version)/Voulez-Vous (Extended Remix, 1979 US Promo)*

France: Polydor 532 152-9 (2009).

31.08.09: **4-4-4**-5-**4**-7-9-7-14-20-15-16-23-26-29-30-27-35 (Compilations chart)

Belgium
12.09.09: 29-34-**20**-26-27-32-32-34-43-66-72-73-90-99-98-x-x-87-72-x-82-85-x-93-98

This compilation was only released in France and Belgium, where it charted at no.4 and no.20, respectively.

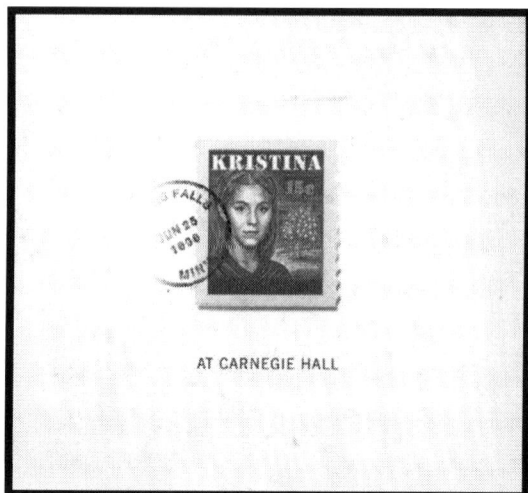

Act 1: *Overture/Path Of Leaves And Needles/Where You Go I Go With You/Stone Kingdom/Down To The Sea/A Bad Harvest/No!/He's Our Pilot/Never/Golden Wheatfields/Down To The Sacred Wave/We Open Up The Gateways/Peasants At Sea/Lice/In The Dead Of Darkness/A Sunday In Battery Park/Home/American Man/Dreams Of Gold/Summer Rose*

Act 2: *Emperors And Kings/Twilight Images Calling/Queen Of The Prairie/Wild Grass/ Gold Can Turn To Sand/Wildcat Money/To The Sea/Miracle Of God/Down To The Waterside/Miscarriage/You Have To Be There/Here I Am Again/With Child Again/Rising From Myth And Legend/I'll Be Waiting There*

Sweden: Mono MMCD 026 (2010).

23.04.10: **31**-55

Kristina: A Concert Event, an English version of Benny and Björn's musical *Kristina Från Duvemåla*, played at New York City's Carnegie Hall on 23rd and 24th September 2009. The cast included Helen Sjöholm as Kristina, Russell Watson as Karl, Kevin Odekirk as Robert and Louise Pitre as Ulrika.

The accompanying album, *KRISTINA AT CARNEGIE HALL*, was released in Sweden, Russia and the USA, but only charted in Sweden where it peaked at no.31 and spent just one week in the Top 40.

75 ~ *O KLANG OCH JUBELTID* by Benny Anderssons Orkester with Helen Sjöholm & Tommy Körberg

O Klang Och Jubeltid/Kära Syster/Månstrålar Klara/Midsommarpolka/Allt Syns När Man Är Naken/Alla Goda Ting/En Dag I Sänder/Flickornas Rum/De Ljuva Drömmarnas/ Jag Hör.../Sorgmarsch/Vilar Glad. I Din Famn/Brudmarsch

Sweden: Mono MMCD 027 (2011).

24.06.11: 3-7-4-6-5-**1-1**-4-3-3-5-7-9-5-5-5-10-9-13-19-20-22-29-36-32-35-32-31-32-22-5-9-16-15-19-20-29-28-43-40-55-53-50-44-57-45

O KLANG OCH JUBELTID ('Oh Sound And Time Of Jubilation') was the fourth studio album by the Benny Andersson Orkester, with vocalists Helen Sjöholm and Tommy Körberg also credited. This time, however, they were joined on three tracks by a third vocalist, Kalle Moraeus.

Benny composed 12 of the 13 tracks on the album himself, the one exception *Månstrålar Klara* being a traditional folk song, with Swedish lyrics by Arvid Ödmann. This was the first time since 1973, when ABBA recorded Agnetha's *Disillusion*, Benny recorded a song he didn't compose himself. Björn penned lyrics for six of the eight vocal tracks on the album.

Boosted by eight concerts they played in the second half of July, *O KLANG OCH JUBELTID* gave the Benny Andersson Orkester their third no.1 album in Sweden, which is the only country where the album was released.

76 ~ COLLECTED by ABBA

CD1: *Ring Ring/People Need Love/Love Isn't Easy (But It Sure Is Hard Enough)/She's My Kind Of Girl/Waterloo/Honey Honey/Dance (While The Music Still Goes On)/Sitting In The Palmtree/So Long/Crazy World/I've Been Waiting For You/I Do, I Do, I Do, I Do, I Do/S.O.S/Mamma Mia/Medley (Pick A Bale Of Cotton/On Top Of Old Smokey/Midnight Special)/Fernando/Dancing Queen*

CD2: *Money, Money, Money/When I Kissed The Teacher/Happy Hawaii/Knowing Me, Knowing You/The Name Of The Game/Hole In Your Soul/I'm A Marionette/Lovelight (Original Version)/Take A Chance On Me/Eagle/Thank You For The Music/Summer Night City/Chiquitita/Does Your Mother Know/Voulez-Vous/Gimme! Gimme! Gimme! (A Man After Midnight)*

CD3: *I Have A Dream/Angeleyes/The Winner Takes It All/Super Trouper/Happy New Year/ The Piper/And On And On And On/Our Last Summer/Elaine/Put On Your White Sombrero/One Of Us/Head Over Heels/The Day Before You Came/Under Attack/When All Is Said And Done/You Owe Me One/I Let The Music Speak*

Netherlands: Polydor 533 377-7 (2011).

25.06.11: 50-46-39-21-28-**18**-21-29-35-43-49-51-58-82-x-73
5.01.13: 86
8.06.13: 19-25-33-40-64-74-x-93-97-96

Belgium
6.08.11: 29-21-19-17-24-**15**-21-26-29-36-56-41-31-30-19-47-56-59-78-92-75-76-79-71-
  65-54-71-x-x-82

This comprehensive 3CD compilation of 50 ABBA hits and album tracks was only released in Belgium and the Netherlands, where it charted at no.15 and no.18, respectively.

77 ~ 5 CD ORIGINAL ALBUM SERIEN by the Hep Stars

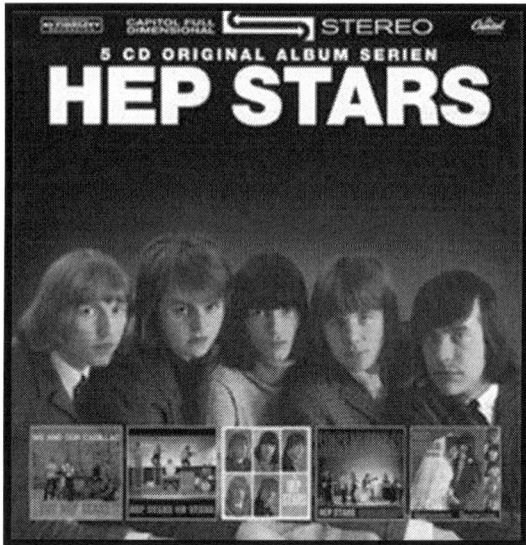

This is a box-set of five Hep Stars albums on CD, dating from the mid-to-late 1960s:

- *WE AND OUR CADILLAC* (1965)
- *HEP STARS ON STAGE* (1965)
- *THE HEP STARS* (1966)
- *SONGS WE SANG 68* (1968)
- *PÅ SVENSKA* (1969)

Sweden: (2012).

3.08.12: **40**

This box-set brought together, on CD, five albums the Hep Stars originally released between 1965 and 1969, two of which achieved Top 40 status in their own right.

The box-set spent a solitary week at no.40 in Sweden, which is the only country where it was released.

78 ~ *TOMTEN HAR ÅKT HEM* by Benny Anderssons Orkester with Helen Sjöholm & Tommy Körberg

Marsch Militaire/Tomten Har Åkt Hem/Julvals/Tomtestomp/Knalle Juls Vals/Tomtarnas Vaktparad/Vinterhamn/Mössens Julafton (När Nätterna Blir Långa)/Trettondagspolkan/ Julpotpurri/Nu Tändas Tusen Juleljus

Sweden: Mono MMCD 029 (2012).

23.11.12: 21-13-12-9-**4**-5-21-53
26.07.13: 53

Benny Andersson Orkester's fifth, and most recent, studio album was released in 2012 – for the third album in a row, vocalists Helen Sjöholm and Tommy Körberg were also credited.

Björn wrote the lyrics for two of the tracks on *TOMTEN HAR ÅKT HEM* ('Santa Has Gone Home'), the title track and *Vinterhamn*.

TOMTEN HAR ÅKT HEM is BAO's least successful studio album to date, peaking at no.4 in Sweden during a comparatively short chart run. As with previous BAO albums, *TOMTEN HAR ÅKT HEM* was only released in Sweden.

79 ~ THE ESSENTIAL COLLECTION by ABBA

CD1: *People Need Love/He Is Your Brother/Ring Ring/Love Isn't Easy (But It Sure Is Hard Enough)/Waterloo, Honey Honey/So Long/I Do, I Do, I Do, I Do, I Do/S.O.S/ Mamma Mia/Bang-A-Boomerang/Fernando/Dancing Queen/Money, Money, Money/ Knowing Me, Knowing You/That's Me/The Name Of The Game/Take A Chance On Me/Eagle/One Man, One Woman/Thank You For The Music/Summer Night City*

CD2: *Chiquitita/Does Your Mother Know/Voulez-Vous/Angeleyes/Gimme! Gimme! Gimme! (A Man After Midnight)/I Have A Dream/The Winner Takes It All/Super Trouper/On And On And On/Lay All Your Love On Me/Happy New Year/One Of Us/When All Is Said And Done/Head Over Heels/The Visitors/The Day Before You Came/Under Attack*

DVD (2CD/DVD Edition only): *Waterloo/Ring Ring/Mamma Mia/S.O.S/Bang-A-Boomerang/I Do, I Do, I Do, I Do, I Do/Fernando/Dancing Queen/Money, Money, Money/Knowing Me, Knowing You/That's Me/The Name Of The Game/Take A Chance On Me/Eagle/One Man, One Woman/Thank You For The Music/Summer Night City/ Chiquitita/Does Your Mother Know/Voulez-Vous/Gimme! Gimme! Gimme! (A Man After Midnight)/On And On And On/The Winner Takes It All/Super Trouper/Happy New Year/ When All Is said And Done/One Of Us/Head Over Heels/The Day Before You Came/ Under Attack/When I Kissed The Teacher/Estoy Soñando (I Have A Dream, Spanish Version)/Felicidad (Happy New Year, Spanish Version)/No Hay A Quien Culpar (When*

All Is Said And Done, Spanish Version)/Dancing Queen (Live at the Swedish Royal Opera)

Europe: Polydor 06025 2799372 (2012), Polydor 06025 27993751 (2CD/DVD Edition, 2012).

Austria
15.06.12: 53-**47**

Germany
8.06.12: 41-**16**-24-42-58-63-84-51-89-97

Spain
16.09.12: **53**-68-78-100-93
26.05.13: 67-83-94-96

Sweden
4.01.13: 56-30-**29**-55-48

Switzerland
1.07.12: **94**

THE ESSENTIAL COLLECTION was a re-titled, re-packaged version of *THE DEFINITIVE COLLECTION*, which was released in Europe only.

The track listing was very similar to that of *THE DEFINITIVE COLLECTION*, however, some minor changes were made. The two bonus tracks on *THE DEFINITIVE COLLECTION*, the 1974 remix of *Ring Ring* and the extended remix of *Voulez-Vous*, were omitted, and four tracks were added: *Bang-A-Boomerang*, *That's Me*, *One Man, One Woman* and *Happy New Year*. At the same time, *Thank You For The Music* was moved from last on *THE DEFINITIVE COLLECTION*'s track listing, to its correct chronological place after *Eagle* on *THE ESSENTIAL COLLECTION*.

Two editions of *THE ESSENTIAL COLLECTION* were released, the standard 2CD edition and a 2CD/DVD edition, with the DVD including the music videos for the tracks on the two CDs, the music videos for three Spanish recordings, plus ABBA's live performance of *Dancing Queen* at the Swedish Royal Opera, at the wedding reception of Sweden's **King Carl XVI Gustaf and Queen Silvia.**

Only in a minor hit, *THE ESSENTIAL COLLECTION* charted at no.16 in Germany, no.29 in Sweden, no.47 in Austria and no.53 in Spain.

80 ~ A by Agnetha Fältskog

The One Who Loves You Now/When You Really Loved Someone/Perfume In The Breeze/I Was A Flower/I Should've Followed You Home/Past Forever/Dance Your Pain Away/ Bubble/Back On Your Radio/I Keep Them On The Floor Beside My Bed

Sweden: Universal 06025 3732184 (2013).

17.05.13: **2**-3-**2**-**2**-5-4-8-7-9-11-10-9-6-5-4-6-10-35-35-41-54-x-56
27.12.13: 23-14-36-40-13-28-39

UK: Universal 06025 3732184 (2013).

25.05.13: **6**-21-33-43-**6**-18-26-36-38-46-58-71-86-88-80
11.01.14: 79

Australia
26.05.13: **3**-9-13-22-48-60-82-5-8-9-13-20-22-36-54-70-85

Austria
24.05.13: **8**-27-28-31-74

Belgium
18.05.13: 96-**35**-75-88-91

Finland
18.05.13: **15**-22-29-43

France
25.05.13: **85**

Germany
24.05.13: **3**-9-8-15-24-36-41-45-51-71-74-88-x-88-x-x-x-28-50-83
6.12.13: 75
18.01.14: 88

Netherlands
18.05.13: **14**-34-53-76-69-90-97
11.01.14: 90

New Zealand
17.06.13: 40
14.10.13: **27**

Norway
25.05.13: **3**-8-9-34-x-x-35-x-31
18.10.13: 31-26

Switzerland
26.05.13: **2**-22-17-28-48-51-x-75
22.09.13: 79

Following 2004's *MY COLOURING BOOK*, Agnetha quietly retired from the music scene, and no one expected her to return with another album – least of all Agnetha herself.

Agnetha celebrated her 60th birthday in April 2010, and the following year a good friend contacted her. 'She called me up and told me that Jörgen Elofsson and Peter Nordahl wanted to play me some music,' she said. 'They came to my house and played me three songs, and I thought, "Oh, God – I have to do this!" It felt like a challenge.'

Titled simply *A*, Agnetha's fifth English album – her first new album for nine years – was recorded between January and October 2012, but it wasn't released until the following spring. Jörgen Elofsson wrote or co-wrote all ten tracks Agnetha recorded for the album, with Agnetha co-writing one track, the intriguingly titled *I Keep Them On The Floor Beside My Bed*.

The Only One Who Loves You Now, When You Really Love Someone, Dance The Pain Away and *I Should've Followed You Home* were all promoted as singles in various countries but, as they were only availably digitally in most cases, none achieved Top 40 status anywhere.

I Should've Followed You Home was a duet with Take That's Gary Barlow. Agnetha joined Barlow on stage in London, on 12th November 2013, to perform the duet during the *BBC Children in Need Rocks* charity concert – this was her first live performance for 25 years. A week later, *I Should've Followed You Home* sneaked into the UK's Top 100 at no.99, but it didn't climb any higher.

Unusually, the normally publicity-shy Agnetha made several other appearances to promote *A*, which charted at no.2 in Sweden and Switzerland, no.3 in Australia, Germany and Norway, no.6 in the UK, no.8 in Austria, no.14 in the Netherlands, no.15 in Finland, no.27 in New Zealand and no.35 in Belgium.

In the UK, where *A* was her highest charting album, Agnetha filmed a documentary for the BBC, *Agnetha: ABBA And After*, which aired on 11th June 2013. The following week, *A* rebounded up the chart to equal its debut position of no.6, and in January 2014 the album became Agnetha's first to go gold in the UK, denoting sales of 100,000.

CELEBRATES ABBA by André Rieu

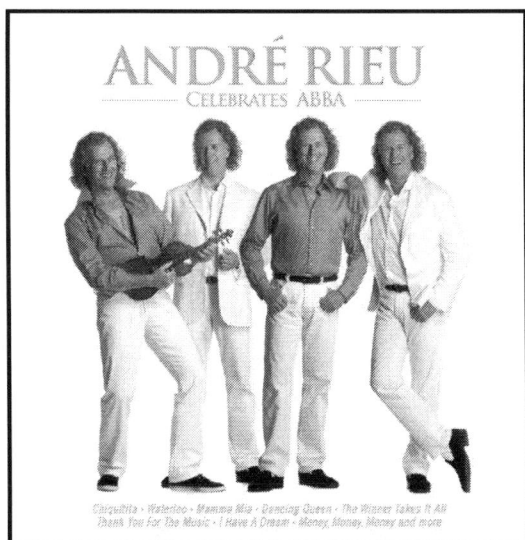

CD1: *Chiquitita/Mamma Mia/Fernando/Money, Money, Money/The Winner Takes It All/ Waterloo/I Have A Dream/Arrival/Dancing Queen/The Way Old Friends Do/Thank You For The Music/Thank You ABBA Medley (Money, Money, Money/Dancing Queen/Mamma Mia/Waterloo)*

CD2: *MUSIC OF THE NIGHT* (no ABBA connection)

Europe: Polydor 375 368-1 (2013).

Australia
11.11.13: **10**-18-28-30-34-30-25-31-63-66-93

Austria
8.11.13: 69-43-**32**-59

Germany
13.12.13: 56-44-**42**-50

Netherlands
2.11.13: 42-49-44-40-42-**24**-41-44-30-42-75

New Zealand
18.11.13: **34**

Switzerland
10.11.13: **67**-71-100-x-83-96-95-88

André Rieu is a hugely popular and successful Dutch conductor and violinist. Known as the 'Waltz King', he created the Johann Strauss Orchestra in 1987, and since then he and the orchestra have released literally dozens of albums and played hundreds of concerts. Every year between 2009 and 2013, his tours ranked among Billboard's Top 25 tours of the year.

In most countries, Rieu's tribute to ABBA was released as part of a two CD package with *MUSIC OF THE NIGHT* – in the UK, the latter was released and charted as a stand-alone album.

CELEBRATES ABBA charted at no.10 in Australia, no.24 in the Netherlands, no.32 in Austria, no.34 in New Zealand and no.42 in Germany.

THE ALMOST TOP 40 ALBUMS

Here is a round-up of the ABBA and ABBA-related albums that made the Top 50 in one or more countries, but failed to enter the Top 40 in any:

ABBA LIVE by ABBA

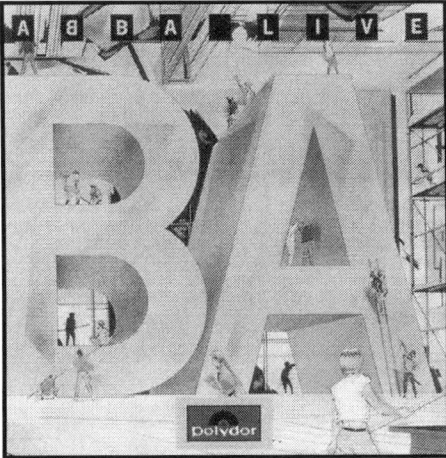

ABBA didn't release a live album while they were still active as a group, but this live album – mostly recorded at London's Wembley Arena in November 1979 – was released in 1986. It charted at no.47 in the Netherlands and no.49 in Sweden, but it failed to achieve Top 40 status anywhere.

THE VERY BEST OF by ABBA

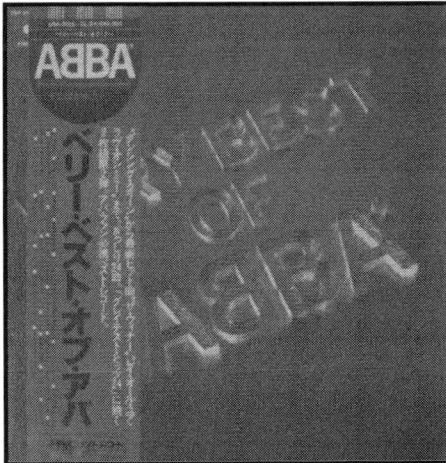

This 2005 compilation was released exclusively in Japan, where it charted at no.44.

***50th ANNIVERSARY 1964-2014* by the Hep Stars**

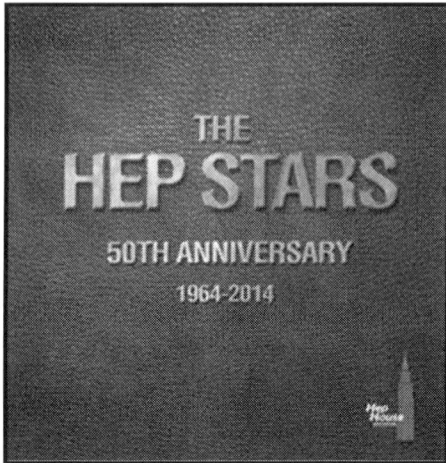

This compilation, which marked the Hep Stars' 50th anniversary, was only released in Sweden – it made its chart debut at no.45, but climbed no higher.

THE TOP 40 ABBA & ABBA-RELATED ALBUMS

The best-selling ABBA album, not surprisingly, runs away with this Top 40, which has been compiled according to the same points system used for the Top 40 Singles listing.

Rank/Album/Artist/Points

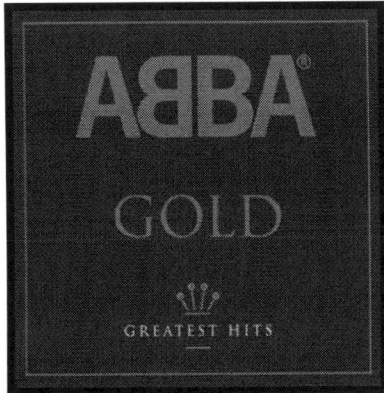

1   *GOLD* | ABBA – 4873* points

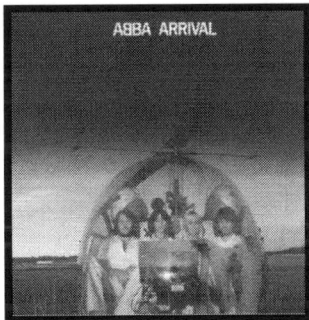

2   *ARRIVAL* | ABBA – 2957 points

3   *VOULEZ-VOUS* | ABBA – 2312 points

Rank/Album/Artist/Points

4 *THE ALBUM* | ABBA – 2140 points

5 *SUPER TROUPER* | ABBA – 2129 points

6 *MAMMA MIA! – THE MOVIE SOUNDTRACK –*
2063 points

7 *THE VISITORS* | ABBA – 1899 points

8 *GREATEST HITS VOL.2* | ABBA – 1710 points

9   *ABBA* | ABBA – 1690 points

10   *THE BEST OF* | ABBA – 1422 points

11. *GREATEST HITS* | ABBA – 1336 points
12. *THE SINGLES- THE FIRST TEN YEARS* | ABBA – 1214 points
13. *CHESS* – 1099 points
14. *THE DEFINITIVE COLLECTION* | ABBA – 1074 points
15. *MORE GOLD* | ABBA – 1073 points
16. *SOMETHING'S GOING ON* | Frida – 977 points
17. *A* | Agnetha Fältskog – 976 points
18. *WATERLOO* | ABBA – 937 points
19. *WRAP YOUR ARMS AROUND ME* | Agnetha Fältskog – 914 points
20. *NUMBER ONES* | ABBA – 737 points

21. *MY COLOURING BOOK* | Agnetha Fältskog – 729 points
22. *A WIE ABBA/A VAN ABBA* | ABBA – 659 points
23. *18 HITS* | ABBA – 538 points
24. *LOVE STORIES* | ABBA – 522 points
25. *THE ALBUMS* | ABBA – 428 points
26. *I STAND ALONE* | Agnetha Fältskog – 395 points
27. *MAMMA MIA!* | Original Cast – 380 points
28. *EYES OF A WOMAN* | Agnetha Fältskog – 378 points
29. *THE ABBA STORY* | ABBA – 372 points
30. *SHINE* | Frida – 356 points

31. *THE VERY BEST OF* | ABBA – 355 points
32. *RING RING* | Benny Björn & Agnetha Frida – 354 points
33. *I LOVE ABBA* | ABBA – 317 points
34. *THE COMPLETE SINGLES COLLECTION* | ABBA – 301 points
35. *FOREVER GOLD* | ABBA – 275 points
36. *THE HEP STARS* | Hep Stars – 269 points
37. *DJUPA ANDETAG* | Frida – 254 points
38. *THE BEST OF – THE MILLENNIUM COLLECTION* | ABBA – 247 points
39. *KRISTINA FRÅN DUVEMÅLA* – 246 points
40. *STORY OF A HEART* | Benny Andersson Band – 237 points

* *GOLD* was still charting in Austria at the cut-off date for publication.

As with singles, ABBA dominate the Top 40 albums, taking 11 of the Top 12 places, with only the *MAMMA MIA!* movie soundtrack breaking into the Top 10.

Interestingly, ABBA's *THE BEST OF* ranks higher than their *GREATEST HITS*, with *GREATEST HITS VOL.2* topping them both – largely because it charted in more countries.

Frida's highest entry is *SOMETHING'S GOING ON* at no.16, with Agnetha's most recent album *A* just one point and one place behind her. The Hep Stars make the list at no.36, and the Benny Andersson Band sneak in at no.40.

The make-up of the Top 40 is as follows:

26 albums	ABBA
5 albums	Agnetha
4 albums	Benny & Björn (musicals/film)
3 albums	Frida
1 album	Hep Stars
1 album	Benny Andersson Band

ABBA's total includes *RING RING*, which was originally credited to Benny Björn & Agnetha Anni-Frid.

ALBUMS TRIVIA

To date, an impressive 80 ABBA and ABBA-related albums have achieved Top 40 status in one or more of the countries featured in this book, and their success may be summarised as follows:

ABBA	43 albums
Agnetha	10 albums
Benny & Björn	10 albums (musicals & film)
Benny	9 albums (solo and with Benny Anderssons Orkester/Band)
Frida	4 albums
Hep Stars	4 albums

A little surprisingly, the Hootenanny Singers haven't scored a single Top 40 album anywhere, not even in their native Sweden. Björn is the only member of ABBA to never release a solo album.

ABBA only released eight studio albums, but has accumulated 43 Top 40 albums to date, thanks to the large number of compilations released over the years.

There follows a country-by-country look at the most successful ABBA and ABBA-related albums, starting with the group's homeland.

ABBA IN SWEDEN

ABBA & ABBA-related No.1s

There have been 19 ABBA & ABBA-related no.1 albums in Sweden, nine by ABBA, three each by Frida, Agnetha Fältskog and Benny Anderssons Orkester, and one concept album, plus one no.1 with an ABBA connection:

1974	*WATERLOO* – ABBA	
1975	*ABBA* – ABBA	
1975	*GREATEST HITS* – ABBA	
1976	*FRIDA ENSAM* – Anni-Frid Lyngstad	
1976	*ARRIVAL* – ABBA	
1977	*THE ALBUM* – ABBA	
1979	*VOULEZ-VOUS* – ABBA	
1980	*SUPER TROUPER* – ABBA	

1981	*THE VISITORS* – ABBA
1982	*SOMETHING'S GOING ON* – Frida
1983	*WRAP YOUR ARMS AROUND ME* – Agnetha Fältskog
1984	*CHESS*
1987	*I STAND ALONE* – Agnetha Fältskog
1992	*GOLD* – ABBA
1996	*DJUPA ANDETAG* – Frida
1999	*THE ABBA GENERATION* – A*Teens
2001	*BENNY ANDERSSONS ORKESTER* – Benny Anderssons Orkester
2004	*MY COLOURING BOOK* – Agnetha Fältskog
2004	*BAO!* – Benny Anderssons Orkester
2011	*O KLANG OCH JUBELTID* – Benny Anderssons Orkester

GOLD returned to no.1 in 1999.

Most weeks at No.1

ABBA spent 92 weeks at no.1 on the album chart in Sweden, Agnetha Fältskog 14 weeks, Frida 12 weeks and Benny Anderssons Orkester four weeks. The albums with the most weeks at no.1 are as follows:

18 weeks	*ABBA* – ABBA
12 weeks	*WATERLOO* – ABBA
12 weeks	*ARRIVAL* – ABBA
12 weeks	*GOLD* – ABBA
10 weeks	*VOULEZ-VOUS* – ABBA
8 weeks	*GREATEST HITS* – ABBA
8 weeks	*SUPER TROUPER* – ABBA
8 weeks	*I STAND ALONE* – Agnetha Fältskog

Most Hit Albums

19 albums	ABBA
10 albums	Agnetha Fältskog
9 albums	Benny Andersson / Benny Anderssons Orkester
4 albums	Frida
3 albums	The Hep Stars

Most Weeks

478 weeks	ABBA

272 weeks	Benny Andersson / Benny Anderssons Orkester
162 weeks	Agnetha Fältskog
92 weeks	Frida
14 weeks	The Hep Stars

Albums with the most weeks

135 weeks	*GOLD* – ABBA
85 weeks	*KRISTINA FRÅN DUVEMÅLA*
55 weeks	*BENNY ANDERSSONS ORKESTER* – Benny Anderssons Orkester
55 weeks	*BAO!* – Benny Anderssons Orkester
46 weeks	*O KLANG OCH JUBELTID* – Benny Anderssons Orkester
42 weeks	*GREATEST HITS* – ABBA
40 weeks	*FRIDA ENSAM* – Anni-Frid Lyngstad
36 weeks	*MAMMA MIA! – PÅ SVENSKA*
34 weeks	*MORE GOLD* – ABBA
34 weeks	*BAO 3* – Benny Anderssons Orkester

ABBA IN AUSTRALIA

ABBA & ABBA-related No.1s

There have been four ABBA no.1 albums in Australia, and one no.1 album with an ABBA connection:

1975	*ABBA* – ABBA
1976	*THE BEST OF* – ABBA
1976	*ARRIVAL* – ABBA
1992	*GOLD* – ABBA
2008	*MAMMA MIA! – THE MOVIE SOUNDTRACK*

Most weeks at No.1

ABBA spent 39 weeks at no.1 in Australia. The albums with the most weeks at no.1 are:

16 weeks	*THE BEST OF*
11 weeks	*ABBA*
8 weeks	*ARRIVAL*

Most Hit Albums

23 albums   ABBA
 4 albums   Agnetha Fältskog
 1 album   Frida

Most Weeks

799 weeks   ABBA
 24 weeks   Agnetha Fältskog
 11 weeks   Frida

Albums with the most weeks

226 weeks   *GOLD* – ABBA
 99 weeks   *THE DEFINITIVE COLLECTION* – ABBA
 93 weeks   *18 HITS* – ABBA
 70 weeks   *THE BEST OF* – ABBA
 65 weeks   *ABBA* – ABBA
 44 weeks   *MAMMA MIA! – THE MOVIE SOUNDTRACK*
 42 weeks   *WATERLOO* – ABBA
 35 weeks   *ARRIVAL* – ABBA
 33 weeks   *THE COMPLETE GOLD COLLECTION* – ABBA
 31 weeks   *RING RING* – ABBA

ABBA IN AUSTRIA

ABBA & ABBA-related No.1s

There have been three no.1 albums by ABBA in Austria, plus one no.1 album with an ABBA connection:

1976   *THE BEST OF* – ABBA
1981   *A WIE ABBA* – ABBA
1992   *GOLD* – ABBA
2008   *MAMMA MIA! – THE MOVIE SOUNDTRACK*

Most weeks at No.1

ABBA spent 23 weeks at no.1 in Austria. Their albums with the most weeks at no.1 are as follows:

8 weeks	*THE BEST OF*
8 weeks	*A WIE ABBA*
7 weeks	*GOLD*
6 weeks	*MAMMA MIA! – THE MOVIE SOUNDTRACK*

Most Hit Albums

18 hits	ABBA
2 hits	Agnetha Fältskog
1 hit	Frida

Most Weeks

570 weeks	ABBA
8 weeks	Agnetha Fältskog
2 weeks	Frida

Albums with the most weeks

197 weeks	*GOLD* – ABBA
78 weeks	*MAMMA MIA! – THE MOVIE SOUNDTRACK*
52 weeks	*THE BEST OF* – ABBA
34 weeks	*GREATEST HITS VOL.2* – ABBA
40 weeks	*THE ALBUM* – ABBA
40 weeks	*VOULEZ-VOUS* – ABBA
34 weeks	*SUPER TROUPER* – ABBA
32 weeks	*ARRIVAL* – ABBA
24 weeks	*A WIE ABBA* – ABBA
19 weeks	*THE COMPLETE SINGLES COLLECTION* – ABBA

* = still charting at publication date

ABBA IN BELGIUM (Wallonia)

ABBA & ABBA-related No.1s

Since 1995, when the Ultratop albums chart was launched, there hasn't been any ABBA or ABBA-related no.1 albums.

Most Hit Albums

9 hits   ABBA
1 hit   Agnetha Fältskog

Most Weeks

152 weeks   ABBA
  5 weeks   Agnetha Fältskog

Albums with the most weeks

69 weeks   *GOLD* – ABBA
31 weeks   *MAMMA MIA! – THE MOVIE SOUNDTRACK*
28 weeks   *COLLECTED* – ABBA
21 weeks   *LES NO.1 DE ABBA* – ABBA
13 weeks   *THE ABBA STORY* – ABBA

ABBA IN CANADA

ABBA & ABBA-related No.1s

There have been no ABBA or ABBA-related no.1 albums in Canada.

Most Hit Albums

13 albums   ABBA

Most Weeks

490+ weeks   ABBA

Albums with the most weeks

130+ weeks *THE BEST OF – THE MILLENNIUM COLLECTION*
 95+ weeks *GOLD*
 58 weeks   *GREATEST HITS*
 52 weeks   *VOULEZ-VOUS*
 33 weeks   *GREATEST HITS VOL.2*
 30 weeks   *THE ALBUM*
 27 weeks   *ARRIVAL*
 24 weeks   *SUPER TROUPER*
 19 weeks   *THE SINGLES – THE FIRST TEN YEARS*
 11 weeks   *THE VISITORS*

Note: Chart action from around 2000 onwards is incomplete.

ABBA IN FINLAND

ABBA & ABBA-related No.1s

There have been three ABBA and ABBA-related no.1 albums in Finland, two by ABBA and one movie soundtrack:

1979   *VOULEZ-VOUS*
1992   *GOLD*
2008   *MAMMA MIA! – THE MOVIE SOUNDTRACK*

GOLD returned to no.1 in 1999, however, it is not known how many weeks *VOULEZ-VOUS* or *GOLD* spent at no.1. *MAMMA MIA! – THE MOVIE SOUNDTRACK* was no.1 for three weeks.

Most Hit Albums

16 albums ABBA
 3 albums Agnetha Fältskog
 2 albums Frida
 1 album   The Hep Stars

Most Weeks

444 weeks ABBA

35 weeks	Agnetha Fältskog
19 weeks	Frida
8 weeks	The Hep Stars

Albums with the most weeks

159 weeks	*GOLD* – ABBA
57 weeks	*ARRIVAL* – ABBA
36 weeks	*GREATEST HITS* – ABBA
34 weeks	*MAMMA MIA! – THE MOVIE SOUNDTRACK*
24 weeks	*WATERLOO* – ABBA
24 weeks	*THE ALBUM* – ABBA
20 weeks	*VOULEZ-VOUS* – ABBA
20 weeks	*SUPER TROUPER* – ABBA
19 weeks	*MY COLOURING BOOK* – Agnetha Fältskog
16 weeks	*ABBA* – ABBA
16 weeks	*GREATEST HITS VOL.2* – ABBA
16 weeks	*THE VISITORS* – ABBA
16 weeks	*SOMETHING'S GOING ON* – Frida

ABBA IN FRANCE

ABBA & ABBA-related No.1s

There have been two ABBA no.1 albums in France:

| 1990 | *ABBA STORY* |
| 1992 | *GOLD* |

GOLD returned to no.1 in 1996, and again in 2008.

Most weeks at No.1

GOLD topped the chart for 8 weeks in 1996/2008, and for an unknown number of weeks in 1992. *ABBA STORY* was no.1 for an unknown number of weeks in 1990.

Most Hit Albums

| 20 albums | ABBA |
| 2 albums | Agnetha Fältskog |

1 album   Frida

Most Weeks

475 weeks   ABBA

It is not known how many weeks Frida's *SOMETHING'S GOING ON*, or Agnetha's *WRAP YOUR ARMS AROUND ME*, charted for.

Albums with the most weeks

132 weeks   *GOLD* – ABBA
 66 weeks   *FOREVER GOLD* – ABBA
 61 weeks   *18 HITS* – ABBA
 54 weeks   *MAMMA MIA! – THE MOVIE SOUNDTRACK*
 27 weeks   *GOLDEN DOUBLE ALBUM* – ABBA
 25 weeks   *THE ABBA STORY* – ABBA
 22 weeks   *MORE GOLD* – ABBA
 16 weeks   *VOULEZ-VOUS* – ABBA
 16 weeks   *THE DEFINITIVE COLLECTION* – ABBA
 15 weeks   *ABBA STORY* – ABBA

ABBA IN GERMANY

ABBA & ABBA-related No.1s

There have been seven ABBA and ABBA-related no.1 albums in Germany, all seven by ABBA:

1976   *THE BEST OF*
1977   *ARRIVAL*
1979   *VOULEZ-VOUS*
1980   *SUPER TROUPER*
1981   *A WIE ABBA*
1981   *THE VISITORS*
1992   *GOLD*

Most weeks at No.1

ABBA spent 45 weeks at no.1 in Germany. The albums with the most weeks at no.1 are as follows:

14 weeks   *ARRIVAL*
11 weeks   *GOLD*
 5 weeks   *A WIE ABBA*
 5 weeks   *THE VISITORS*

Most Hit Albums

23 albums   ABBA
 5 albums   Agnetha Fältskog
 2 albums   Frida

Most Weeks

1067 weeks ABBA
  68 weeks Agnetha Fältskog
  18 weeks Frida

Albums with the most weeks

239 weeks   *GOLD* – ABBA
107 weeks   *THE DEFINITIVE COLLECTION* – ABBA
 88 weeks   *THE VERY BEST OF* – ABBA
 84 weeks   *THE BEST OF* – ABBA
 76 weeks   *ARRIVAL* – ABBA
 70 weeks   *GREATEST HITS VOL.2* – ABBA
 57 weeks   *VOULEZ-VOUS* – ABBA
 56 weeks   *MAMMA MIA!* – German Cast Recording
 55 weeks   *THE ALBUM* – ABBA
 51 weeks   *SUPER TROUPER* – ABBA

ABBA IN JAPAN

ABBA & ABBA-related No.1s

Only one ABBA album has achieved no.1 in Japan:

1979   *VOULEZ-VOUS*

VOULEZ-VOUS spent two weeks at no.1, while ABBA's *GREATEST HITS VOL.2* was no.2 for five weeks.

Most Hit Albums

12 hits   ABBA

Most Weeks

478 weeks   ABBA

Albums with the most weeks

123 weeks   *ARRIVAL*
 72 weeks   *GREATEST HITS 24*
 66 weeks   *THE ALBUM*
 51 weeks   *GREATEST HITS VOL.2*
 37 weeks   *VOULEZ-VOUS*
 35 weeks   *S.O.S. – THE BEST OF*
 23 weeks   *SUPER TROUPER*
 18 weeks   *THE VISITORS*
 14 weeks   *ALL ABOUT ABBA*
 14 weeks   *GOLD*

ABBA IN THE NETHERLANDS

ABBA & ABBA-related No.1s

There have been seven no.1 albums in the Netherlands by ABBA, and one no.1 album with an ABBA connection:

1976   *ARRIVAL* – ABBA
1978   *THE ALBUM* – ABBA
1979   *VOULEZ-VOUS* – ABBA
1080   *SUPER TROUPER* – ABBA
1981   *A VAN ABBA* – ABBA
1981   *THE VISITORS* – ABBA

1999	DE GROOTSTE HITS IN NEDERLAND – 25 JAAR NA 'WATERLOO' – ABBA
2004	MAMMA MIA! – Dutch Cast Recording

Most weeks at No.1

ABBA spent 37 weeks at no.1 in the Netherlands. The albums with the most weeks at no.1 are as follows:

9 weeks	*SUPER TROUPER*
8 weeks	*A VAN ABBA*
7 weeks	*ARRIVAL*
5 weeks	*THE ALBUM*
5 weeks	*VOULEZ-VOUS*

Most Hit Albums

21 albums	ABBA
5 albums	Agnetha Fältskog
2 albums	Frida

Most Weeks

532 weeks	ABBA
48 weeks	Agnetha Fältskog
16 weeks	Frida

Albums with the most weeks

82 weeks	*GOLD* – ABBA
55 weeks	*MAMMA MIA!* – Dutch Cast Recording
52 weeks	*DE GROOTSTE HITS IN NEDERLAND – 25 JAAR NA 'WATERLOO'* – ABBA
49 weeks	*VOULEZ-VOUS* – ABBA
38 weeks	*MAMMA MIA! – THE MOVIE SOUNDTRACK*
37 weeks	*THE ALBUM* – ABBA
33 weeks	*ARRIVAL* – ABBA
31 weeks	*THE DEFINITIVE COLLECTION* – ABBA
26 weeks	*GREATEST HITS VOL.2* – ABBA
25 weeks	*COLLECTED* – ABBA

ABBA IN NEW ZEALAND

ABBA & ABBA-related No.1s

There have been four ABBA and ABBA-related no.1 albums in New Zealand, all by ABBA:

1976	*THE BEST OF*
1977	*ARRIVAL*
1978	*THE ALBUM*
2007	*NUMBER ONES*

Most weeks at No.1

ABBA spent 38 weeks at no.1 in New Zealand. The albums with the most weeks at no.1 are as follows:

18 weeks	*THE BEST OF*
12 weeks	*ARRIVAL*
5 weeks	*THE ALBUM*

Most Hit Albums

16 albums	ABBA
1 album	Agnetha Fältskog

Most Weeks

409 weeks	ABBA
2 weeks	Agnetha Fältskog

Albums with the most weeks

84 weeks	*THE BEST OF* – ABBA
84 weeks	*GOLD* – ABBA
71 weeks	*ABBA* – ABBA
49 weeks	*ARRIVAL* – ABBA
30 weeks	*CHESS*
20 weeks	*VOULEZ-VOUS* – ABBA
17 weeks	*THE ALBUM* – ABBA
17 weeks	*GREATEST HITS VOL.2* – ABBA

17 weeks   *SUPER TROUPER* – ABBA
13 weeks   *NUMBER ONES* – ABBA

ABBA IN NORWAY

ABBA & ABBA-related No.1s

There have been ten ABBA and ABBA-related no.1 albums in Norway, nine by ABBA and one by Agnetha Fältskog, plus one no.1 with an ABBA connection:

1974   *WATERLOO* – ABBA
1975   *ABBA* – ABBA
1976   *GREATEST HITS* – ABBA
1976   *ARRIVAL* – ABBA
1977   *THE ALBUM* – ABBA
1979   *VOULEZ-VOUS* – ABBA
1980   *SUPER TROUPER* – ABBA
1981   *THE VISITORS* – ABBA
1983   *WRAP YOUR ARMS AROUND ME* – Agnetha Fältskog
1992   *GOLD* – ABBA
2008   *MAMMA MIA! – THE MOVIE SOUNDTRACK*

Most weeks at No.1

ABBA spent 65 weeks at no.1 in the Norway, and Agnetha Fältskog five weeks. The albums with the most weeks at no.1 are as follows:

20 weeks   *ARRIVAL* – ABBA
14 weeks   *ABBA* – ABBA
 7 weeks   *THE VISITORS* – ABBA
 6 weeks   *WATERLOO* – ABBA
 6 weeks   *VOULEZ-VOUS* – ABBA
 5 weeks   *THE ALBUM* – ABBA
 5 weeks   *WRAP YOUR ARMS AROUND ME* – Agnetha Fältskog

Most Hit Albums

18 albums   ABBA
 5 albums   Agnetha Fältskog
 3 albums   Frida

2 albums	The Hep Stars
1 album	Benny Andersson Band

Most Weeks

427 weeks	ABBA
40 weeks	Agnetha Fältskog
22 weeks	Frida
22 weeks	The Hep Stars
5 weeks	Benny Andersson Band

Albums with the most weeks

103 weeks	*GOLD* – ABBA
62 weeks	*ABBA* – ABBA
62 weeks	*GREATEST HITS* – ABBA
48 weeks	*MAMMA MIA! – THE MOVIE SOUNDTRACK*
35 weeks	*ARRIVAL* – ABBA
31 weeks	*CHESS*
29 weeks	*SUPER TROUPER* – ABBA
24 weeks	*WATERLOO* – ABBA
21 weeks	*THE HEP STARS* – The Hep Stars
21 weeks	*VOULEZ-VOUS* – ABBA

ABBA IN SOUTH AFRICA

Note: the official South African album chart didn't commence until December 1981.

ABBA & ABBA-related No.1s

Only one ABBA album achieved no.1 in South Africa, as the launch of the album chart came after all but one of the group's studio albums were released:

1983   *THE SINGLES – THE FIRST TEN YEARS*

THE SINGLES – THE FIRST TEN YEARS spent three weeks at no.1.

Most Hit Albums

2 albums   ABBA

1 album   Agnetha Fältskog

Most Weeks

36 weeks   ABBA
 4 weeks   Agnetha Fältskog

Albums with the most weeks

23 weeks   *CHESS*
18 weeks   *THE VISITORS* – ABBA
18 weeks   *THE SINGLES – THE FIRST TEN YEARS* – ABBA

ABBA IN SPAIN

ABBA & ABBA-related No.1s

There have been two ABBA and ABBA-related no.1s in Spain, one by ABBA and one soundtrack:

1992   *GOLD* – ABBA
2008   *MAMMA MIA! – THE MOVIE SOUNDTRACK*

GOLD returned to no.1 in 1999, and spent a total of five weeks at the top.

Most Hit Albums

10 albums   ABBA

Most Weeks

323 weeks   ABBA

Albums with the most weeks

100 weeks   *GOLD* – ABBA
 88 weeks   *TODO ABBA* – ABBA
 45 weeks   *MAMMA MIA! – THE MOVIE SOUNDTRACK*
 28 weeks   *18 HITS* – ABBA
 23 weeks   *SUPER TROUPER* – ABBA

21 weeks	*VOULEZ-VOUS* – ABBA
21 weeks	*GRACIAS POR LA MUSICA* – ABBA
16 weeks	*THE VISITORS* – ABBA
10 weeks	*THE SINGLES – THE FIRST TEN YEARS* – ABBA
9 weeks	*THE ESSENTIAL COLLECTION* – ABBA

ABBA IN SWITZERLAND

ABBA & ABBA-related No.1s

There have been five ABBA no.1 albums in Switzerland, and one no.1 with an ABBA connection:

1978	*THE ALBUM* – ABBA
1979	*VOULEZ-VOUS* – ABBA
1980	*SUPER TROUPER* – ABBA
1981	*THE VISITORS* – ABBA
1992	*GOLD* – ABBA
2008	*MAMMA MIA! – THE MOVIE SOUNDTRACK*

GOLD topped the album chart for 10 weeks, however, no information is available on how many weeks pre-1984 albums spent at no.1.

Most Hit Albums

20 albums	ABBA
3 albums	Agnetha Fältskog
2 albums	Frida

Most Weeks

677 weeks	ABBA
20 weeks	Agnetha Fältskog
15 weeks	Frida

Albums with the most weeks

303 weeks	*GOLD* – ABBA
48 weeks	*THE BEST OF* – ABBA
47 weeks	*MAMMA MIA! – THE MOVIE SOUNDTRACK*

46 weeks	*ARRIVAL* – ABBA
36 weeks	*THE ALBUM* – ABBA
34 weeks	*THE DEFINITIVE COLLECTION* – ABBA
26 weeks	*VOULEZ-VOUS* – ABBA
26 weeks	*SUPER TROUPER* – ABBA
24 weeks	*THE COMPLETE SINGLES COLLECTION* – ABBA
23 weeks	*GREATEST HITS VOL.2* – ABBA

ABBA IN THE UNITED KINGDOM

ABBA & ABBA-related No.1s

There have nine ABBA and ABBA-related no.1 albums in the UK, all nine by ABBA:

1976	*GREATEST HITS*
1977	*ARRIVAL*
1978	*THE ALBUM*
1979	*VOULEZ-VOUS*
1979	*GREATEST HITS VOL.2*
1980	*SUPER TROUPER*
1981	*THE VISITORS*
1982	*THE SINGLES – THE FIRST TEN YEARS*
1992	*GOLD*
2008	*MAMMA MIA! – THE MOVIE SOUNDTRACK* (Compilations chart)

GOLD returned to no.1 in 1999 and 2008.

Most weeks at No.1

ABBA spent 57 weeks at no.1 on the albums chart in the UK. The albums with the most weeks at no.1 are as follows:

11 weeks	*GREATEST HITS*
10 weeks	*ARRIVAL*
9 weeks	*SUPER TROUPER*
8 weeks	*GOLD*
7 weeks	*THE ALBUM*

MAMMA MIA! – THE MOVIE SOUNDTRACK spent 11 weeks at no.1 on the Compilations chart.

Most Hit Albums

19 albums   ABBA
5 albums   Agnetha Fältskog
2 albums   Frida

Most Weeks

1316 weeks   ABBA
38 weeks   Agnetha Fältskog
8 weeks   Frida

Albums with the most weeks

682 weeks   *GOLD* – ABBA
130 weeks   *GREATEST HITS* – ABBA
96 weeks   *MAMMA MIA! – THE MOVIE SOUNDTRACK*
92 weeks   *ARRIVAL* – ABBA
63 weeks   *GREATEST HITS VO.2* – ABBA
61 weeks   *THE ALBUM* – ABBA
55 weeks   *18 HITS* – ABBA
43 weeks   *VOULEZ-VOUZ* – ABBA
43 weeks   *SUPER TROUPER* – ABBA
42 weeks   *MAMMA MIA!* – Cast Recording

BPI (British Phonographic Industry) Awards

The BPI began certifying albums in 1973, and between April 1973 and December 1978, awards related to a monetary value and not a unit value. Thanks to inflation, this changed several times over the years:

- April 1973 – August 1974: Silver = £75,000, Gold = £150,000, Platinum = £1 million.
- September 1974 – December 1975: Gold raised to £250,000, others unchanged.
- January 1976 – December 1976: Silver raised to £100,000, others unchanged.
- January 1977 – December 1978: Silver raised to £150,000, Gold raised to £300,000, Platinum unchanged.

When this system was abolished, the awards that were set remain in place today: Silver = 60,000, Gold = 100,000, Platinum = 300,000. Multi-Platinum awards were introduced in February 1987. *Note:* the certification levels are double for budget albums.

In July 2013 the BPI automated awards, and awards from this date are based on actual sales since February 1994, not shipments.

14 x Platinum *GOLD* – ABBA (July 2013) = 4.2 million
4 x Platinum *MAMMA MIA! – THE MOVIE SOUNDTRACK* (July 2013) = 1.2 million
Platinum *THE ALBUM* – ABBA (January 1978) = £1 million
Platinum *SUPER TROUPER* – ABBA (December 1980) = 300,000
Platinum *THE SINGLES – THE FIRST TEN YEARS* – ABBA (November 1982)
= 300,000
Platinum *MORE GOLD* – ABBA (July 1999) = 300,000
Platinum *18 HITS* – ABBA (July 2013) = 300,000
Platinum *MAMMA MIA! – ORIGINAL CAST RECORDING* (July 2013) = 300,000
Gold *THE HITS VOL.2* – ABBA (June 1990) = 200,000 (budget album)
Gold *THE NAME OF THE GAME* – ABBA (July 2013) = 200,000 (budget album)
Gold *THE MUSIC STILL GOES ON* – ABBA (July 2013) = 200,000
(budget album)
Gold *ABBA* – ABBA (January 1977) = £300,000
Gold *GREATEST HITS* – ABBA (May 1976) = £250,000
Gold *ARRIVAL* – ABBA (November 1976) = £250,000
Gold *VOULEZ-VOUS* – ABBA (May 1979) = 100,000
Gold *THANK YOU FOR THE MUSIC* – ABBA (December 1983) = 100,000
Gold *CHESS* (March 1985) = 100,000
Gold *ABSOLUTE ABBA* – ABBA (November 1988) = 100,000
Gold *THE DEFINITIVE COLLECTION* – ABBA (July 2013) = 100,000
Gold *NUMBER ONES* – ABBA (July 2013) = 100,000
Gold *A* – Agnetha Fältskog (January 2014) = 100,000
Silver *WATERLOO* – ABBA (February 1976) = £100,000
Silver *GREATEST HITS VOL.2* – ABBA (November 1979) = 60,000
Silver *THE VISITORS* – ABBA (December 1981) = 60,000
Silver *SOMETHING'S GOING ON* – Frida (December 1982) = 60,000
Silver *THE COLLECTION* – ABBA (October 1990) = 60,000
Silver *MY COLOURING BOOK* – Agnetha Fältskog (April 2004) = 60,000
Silver *THE ULTIMATE COLLECTION* – ABBA (February 2005) = 60,000
Silver *FOREVER GOLD* – ABBA (July 2013) = 60,000
Silver *THE ALBUMS* – ABBA (July 2013) = 60,000

ABBA IN THE UNITED STATES OF AMERICA

ABBA & ABBA-related No.1s

There has only been one ABBA-related no.1 in the USA, which topped the album chart for just one week:

2008   *MAMMA MIA! – THE MOVIE SOUNDTRACK*

Most Hit Albums

9 albums   ABBA
1 album   Frida

Most Weeks

221 weeks   ABBA
 13 weeks   Frida

Albums with the most weeks

61 weeks   *GOLD* – ABBA
48 weeks   *MAMMA MIA! – THE MOVIE SOUNDTRACK*
33 weeks   *THE ALBUM* – ABBA
29 weeks   *SUPER TROUPER* – ABBA
26 weeks   *ARRIVAL* – ABBA
20 weeks   *GREATEST HITS* – ABBA
19 weeks   *VOULEZ-VOUS* – ABBA
14 weeks   *THE SINGLES – THE FIRST TEN YEARS* – ABBA
13 weeks   *SOMETHING'S GOING ON* – Frida
11 weeks   *THE VISITORS* – ABBA

RIAA (Recording Industry Association of America) Awards

The RIAA began certifying Gold albums in 1958, Platinum albums in 1976, and multi-Platinum albums in 1984. Gold = 500,000, Platinum = 1 million.

Note: awards are based on shipments, not sales, and each disc is counted individually (so, for example, a double album has to ship 500,000 to be eligible for Platinum).

6 x Platinum   *GOLD* – ABBA (June 2002) = 6 million

Platinum	*GREATEST HITS* – ABBA (July 1978) = 1 million	
Platinum	*THE ALBUM* – ABBA (August 1978) = 1 million	
Platinum	*MAMMA MIA! – ORIGINAL CAST RECORDING* (February 2004) = 1 million	
Platinum	*MAMMA MIA! – THE MOVIE SOUNDTRACK* (August 2008) = 1 million	
Gold	*ARRIVAL* – ABBA (April 1977) = 500,000	
Gold	*VOULEZ-VOUS* – ABBA (November 1979) = 500,000	
Gold	*GREATEST HITS VOL.2* – ABBA (April 1980) = 500,000	
Gold	*SUPER TROUPER* – ABBA (February 1981) = 500,000	
Gold	*THE BEST OF – THE MILLENNIUM COLLECTION* – ABBA (March 2003) = 500,000	

ABBA IN ZIMBABWE

ABBA & ABBA-related No.1s

There have been six no.1 albums by ABBA in Zimbabwe:

1975	*I DO, I DO, I DO, I DO, I DO* (aka *ABBA*) – ABBA
1976	*GREATEST HITS* – ABBA
1976	*ARRIVAL* – ABBA
1979	*VOULEZ-VOUS* – ABBA
1981	*SUPER TROUPER* – ABBA
1982	*THE VISITORS* – ABBA

Most Hit Albums

11 albums   ABBA

Most Weeks

256 weeks   ABBA

Albums with the most weeks

57 weeks	*THE ALBUM*
37 weeks	*I DO, I DO, I DO, I DO, I DO*
30 weeks	*GREATEST HITS*

29 weeks	*VOULEZ-VOUS*
25 weeks	*ARRIVAL*
22 weeks	*THE VISITORS*
18 weeks	*GREATEST HITS VOL.2*
14 weeks	*GOLD*
12 weeks	*WATERLOO*
10 weeks	*SUPER TROUPER*

Author's Note

There are several advantages to independent publishing, not least of which is that any errors and omissions can be readily corrected. Further, up-dates and additional information can be added at any time. If you spot any errors or omissions in this book, or can provide additional information on countries already included in this book or have chart action (ideally, full chart runs) for countries not included at the moment, please contact me via the 'Contact' icon at www.cadman-halstead-musicbooks.com.

Printed in Great Britain
by Amazon